Plea
for a Measure
of Abnormality

Plea
for a Measure
of Abnormality

JOYCE McDOUGALL

INTERNATIONAL UNIVERSITIES PRESS, INC.

New York

Library of Congress Cataloging in Publication Data

McDougall, Joyce.
    Plea for a measure of abnormality.

    Translation of Plaidoyer pour une certaine anormalité.
    1.   Psychoanalysis.   2.   Psychology, Pathological.
I.   Title.
RC506.M2313   616.85'83   80-23586
ISBN 0-8236-4139-2

Contents

v

Preface

When an analyst publishes a "psychoanalytic" book he reveals a fragment of himself.

This book contains a trajectory of reflection on the psychoanalytic experience I have shared with my analysands over a period of many years, for the psychoanalytic adventure, like a love affair, requires two people. It is not an experience in which one person "analyzes" another; it is the analysis of the relationship between two persons. The analyst's participation, forged from his own psychic strengths and weaknesses, enables him to feel and understand something of what his patients are experiencing; at times he identifies with them — the child as well as the adult, and the man as well as the woman in them — while at other moments he finds himself experiencing the thoughts and feelings of those figures of the past who have left an indelible mark on the analysand's psychic world. His most precious guide in this difficult voyage without maps is his intimate if fragmentary acquaintance with his own psychic reality. Thus the analyst shares with his analysand an experience that is in certain ways more private, at times more intense, than his relationships with those near and dear to him.

What imeplled me to write this book? The various chapters were not written at those moments when my pleasure in being an analyst was at its keenest; on the contrary, it was frequently the need to rediscover this pleasure that led me to pour out the uneasy feelings and anxious questionings that every analyst comes to know in the course of his work. That intimate relationship in which two individuals are working together in order to better understand the mental conflict and way of functioning of one of them sets in motion an innovative experience in which something is going to be felt and put into words for the very first time in the life of the analysand — and occasionally in the psychic experience of the analyst also. However the complexities of the venture are such that in every psychoanalysis come fallow moments in which this creative process appears to be at a halt. Should these sterile stretches continue, in time both analysand and analyst become ill at ease. Whenever I find myself in difficulty with my work, failing to communicate my understanding, no longer understanding anything of the inner drama concealed in my patient, or still more troubling, when I have the impression of having understood, or having shared this understanding, and am obliged to accept that, in spite of our combined efforts, the psychoanalytic process, far from unfolding, seems hardly to exist — then I begin to take notes, and have done so for many years.

But one rarely writes for oneself alone. Although many of those spontaneous pages have never seen the light of publication and never will, others have been lengthily rewritten in response to requests for articles in psychoanalytic journals; others again have been used extensively in seminars for analysts in training, in which I have tried to share my reflections and perplexities. The seminars were at first focused on the transference-countertransference relationship, a theme destined to lead to a deeper exploration of the factors that create difficulties in psychoanalytic practice and more particularly of those that tend to escape the analytic process, that is to say when the tensions involved are expressed in preverbal ways outside the analytic situation instead of being elaborated within its context. In addition to an interrogation of the limits of the psychoanalytic method itself, this stimulated a constant questioning of the limitations of the patient as well as the analyst. For the analyst readily becomes a prisoner of his psychoanalytic training. His rather special sort of knowledge, itself acquired "transferentially" and ineluctably marked by transference affects of both a positive and negative kind, threatens not only to generate a kind of "terrorist super ego" — which hampers the analyst's capacity to think and to question — but also interferes with his clinical understanding. Everything the analyst has failed to explore in his own psychoanalysis — either during his necessarily long years of personal analysis or in his continuing self-analysis — is the basis of his psychic deafness and blindness to his own patients. Thus he finds himself constantly constrained to re-examine his countertransference feelings and attitudes if he hopes to conduct his patients as far as possible on their analytic journey.

This early interest in the interaction between analyst and analysand has left its imprint on almost every chapter of this book. But the difficulty of the psychoanalytic relationship is not the sole impediment to trammel up the forward march of analytic work. Over the years I have observed a subtle change in the nature of the demands analytic patients make, explicitly or implicitly, on the treatment. This "widening scope" noted by many colleagues in many different countries may be subsumed in the statement that "good classical neuroses" seem to be on the wane. A brief might be held for the notion that "classical neurosis" as a pure entity was never more than a figment of the imagination, a thought-saving element for the psychoanalytic theoretician. Although neurotic symptoms and suffering undoubtedly continue to exist, it is nevertheless a common finding that today the analyst's consulting room is filled with patients who have no organized hysterical or obsessional symptoms but complain instead of diffuse feelings of depression or anxiety, of repetitive failures, or other symptomatic expressions such as addictions and psychosomatic maladies.

The term "acting-out neuroses" has sometimes been employed to describe this kind of problem. The phrase is a neat one, but contains an inherent contradiction in terms from the point of view of the psychic economy. For this reason, I prefer to refer to these manifestations as "action symptoms," in the hope of highlighting the fact that these acts take the place of repression and other forms of psychic elaboration of the ideas and affects that make up a neurosis. Instead of being dealt with psychically, the tension and dynamics of the psychic conflict are expressed in action either in the outside world or, in the case of psychosomatic mani-festations, outside the psyche and into the soma.

The observed changes in clinical psychoanalysis have various roots. The large-scale application of psy-choanalysis and its many "psychoanalytically oriented" therapeutic ramifications has had the effect of bringing to the analyst's consulting room many patients who would not have been considered formerly as suitable candidates for "classical" psychoanalysis. (In passing, we might well ask ourselves at what point analysis — and neurosis — become "classical.") In addition, psy-choanalyses today frequently last many years, thus giv-ing so-called "neurotic" analysands time to discover the "psychotic core" hidden within their character traits, their psychosomatic symptoms, or their inhibitions in creative and intellectual spheres.

I have also come to discover — and I am certainly not the sole analyst to have made this observation — that the "good neurotic" with his "strong ego" often turns out to be so well defended psychically as to be virtually inaccessible to the psychoanalytic process, whereas many an analysand with a more nebulous psychic structure, more narcissistic, more projective, albeit en-dowed with a "fragile ego," will often make of his psy-choanalytic voyage a fascinating and fertile exper-ience, rewarding to patient and analyst alike. Such pa-tients — for whom I have no name, so diversified is their symptomatology (let us call them "difficult cases") — have made me understand, through their very *re-sistance to the analytic process* (while clinging tena-ciously to the experience) just how much was at stake in their quest. Their character shell existed not only to protect their sexuality and their adult capacity to love and to work, which marks neurotic organizations, but served above all to protect their psychic existence. Although all psychological symptoms are attempts at self-cure, with these sensitive and complicated patients the defensive ramparts serve to protect their inner selves from the danger of dedifferentiation, the loss of identity feeling, and the threat of implosion from others. In order to safeguard the right to exist — among others, or alone — without fearing the loss of one's sense of being, or of sinking into states of depression or overwhelming anxiety, such patients have created a psychic edifice from magical infantile bricks; these megalomanic childlike structures are marshalled together in an attempt to cope with the life of an adult. The way in which these analysands conduct their lives may appear to others to be incoherent or "crazy," and the individual may seem unusually agitated or withdrawn. But he who lives within this edifice, even when its narrow and tortuous construction renders it practically uninhabitable, is not going to give it up lightly — unless he decides to give up living — for at least within its precincts survival is possible.

This book begins where my questioning of the creative aspects of psychological symptoms started — with an attempt to understand the meaning of the inventions of sexual deviants. These well-built neosexual constructions rendered any extensive excavation into their underlying structure and their role in the psychic economy a laborious venture. Yet this is familiar psychoanalytic territory. Freud wrote his well-known essay on "The Sexual Aberrations" in 1905 (*Three Essays on Sexuality*), and all his brilliant new findings of the time are still there to be corroborated. My first years of clinical experience brought me constant confirmation of the operative factors designated by Freud in this and subsequent writings on the subject: the role of castration anxiety; traumatic childhood events; pregenital fixations and the tolerance of erotic expressions that are excluded in neurotic structures; the return of superego attacks, with persecutory force, from the external world into which the individual has projected his feelings of guilt and depression. These factors all combine to give coherence to the form and content of sexual deviations. In addition, my patients cooperated in this piecing together of their distressful childhood past, and helped me discover, by way of their associations, the significant themes and images that gave meaning to their erotic inventions, aims, and object choices. But although many things changed, the fundamental suffering continued — and in certain cases the compulsive force of their sexual deviation also. Something more was needed. I had certainly found food for thought in the celebrated Freudian dictum that "neurosis is the negative of perversion" — a formula confirmed by clinical observation — yet I was forced to admit that this dynamic notion was insufficient to understand the unwavering and compulsive dimension to sexual perversions. Similarly, the economic hypothesis of a "libidinal force," a theoretical model that gives illuminating insight into the secret satisfactions of neurotic symptomatology, does not throw the same searchlight on the complex paths of sexual deviation, in spite of the fact that the latter have arisen in the place where a neurotic solution might also have resulted. In other words, deviation from the original instinctual trajectory (*de via*: another route) cannot be reduced to a simple detour on the path to pleasure. There is a dimension of urgency and despair, and a sense of vital need attached to the practice of sexual perversions when they are stable and organized. Indeed, one frequently has the impression that the dimension of need outweighs that of desire. More exactly, another desire is being pursued, one that is more global and more archaic, so that in many cases it may bypass the aim of orgastic end pleasure and the dimension of love. In contradistinction to the phallic-oedipal tensions that lie behind neurotic symptomatology, the subject is threatened here with a primordial form of anguish that may be represented by a double polarity of terror: that of losing one's psychic and bodily limits and dissolving into the Other, and that of *desiring* this fusional form of psychic death. The fragile and child-like being who laid the first foundation stones of his future sexual inventions was mobilized to construct what he could with the elements provided by the environment, in his need to escape this danger. Thus sexual as well as character perversions emerge. In order to protect himself, the sexual deviant seeks erotic control over the Other, whereas the character pervert seeks to master through deliberate cruelty or other perverse manipulation the threat the Other represents.

Perversions furnish a reply to a dual exigency: the individual, caught between his desire to exist as a separate being and the impossibilty of doing so without great violence, must find in his neosexual scenario a scene of action apt to contain this violence; at the same time he has elaborated an erotic ritual that allows of sexual sharing with another human being even though this contact be fleeting and partial in many cases. For some, even the presence of a partner is too dangerous but there remains some form of erotic pleasure albeit restricted and heavily conditioned. Thus, in one complex invention, the pervert avoids the danger of losing all access to the satisfaction of instinctual desire and the threat of losing himself in relation to another. In this exchange (with a real or fantasied object) the subject recovers not only his self-image and identity feeling, but also the assurance that no one is destroyed. This latter guarantee is a cardinal element in that the fierce wish to attack the threatening object of desire is aimed, in the unconscious, at the earliest and most beloved objects. Such is the drama that gives its force to the exploit of the infant creator of these imaginary solutions that become, at adolescence, sexual perversions.

This book opens with the story of Professor K, or rather with a thin sliver of his psychoanalytic history, with the aim of illustrating the above hypotheses. All that was unique to K himself is not contained in these pages; what has been retained is his characteristic way of functioning and his family history insofar as these were found in other patients who suffered from similar problems and had found similar solutions to the same anguish and despair. The specific mental pain that goes beyond the so-called "castration" anxiety of neurotic suffering (though castration anxiety is certainly not lacking) is more concerned with the catastrophe in which the "I" of the speaking subject runs the risk of losing its narcissistic identification points and hence its meaning for him and for his relations with others. The attempt to erect a bulwark against the ensuing threat of disintegration and psychic death, since it is built from massive stones placed once and for all in early childhood, gives to the structure a certain immutability, and to the erotic act, keystone of this elaborate edifice, a terrifying and ineluctable quality. Should it fail to hold, the whole construction might fall with it.

In a more theoretical approach to similar questions (Chapter II) I have tried to conceptualize some of these notions and to define the psychic functioning that might permit the maintenance of such a delicate balance.

This initial exploration of the unconscious significance and the economic role in the psychic structure of stable sexual deviations opened the way to other questions. Many sexual perversions might appear to be nothing more than unusual systems of masturbation. Certain reflections on masturbation as a universal phenomenon in man, and upon its role as a privileged expression of psychic bisexuality and erotic omnipotence, are contained in Chapter IV. Though true bisexuality may be a privilege reserved for gods and earthworms, Hermaphrodite occupies an important space in man's imagination.

It is often said, with little observational data to support the contention, that perversions other than homosexuality are limited to the male sex. Although it may be held that homosexuality is in certain ways distinct from other perversions, exclusive and organized homosexuality contains many of the same essential features insofar as its libidinal and narcissistic economy and oedipal structure are concerned. I thought it worthwhile to include in this volume a chapter dealing with female homosexuality from this point of view. Chapter III on "The Homosexual Dilemma" resumes and extends ideas contained in earlier articles on female homosexuality that have been published elsewhere.

In "Creation and Sexual Deviation" (Chapter V) the notions of perversion and sublimation are examined in order better to understand their paradoxical relationship to each other, for curiously enough they are defined by Freud in almost identical fashion. This interrogation opens many vistas that require further research. The dynamic and economic problems involved remain for me an open question of fascinating dimensions.

In the course of my reflections on the puzzle of perversion I came to use the notion of "addictive" sexuality in which sexual pursuits perform the function of a drug. This led me to speculate about the possibility that many sexual relations, which in the light of clinical observation are neither neurotic nor perverse, might be performing a similar function in the psychic economy and the maintenance of ego identity as the sexual deviations. Specifically, my interest in the unfathomed mysteries of psychosomatic phenomena in psychoanalytic practice had enabled me to observe that patients who invariably produced such symptoms at times of stress frequently demonstrated what I would call "operational" or "addictive" sexuality and love relationships. From a phenomenological point of view these characteristics contributed to the impression that there existed a "psychosomatic personality." I came to question the validity of this notion, based as it is on the idea of something that is lacking in the psychic structure (fantasy, affect, etc.) since my analytic experience demonstrated that this operational sexuality and way of relating cloaked feelings of profound and terrifying dependency. The question then arose as to the probable failure of earlier defensive maneuvers against this danger, in particular the defensive function of neosexual inventions. Chapter X, "The Body and Language and the Language of the Body," gives a verbatim account of an analytic session that reveals various attempts at self-cure that had been found and lost again, including a sexual invention intended to contain the patient's overwhelming castration anxiety as a child. It is feasible to propose that these losses may have facilitated the later development of his severe psychosomatic symptoms.

These observations and the attempt to conceptualize them led to an increasing interest on my part in the narcissistic economy as such, and its eventual permutations in those who struggle ceaselessly to preserve their feeling of subjective identity and intrinsic value. In the wish to understand and identify with these analysands in their psychotic fears of disintegration and loss of self, the analyst finds himself engaged in an exploit of psychic speleology, a shared anguish in which he is enabled to discover that this route opens onto a void so terrifying that any path of escape is worth taking in order to avoid it: flight to others who shall be gulped down like a drug; flight from the others into narcissistic autarchy; and when the endeavor to live through someone else or to live wrapped up within oneself fails, the subject, once more on the edge of the abyss that cannot be represented mentally, runs the risk of precipitating himself into acts such as automutilation or toxicomania, with suicide on the horizon as the final solution.

We are therefore not surprised to find, in those patients in whom this kind of suffering has led to their undertaking psychoanalysis, that they are more apt than others to resist fiercely the psychoanalytic protocol with its austere atmosphere and its invitation to say everything and allow feelings to flood the mind, without any recourse to action. I am not referring here to those recommended for "psychoanalytic psychotherapy" in which the analyst has reservations as to the capacity of the patient to use the psychoanalytic relationship creatively, to be able to contain and work through the intense emotions that will be aroused, and to be sufficiently strong to receive no other communication than interpretations. Admittedly, to put up with such a relationship requires a fair measure of psychic health! It so happens that many patients begin an analysis in the light of their neurotic symptomatology, whereas in fact the psychotic dimension of the personality structure outweighs the neurotic part. The defense against the explosion of psychotic anxiety is maintained rigidly in the potential space in which analysand and analyst should meet. This frequently gives rise to acting out outside the analytic situation, or to impulsive acts within it — or again, to psychoanalytic treatment of fierce but empty affect or of deadly monotony, in which the sessions go steadily on while the unfolding of the psychoanalytic process remains totally blocked.

It was inevitable that I should discover that analytic work with such patients mobilized the analyst's fears of psychotic thought and feeling, within his own psychic structure. In the stagnation of the psychoanalytic work it is in fact the analyst who runs the risk of losing his feeling of identity, that is to say, his *identity as an analyst,* for such patients do not permit him, for long periods of time, to *function* as an analyst. At such moments one is impelled to "invent" some other form of intervention in order to communicate if one wishes to avoid a stalemate. This is where the analyst begins to question himself and to search out new working hypotheses: another way of listening, free-associating and fantasy-making in the analysand's place, a gesture or motivated change in the analytic protocol, a more profound reflection about himself and his relationship with his patient, a placing in question of the possible collusion — or collision — between the inner world of the analyst and that of the analysand. This aspect of the psychoanalytic adventure is explored more particularly in Chapter VI, "The Anti-Analysand in Analysis," and Chapter VII, "Countertransference and Primitive Communication."

But the analyst's self-analysis does not provide the only key to this form of psychoanalytic puzzle. Why was I able to succeed in bringing Annabelle Borne, the central personage of the "Primitive Communication" back to life, and why did I fail so lamentably to do the same for Mrs. O of the "Anti-Analysand"? The conclusion would seem to be that there always remains a countertransference mote in the analyst's eye! It is no surprise to discover in the course of an analysis that the form of relationship created with the analyst is reflected in the markedly incoherent object relations of these patients with those who are close to them. Nevertheless, it is part of the analyst's task to discover the hidden meaning of this incoherence, in spite of lack of cooperation from his patient — and he frequently manages to piece together the childhood tramauta, the incoherent communications and relations of infancy, gratifying one moment and frustrating the next; the experiences of abandonment, perversion, illness or death of parents, all of which certainly contributed to plunging the small child into situations of loss which could not be mourned, thus endangering his psychic integrity. The infant, caught up in the web of his parents' unconscious wishes and conflicts, as well as in real traumatic events, suffers from rage and narcissistic mortification to such an extent that he can neither elaborate these feelings, nor find a system of thought (other than a psychotic reconstruction) to give them significance. Thus they remain in an embryonic state until adulthood, at which time, despite the maintenance of massive defense against violent and destructive wishes, they will manage to seek satisfaction in roundabout ways. Although a psychotic "solution" may be avoided, primitive psychic mechanisms nevertheless infiltrate every relationship. Such people come to lose all hope of maintaining love relationships that will not eventually be destroyed by hate. Destruction of oneself, or destruction of the other? In a sense, in this almost fusional internal world, there is little difference. Yet with every new failure the subject finds a confirmation of his fantasy—that each encounter can only promise further rejection, denigration, treachery, and abandonment. Thus he is drawn into a repetitive circle which begins with an idealization of the Other as the object destined to fulfill any longing and every desire; this high hope, once lost, is followed by fury and murderous rage. In his determination to make an eternal tie to the Other, the individual creates an imaginary ideal relationship which cannot but fail to meet the great expectations that surround it. The illusion, which holds the subject transfixed, is finally broken by the creator himself who exercises an almost super-human force to escape from its power in order to leave his imaginary paradise. In this way he attempts to smash the mirror that no longer gives back the demanded reflection; but it is at this precise moment that his own image falls apart. Overwhelmed by the ensuing anguish, the author of this sinister drama beats a retreat before the world and cloaks himself in bitter solitude. In the face of such a catastrophe, certain people no longer care to take the risk of entering into the universe of others; henceforth they reject the servile dependence on the supposed object of desire, and the eternal terror of losing this Other—that is to say, not only the loss of the gratifying object, but also and more particularly the loss of the object's power of reflecting to the subject the guarantee that he himself exists, that this existence has value, and that life is worth living. I have tried in "Narcissus in Search of a Reflection" (Chapter VIII) to highlight, with the aid of fragments of analysis, two fundamental, seemingly opposite "solutions" chosen by many individuals to resolve this vital psychic conflict. If one of these solutions may be said to be constructed around the determination to maintain absolute control over *oneself*, the other seeks to gain absolute control of the *object*. In such fashion each tries in his own way to escape the ever-present threat of psychic death.

My evolving thoughts about man's narcissistic libido, with its precarious economic balance, brought me face to face with its most regressive expression (albeit one of its most banal manifestations): psycho-

somatic "creations." These explosions of psychic tension in the somatic self tend to indicate that people,
while struggling blindly for life, are nevertheless
capable of taking as their thinking apparatus that implacable computer, the soma, and thus place themselves on the side of death. This fault-line in the psyche
that divides it from the soma is not a missing element
that can be represented mentally; it does not resemble
that lack of the object which creates a representation
that mobilizes desire and creativity; sublimatory activity, neurotic, psychotic, perverse, and other action
symptoms — all are evidence of psychic creativity.
When it falls to the soma alone to find its (inevitably)
biological response to psychic conflict and mental pain,
its inventions by definition are unrecountable in
words. Here the analyst finds himself listening to something ineffable, an unspeakable nothingness, rather
like a metaphor of death. The chapters that deal with
the psychosoma and its psychoanalytic expression
(IX–XI) contain highly hypothetical notions. The Ger-
man poet Novalis once wrote that hypotheses were like
nets; he who casts none catches nothing. I have spread
out my nets with the hope that others might come to
my aid and help me pull them to shore and evaluate
their contents. This attempt to explore the limits of the
analyzable has led me to an appreciation of psychic
vitality in all its forms, even those creations generally
regarded as pathological manifestations. Might it be
that our final choice is between creation and dying?
The human psyche is structured around the *forbidden*
and the *impossible*, therefore people must struggle as
best they can to maintain their illusions, their personal
identity and their capacity for instinctual gratification,

but in many cases the price paid is exorbitant.

Between the bright promise of infancy and the fulfillments of adult life there are pitfalls other than neurosis, psychosis, and action symptoms. The incestuous infant and the megalomanic nursling who make known their demands in these forms have perhaps avoided another fate, and one that is even more widespread, namely that of the child who has learned too soon and too well how to bend to the will of the world around him, with the risk of losing his essential uniqueness by *overadaptation* to external reality; "pathological normality," under its faded colors, is just as poignant as the brilliance that colors the paths of madness.

If the child hidden within each grown adult is the cause of his mental suffering, this child is also the source of art and of the poetry of life. On his continuing existence rests the ever-present promise of a fresh perception of the world, the revelation of unsuspected mystery in the everyday scene, the maintenance of a personal and private folly to offset the deadening specter of "normative normality" which adulthood might bring. It is the task of each of us to know how to keep in touch with the magical and narcissistic child within, so that he may not be stifled. To see this exchange take place with the patient in analysis is a moving experience; to see it fail, a tragedy. This is the thought I hope to have transmitted in my final chapter, which gives this book its title: *Plea for a Measure of Abnormality*.

Each man in his psychic complexity is a masterpiece, each psychoanalysis an odyssey. My patients never cease to surprise, enlighten, and affect me. To all those who have allowed me to accompany them on their psychoanalytic voyage, this book is dedicated.

Chapter I

The Sexual Scene and the Anonymous Spectator

"Life! It's a game and I know all the rules. Whether I win or lose, I don't give a damn. Let's say I find life amusing." Listening to this patient, I was struck by his dry, serious tone of voice, his stiff carriage, and the expression on his face, tight with anxiety, and showing no trace of the amusement that life supposedly brought him. Why such a denial of life's importance, and indeed of his own? There was something distinctly defiant about his statements, but to whom were they directed, and why? Looking back on this first meeting with Professor K, I can now answer that question in part. His idea that life was a game which he knew how to play, even if he did not get much out of it, was a desperate attempt to give some *meaning* to his life. We were to discover subsequently that he felt it had none, that the necessary signposts were missing, and that he often wished he could put an end to his miserable game. But there was no way out of his compulsive existence. In a sense, he was saying, "I have to live my life

21

as though it were a futile game. Otherwise I shall not be allowed to go on living."

Toward the end of this first interview he replied, "You ask what would happen if I should take myself seriously. Let's suppose I really finished this book I've pretended to work on for years — well, I feel I would be taking a senseless risk. It sounds crazy, but if the book were a success that would be the end of everything."

The paradoxical answer to fulfilling his life goals was of the order of castration, aphanasis, and death. Having decided he was only playing, somehow enabled him to get by. We were to discover that this *modus vivendi* touched every aspect of his life — his friendships, his work, his beliefs, his sexuality. He did nothing "really," and was ironic about those who did, including analysts. The illusion that nothing he did was serious or quite real allowed him in fact to begin his analysis. In his first session, after a few desultory remarks on the oddness of the situation, he stopped abruptly: "I say, am I playing it well, this psychoanalytical game?"

Behind the playful camouflage, K was able to reveal glimpses of another reality. "My life is a continual degradation. My intellectual work suffers. Everything I do is accomplished under pressure at the last possible minute. In front of my public I have the constant impression that I'm cheating, fooling them. . . . I live in dread of being unmasked one day and condemned forever. By the way, perhaps I should tell you about some of my little sexual obsessions — that is, if it interests you."

In the sessions that followed, this theme was employed like a tantalizing game as K let fall here and there a veiled hint relating to his sex life, stopping from time to time to ask if I had "understood." His sexual practice, in fact, consisted in beating his girlfriend on the buttocks with a whip, in a highly detailed and ritualistic scene.

"There you are. Now I've shown you my sexual degradation, something which is beyond my own understanding. Oh but don't imagine that I want to do away with it. These are my favorite games." Despite his feeling of sexual failure, it was evident that K did not wish to lose or to modify his erotic activity. This would in fact have been the unconscious equivalent to castration, since the erotic ritual was his only path to potency. But it now transpired that K used his sexual deviation to deny or bypass the ever-present terror of being "unmasked and condemned forever" for an *unknown act or crime.*

With regard to his work failure, on the other hand, K genuinely wished to change. His inability to finish anything had been his ostensible reason for coming into analysis. Yet in attempting to render intelligible his anxiety regarding his work problems, he succeeded in revealing that they too were closely connected with his sexual inhibitions. Talking of his difficulty in taking his work seriously, he used imagery evocative of disquieting sexual fantasies:

"I seem incapable of penetrating, of really getting inside my work. It's as though I dare not go right to the end. I never reach the bottom. Even to get started I have to plunge in with my eyes closed. Nevertheless I get there somehow or other, at least with the bare essentials, but it's a terrible strain. I have a stack of little tricks to help me. First of all I put myself into a position where I can't back out. I have to go through with it then, because that's what's expected. . . . It's the fact that others are always watching which obliges me to produce. *In front of a public I always perform well!"*

K's "stack of little tricks" for overcoming his work inhibitions found its counterpart in the whips and ritual clothing of his theatrical fetishist scenes, but "the others who were always watching" were less easy to identify. These anonymous others were often referred to as though they were a single individual. "I constantly have my eye on the Other," K would say. This "Other" became an ever-present and important personage in K's analytic discourse. Thanks to his watchful presence, K's painfully accomplished professional tasks became brilliant "performances" that brought him some renown and a feeling of having triumphed over terrible odds. But his triumphs were also accompanied by the nagging feeling of having fooled "the Other." Although he described his public success as "an orgastic moment," the more so since he took nothing seriously as "well-intentioned folk" did, his tenuous feeling of superiority invariably gave way to depression and the feeling that nothing he did was quite real: "This feeling of unreality—I think it's part of my game. I sometimes wonder if I'm not utterly childish to live my life the way I do. . . . Yet I've always made others feel that they were childish to take life so seriously and that I was the one who had the real secret."

But what was his secret? My patient was far from being able to pin it down except to say that he played "the game" and was fully aware of what he was doing. He did not fool himself like "the others." Nevertheless it was never clear what the game in question really was. Claparède's definition of play as "a free pursuit of fictitious goals" would have met with K's approval, and indeed seemed to characterize his philosophy of life. He was constrained to present all his life goals as fictitious, and it seemed doubtful that he could ever permit himself to act as though they were real. His playing-at-living carried an element of conjurer's magic which implied someone was always watching. This "someone" in contradistinction to himself, had to believe, had to be fooled, as the child is fooled by the adult. In this fashion K projected on others his own confusion, with the result that he, the "adult," played while "the others," mystified and serious, watched him. Thanks to his role as magician he regarded himself as "an eccentric" who could take liberties where others could not, and override certain social conventions the others had to respect (the serious children).

As his analysis proceeded, K began to view himself with new eyes: "For the first time, I'm beginning to realize that I'm not a cunning clown. On the contrary, I'm rigid and compulsive. I control everything I do. I don't believe I've ever made a single spontaneous gesture in my life! And I paralyze every attempt to get free. My analysis is making that clear. Do I or don't I want to change? Will I ever be able to tell you, truly, the thoughts that come to my mind? I even fool myself. Who am I anyway?" After a short silence he took up his old refrain: All week he had only "played at working"; things had not changed for months, for years, in fact. Every success increased his complaints of failure and his sense of degradation. Within the session he expressed his wish to "get into his work" to "get going and do something" and at the same time insisted on his total and continual failure to move. I suggested to

him that he was seeking to reassure me of his innocence; he would not move, would not "penetrate" further, into whatever he undertook. Whether he discussed his work or his sexual games, he showed me that
he always postponed to the limit the final accomplish-
ment, the end pleasure.

K was beginning to discover that this disarming
"game" that was his life obeyed iron-clad rules to
which he was a slave — an astonishing fact he had never
before recognized. His relations to his "public," his desire to dazzle and to mystify, revealed the existence of a
powerful and immutable fantasy whose meaning elud-
ed him. The stage setting, equally immutable, of his
erotic fantasies, also began to reveal itself. The cast of
characters frequently included two women, in which
the elder, perhaps a mother, was beating her daughter
on her bare buttocks. "And what about the public?" I
asked, thinking back on all he had hinted at with regard to the mysterious Other. This intervention provoked a moment of intense anxiety: "How did you
guess about the public? Who told you it was important?"

The anonymous onlooker rapidly worked his way into the transference situation and became installed
there as a powerful source of resistance. "You, you
watch me all the time, and seated where I can't see
you. Who are you anyway? Who am I really talking
to?...If this goes on I shall be obliged to take you seriously. The idea horrifies me....I hope you understand, I no longer find this very amusing!" I said,
"What will happen if your psychoanalysis no longer
amuses you, is no longer a game?" He responded,
"Words like abyss, chasm, and void come to my mind.

I no longer see anything. I'm frightened."

K, who never admitted to anxiety or fright, caught himself up quickly and added, "But don't worry, I can stand any amount of fear." I replied, "Could we say you turn fear itself into a game?" K said, "Have I ever done anything else but that? All my procrastination, my balancing tricks to put off everything to the last possible moment, till I can no longer draw back. . . . I'm like a man playing with death."

After a long pause I drew K's attention to the fact that he had fallen silent on evoking the idea of death. "Odd, I wasn't thinking of my work problems any longer, but of my sexual games. The whip is a source of anxiety for me, but it is also the means of triumphing over it."

If the whip evoked in K the threat of castration, it was also the element in the game that allowed him to master that anxiety. "Castration" took on the form of the female genital, the "abyss," the "void" he could not face—a deathlike threat to the little boy who was "playing at sexual relations."

The associations that followed were enlightening: "Is there some link between fear and disgust? I began to think of my feeling of disgust for everything that I imagine is inside a woman's sex organ." (K seemed to be seeking an anal defense against the anxiety produced by the "void.") "I never could touch a woman's sex! Nor look at it either! I always hide it from sight as I told you—yet I love to expose that disgusting sex at the same time." "To whom?" I asked. K gave a short dry laugh and replied, "Oh, no doubt to my 'public,' my unnamed spectators. In telling you that, I feel suddenly upset. The anxiety, shall we say, is precisely *there*.

But why?" He added rapidly, "But that's alright. Anxiety increases my sexual excitement." So anxiety became an integral part of the game, and was intimately linked to the unknown Other.

Whether the game concerned K's professional activity, his love relations, his need to fascinate and dominate the audience, or his masturbatory games in front of the mirror, the scene was always a spectacle, an offering to the same anonymous spectator. In the weeks that followed, it became possible, through the transference relationship, to outline more accurately the role of the unknown onlooker. One day K explained at length that he could not continue to reveal his erotic game without some encouragement on my part. Since these revelations were torturing to him, it was essential that I assure him of their interest to me. In other words, I had to desire his recital and take pleasure in it. Implicitly I was offered the role of the *voyeur*. K found this interpretation "exact and disquieting," the more so since he had said to himself just the other day, "Well, if she *wants* to hear all this she'll certainly be disappointed. I shall show and I shall also hide just whatever I please."

It was essential that the Other watch, but equally important that he be duped. This was an indispensable thread in the fabric of K's fantasy. With minor variations, the scene always involved the punishment of an innocent victim, a child chastised by her mother, a wife beaten by her husband, a mistress by her lover. The innocent-guilty victim would be publicly whipped "in front of a crowd," or "the Other." The unnamed spectator would be doubly fooled, first as to the *significance* of what he saw, insomuch as the scene which purported to be a punishment was at the same time the very condition of sexual excitement to the "victim." Second, the spectator unknowingly played the role of *an accomplice* since the fantasy of his presence was necessary to the orgasm that ended the drama.

It does not escape us that the patient was also duped by his own game. His insistence on the fact that the girl victim *ardently desired the beating* (this being a constant theme whether attached to K's masturbation fantasy or enacted with his girl friends) reveals the importance attached to the partner's orgasm as a way of validating both his fantasy and the means by which satisfaction was achieved. The partner was thus required to prove that K had indeed stumbled upon the secret of sexual intercourse. So the game became reality, and the whip (fetish, factitious sex) became endowed with authentic phallic qualities.

K's insistence that the girl desired the beating became intense when certain partners proclaimed indifference or even indignation at his sexual requests. We were able to reconstruct the truth in this respect, and K was overwhelmed to discover that he projected upon his girl friends his *own* excitement at the idea of being whipped in order to identify with their supposed ecstasy. This reconstruction enabled K to say to me, for the first time, that he would sometimes flagellate himself before the mirror, watching excitedly for the whip marks, just as he did when he could play the scene out with a girl friend. Later he came to speak of "the pleasure of being penetrated by pain." It might be added here that the whip marks were symbolic of castration, a playful castration of which he was the master, and which reduced to naught his profound anxiety.

The castration threat was finally rendered derisive in that the "castration game" had become the means to orgasm. At the same time pain was represented psychically as "penetrating" and served also to enact the fantasied possession of the paternal phallus desired by the woman, mother-substitute, in K's unconscious. "It is finally clear to me that I disguise myself as a woman in order to become a man! As though I don't possess my own penis or as though I need to get hold of a very special one. What's wrong with me? Am I a homosexual?"

But this was not the answer to K's dilemma. There was no vagina in K's sexual stage play, but there was no penis either. His fantasy obviously contained homosexual as well as heterosexual significance, but what was more particularly denied (actually disguised in his erotic act, and also hidden from him physically) was *the difference between the sexes, and its significance with regard to sexual reality.* The sexual relationship was reduced to a game of whipped buttocks (a classic illustration of the role of *disavowal* so well described by Freud in his writings on fetishism). In disguising the sexual organs with ritualistic clothing, K disavowed their destiny, namely to complement each other. Even more important was the need to camouflage the identity of the participants in his play. The dramatic exchange between the woman and the girl, before the gaze of the unknown onlooker, indicated a transposition of the oedipal constellation.

Perhaps this is the moment to focus attention on K's parents, or at least on the manner in which he presented them. He let drop so little concerning his family that I had the impression he was a child without a past. For two years I was not sure whether his father was dead or alive, or whether he had any brothers or sisters. I refrained from asking questions in the beginning, and constructed erroneously from the information so sparingly offered that he was the only child of a lonely mother: "In my pastel-colored trousers, long after the normal age, I was still her little Prince Charming. *We were as one against the world.*" "There was no one else in this world?" I asked. K answered: "Well, yes, the rest; in a way we formed a couple against my father I suppose.... She always used to tell me I was a real little man.... She was very ambitious for me. Her dearest desire was that I should one day resemble *her own father*. He had been a writer and she held him in boundless admiration. Tall, strong—quite the opposite of my own father.... You say my father is totally absent whenever I talk of my childhood. But it's true, he simply didn't count. Sure, he was always there, but *like a continual absence*. I have no clear picture of my grandfather either, except through the eyes of my mother. There was one story about him that I loved. She would tell it over and over for me. One day grandfather chased her with a whip in his hand, and she fled into the toilet at the bottom of the garden. I see myself as a little boy sitting in grandfather's garden, imagining the scene. I used to spend hours like that."

I was to learn later that K, at the age of nine, daydreaming in his grandfather's garden, had already constructed, down to the tiniest details, the erotic fantasies which, thirty years later, were still the cornerstone of his sexual edifice. The ritualistic clothing was none other than the garments worn by the mother on this famous day. Years later the very thought of the whip or the garments was sufficient to excite a powerful desire

in my patient. What was this desire? From the time of
the screen memory, the whip stood for the total event,
violent and exciting, which the little boy imagined had
transpired between mother and grandfather. To his
mind the whip symbolized his grandfather's penis — the
idealized, exclusive, in fact the only possible model and
sole object of his mother's sexual desire. "You are
mother's real little man" in no way evoked in the small
boy a comparison with his own father. The latter,
denigrated in the eyes of the mother, had become a
negative value, an absence, the very image of castration. It was not toward this father that K could turn to
find the phallic image with which he could identify.
Only through his mother could he hope, eventually, to
have access to it. Thus his masculine identifications
were at this point split in two. Although certain of his
hobbies were an attempt on K's part to identify with
the idealized grandfather, in his creative and professional life he seemed constrained to identify with the
castrated father, at the same time trying to cloak the
ensuing depression in the fiction of playing an eternal
game. In his erotic life, on the other hand, he identified with the masculine image offered by the mother —
the phallic grandfather with a whip in his hand — but
on a deeper level this necessitated an identification
with his mother, who alone had the right to the paternal phallus. The theatrical fetishist scene served to hide
the feeling of deception and emptiness. In an atmosphere of anguish mixed with delight, he imagined
himself penetrated by the whip, external representation of the grandfather's penis, while he disguised
himself as a woman in order to have the right to possess
it. It was some time later that this role was in its turn

camouflaged and attributed, in the ritualistic sex act, to his girl friend, thus allowing him to identify with the mother's pleasure in receiving the whipping in order to reach orgasm. By means of this devious path, K was able to recover narcissistically the phallus of which he had been deprived.

The fantasy of absorbing magically, into one's body, the highly valued penis, is typical of the anal stage of libidinal development. During this phase the possession of phallic power is represented, in the imagination of children of both sexes, as an anal incorporation of the father's penis. (Clinical work brings many examples of this, and the games of young children are even more explicit.) However, the way in which the child comes to terms with his desire for the symbolic phallus, and his fantasy incorporation of the father's penis, will depend to a large extent on the unconscious attitudes of his parents, and his relation to them. The wish may be felt as permitted, in which case it will become integrated within the ego and its identificatory system, thus opening the way to secondary identification and genital sexuality. But such wishes may also be regarded as dangerous, forbidden, and fraught with the risk of castration—castration of the father, of the mother, or of the child himself. For my patient sexual desire was only permissible in the form of a game, a game which then became his only solution to the enigmas of the sexual relationship. It is evident that this "solution" structured the whole of his psychic life.

Later, K was to recall the pain he experienced as a child believing he was different from the others. He relived a memory of being in the center of a group of children of his age shouting with joy, while he stood silent and frightened searching for his mother's face: "Nothing else in this world counted. I couldn't understand the other children, and what's more I didn't want to understand them!" *Understanding them* would have meant identifying with them and thereby renouncing his privileged place as Prince Charming at his mother's side—the queen-mother of his inner kingdom in which there was no place for a king. Thirty years later "to be like the others" still signified castration; "to be accepted by the others" was equivalent to losing his identity. He would then be forced to go over to the other side, the side of the brothers—and the fathers. To make such a move would mean the risk of losing all hope of possessing the mother's phallic secret and thus one day possessing the means of totally satisfying her. It also meant losing the illusion of an idealized, magical, and all-powerful father, and losing the sense of mystery and sacrament. Worse, his feeling of identity would be reduced to nothing. *For K could only find his identity in the eyes of his mother.* Only through her could he hope to acquire his manhood. His wish for his father's love and for the right to identify with him and thereby introject an authentic paternal-phallic image was felt to be forbidden by his mother, and had therefore to remain unconscious. His mother remained sole guardian of his narcissistic integrity.

Each movement in the analysis toward integrating his father into his personal history immediately mobilized anxiety, and K would again seek refuge in the tender and nostalgic memories of the maternal paradise. And each return found him back in the same *cul-de-sac*: "Often when I was a child I would have a hard knot in my throat and I would then have to find my mother and cry on her shoulder. She only had to make a gesture and the knot would be gone. Those moments were a secret joy. But there came a time when I could no longer ask this of my mother. Whatever hard knots arose in my throat from then on I just had to swallow. Later I constructed a system in which, no matter what happened to me, *I never needed anybody*. It became my ideal to be entirely self-sufficient. My system was well in place by the time I was nine. Why nine? I can't tell you. . . . But I can tell you one thing! I'm sick of it! Sick of all my phoney independence! I've got to get out of it, do you see! All my life I've looked for a miracle, something that would change the unreality of my existence into something real, something that would make sense out of my pain. . . . I am lost in a world in which I don't know the rules of the game."

In letting slip the defensive function of playing-at-living, K revealed for the first time how much his disordered oedipal situation provided him with a twisted image of relationships and sexual realities in general as well as confusion about his own sexual role in the scheme of human relations.

K said, "It would require a catastrophe to get me out of all my subterfuge, my mess of failures, and wasted years — I need something that would put my back to the wall. We once worked out that I refused to take any risks of any sort. It's true! Somehow, whenever there's any challenge, any tests to pass, I just make a sort of turn about and get myself onto the other side by cheating — without ever passing the test."

"Perhaps this obliges you to have to go on pretending, to be constantly on the lookout for fear of being caught?" I proposed.

"Exactly! I'm fed up with it, fed up with my fallacious personality. Always the usurper. If I could only do what I really want to do instead of playacting; if I could only feel that the others really existed and that I counted among them. But not me! I'm the one who always sneaks in, always looking for a secret opening that the others don't know. Nothing but a cataclysm could destroy my carefully constructed system." After a long pause he continued: "I don't know why, but I was thinking back to the time of the war.

"There was a catastrophe that made a number of things possible for you," I said.

"It sure was. In my father's absence I felt I was a man. Suddenly everything seemed easy. Yet I waited day after day for the real catastrophe to hit me. And it never came. I've been deprived of my catastrophe! That sounds silly, and yet it feels profoundly true. It's as though I never signed my peace theaty with the enemy. As though it were too humiliating to give in. I just sneaked away, treaty unsigned."

"Could we say that you drew up the clauses of the treaty and ratified it yourself?" I suggested.

"That's right. The whole thing's a forgery. Like all my diplomas, all my accomplishments. All totally false! And now I'm waiting for *you* to provoke this catastrophe, to say something that will throw me completely off balance."

The long-awaited "catastrophe," K did not yet realize, would require him to give up his belief in the omnipotence of infantile wishes. The little usurper would have to renounce his fraudulent claim to the object of incestuous desire, would have to give up his ill-gotten kingdom, and would have, finally, to fulfill the clauses of the humiliating treaty he never signed with his father. For K had invented his own solution to the oedipal conflict. In rendering his father inexistent (helped, no doubt, by the complicity of his mother) K had kept intact his illusion of being his mother's sole love object. His "phony diplomas" procured him certain rights, but they had cost him dearly. In spite of his increasing feeling of depression, K could neither give up the "diplomas" (by now an integral part of his identity) without pain, nor could he precipitate the "catastrophe" without anxiety. He sought reassurance in the eyes of the onlookers: "I'm perfectly capable of being the star of the show provided I have the public in front of me. *The star only exists in the eyes of the spectators.* So there I am in my element. I play the game and cheat when necessary."

But at other times all of this seemed to K empty of meaning; he would then spend hours composing long erotic fantasies, such as: "My girl friend writes to her mother and tells her she has been beaten by me and that everyone knows about it, but that I refuse to admit this. All the neighbors gaze at her, but she doesn't care a damn. . . . You're right, the 'public' is always there — and indispensable to my excitement!"

Hidden behind his partner's complicity, contained in the varied beating fantasies, or concealed in his masturbation rituals in front of the mirror, there was alway the fantasy of the unknown Other, or Others, who watched: "This spectator, whoever he is, is the culminating point of my excitement — and also of my anxiety. I am terrified of his gaze." In the session following this remark, K brought one of his rare dreams: "I was in the home of my childhood, and you were with me in the bed. You said 'Those spots on the sheets are all my fault. Someone might see them.' Then you added in a solemn voice 'We're anxious, both of us.' It was exciting and terrifying at the same time, waiting for the other person to come and catch us."

In his spontaneous associations to the dream, K said the bedroom recalled his mother's room in which, in the past, she had often shared confidences with him in respect to disputes and disagreements she had with his father. Among the different possible interpretations of the dream it seemed to reveal an appeal to the oedipal father, and the mother having been replaced by the analyst as the object of sexual desire. The mother's guilt is also underlined. The whole scene is anxiety-arousing in that the father might castrate the incestuous son, but at the same time exciting because the son has triumphed over him. K, however, saw no connection between his dream and the memory of his mother's confidences concerning the father; he still maintained a blank in the place of that Other before whom the guilty couple trembled. Instead, the anonymous crowd concealed the disavowed father. K went on to say how he regarded all men with a wary and mistrustful eye, then, waving his false diplomas once more in the air he concluded: "But after all I'm a shining example of superadaptation to others. I never stumble over my words or lose my presence of mind because whatever the others, all those well-intentioned folk do, has no meaning for me. Sure, I'm the one that wipes out the meaning. And so much the better. The collective spirit repulses me. I've avoided it since I was six. Why six? I don't know. I've always needed a maximum of independence in respect to others...eating, drinking, masturbating, daydreaming—that's *my* world, the only real one." K's "real" world was in fact the imaginary one of childhood which he shared with his mother, and from which the Other was excluded. K had "wiped out the meaning" of his father's role in the family constellation. His inexplicable presence and activities were projected onto all the "well-intentioned folk"—the castrates—with whom K wished to have no relation. Thus his world was split into two: an outer one, where all was treachery and deception and where he had to control his every word and movement to achieve his "superadaptation" to it, and an inner world, the "real" one, where he was alone with his body and his fantasies. I attempted to put into words the two worlds he had so carefully delineated for me in the last few sessions: one valueless, colorless, controlled, and kept at distance, and the other, intimate and sensual, the kingdom of sexual desire in which he was the sole sovereign.

"It's true, absolutely true! And I'm fed up with it! For God's sake let me out!...But I'm afraid, especially afraid of stumbling in the world of the others. If only I dared take the risk. I'm alone wherever I go. Even with my girl—and we've been together for years—I'm never really with her. She doesn't even know what's going on inside me. I'm ashamed to admit this, but I've never given her the power to make me suffer." This last phrase was a paradigm of K's relationships in general, including the position he attempted to maintain in the analytic relationship. Here he revealed that his girl, substitute for the collusive mother, was also to be feared. K began to discover that hidden behind the image of the mother with her seductive complicity was another who could cause pain and suffering, who cheated while pretending to believe in the reality of childhood illusions.

The third year of analysis brought certain changes in K's professional and sexual life, and he began to feel threatened: "I don't like to admit it to you, but for some time I've been working better, writing freely, even getting pleasure out of it. That may seem childishly simple, but I've never in my life felt like that. For me to be able to complete any project I had to render it valueless, treat it like a game, of no consequence. That I might want to create something and that it might have importance makes my head reel. This recent triumph (it concerned a literary success) I owe to you, and this irritates me. I don't wish to be beholden to you for anything. Also my success frightens me; I'm sick with anxiety and I hold this against you."

Success carried a double danger for K. Unconsciously it signified phallic potency, and thus exposed him to castrative retribution. At the same time it implied his need for public recognition, and thus revealed his dependence on others. The latter danger was accessible to K's consciousness, and went counter to his lifelong ego ideal of being utterly sufficient unto himself, independent of the wishes of others as of their judgments. Each success was followed by a swift retreat to his old defenses. At these times he would pass whole sessions denigrating his work, accusing himself of worthlessness or damning his destiny. I remarked that he seemed to be "proving his innocence" once more, assuring me that he would never fulfill a single desire. "It's true. I hesitated to tell you, but for a certain time now I've been making love differently, normally you might say, and with pleasure."

Feeling alive, working seriously, making love with pleasure remained nevertheless dangerous activities. Not only were they felt to be deeply forbidden by the inhabitants of his inner world, but they also involved the immense risk of becoming dependent upon others. Around this time it became clear that K used his ritualistic fetishist scenario for other than merely sexual purposes. Each time he had to face a new work project, terminate a report on time, meet people whom he felt he had to control, that is, in the face of any threat, he would seek refuge in his private erotic kingdom. At the same time his analytic associations colored and clarified the fuzziness of his childhood memories. His father had played a more predominant role than he had so far realized; the tender and loving image of his mother became tinged with hostility.

Before citing a last clinical fragment I would like to summarize certain elements of the oedipal constellation revealed in K's analysis, not because they are specific to this patient but, on the contrary, because they are, in my experience, *an essential and invariable element in personality structures whose balance is maintained through perverse sexuality.* The oedipal situation with its accompanying anxieties had never been faced; it was simply circumvented. This was achieved largely through two major defenses — disavowal and the disguise of "play." These served *to deny the primal scene through inventing a counterfeit couple* and also *to convert castration anxiety into its opposite by treating it as a game.* With regard to the parental imagos, the father's image is marked with

negative value, and this factor is counterbalanced by
an ambiguous image of the mother in which the attributes of both sexes are condensed. The fear and hatred
that such an image will inevitably awaken are held in
repression through idealization. In such a "telescoped"
oedipal situation the mother becomes both seductive
and forbidding at the same time. She arouses sexual
desire while constituting in the same moment the obstacle to its fulfillment. For the child, she is contradiction itself, the very image of perversity. She is also
the mainstay of an illusion, for he comes to believe that
he may escape the destiny of Oedipus. Deprived of the
solution which allows identification with the father, he
sees *himself* as the object of his mother's desire and her
true complement. He comes to believe he can avoid the
human sexual dilemma. He gets the diploma without
passing the examination. But this is his bitter reward—
he keeps it on condition that he never uses it. Nevertheless the fraudulent diploma, stolen from a repudiated
father, is the only reference that permits him to avoid
the "solution" of psychosis. A paper king with an imita-
tion scepter, he must thereafter protect this identity
and convince the others that his illusory world is real.
Of necessity, he must deceive them—the public, his
sexual partner, and, finally, himself—in the same way
that, in fantasy, he deceived the father. From there on
the fear of being unmasked and punished for an unnamed crime becomes a consuming preoccupation. He
must keep a close control on everything. Thus the *fear
of losing control* is added to the anxiety of losing his
fragile identity. He fears losing control not only of
himself, but also of the Other, the anonymous spectator in whose eyes the false identity must be main-

tained. The image of the Other, projected onto the world of men, renders the public, all the Others, a constant threat to his position as chosen king. The menacing father is thus ejected from his inner world and kept at bay embodied in the world at large, while in the intimate erotic world he is endlessly duped and humiliated.

Nevertheless, illusory control of the external object world and rigid self-control are insufficient to master the intense castration anxiety of these patients. Other defenses are needed to maintain the delicate balance of their inadequate solution to the Oedipus complex, one of the most important being regression in instinctual aims. Mastery, control, humiliation, and defiance play a predominant role. That is to say, the edifice is indelibly marked by anal defense work. The primal scene, divested of its genital significance, becomes an anal-narcissistic struggle. Orgasm is then equivalent to a *loss of control*, and must frequently be retarded or even warded off altogether. In the latter case sexual pleasure is often experienced vicariously through the orgasm of the partner — another means of overcoming castration anxiety. Thus instead of confirming his feeling of sexual identity through the sexual act, the sexual deviant manages only to delimit himself in space and time as distinct from his partner. There is no losing of oneself in the other to threaten either the individual or his partner. Although the latter is frequently treated as a part object, the individual must reassure himself that he has not destroyed this object nor been destroyed by it. This is particularly evident when the sexual couple is reduced solely to the subject himself and the fetish-object. The need to control, which these patients maintain both in their sexual relations and their relationships in general, acts as a barrier to profoundly disturbing feelings of depression or persecution, while at the same time conferring on the sexual act a compulsive and ritualistic character.

One further aspect of the anal component is expressed in the importance of the *secret* in sexual perversions. Anxiety attached to the *visible* — the penis or the lack of one — is considerably reduced by displacing interest to the invisible. The anal object, hidden from view, allows one to maintain the fiction of possessing a secret penis and also permits of a secretive erotic relation with the mother. Like all secrets, it can be exhibited and concealed in turn under cover of the sexual game. It frequently finds a further expression in the creation of a "cult," secret knowledge built around illusion, impalpable and infallible. In the erotic relation built upon illusions of this kind, the presence of the two people concerned is not sufficient to validate the fictitious anal phallus and its oedipal significance. Someone must witness, in imagination, the illicit love between mother and son. This witness is destined, in the unconscious, to be the father; he in turn shall be humiliated and deceived, just as the child once was, when confronted with the irrefutable evidence of his parents' sexual relationship. This "voyeuristic" father plays a double role in the imagined scene. He is also the object of homosexual longings and homosexual identification, *a libidinal phase whose integration has been severely hampered in the patient who has created a sexual perversion.* But this aspect of the relation to the father is usually deeply repressed. We discover in the course of analysis that the father, invariably presented as a castrate, a figure unworthy of identification, conceals his idealized counterpart, that of an uncastratable phallus, the only one capable of completing the mother. But this ideal father and penis are forever out of reach. The only path to identification with such an exalted being is through childhood omnipotence — magic and sleight of hand. This splitting of the paternal object designates the point of rupture in the development of identification with a genital father.

Such total failure to symbolize a valid representation of the father's phallus could only come about in the context of a disturbed relationship to the mother (and the strong possibility of difficulty in the parents' relationship to each other), which leaves traces in the existence of an underlying depressive structure. This in turn must be warded off through the sexual act and gives to the perverse quest the feverish quality of *manic denial*. But before exploring this sector of the analysand's personality structure, it is necessary to construct other versions of the genital relationship than that fabricated by reversal, denegation, and disavowal.

I shall return at this point to K's analysis and to the exploration of another dimension of the oedipal constellation which opened the way to more deeply buried fantasies and feelings. K slowly came to disclose, indeed to discover as though for the first time, feelings of intense anger toward his mother. "Always talking about her wonderful father... the man I was supposed to emulate. Actually it was *she* who wanted to be exactly like him. She told me she had always wanted to be a boy. Well I was supposed to be that boy — not for myself but for her. My grandfather's death must have affected us both, and yet I can hardly remember anything around that period of my life. Let's see, I know I must have been six when it happened. I remember that when my grandfather died my little brother was just learning to walk." After a short silence he continued, "Really I don't understand this hatred I feel for my mother. After all she only wanted the very best for me. If she wanted to keep me all to herself it was only because she loved me so much. The fact that she prevented any possibility of a real relationship between me and my father is not sufficient to explain the hatred I feel."

I repeated, "When my grandfather died my little brother was just learning to walk."

"What do you mean?"

"You tell me your mother adored you, and wanted you all to herself," I said.

"Sure! And I said it isn't a good enough reason to explain all this hatred!"

"Perhaps it is not the sole or even the true reason for your hatred," I said. "It could be that you resented your mother because she *desired other people besides yourself.* When her adored father died (and he must certainly have been a rival for her love) her *baby,* who was just learning to walk, was already beginning to take his place. And this little brother, how does he fit into the idea that your parents had no sexual relationship as far as you were aware? By the way, this is the first time you ever mentioned the existence of a little brother."

"Oh," said K lamely, "I guess I never mentioned it. I'm the oldest of four."

"So she was pretty unfaithful to you one way and another?" I said.

The fatal childhood dates — six years, nine years — which marked the setting up of K's sexual system also marked the birth of two of the rival brothers, but by a powerful act of *disavowal* (for he was well aware of their existence) these cataclysmic events in the life of the little mother-fixated boy had been rendered totally meaningless; thus his illusion was protected. The whip, fictitious phallus, grandfather's idealized penis, became the chosen object of maternal desire, the sole object able to excite his own. In this way he was able to camouflage the fact that his father, and his father's penis, played a vital role in the mother's life and in the existence of the little brothers. Whatever the unconscious wishes of K's mother may have been, we were now able to establish the fact of K's intense childhood demand that his mother exist solely for him.

In the following sessions K recalled scenes from this early period, and one in particular which had the brilliance and clarity of a screen memory. K's mother is nursing the new baby while K watches with fascination: "She was holding him down there, against her sex, where you musn't look. But I could look because the 'void' was covered by *the bare bottom of my baby brother*. I kept staring at his naked buttocks, trying to understand — I don't know what."

In contemplating this scene K realized that not only did the baby bottom take the place of the mother's missing penis, but it also enabled him to deny her breasts which were feeding the rival child. To his childlike gaze the breast and the buttocks became indissolubly linked in unconscious memory. Primordial longings from early childhood began to appear in his dreams and daydreams, and it became clear that the ritualistic and exciting game of beating on the buttocks mimed not only a castrative act, but also *a desire for vengeance upon the faithless breasts.*

To his feeling of having been duped and humiliated, at the height of his oedipal longings, by his most beloved objects, was added the deeper anxiety of having destroyed the mother's breasts and thus lost the source of love and of life. K had struggled endlessly against the recognition of such feelings, fearing that his hate would destroy his love and destroy him too. Every activity became a game; every desire — whether a sexual or a love relationship, or a creative work project — could only be a magical fulfillment. He had managed to persuade himself that life itself was nothing but a game, a game in which you could control everything, provided you never depended on anyone else. Patients such as K often appear unusually undemanding and free of all attachments. In fact, they are forced to deny, on a deep unconscious level, any desire, or even any need of another. This involves the babyhood magic of believing that the mother's breasts are one's personal property, and that one will have them forever. To maintain this illusion it is necessary to divest life of any semblance of seriousness and thus remain out of reach of frustration, guilt, or depression.

The game created out of K's disavowals served not only to lull the castration anxiety attached to his thwarted phallic strivings, but also to control the underlying anxiety concerning the fantasy of having deprived his mother of her life-giving powers. His game therefore became a massive negation of what he felt his life amounted to — a form of inner death. This mechanism recalls in many ways Melanie Klein's concept of *manic defense*, and to my mind forms on an important dimension in all individuals whose psychic equilibrium depends predominantly on a sexual perversion. The extensive denials and denegations procure for the individual a double benefit: In connection with his oedipal strivings (both the heterosexual and the homosexual oedipal desires) he is able to convince himself that the event he fears the most — castration — is the most exciting experience he knows. At a more primitive narcissistic level, he is able to wipe out feelings of intolerable guilt which would otherwise threaten his very right to live. Should the game, the illusion, begin to lose its power, leaving in its wake a feeling of fighting against inacceptable realities, that is, *should the manic defense cease to operate*, the sufferer may then decide to seek analytic help. He rarely, if ever, comes in order to be rid of his sexual deviations (or if he does, we are dealing with a more common neurotic personality structure). It would be closer to the truth to say that under cover of being concerned about his sexual practices he hopes to acquire the right *to cease playing at living as the only path to survival.*

The aim of this chapter has been limited to the exploration of certain aspects of the oedipal constellation in sexual perversion: to an attempt to formulate, through a clinical case history, the basic fantasies to which the oedipal "solution" of the sexual deviant gives rise, and finally the economic means through which the ensuing ego identity is maintained. Although the clinical example provided by K's analysis was rich in individual detail, this has been set aside in order to concentrate on those aspects which are typical of the psychic structure underlying sexual perversion in general. The following points seem to me important: The fantasy that is directed to the phallic castration of the paternal imago hides another which is the castration of the feeding mother. If the first wish may be said to threaten the individual himself with castration, the second produces anxiety linked to depression, to fear of psychic disintegration, and to death.

These aggressive-castrative wishes with their accompanying anxieties are held in check through compulsive sexual behavior which takes on the characteristics of a play, or a game with rigid rules, and leads to a form of object relation dominated by the same defensive mechanisms: disavowal and negation, splitting and projection, instinctual regression, manic defense.

As in childhood, the game functions in the service of mastering traumatic events and states, and permits the individual to play at things he may not carry into action (libidinal and aggressive wishes); it also permits a reversal of roles which often takes the form of controlling the orgastic response of the partner, this "loss of control" being regarded as a castration of the partner, or a reduction of his status to that of a helpless child. He plays in fantasy at being the only one to enjoy the father's penis and the only one to enjoy the maternal breasts; in consequence, he may possess and punish these objects. Thus the desperate sexual game allows the recovery in fantasy of lost objects as well as the erotization of the defenses against the forbidden wishes.

In the case history which forms the core of this chapter, the loved-hated objects (paternal penis, maternal breasts) were disguised by being displaced onto the whip and the buttocks, where they were able to be controlled and castrated, and above all, brought back to life again. The very act of attacking and controlling the beloved objects through their partial representations was in itself a way of proving that they still lived and that the son was protected from their vengeance and from his guilt.

If the stage play of the pervert is a gesture of defiance (of the father, of society as a whole), it is also an attempt to recover this lost internal object. To deceive and humiliate the father is one way of ensuring that he exists. In no matter what form the perverse act may manifest itself it aims always to capture the eye of the "anonymous spectator," external representative of the phallic image, the third dimension. Thanks to this shadowy third, though reduced to a truncated inner object or inanimate symbolic object, the individual is able to maintain his feeling of identity and to annul the ever-present risk of depression or persecutory anxiety during which time his ego identity is threatened and may be drawn into the psychic void represented by the limitless omnipotent world of the mother — psychosis. Such is the fate the pervert fears should he shake off the bonds which make his sexual — and sometimes his total — life an anguished tightrope-walking exploit. For the anonymous spectator can only cede his place to the specter of psychic death.

Chapter II

The Primal Scene
and the Perverse Scenario

Before discussing the unconscious meaning of sexual perversion and the possible elements of what might be called a "perverse" structure, I should like to delimit the clinical concept of such a structure as opposed to a neurotic or a psychotic one. This presents some difficulty since a perverse organization cannot necessarily be deduced from, or defined simply in terms of, the incidence of deviant sexual behavior. Sexual aberrations occur in people with differing psychic structure and the same sexual act may have a significantly different meaning and function according to the personality. Nor may such a structure be said to include people whose sexual relations or whose masturbation is regularly accompanied by what might be termed perverse fantasy, since this is in no way specific and might be considered by many to be the prerogative of the neurotic. In contradistinction, the individual whose sex life is expressed mainly through manifest and organized perversion usually displays a singularly impoverished fantasy life. This may mean that his inner object world allows him to imagine sexual relations solely from one limited perspective (Sachs, 1923). In addition, his ego structure is such that he usually feels compelled to carry into immediate action most of what he imagines. On the whole he has little erotic freedom, whether in act or fantasy. Nor may we include in the category of a stable perverse organization those patients, often of hysterical structure, who have engaged in incidental homosexual adventures, nor the obsessional analysands who recount perverse phases such as fetishist or anal erotic experiments. These have a qualitatively different meaning and function. *The erotic expression of the sexual deviant is an essential feature of his psychic stability, and much of his life revolves around it.* A similar qualitative distinction is to be made for people whose ego and object relations are predominantly psychotic. Such individuals sometimes seek out homosexual or other perverse relations in an attempt to escape anxiety of psychotic origin or to find some delimitation through erotic contact. These factors may well enter into a perverse relationship too, but they are not the leading elements.

In the long run it is no simple matter to designate what is and what is not perverse. And even so, it is easier to define what we mean by a perversion than what we mean by a pervert. Freud early drew attention to the fact that we are all perverts under the skin where the pervert-polymorph childish parts of ourselves are hidden. It follows from this that activities which are commonly regarded as perverse — voyeurism, fetishism, exhibitionism, interest in a diversity of possible erotic zones — all might form part of the experience of a normal love relation. *One factor which would appear to characterize the pervert from this point of view is that he has no choice; his sexuality is fundamentally compulsive.* He does not choose to be perverse and cannot be said to choose the form of his perversion any more than the obsessional could be said to choose his obsessions or the hysteric his headache and phobias. The compulsive element in deviant sexuality also leaves its imprint on the object relationship, the sexual object being called upon to fulfill a restricted and rigidly controlled role — even an anonymous one. The role of the partner, though frequently reduced to that of a partial object, nevertheless is highly invested and fulfills a magical function. But this might also be said to apply to many an ordinary love relationship where illusion is never lacking. In addition, if we agree that the psychotic often seeks erotic contact as a bulwark against anxiety, or as a prop for his ego, then we should add that ordinary genital heterosexuality also contains an important element of narcissistic enhancement and considerable reassurance against the slings and arrows of existence. There is a fantasy of self-reparation and omnipotence in everybody's love-making; it is not, however, the sole or the dominant factor in most cases. Not only are the nonsexual aspects of the relationship of importance, but the sexual relation itself plays a different dynamic role in the libidal economy from that found in perverse or psychotic personality patterns.

No reference will be made here to perverse character traits or to other "acting-out" structures comparable to the perversions (such as addictions or delinquency); all of these clinical categories have something in common with sexual deviation and may be different methods of solving the same basic unconscious conflicts, but they lack the specific quality of conscious erotization of defenses. The aim of this chapter is to examine certain characteristic elements of the structure that is maintained through overt and relatively consistent sexual perversion. In particular, attention will be directed to the relation of the subject, and his act, to the primal scene (this term being taken to connote the child's total store of unconscious knowledge and personal mythology concerning the human sexual relation, particularly that of his parents).

Background to this study

I became interested in the unconscious significance of organized sexual perversion through one of those coincidences which occur in all analytic practices: I had three homosexual women in analysis during the same period of time. Before these long analyses were terminated I had acquired two more. All these patients suffered periods of intense depression connected either with failure in their love relations or in their work. (All were engaged in professional or artistic work, and none worked well. This was sometimes the reason for seeking analytic help. None came because of her homosexuality.)

In these clinical pictures, characterized by a mixture of neurotic and psychotic manifestations, I came to understand that the sexual love relations of these analysands were often a frantic screen in which the partner was to act as a sheltering wall against the danger of depressive feelings or loss of identity, and equally as a magic shield against fantasied attack from men. The highly ambivalent relationship itself was also constantly threatened from within.

Apart from these similarities in ego structure and in the defense mechanisms used to maintain this precarious equilibrium, these patients showed striking homogeneity in the way they presented their parents. The over-all picture was of a father who failed to fulfill his paternal function and a mother who more than fulfilled hers. I was struck by this curious splitting of good and bad qualities along a line of sexual demarcation and tried to sort out my impressions with regard to the inner fantasy world and its relation to the external sexual object. From there, I developed certain theoretical ideas concerning the role of homosexuality in the maintenance of psychic equilibrium and ego identity (McDougall, 1964, 1970).

We might sum up the psychic economy of female homosexuality as an attempt to maintain a narcissistic equilibrium in the face of a constant need to escape the dangerous symbiotic relationship claimed by the mother imago, through conserving an unconscious identification with the father, this being an essential element in a fragile structure. Costly though it may be, this identification helps to protect the individual from depression or from psychotic states of dissociation, and thus contributes to maintaining the cohesion of the ego.

I became interested in the fact that male homosexual patients displayed many of the same basic structural features as the homosexual women, particularly with respect to imago patterns and affective splitting of objects according to their sex; but where the homosexual woman seeks to recover her own essential femininity from her idealized female partner, the male homosexual seeks an idealized penis on another man. The dangerous destructive aspects of the parent of the same sex are projected in each case onto the opposite sex. Homosexuals of both sexes unconsciously seek protection from the primitive "oral" or "anal" mother of the pregenital phases, and both try desperately to maintain some form of "phallic barrier" — either through identification (in the case of the girl) or object choice (in the case of the boy) to some inner or outer representation symbolizing the father. Meanwhile the real father is invariably held to be valueless or regarded as absent.

The specificity of this unbalanced oedipal organization and the unconscious personality structure to which it gives rise received further confirmation in the study of two fetishist patients and in the discussion of similar cases with colleagues. I became more aware of the sadistic fantasied attacks against both parents, particularly the idealized mother, and continued to be preoccupied with the fate of the father imago and the role of the symbolic phallus in the structurization of the personality. These reflections are contained in Chapter I.

I would suggest that certain essential features to which my work on female homosexuality and fetishism drew attention are to be found in all organized perverse formations and may provide elements of differentiation between these and neurotic or psychotic organizations. I do not wish to give the impression that the varying forms of perverse sexuality are without theoretical significance; the relation between fetishism and transvestism, for example, or the link between fetishism and sadomasochistic wishes, is evident and important for our analytic understanding of these patients. The same is true of voyeurism and exhibitionism, and more particularly significant is the difference between all these sexual expressions and homosexuality. It is obvious that the homosexual has a specific problem concerning the narcissistic body image and a compulsion to repair his own image through a partner of the same sex. In contradistinction, the non-homosexual pervert frequently displays as many defenses against homosexual wishes as does the neurotic. An example of this was given by a fetishist patient who paid prostitutes to whip him and stamp on his genitals. In one session he reported meeting another client of the same brothel who suggested they had much in common since he too paid to be whipped on the genitals — but by boys. My patient became highly anxious and said, ". . . but that man's crazy. We have absolutely nothing in common. Why, he's a homosexual!" My analysand's remark also highlights the fact that all perversion is built around essential illusions that must not be touched, and raises the question as to what is considered as "real" or significant in this sexual microcosm where negation and denial play a predominant role.

For the purpose of this chapter, however, I am more concerned with the pervert as a person and with his unconscious structure than with the form of his perversion. Beginning with the oedipal constellation and the parental imagos, we have seen that the mother holds an idealized place, while the father plays a curiously

negative role in the inner object world. Complicity and
seduction are attributed to the mother, while the
father is represented as a cipher or in any case inapt to
be chosen as a model for identification. Thus we find a
false splitting (Meltzer, 1967) of an unusual kind in
which the mother becomes an unattainable phallic
ideal and the father a denied or denigrated object. In
the unconscious counterparts to these ostensible family
portraits the mother is felt to be mortally dangerous to
her child, the hatred and aggression attached to her
image being deflected onto other objects. Behind the
image of the denigrated father, equally split, lies an
idealized father (a role frequently attributed to the
mother's own father, or to a religious figure, or God
himself) or more often, the fantasy of an idealized
phallus. This plays an important structuring role in the
personality despite its split-off quality (Kurth and
Patterson, 1968). It is also represented in a variety of
ways in the deviant sex act where there is invariably revealed an attempt to gain, to retain, or to control this
idealized paternal phallus. It is only defensively attributed to the mother, hidden so to speak behind her
own primordial phallic role as the first object of desire
and giver of life. This eternal quest for the father, for
something which stands between the child and the
omnipotent mother, contributes of the compulsive
character of perverse sexuality. It also gives the psychic
structure a bulwark against psychosis and at the same
time marks the possible fragility to the perverse structure. *That which is missing in the internal world is*
sought in an external object or situation, for there is a
vital lack or blank in the ego structure of the subject,
and this in turn is due to a failure in symbolization.

This failure concerns the meaning of the primal scene, and the role of the father's penis. The effacement of certain associative links tends to weaken the individual's relation to reality, at least in this circumscribed area, and thus leads to a "psychotic solution," to oedipal conflict and castration anxiety; this is in turn eroticized, thus contributing a partial solution also to problems of instinctual discharge.

Apart from specific features in the unconscious oedipal and preoedipal organization, perversion offers a rich and interesting study of the growth of human desire and the varied objects through which it may be mediated. By the same token it offers an important field of research into the problem of human identity. Since the deviant by definition shows disturbance in his sexual identity we might well question what role deviant sexuality plays in maintaining ego identity. Lichtenstein (1961) suggests that one of the chief functions of nonprocreative sexuality is the maintenance of identity feeling. I would suggest that this is equally true for the sexual deviant. His constant search for identity confirmation (to stem the panic that accompanies a threatened loss of identity feeling) may even predominate over the libidinal and aggressive aims in his ritualized sexual scene. Thus, through a complicated system of negation, disavowal, and displacement, he will often claim that he is not perverse, that he was born homosexual, transvestite, etc., that is to say, his sexual pattern is a necessary part of his identity. André Gide's *Corydon* (1920) is an outstanding example of this. The pervert frequently believes too that he holds a special secret concerning sexual desire and may even claim that he has discovered the true secret (we shall examine the unconscious basis of this secret later). Supported in his own sexual identity, he often reserves scorn for the "straight" people who make love in the old-fashioned way — the way of the despised and denigrated father. Paradoxically, the ordinary heterosexual is thought of as deprived (unconsciously, the castrated victim of paternal and social pressure), and as a representative of the castrated paternal imago. The son has discovered, as one analysand put it, "a more spicy dish." (This patient, whose problems were also reflected in his alcoholism, paid prostitutes to urinate on him. He felt that others were envious of his special formula.) This feeling of being "in the know," chosen over the heads of ordinary mortals to receive the secret of the gods, marks the illusion of the incestuous child who believed himself to be the apple of his mother's eye — to the detriment of the scorned father who is relegated to the child's place as the excluded one, the castrate. But the incestuous child is able to continue his illusion of being mother's sole object of desire *on condition that he agrees only to play at sexuality.*

Childhood's end

Some perverse patients are more keenly aware than others of the depression that lies behind this frantic play, thus closer to remembering that inevitable moment of disillusion when the house of cards of incestuous promise came tumbling down. In an attempt to fill the sudden void thus created in identity feeling, the sexual game becomes a desperate attempt to ward off rage and murderous or suicidal impulses. Sexual perversion admits and exhibits its excited, libidinal aim but draws a veil of silence over its more frightening aspects. "Kinky sex" is widely displayed as a technicolor diversion; the "gay" world of the homosexual is paraded in many a bar, but the color and the "gaiety" thinly disguise its depressive and often persecutory counterpart. Since it is suggested here that these complex sexual anomalies are built on the ruins of crumbling illusion, one question clamors for elucidation. If sexual perversion is an answer to incestuous wishes and the frustrated rage that greets their nonfulfillment, little is explained, since these disappointments form a universal trauma, an integral part of the human predicament. Why are these children specially marked for disillusion?

In analysis these patients reveal to us the way in which they have woven their identity, especially in its sexual aspects, from the strands of silent clues picked up from the parents' unconscious wishes and conflicts; they are, in particular, consciously aware of the place they occupy in their mother's eyes. Many analytic papers have been written on this subject — the mother's complicity and its effect on the creation of a deviant superego model (Bak, 1956; Gillespie, 1956a, 1956b; Segal, 1956; Sperling, 1955; Stoller, 1968). I should like to take up the counterpart to this and examine *the child's part* in the outcome, an outcome in which a new sexuality is created and the primal scene reinvented. Although a reaction to parental problems, this is the child's creation, not the mother's. It is made from scraps of childhood magic (the elements of infantile sexuality) and tailored to fit childlike desire (the wish to annihilate the primal scene and the complementary wish to be the sole object which completes the mother). Yet in the very creation of his perversion, the child breaks the maternal bonds and *triumphs over the internalized mother*. In the course of analysis these patients came to recall quite vividly the discovery of their deviant "solution": the creation of their private erotic drama. This is usually assigned to the latency years, or around puberty, and is often presented as a "revelation" of their true sexual nature. Precipitating factors, which in many cases have the force of screen memories, are often family events such as the birth of a sibling, a rift in the parental relationship, or a remarriage. Two of my female homosexual patients claimed to have "discovered" their sexual vocation after the birth of a second child when they were 10 or 11 years old. Freud's case of female homosexuality (1920) also followed this pattern. A fetishist patient and another with elaborate sadomasochistic rituals dated the different elements of their sexual system from the time of the birth of brothers and sisters—incontrovertible proof of the mother's infidelity.

Some searing memory is invariably utilized to account for the final crumbling of incestuous illusion, and this is just as frequently a frank disparagement of the child's immature sexual being by the seductive mother who denies any sexual awareness on the part of her offspring. The mother in *Portnoy's Complaint* is almost classical. "What? For your little thing?" she says when Portnoy wants a jock-strap in his trunks. As Portnoy tells his analyst, "Maybe she only said it once—but it was enough for a lifetime!" A similar experience was recounted by one of my patients with homosexual problems. "I was 11 and I slipped naked into bed with mother as I had often done. This time she pushed me out brutally and said: 'Whatever do you think you're doing, you rude boy!' About the same time my father took me aside and explained how babies were born. I burst into tears."

It is astonishing to learn how long these children have been able to believe that they were "mother's little mate" and even believe that they would one day have sexual relations with her. The rage and bewilderment that these disenchantments inspire are slowly released from repression in analysis; but this is only a beginning. These recovered traumas are merely the last link in a very long chain. The mother-attached child has reached a point of no return. He makes a desperate attempt to free himself through erotic relations of various kinds, but the apparent solution to his conflict is already determined. His sexual illusions remain intact; they have simply found new disguises. Important links concerning sexual truth have been distorted or destroyed in the primitive preoedipal relation, the stage set perhaps at the breast. Indeed it is no surprise to learn that the "castrator" in the perverse structure is invariably the mother, not the father. She is the seducer who awakens desire and at the same time acts as the barrier to its fulfillment. To her child she is the very portrait of perversity. What does she want? Children who have idealized the mother's image have believed that in some sense they too were "ideal" children, the center of her universe — up until the fatal revelation that they are not the answer to the mother's desire. Now they no longer know just who they are, nor what will satisfy her. There must be, somewhere, an "ideal" phallus; but it is abundantly clear that it is not

in the father's possession. He has rarely been acknowledged as an object of sexual desire for the mother, so
there is little wish on the child's part to turn to him or
to identify with him. This factor, reinforced by conscious and unconscious attitudes on the mother's part,
fits in only too well with the child's wish to believe in
the myth of a castrated or nonexistent father. (It
should be noted that a father actually absent, or even
dead, does not necessarily prevent the child's creating a
valid internal phallic image if the maternal relation
allows of it.) The fathers of these unfortunate children
would appear also to contribute to their own exclusion,
or reveal themselves as incapable of modifying those
personality aspects that alienate them from their children. Thus *oedipal jealousy and the castration complex
become a disorganizing experience rather than the reverse* (i.e., the nodal point for a new and more mature
reorganization of the whole personality). But the children with whom we are concerned here have found no
dissolution to oedipal conflict; instead a deviant way
around the problem has been contrived. To understand its nature, we must now turn to a study of the
sexual scenario.

Perverse scenario and dream scene

What is the unconscious meaning of a sexual act
from which pain and anxiety are rarely absent (or at
most frantically denied)? What role does the sexual object play in this partnership which, more often than
not, is detached from any love relationship? And what
material does the sexual deviant use to write his curious

script? As Gillespie (1956a) pointed out, although perversions are created out of the constituent elements of childhood sexuality, it is both clinically and theoretically untenable to maintain (as Freud's early writings on the subject might have led one to believe) that organized perversion is simply the persistence into adult life of id impulses that have escaped repression. In many ways the perverse play is comparable to a dream. Let me cite a clinical example.

My patient asks his wife to dress in ritualized clothing which hides her genitals but reveals her buttocks; he then whips her on the buttocks and the sight of the marks brings him to a sexual climax. When he is alone the patient will sometimes don the clothing and whip himself on the buttocks in front of the mirror, watching anxiously for the whip marks. This scene, like a dream, resembles a stage play in which some vital links are missing (and its air of theatricality is common to many a perverse scenario). It is a manifest content, making use of primary-process thinking, reversals, displacements, and symbolic equivalents. But the chief actor himself has invariably lost the clues and will frequently attempt to make a secondary revision of the elements of his act (like the dreamer) in an attempt to explain the attraction of the deviant object or the deviant situation. In the above example, the analysand, instead of questioning the sexual conjunction of a whip and a pair of buttocks in which the whip would appear to play the role of a fictitious penis and the buttocks to replace the female genitals, explained that he had a particular interest in whips of all kinds, and sometimes he even photographed them. He also proclaimed a fascination for relationships of force between parents and children. He has written many versions of a story (a classical fetishist script) in which an older woman publicly whips her daughter. He has been polishing this erotic script for some 20 years, and this is what he imagines in his sexual play in which he takes the role of either mother or daughter, although he claims to be merely a spectator. While attempting to justify the elements of his personal myth of sexual intercourse, he once broke off to say: "By the way, did I ever tell you about my passion for the study of science fiction?" In that session he was able to see that he had no idea what his sexual script was all about and that in all probability it too was a piece of science fiction.

A different type of secondary revision, one concerning a deviant aim rather than a deviant object, was given by another analysand. He described in minute detail his need to pay prostitutes to stamp on his genitals while wearing a particular kind of high-heeled shoe, during which time he watched the procedure anxiously in a mirror. He interrupted his description to say: "By the way, I hope you don't think I'm a masochist — you see, this gives me intense pleasure." Now the point is that both these patients recognized the idiosyncratic nature of their sexual creation and felt it needed some justification; they were not psychotic. In contrast, a third patient (and this one did pass through a psychotic episode during his analysis) felt no such need; he imposed his inner reality on the world. In his first interview he said: "I am, of course, a homosexual. As I expect you know, all men are homosexual but the majority simply lack the courage to admit it." I shall refer later to this patient's psychotic phase, since I believe it was precipitated by an interpretation touching a vitally important element in the perverse organization, the contact with a phallic object which was keeping psychotic confusion at bay.

Theme and variations

Thus the pervert attempts to convince himself and others that he holds the secret to sexual desire. This is then played out in his sexual creation. What in fact is his secret? What is his sexual play trying to prove or achieve over and beyond its value as a path of libidinal discharge? The secret may be reduced to the relatively simple proposition that there is no difference between the sexes. More precisely put, his secret is this: *there are perceptual differences between the sexes, but these are without significance;* and *above all this difference is neither the cause nor the condition of sexual desire.* It is a denial of a vast order and includes the denial of the primal scene. Through an infinity of symbolic displacements and the cutting of certain associative links, sexual desire is furnished with new objects, new zones, and new aims.

The new primal scene of which the pervert is the author merits attention. Although the decor, actors, and objects vary considerably, the theme is immutable: it is the drama of castration, and the mastery of its associated anxiety. Whether this be the script of the sadomasochist with his concentration on pain, often aimed directly at his genitals or those of his partner, or the fetishist who reduces the game of castration to beaten buttocks and bodily constriction (the important bodily marks that symbolize castration but are so readily effaced) or the transvestite who makes his own genitals vanish while he infiltrates himself into his mother's garments in order to take on her identity, or again the homosexual with his restless quest for more and more penises which he magically absorbs, orally and anally, thus repairing his own fantasied castration and at the same time castrating and repairing the partner through controlling his orgastic response — in every instance the plot is the same: castration does not hurt and in fact is the very condition of erotic arousal and pleasure. When anxiety appears nevertheless (and it is rarely absent) it is in turn erotized and becomes a new condition of sexual excitement. One cannot escape the impression that these people resemble children *playing at sexuality,* but the game is a desperate one; castration anxiety of an intense order has to be warded off by means of the sexual play (and in these individuals with their relatively fragile ego structure, any of life's irritations and disappointments are liable to arouse inadequacy feelings which call for immediate solution through the magical sex act); in addition, the invented primal scene has to be validated. There is always a spectator to this stage play — a role which the individual will frequenty play himself as he watches in the mirror the production of his special sexual scene. There is an important reversal of roles here; the child, once victim of castration anxiety, is now the agent of it, the dealer in castration (like the child with the cotton-reel mastering the drama of separation). The excited child, once the helpless spectator of the parents' relationship, or victim of unusual stimulation which could not be dealt with, is now the controller and producer of excitement, whether his own or his partner's. In fact, many perverts are uniquely interested in manipulating the other person's sexual response. This rather important element of actively making the object suffer what one once passively endured finds its correspondence in certain psychotic ways of handling relationships, as Hanna Segal (1956) pointed out in her paper on "Depression in the Schizophrenic" in which the patient subtly contrived to make the mother feel like "the infant experiencing sexual excitement, greed, frustration, rage and guilt." Added to these essential reversals of early traumatic experiences is the all-important negation of the genital relation between the parents. The father's penis thus has no role in the mother's sexual life. Instead, sexual pleasure comes to her through being whipped, chained up, or urinated upon, or through exhibiting herself, defecating or urinating on the father, beating him, etc. — or so we are invited to believe. To the multiple variations on the castration theme must therefore be added its counterpoint — that the genital organs of the parents are not intended to complete one another and mutual desire is nonexistent. Such is the fiction that must continue to be reaffirmed. In his attempt to know nothing of the relation between the parents, that is, to maintain a fictional introjected primal scene, the pervert is facing a losing battle with reality. Like trying to repair a crumbling wall with scotch tape, it has to be redone every day. In this perspective his sexual act is a form of continuous acting out of a compulsive kind, for the pervert has created a sexual mythology whose true meaning he no longer recognizes, like a text from which important pieces have been removed. As we shall see, these missing pieces are not repressed, for this would have given rise to neurotic symptoms; instead they are destroyed, rather in the style of someone cutting the telephone wires when the news is bad. Thus many perverse patients complain of not understanding human sexuality. A voyeurist patient told me he felt like "a man from Mars" when he heard other men talking about their interest in women. The fetishist patient who was interested in science fiction remembered his amazement when his adolescent companions would talk about sex and girls and tell risqué stories. He faced this unequal situation as he faced all disturbing experiences, by careful mastery and manipulation of it. He became the school expert on naughty stories and invented more and wickeder ones than the others. His personal pleasure in controlling the sexual excitement of his companions was intense, as was his pride in the fact that he "felt nothing." Like the "man from Mars" he had difficulty in believing in other men's sexual objectives, so total was his denial of sexual reality with all its alienating consequences for his own sexual desire and sexual identifications. This same patient also came to say: "I feel as though I were cursed in childhood. I never chose my sexuality, it was cast upon me like a spell." Yet in this same session he added: "...but don't imagine that I want to change. As you well know, these are my favorite games." And therein lies the dilemma of the pervert. To give up his ritualized, anxious, and highly conditioned form of sexual expression would be equivalent to castration and open the door in many cases to perilous moments of loss of ego identity. A homosexual woman patient said recently: "...at least when I'm with her I know I *exist*...it was like that with my mother when I was young. I only existed in her eyes."

It is evident that behind the anxieties of the phallic phase and the narcissistic wounds of the primal scene lie deeper terrors concerning separation and individual identity. With all these patients, the father, though usually present, is represented as an absence. This lack in the internal representational world is of itself deeply threatening to identity feeling. Only the perverse or mythical sexual act permits some illusory recovery of the paternal phallus, albeit in idealized and disguised forms; it thus fulfills an essential function in affirming separate identity and affords some protection against the overwhelming dependence on the maternal imago, and the equally dangerous desire to merge with her. But how does this magic sexual system function? How do these individuals manage to destroy their knowledge of sexual reality and to replace it with a new, illusory act? The primitive mechanisms which this requires, while normal in very small children, are, in the adult, the hallmark of psychosis. Yet the pervert is not psychotic; for what has been denied or disavowed has not been recovered in the form of delusions, but is, in a sense, retrieved through a form of *illusion* contained within an act. There is evidence of some breakdown in the capacity to symbolize and to create an inner fantasy world to deal with intolerable reality; thus the illusion must be acted out endlessly, and this helps to avoid the danger of recuperation through delusion.

Let us re-examine Freud's concept of the maturation of sexual knowledge in the young child, and the series of fantasies through which it is mediated (Freud, 1923, 1924a, 1925, 1927, 1940). In the first place the child believes there is only one sexual organ — the penis. At a later stage he cannot avoid the perception that the female genital has no penis; at this point he *disavows* the unacceptable perception. "There is a penis there; I saw it." As Freud points out, this is in itself an affirmation of the child's perception of the sexual difference. Later still, the child's developing reality sense will not permit him to maintain that there is no perceptual difference between the sexes, and at this point begins a most important psychic adaptation to the unwelcome sexual reality — the child starts to *elaborate a series of fantasies* to account for it. "She hasn't a penis now, but it will grow later...other women don't have one but my mother does... or did, but father took it away... or else it's hidden up inside her," etc. There is no longer the disavowal of an external sense perception, but something infinitely more mature and sophisticated — another kind of disavowal. Anna Freud (1936) describes in detail the distinction between *denial in word and act* and *denial in fantasy.* Freud goes on to describe a fourth stage where children develop neurotic avoidance of the unacceptable sex organ through reaction formation or phobia in which the female genital becomes dirty or dangerous, or in which femininity in general is despised. In any case, the mother's open sex is known and counterinvested; it is no longer an object of fascination but a place of disquiet which temporarily bars the gateway of desire. If the disquieting fantasies are simply repressed at this stage, the child will make an apparent resolution of his oedipal wishes, but the door is open to later neuroses. In the best of all possible worlds the child will of course eventually accept that what he wishes were true will never be true; that the secret of sexual desire lies in the mother's missing penis; that only the father's penis will ever complete her genital, and that he will be forever alienated from his primary sexual desire and his unfilled narcissistic wishes. But to arrive at such a landing point one needs two "good-enough" parents, and we have every reason to suppose that the future pervert did not have them. He appears at times to be trying to solve his parents' problems as well as his own with his aberrant solution to oedipal distress. The perverse "solution" to oedipal problems is no solution at all; it is nevertheless an effective way out of certain serious "pre-oedipal" conflicts (Glover, 1933). The perverse solution is stuck somewhere between stage two (disavowal of perception) and stage three (denial through fantasy) of Freud's maturational model. Stage two (there is a penis there — I saw it) is magic denial and can only be dealt with by the creation of a new reality to fill the gap, followed by some manipulation of the outer world (Freud, 1924b). Stage three (there is no penis but. . .) does not destroy the information gathered from outer reality; it takes account of it and autoplastically creates imaginative, internal fantasy ways of dealing with the painful knowledge. The difference between the neurotic and the perverse solution is situated at this point. However, the factors that predispose a child to deal with sexual reality by magic denial, by the disavowal of sexual difference rather than through fantasy elaboration, *are operative long before this phase* of development.

What exactly is *disavowal?* This term, chosen for the *Standard Edition* to translate *Verleugnung* (Freud, 1923, p. 143 n.), seems to express more adequately the forceful "denial of reality through word and act"; it implies the notion of "avowal" followed by a *destruction of meaning*, through the cutting of associative links. It forms part of what Bion (1962, 1963) has designated as minus-K phenomena. Bion (1962) writes: "Before an emotional experience can be used for a model its sense data have to be transformed into alpha-elements to be stored and made available for abstraction. In minus-K the meaning is abstracted, leaving a denuded representation" (pp. 74–75).

In the particular case under consideration (in which the "model" concerning the truth about sexual difference and sexual relations becomes distorted) the "denuded representation" is not only the mother's empty vagina but also *the significance which should have been attached to this discovery*. The child of course comes to recognize the perceptual difference, and to know that his mother has no penis, but its mental representation leads to little else; it remains nonsignificant. The perception of the female genital is not only capable of arousing the fantasy described by Freud, namely that castration can happen to a little boy, or has happened to a little girl. It inevitably awakens the intuitive knowledge that the missing penis marks the place where a real penis comes into its true phallic function; this intuition makes room for learned knowledge concerning the sexual relation. Thus the mother's genital provides the proof of the role of the father's penis. But the child wishes to know nothing about this; he prefers to hallucinate a penis, thus destroying his recognition of sexual difference, rather than accepting that the genitals of his parents are different and complementary, that he is forever excluded from the closed circle, and that, should his desire persist, he must face the threat of castration. The concept of castration may be considered the equivalent of *reality* in this context, and thus acceptance of it leads the child to the various fantasies we have described as stage three of Freud's model. They are all ways of coping with castration fear and the prohibition of incest. The child who finds a perverse way out makes light of these inescapable realities but at the costly price of attacking a part of his own ego and therefore detaching himself, in a limited area, from external reality. He proclaims instead: "It is not true; my father is of no importance either to me or my mother. I have nothing to fear from him, and besides my mother loves only me." Thus the father's penis loses symbolic value and an important piece of knowledge is effaced.

The feeling of this gap-in-knowing, and its consequences, may perhaps be evoked in the following dream of a fetishist patient. "I was lying beside a woman and was asked to look at her legs. I stared for some time but couldn't make out what I was supposed to reply. It seemed to be a problem in logic. Finally I said that I would never find the answer because I never had been good at mathematics." In his associations the patient recalled his adolescent "flirtations" and the first time he kissed a girl. He was disquieted to find that he had no reaction; in place of sexual desire he was aware only of slight disgust. One is reminded of Oscar Wilde's likening women to "cold mutton" in comparison with the attraction of a homosexual object choice.

In his paper on the splitting of the ego Freud (1940) says, essentially that, faced with the gap where the mother's penis should have been, the child may create either a fetish or a phobia to fill it up — or a bit of both (this being the nodal point for a possible "third" structure, partaking both of neurotic and psychotic defense mechanisms. In other words, the ego "splits" its defensive forces in its attempt to face the truth of sexual desire and the futility of narcissistic demands. It disavows what it does not wish to know). Depending on the extent to which the child is unable to internalize and symbolize reality, he will evolve either toward a psychotic organization (disavowal not only of the significance of sexual difference but also refusal to accept and compensate for separateness itself), or else toward a deviant adaptation. This does not necessarily lead to the solution of sexual perversion. Many cases of addiction, of delinquency, of severe acting-out character pathology show similar mental mechanisms (McDougall, 1970; Sperling, 1968).

Fetishism is paradigmatic of all perverse formations, i.e., it demonstrates in exemplary fashion the way in which the gap left by the disavowal or destruction of sexual truth is subsequently compensated. In a sense it is an act of utter lucidity. Faced first with the fact of separate identity and then with sexual difference and its oedipal implications, the future pervert finds no veils thick enough to blur the outlines of insupportable reality as the neurotic is able to do. He can only obliterate the problem and find new answers to sexual desires. In the analyses of these patients one has the impression that they have been prematurely exposed to sexual stimulation and subsequently rejected and misinformed, or fed with illusory knowledge. One might recall here Hellman's (1954) paper on the mothers of children with intellectual inhibitions in which the children could not know things their mothers could not tolerate their knowing. In the child destined to a perverse solution of sexual desire the mother's unconscious plays a vital role. One is tempted to surmise that the mother of the future pervert herself denies sexual reality and denigrates the father's phallic function. It is possible that she also gives the child the feeling that he or she is a phallic substitute. In the histories of these patients we frequently find that another model of virility was held up to the child, sometimes the mother's own father or brother, sometimes a religious figure or God is the one phallic object of value. Nevertheless these are only partial explanations for the complicated psychic system that results, and they are of limited help in the analysis of sexual perversion.

Some of the factors noted by Bion (1967) in relation to psychotic formation and schizophrenic thought seem to me to apply also to those children who become perverse. Premature object relations and a hatred of reality are clinically evident in most cases. Phallic castration anxiety and oedipal jealousy are terminal rather than originating factors in promoting a perverse outcome to reality problems. Anxiety arises in the *absence of an object.* Behind the trauma of the mother's missing penis lies the global shadow of the missing mother; the ways in which the child was helped or hindered in compensating for this vital gap lay the foundation for the way in which he will approach the conflicts of the classical oedipal phase. Separation anxiety is the prototype of castration anxiety, and the mother's presence and absence are the factors around which the earliest oedipal structure will be erected. Rosenfeld (personal communication) has suggested that the nursling may already have established a "perverted" relationship with the nipple. I would agree with this in a broad metaphorical sense. Early castration trauma which expresses itself in the form of fear of bodily disintegration and fear of loss of identity is invariably revealed in sexual perversions, but it is not specific to these. When early separation experiences have been traumatic there are still many possible outcomes, ranging from psychosis and psychosomatic illness to addiction and other acting-out pathology. The crucial mobilizing factors that set the stage for later sexual deviation arise in the true oedipal phase; the infra-structure begins at the breast. The incidence of psychosomatic disorders (particularly allergic) appears clinically to be unusually high in patients with structured perversion. Sperling (1968) has studied the alternation of perverse and somatic expression in these analysands. This suggests other premature "gaps" where fantasy should have been, other areas of minus-knowledge in which affect and attempted thought have only been able to find expression directly through the body, without the mediation of a sufficiently elaborated fantasy world (neurosis). This is also the point at which perversion formation shades off into psychotic formations and where disavowal shades off into the *repudiation or abolition of perceptual truth* postulated by Freud (1911) as a basic psychotic mechanism in the Wolf Man and the Schreber case. In seeking to understand Schreber's psychotic homosexuality attached to Flechsig and God, Freud writes:

> It was incorrect to say that the perception which was suppressed internally is projected outwards; the truth is rather. . .that what was *abolished internally returns from without* [p. 71, italics added].

This fundamental differentiating mechanism which either facilitates or bars access to the truth about the world of human reality has been particularly studied by Bion (1962) within the concept of minus-K phenomena and in France by Lacan (1956, 1959), who has chosen the term "foreclosure" (*forclusion*) to designate this mechanism. The psychotic must recover in delusional form the projected knowledge whose links have been abolished. The pervert makes a considerable advance on this position in that he too recovers from the outside what has been lost, but by means of an *illusion he controls and delimits*. He is not deluded. The minus-knowledge concerning sexual difference and the primal scene in the perverse structuration is able to reduce the "influencing machine" (Tausk, 1919) of psychotic sexuality to a whip, a hank of hair, another man's penis. These tiny influencing machines are perhaps a miniature psychosis, but they serve to protect the individual's sanity. They also serve to protect *the object* (Gillespie, 1956a).

Let us return once more to the concept of disavowal. The destruction of associative links which it implies is a violent psychic act and is probably precipitated in moments of intense rage that finds no bodily discharge to deal with it. Here is a scene taken from everyday life: a small boy of two and a half has heard much talk about the coming baby in the family. One day he suddenly taps his nine-months pregant mother on the belly and shouts: "It isn't true that Mummy's as full as a bottle!" This is no simple negation; it is denial or disavowal of the little boy's own sense perception, a last determined effort to destroy the frightening reality that there is something which stands between him and his mother, right there inside her where he would often like to be. He knows it is a rival child; he knows too that it concerns daddy's penis; and he would like to destroy both baby and penis in that moment. But he protects his father and his mother from the fantasied onslaught. He denies reality instead. Of course the little boy's reaction is perfectly age-adequate. What he does afterward is what counts. What strands will he use to mend the hole left by his disavowal? Many roads are still open to him, as we have already seen in discussing Freud's maturational scheme of the apprehension of sexual reality.

The pervert, like the little boy, in destroying part of his perceptual and intuitive knowledge, protects his object from destructive hatred. And this too must be contained in his self-invented primal scene. The object (partner, penis, fetish, etc.) must not be destroyed. Depending on his inner fantasy world this will take one of two possible forms: he will seek either to *repair the object* (depressive aspect) or to *protect himself from being destroyed* (paranoid fear) by dominating the object erotically.

A passage in Painter's (1965) biography of Marcel Proust displays a sensitive understanding of the more violent aspect of Proust's homosexuality. In this chapter Painter describes Proust's giving first his dead parents' furniture and then their portraits to Albert's brothel, so that his young homosexual friends might insult these exalted beings. In front of Proust's favorite portrait of Princesse Hélène de Chimay, they had to shout: "Who the hell's this little tart?" Painter goes on to describe Proust's need to watch rats being tortured and the search for young men to torture them as part of an orgiastic ritual:

"Proust's search for cruelty in these young men was only in part a conscious craving for the imaginary beauty of strength and amorality. He was also performing symbolic acts of revenge for an injury inflicted in remote childhood. . . . It was when he was only 22 months old, and his brother Robert was born, that it became forever impossible for him to possess his mother's undivided love. Robert was not to blame, and Marcel had almost entirely forgiven his brother in the very early years; but a diabolical part of him had never forgiven his mother. . . . The hitherto unresolved abscess of infantile aggression burst, by a fistula cut through 44 years of time" (p. 267).

Thus Proust, like many another homosexual, played out his revenge on the faithless parents who, contrary to all he had been led to believe, and contrary especially to what he wanted to believe, had sexual relations together. The tortured rats are one more dreamlike image of the father's penis and of the eternal theme that castration does not hurt. Neither he nor the loved-hated objects are ever really destroyed — as long as the fictitious primal scene can continue functioning. The fetish (which comes from the French *factice*, meaning fictitious or artificial), fictitious phallic object, whose psychic representation has been severely damaged in the inner object world, must be eternally revived, there to be repaired or mastered, in the perverse sexual scene. To castrate, humiliate, and deny the father is nevertheless a proof of his existence.

Thus there is a condensed primal scene involving three people in every perverse act; this in turn depends on the individual's having the capacity to use external objects symbolically, to fill the internal gap where there has been symbolic failure, foreclosure, or minus-knowledge. Segal (1956) states that the child's capacity to symbolize "can be used to deal with earlier unresolved conflicts by symbolizing them." It seems to me that the pervert is attempting to resolve various problems from different layers of psychic life through the magical and symbolic aspects of his sexual act. Failure to use what might be called symbolic play may lead instead to a psychotic resolution. For example, the transvestite who wants to merge into his mother's identity will play at being in her skin by dressing up in female clothes; he will then play out the fantasy of attracting to himself the phallic father, thus accomplishing, symbolically, a double desire. In contrast to this, the man (whose case made newspaper headlines) who killed his girl friend in order to wear her skin for erotic purposes was psychotic, not perverse. The same may be said of the transsexuals who undergo physical castration in order to escape anxiety and to be able to accept a homosexual solution. Faced with the lack of an internalized phallus (other than the omnipotent early mother), the child must be capable of finding some external symbolic father object to prevent him from merging into the limitless oral universe where self and object are as one. It seems that this is what Khan (1969) is expressing when he writes: "One of the achievements of the collated internal object in the psychic reality of the pervert is that it enables him or her to establish a paradox in inner reality which protects him from being completely overwhelmed in his person by the intrusive omnipresence of the mother's unconscious in his childhood experience" (p. 564). He goes on to suggest, following Winnicott, that the embodiment of the sexual fantasy in a real person may protect the individual from suicide. Using Khan's metaphor of the collated object as disparate aspects of the father and mother imago, I would suggest that when certain vital father bits of this "collage" come unstuck, the door is open to suicide, or to psychotic dissociation.

In the same way, the sudden re-entry into consciousness of that which has been rendered inanimate, or forcibly ejected, can be dangerously disruptive. I would like to quote an incident in the analysis of a homosexual patient in this respect. His usual sexual pattern was to collect a number of different male partners for fellatio purposes, always in the belief that one day he would find "someone he really loved." He reported in one session that the previous night's search had brought him a terrible experience. He had gone home with a man much older than himself, which was unusual, and to his surprise he found himself becoming more interested in the man than in his penis. He became panic-stricken and sought an excuse to get away. Since he had always convinced himself he was in love with his companions of fortune, he was distraught to discover that they barely existed as persons, only as penises. Following his associations to the older man, dove-tailing with his current paternal transference in the analytic situation, I was able to show him that it had been necessary to avoid being interested in his partners in order not to know that the one penis he was seeking to possess was his father's. He wished to be nourished and strengthened by his father's penis but he did not want his father to suffer from the castration this implied. Following the session in question he abruptly ceased all his homosexual adventures and involved himself in a relation with a woman older than himself—but he discovered that whenever they ate meals together he became monstrously swollen. He exhibited these imaginary swellings to all his friends as well as to me. At the same time he complained that his bedroom was filled with ghosts. Everyone was alarmed. There are many possible interpretations of this incident: for one thing the removal of his disavowal concerning the father and his relation to the mother brought an intolerable flooding with painful affect; in addition it would seem that he had abruptly reintrojected a series of split-off images of the father's penis which had been play-acted in his homosexual activities (and now turned up as ghosts); finally, in giving up the last vestiges of his illusory recovery of the "ideal phallus" he merged completely with the mother figure —by swallowing her up! I shall leave aside the pregnancy fantasies that developed subsequently and disappeared when the patient decided to go back to real penises once more. I trust this vignette may epitomize the theme of this chapter: the reinvented primal scene, a privileged form of manic defense, is preferable to madness.

Chapter III

The Homosexual Dilemma:
A Study of Female Homosexuality

I hope to show in this chapter that female homosexuality is an attempt to resolve conflict concerning the two poles of psychic identity: one's identity as a separate individual and one's sexual identity. The manifold desires and conflicts that face every girl with regard to her father have, in women who become homosexual, been dealt with by giving him up as an object of love and desire and identifying with him instead. The result is that the mother becomes once more the only object worthy of love. Thus the daughter acquires a somewhat fictitious *sexual identity;* however, the unconscious identification with the father aids her in achieving a stronger sense of *subjective identity.* She uses this identification to achieve a certain detachment from the maternal imago in its more dangerous and forbidding aspects. As far as the idealized aspects of the mother image are concerned, these now seek satisfaction in a substitute relationship with a homosexual partner. This oversimplified statement of the "homosexual solution" to oedipal distress, as well as to pre-oedipal conflict and narcissistic integrity, raises many questions. I hope to offer partial answers to some of them.

What are the reasons that might force a small girl to give up her love for her father? And by what means does she arrive at an identification with him instead? Why is the mother felt to be so dangerous? What factors have hindered identification with the genital mother who has sexual relations with a man? What lies behind the frantic idealization of women? And what does she have to offer to her idealized women partners?

Over and beyond these questions which relate basically to the inner object world and the oedipal structure, are others which concern female sexuality in general. What is the role of "penis envy" and of "castration anxiety" in homosexuality? And what of the body image itself? How is it possible to maintain the illusion of being the true sexual partner to another woman? When we have some tentative answers to these questions, we shall be better equipped to broach the investigation of the homosexual relationship and all that it unconsciously represents. But let us first glance back some forty years to the earliest psychoanalytic paper ever published on the subject.

"No prohibitions and no supervision hindered the girl from seizing every one of her rare opportunities of being together with her beloved, of ascertaining all her habits, of waiting for her for hours outside her door or at a tram-halt, of sending her gifts of flowers, and so on. It was evident that this one interest had swallowed up all others in the girl's mind." Thus Freud (1920, p. 147) describes the passion of a young homosexual patient for an older woman. In reconstructing the genesis of his patient's homosexuality, Freud reveals that the daughter, having reached a "normal oedipal attachment" to her father, renounced all love for him at a period when she unconsciously desired a child from him. This period coincided with the mother's pregnancy. Thus it was the mother — unconsciously hated rival for the father's love — who gave birth to the child longed for by the daughter. The traumatic effect of this event appears to have led the young girl to a bitter rejection of all men, while she herself "changed into a man, and took her mother in place of her father as the object of her love" (p. 158). From this time onward, she pursued with amorous devotion women slightly older than herself. At the time of her consultations with Freud, she was enamored of a lady of doubtful morality, albeit of distinguished family, and of whom her father particularly disapproved. The young woman nevertheless arranged to be seen by her father in the company of her beloved. He turned upon her with a look of hatred which she construed to mean: "You are forbidden to love this woman." But to her unconscious mind the silent message read: "And you shall not have me either." Following the exchange of angry glances between father and daughter, the woman friend was enraged at finding herself an object of disapproval, and ordered the girl to leave her and to refrain from ever addressing her again. In the girl's mind, both man and woman refuse her the right to sexual possession of a woman, but unconsciously, as Freud's paper shows, the daughter takes this prohibition to mean that she has no right to take her mother's place and to desire her father's love for herself. Faced with rejection by both father and mother, she makes a final symbolic gesture in an attempt to possess and punish the two objects of her desire—she throws herself onto the railway cutting with the intention of committing suicide. In this tragic fashion she hurls a protest against the double abandonment, her feeling of utter helplessness, and her belief that there is nothing left to live for.

Freud elicits from this fragment of analysis an insight into the young girl's secret sexual wishes toward her father and her symbolic attempt, through her suicidal gesture, to compel him to give her a child. It is an oedipal drama. Freud's conclusions might lead us to suppose that narcissistic mortification alone explains the young woman's suicidal leap. However, oedipal rage and pain in the face of the fact that one is barred forever from the fulfillment of incestuous childhood wishes is a universal sexual trauma. Why is this young patient, and many others like her, so specially marked by the traumatic nature of human sexuality and oedipal disillusionment? Why such a desperate solution? Although her suicide is mobilized by oedipal distress, we are witnesses at the same time to a *preoedipal* drama which Freud does not explore. This paper predates by some ten years Freud's startling discovery of the little girl's preoedipal conflicts in her struggle for sexual identification (Freud, 1931, 1933). Long before the classical oedipal phase, she must come to terms with her love-hate relationship with her mother; she must achieve an identification with her as an individual and separate being, as well as identifying with her on a sexual plane. It is evident that her chances of achieving psychic independence, without undue guilt and depression, depend to a large extent on the mother's willingness to allow her girl child to become independent of her and to help her daughter in her sexual identification. This in turn requires the mother to acknowledge her daughter as a rival with feminine aims and desires, and to accept the daughter's love for the father. Clearly this also involves the father's attitude to his little girl, and depends on the extent to which he is willing to offer her his strength and love, and thus help her to disengage herself from her mother. If the parents suffer from unconscious conflicts that *interfere* with the girl's attempts to come to terms with her narcissistic and erotic wishes, and with the necessity to face sexual realities and accept her own sexual identity, then she runs the risk of receiving confusing messages. These will jeopardize her growing feeling of identity, her capacity for reality testing, and affect the structuring of her libidinal and aggressive impulses. Furthermore, it is on the basis of her disturbed early oedipal organization that she must face, and eventually work through, the conflicts of the classical oedipal crisis. It is perhaps justifiable to propose that it requires two problem parents to produce homosexual offspring.

Freud's paper states clearly his thesis that his young patient's suicidal attempt was an unconscious acting out of a phallic union with her father. But we must add to this symbolic reconstruction that she was also enacting the dissolution of her infantile relation to her mother. She is, at last, a woman asserting her right to sexuality and to motherhood, no longer in need of another woman in order to complete her own femininity. She had assigned to her woman friend the role of an idealized mother. Endowed with beauty, surrounded by lovers, she was, to the eyes of the ardent young girl, a perfect portrait of femininity, and thus possessed of manifold gifts which the girl considered were denied to herself and which, in childhood, she had believed were uniquely reserved for her mother. Her conscious wish to be an object of erotic desire for the other woman and to take sexual possession of her masks not only her desire "to be a man," as Freud put it, but also her aggressive wish to obtain the woman's hidden treasure—the right to the man and his penis and to the child he will give her. When her homosexual quest is thwarted, she seeks to punish both the man and the woman, for she demands something from each of them. In her suicidal leap she attempts an ultimate and secret fulfillment of these wishes and, as Freud points out, at the same time obtains punishment for them.

An alternative solution to her conflict might have been the establishment of overt homosexual relations, and in fact Freud's paper leads us to suppose that such was the case with his young patient. Her homosexual activity would then carry the same unconscious significance as her suicide attempt, namely a symbolic fulfillment of wishes, both loving and destructive, originally directed toward the parents. I do not maintain that a homosexual solution to oedipal and narcissistic problems is the equivalent of suicide; on the contrary, such an outcome may serve to ward off states of depression or depersonalization and thus act as a bulwark against suicide or psychic death.

Several homosexual women who were my patients showed striking similarities in ego structure and oedipal background. Their violence was particularly evident, as was the complicated defensive struggle against it, especially when these violent feelings were directed to the sexual partner. Equally striking was the fragility of their sense of identity as expressed in periods of depersonalization, bizarre bodily states, and so on, particularly if the relation to the love partner was felt to be threatened, whether by external circumstances or from within. One patient, for example, on learning that her lover was to leave her unexpectedly for three days, exclaimed: "I felt the room swimming round me when I read her letter; I couldn't think where I was and I had to bang my head against the wall until I came to my senses." On a similar occasion, she stubbed burning cigarettes out on her hands in order to bring to an end the painful sensation of loss of body-ego boundaries (Federn, 1952). Another patient cut her hands with a sharp knife and burned pieces of her skin when deserted by her lover of the moment. These analysands were expressing not only their almost symbiotic dependence on their partners, but also the terror and violent rage which the experience of separation and loss aroused. All these patients manifested equally intense reactions to men — but from men violent attack was anticipated. One of my analysands kept a stiletto in her pocket; another hid a large kitchen knife in her purse. Both claimed to be protecting themselves from attacks by taxi drivers and passersby. In addition to isolated episodes of confusion and depersonalization, all suffered from periods of intense depression connected with failure in their relationships, or with failure in their creative and professional activities. Work failure was frequently the conscious reason for coming to analysis. In my work with these patients, I came to understand that their sexual and love relationships were often used as a manic screen against depressive feelings and persecutory fears, a magic shield against fantasied attacks or threatened loss of identity.

The oedipal story and the oedipal structure

I make a distinction here between the personal family history that emerges through childhood memories, conscious assessments and what we might call the parental imagos, and the unconscious symbolic structures to which the childhood experiences, plus the inner fantasy world of the individual, have given rise. These structures affect not only the ego, its defensive system, and the internalized objects of love and hate, but also relations with external objects. If we give to the concept of *structure* the significance assigned to it by Levi-Strauss (1949), we may readily accept that the *oedipal structure* is a nuclear one in the unconscious basis of the personality. Not only does it determine ego identity in its narcissistic and sexual aspects, it also imprints a pattern on instinctual aims and eventually will structure interpersonal and intrapersonal relations. The profound symbolic significance of the Oedipus complex cannot be reduced simply to the story of the child and his parents. Nevertheless, it is only through piecing together this "story" that we can arrive at any understanding of the symbolic structure of the ego and its sexual objects.

In homosexual men and women, we find a family romance of a specific kind, and one which needs to be carefully analyzed if we are to understand the personality structure which results and the role of homosexual objects in the psychic economy. In addition, therefore, to corresponding factors in ego structure and in the defense mechanisms used to maintain its precarious equilibrium, there is a striking similarity in the way in which these patients present their parents. My female homosexual patients might all have been of the same family, so much did the parental portraits resemble one another. My own clinical observations have been amply confirmed by the findings of other analytic writers on this subject, in particular Deutsch (1932, 1944–1945), Socarides (1968), and Rosen (1964).

The descriptions that follow continue earlier research into the unconscious significance of object relations in female homosexuality (McDougall, 1970). If I cull rather extensively from this paper, it is because I have very little to add to this particular aspect of homosexuality.

The father image

As we shall see, the father is neither idealized nor desired. If not totally absent from the analytic discourse, he is despised, detested, or denigrated in other ways. Intense preoccupation with the noises he makes, his brutality, insensitivity, lack of refinement, and so on, all contribute to giving an anal-sadistic coloring to the portrait. Furthermore, his phallic-genital qualities are contested, since he is often presented as ineffectual and impotent; there is no feeling of a strong, loving father nor of a man whose character might be considered as essentially virile. In the daughter's inner psychic world, the once phallic father has regressed to being an anal-sadistic one.

Olivia, a pretty young woman in her twenties, who in the first years of her analysis lived with an older woman to whom she said she was "married," came one day to her session looking physically ill and brandishing a letter from her father. "I have to go back to Florence for the holidays, to be with the family! It makes me sick. I couldn't sleep all night. Thought I was going to vomit...I can't bear the sound of my father with his horrible throat noises and coughing. He only does it to drive me mad. I can't stand looking at him. He makes little twitching movements with his face. Disgusting." In earlier sessions, she had recalled that his beard used to scratch her when she was little, that his voice was sharp and frightening. In fact, every memory connected with him portrayed his presence as an intrusion of a violent kind. Warmer and more tender memories did not appear until some two years later. As far as Olivia knew at this point in her analysis, she had always hated him and believed he hated her, too. She continued: "I'm so afraid that I shall have an 'attack' when I get back to Florence—and my father hates me more than ever when I'm ill and can't leave the house." Here Olivia refers to a phobia of vomiting, which was sufficiently severe to cripple most of her social relations, and was one of her principal reasons for coming to analysis. Olivia continued to "vomit up" her distressed and hateful feelings about her father. "I'm sure he is responsible for my attacks. He tries to make me ill. You probably don't believe it, but I know he would like to kill me." Olivia had passed through periods when she even imagined her father's plotting with his employees to liquidate her. In her third year of analysis, she amended this belief to: "My father is not aware of it, but *unconsciously* he would like to kill me." At this point Olivia was no longer compelled to go out armed with a knife against the men who might attack her.

Karen, a talented actress, came to analysis because of severe anxiety attacks which stultified her work when she was in front of an audience. As her analysis progressed, she was able to give a fantasy content to her phobic attacks; it was as though she might suddenly defecate or vomit on stage. "When I think of my father I hear him clearing his throat of mucous, blowing his nose, horrible noises which seemed to spread over the dinner table and envelop us all [herself and her sisters]. I used to think I would faint when he spoke to me, as though he were going to spit at me. I'd like to tear his guts out, filthy pig! Makes you want to vomit." On another occasion she said: "As a child I was always afraid of losing control of myself. I used to faint a lot. Every morning before going to school I would pray, 'Please God, don't let me vomit today.' At other times she recalled a frightening fantasy, which persisted for some twenty years, in which her father would creep up behind her to cut off her head. "I think he must have *threatened* to kill me when I was little. I would jump whenever he came up behind me. I always kept a safe distance from him, would never sit beside him in the car."

Eva says: "I can't describe the terrible look on my father's face. Even though I've done nothing I'm always afraid he will shout at me . . . and he's so rude at the table. My heart races as though he's going to kill me. When he's there I'm paralyzed with fright and can't eat or talk."

Sophie, a gynecologist, living with a woman colleague, paints the same basic portrait of the denigrated father in slightly different colors: "He's a rich and successful businessman, but basically he's just a peasant — retarded ideals, no sensitivity. No one could make a move in the household if he were not in agreement. He would throw violent tantrums like a child. He hates women; he would tell with pride of the time he slapped his sister publicly because she was out walking with a boy. No one can look up to such a father."

We see from these examples, which could be multiplied, that the paternal imago is strong and dangerous. Physical closeness to the father gives rise to feelings of fear or disgust. The daughter presents a childhood situation in which the father is kept at arm's length. There follows a fantasy struggle against being invaded by his tics, mucous, angry voice, and similar intrusions. The anal quality of the descriptions is evident, as is the idea of a sadistic attack. The very concentration on the father, his gestures, noises, words, and attitudes gives some indication of the uneasy excitement attached to this image. One has the impression of a little girl in terror of being attacked or penetrated by her father. The emphasis on his dirty, noisy, or unrefined qualities, and the intensity of her repudiation of him as a person, gives us an inkling of the way she has used regression and repression to deal with any phallic-sexual interest he might have aroused. In addition, there is much evidence that the girl-child has been obliged to find psychic defenses to deal with the *unconscious problems of the father* regarding femininity.

These suppositions are further corroborated by the observation that in the early stages of analysis there is rarely any reference to the father's genital sexuality or even to his masculine activity in the outside world. His sexual relation to the mother is totally blotted out, and his achievements in the professional world are despised or minimized. The defensive value of this impotent image is clear: if he is castrated, there is little fear of desiring him as a love object. The reason for this destroyed and denigrated introject, and the manner in which it becomes deprived of all phallic-genital quality remains to be explored. Important at this point, is some insight into the unconscious *identification with the father* which these patients constructed.

At the beginning of her analysis, Olivia always dressed in stained jeans and large thick sweaters. She complained of the women in her environment who criticized her appearance, refusing to accept her for what she was. "I'm scruffy; I look like a grubby boy. I'm convinced you aren't interested in me either; I don't suppose you even want to go on with my analysis!" She asked if many attractively dressed women came to consult me, then dissolved into tears saying she was "dirty, clumsy, and disgusting." At the same time she asserted that it would be impossible for her to be otherwise. "I'd feel ridiculous dressed up like a *woman*. Besides I can't bear to hear them cackling about fashions and make-up. All my life my mother made me get dressed up to go to receptions. I always felt angry and ill."

Olivia applied to herself the identical terms with which she castigated her father. Largely lost to her as an object, except for her passionate hatred of him, she identified with him in the form of a regressed image, possessed of disagreeable and dangerous anal qualities. She wore a thick leather wristband for a time, believing it gave her "an appearance of strength and cruelty," but the extent of her identification was unknown to her, since she projected a large part of this dangerous strength and cruelty onto the world of men in general. She went outside, protected against sadistic attack by her knife; the fact that it was she who wielded the knife and might therefore be considered as dangerous did not occur to her.

Anticipating our discussion of the mother's role in this curious oedipal tangle, we might point out that the partial identification with the father imago was felt to be forbidden by the mother and criticized and despised by other women. Olivia also feared in this session — and indeed for some two years of our analytic work together — that the analyst too would cast her out for those traits in which she unconsciously identified with her father's strength. These elements clearly represented a vital part of her identity, which she had to struggle to preserve. Although her narcissistic identification with a father conceived of in anal-sadistic terms was highly conflictual, it was of cardinal importance to Olivia's self-image and formed an important dimension in her homosexual attachments.

Karen, in her own inimitable style, revealed the same self-portrait, "I'm just a piece of shit, and that's exactly how everyone treats me. But my friend, Paula, saw me quite differently. And that's how I knew she really loved me. She liked my craziness and she didn't treat me like shit." She then added defensively, no doubt wondering if the analyst could love her and accept her as she was: "I haven't had a bath for weeks and I don't give a damn. I smell like a skunk and I love it. Can you smell it?" Clinging narcissistically to her body products and odors, Karen added a style of dress which carried out the same idea. When obliged to wear "feminine" clothing she felt anxious and uncomfortable.

The sadistic intentions imputed to her father were also important elements in Karen's own fantasy life. She often imagined herself killing men. "I'd like to kill some man — any man — and drive a knife right through his belly." She frequently dreamed of chopping men up, and at these times was afraid to go out in the street, unless accompanied by her lover, for fear that men were plotting murder against her.

It is interesting to note that Sophie, who considered her father to be a woman-hater, told me in her first interview that *she* was a misogynist, although exclusively homosexual in her love relations. She too felt "like a castrate" (her own term) if she wore dresses instead of her well-tailored trouser suits. Sophie was more aware than any of my other homosexual patients of the underlying hatred and general ambivalence attached to her homosexual loves, although her identification with an anal-sadistic father was entirely unconscious.

I come now to another essential aspect of the father image, one which has considerable importance for any understanding of the symbolic oedipal structure and its particular fragility. This in turn has momentous consequences for the structure of the ego and the maintenance of ego identity. Behind the "castrated" image, behind the regressive libidinal involvement with an exciting and frightening anal-sadistic father, lies the image of the father who has *failed in his specific parental role*, leaving his small daughter prey to a devouring or controlling and omnipotent maternal image. The mother, usually represented, as we shall see, as the essence of femininity and in no way a masculine-phallic personality, is nevertheless felt to have secretly destroyed the father's value as an authority figure, and to have aided the child in denying his phallic-genital qualities. The primal scene, if acknowledged at all, is conceived of in sadistic terms, and is usually attributed to the mother's tales of sexual brutality to be expected of men.

The mother's apparent complicity in the quasi-total destruction of the masculine image of the father is a constant theme. One mother plotted with her children to steal small sums of money from the father; another aided her child to conceal poor school marks. One patient claimed that her mother refused to allow the father to come near her when she was young, on the grounds that he was disturbing to her because she was "nervous and delicate." Karen's mother frequently discussed with her daughter the eventuality of a divorce from the father, the underlying idea being that she and the mother would be better off alone; another constantly decried the father's family and background. In spite of a childlike delight in believing that they were more important to mother than father, these children bitterly resented the father's exclusion and blamed him for not having played a paternal role to help them become independent of the mother. The extent of the threat, which this destruction of the paternal image represented, was only slowly brought to light in analysis, although detectable in certain anxiety symptoms from the outset.

Karen described a dream thus: "There was a little boy running in front of a car. A woman driver rides right over him and leaves him paralyzed. My father just stands there saying he doesn't know where to go for help. I scream, 'You're a doctor aren't you? You could be hanged for refusing to help someone in mortal danger.' Then I take the baby to a woman doctor myself. She sprays it with ether, but I keep on calling my father to come and help me."

Karen's associations led to angry rantings against the father and to details which identify the damaged baby boy as a representation of herself, and the woman doctor as the analyst. Let us reconstruct the latent meaning of the dream insofar as it pertains to the present discussion. The little boy's accident symbolizes castration in a global sense. He is paralyzed, as Karen feels herself to be most of the time. "My mother's a terrible driver. Never looks where she's going!" But it is also a woman (analyst-mother) who is supposed to repair the grave damage to which the father is indifferent. Homosexual relations will "repair" her and end her own feeling of being paralyzed, providing the longed-for completion of herself. However, the dangers that lurk in the homosexual solution, when lived out in the analytic situation, are revealed in Karen's associations to the woman doctor's "treatment." "Ether," says Karen, "will either lull you into insensibility so you feel no more pain — or else it kills you outright." The analyst-mother, like the homosexual partners, may lull the damaged baby back into the fantasied bliss of the mother-nursling fusion, but this quest may also kill the baby. The rejecting father abandons his child to the overpowering, seductive mother who, in return, offers only psychic death. What was once a phallic-libidinal demand has now regressed to a cry for help; but the father does not heed her appeal.

A dream of Olivia's reveals a similar unconscious picture of the father. In her dream, she watches a mother cat delivering kittens. The kittens are born with their eyes open, and this means they are going to die. She makes desperate attempts to save these babies, first putting them into a box too small for them, where they suffocate. Then she puts them out with the mother cat in the snow, where they continue to fare badly. Her father is there with the mother cat, and she begs him for help. He replies that he is too busy, he has a business meeting. She turns back to the kittens and finds they are all dead. In recounting her dream, Olivia burst into tears, saying the dream was like real life in that her father would not care if *she* died. The kittens doomed to die *because their eyes are open* was a reference, in primary-process thinking, to an early primal-scene memory. Olivia had once observed her parents making love when they believed she was asleep, and she had described her mother, when recounting this screen memory, as "the cat who got the cream." She was three years old at the time; one can detect in the dream story her wish that her mother's babies would die, but what had eventually died in the tiny girl's mind was the hope that she might one day identify with the mother cat and have access to a genital father image and the right to live kittens of her own.

Olivia's associations to this dream all led to a feeling that she was "destroyed" on the inside. At the time of this dream she had suffered for several months from amenorrhoea. Although we were able to understand later that this symptom also signified her desire to have a child, in her fantasy at this time she was empty and finished as a woman; the dead kittens represented herself and her unborn children doomed to extinction. In the dream, it is to her father that she turns to save her from the situation in which her femininity is at stake. He does nothing, and the end result is death.

Behind the conscious wish to eliminate or denigrate the father, all of my homosexual patients revealed narcissistic wounds linked to the image of the *indifferent* father. Strengthened by the conviction that the mother forbade any loving relationship between father and daughter, these women tended to feel that any desire for the father, his love or his penis, was dangerous. Such a wish could only entail the loss of the mother's love and bring castration to the father. Thus the daughter's consciously avowed dislike of the father was experienced as a gift made to the mother. In turn, it gave rise to fantasies of a revengeful and persecuting father, and subsequently to the fear of men in general.

What light do these brief clinical examples shed on the relation of the homosexual to her father? There is practically no trace of the normal neurotic solutions to oedipal wishes. The father has become lost as a love object, and equally lost as a representative of security and strength, barring the way to future genital relations. In addition, in her attempts to deal with her primitive libidinal and aggressive wishes, the small girl's ego has undergone profound modifications. The discarded paternal object has been incorporated into her ego structure never to be given up. No other man ever takes the father's place in the homosexual girl's psychic universe. The renunciation of the father as an object of libidinal investment does not correspond to the relinquishing of the oedipal object that we find in heterosexual women; nor, in consequence, does it lead to the formation of symptoms to deal with frustrated oedipal wishes and castration anxiety which we find in most neurotic structures. Instead there is identification with the father, but this identification, while it might be said to prevent further ego disintegration, itself has crippling consequences for the ego, for it is an identification with a multilated image, possessed of disagreeable and dangerous qualities. The ambivalence inherent in any process of identification is immeasurably heightened; the ego runs the risk of suffering merciless attacks from the superego for these identifications which nevertheless form an essential part of the girl's identity. The depressive reproaches the homosexual so frequently heaps upon herself bear the stamp of the classic reproaches of the melancholic (Freud, 1917). They represent an attack on the internalized father; yet this narcissistically important and zealously guarded object of identification is a bulwark against psychotic dissolution. The pregenital superego results in ego fragility, and an impoverishment or paralysis of much of the ego's functioning.

We are still faced with the question why the little girl, in her attempt to internalize something as vitally important to her ego and to her instinctual development as the phallic representation of her father, is able to do so only at the expense of object loss, ego impairment, and considerable suffering. A fuller understanding of her inner psychic reality requires us to turn now to an investigation of the relationship with the maternal imago.

The mother image

The complicity with the mother has already been noted; however, there is little identification with her. Invariably the mother is described in idealized terms — beautiful, gifted, charming. She is endowed with all the qualities the daughter lacks. What is striking in this unequal situation is that it is taken for granted. There is no conscious envy of the mother. Furthermore, she emerges as the sole safeguard against the dangers of living, dangers coming from the father as well as the outside world. At the same time the mother is frequently felt to be in danger herself; fears of her imminent death are quite common. In fantasy, she is the victim of fatal accidents or illnesses, or the prey of would-be attackers. Coming closer to the source, she is threatened with abandonment or excessive domination by the father. He is believed to make unfair demands on her sexually or otherwise.

Identification with such an imago presents two main difficulties. Any aspiration toward narcissistic identification is doomed to failure because of its excessively idealized qualities: these in turn are maintained in order to repress a fund of hostile and destructive wishes directed toward the internalized mother. She must remain an unattainable ideal at the price of a continuing narcissistic hemorrhage in the daughter's self-image. This attitude is reinforced by the destructive nature of the primal-scene fantasies. There is no trace of an idea that the parents might be complementary to each other sexually, or that the mother is enhanced in any way by her relation to the father. Frequently the parents' sexual relationship is totally disavowed on a conscious plane. Analysis reveals that, behind this denial of sexual realities, there are sadistic and frightening images of the sexual relations and of the father's penis. Thus there is no wish to identify with the mother in her genital role. The wishful fantasy of all these patients might be summed up as a desire for total elimination of the father and the creation of an exclusive and enduring mother-daughter relationship. This fantasy is lived out in the sexual relationship with women partners, who thus become mother substitutes, frequently with alternating roles, each being at times the mother, at times the child. Elaborations of this wish are often reiterated in the early transference situation. Its aggressive elements usually are strongly repressed.

Again, I draw on examples from my analytic experience. Olivia described her mother as "talented and beautiful; she was a public figure and everyone adored her. . . I always wanted to be near her, like they did. Whenever we went out I was haunted by the idea that she would get run over. . . . She's pure and innocent, can't imagine that anyone can have evil thoughts. . . the only trouble is that she can't understand what it is to be ill. She was never sick. . . . Somehow she was never there when I needed her. I wonder if all my stomach troubles weren't a way of keeping her near me."

Eva would say: "I loved her so much; and she looked so pretty. She had lots of beauty treatments and still looks very young for her age. I used to save up all my pennies to buy flowers for her when I was little." (Later she stole money from her father to give flowers to the girls she was in love with at college.) "When she was caring for my little sister I was almost ill with longing for her. Sometimes I would try to be ill so that she would keep me at home with her." Later, she added: "But somehow it was as though you couldn't get close to her. She wasn't mean, but she gave things instead of love."

Before exploring the many layers of the maternal imago, let us briefly recapitulate the parental images as revealed in the early stages of analysis. Father is the repository of all that is bad, dirty, or dangerous, while mother is pure, beautiful, and clean. Above all, she is maintained as a *nonconflictual* object. She is the fountainhead of all security — a security later sought in other women who become objects of sexual desire. She is thought to possess highly valuable feminine attributes, but these evoke no conscious jealousy. The daughter hopes to have access to some of these qualities later by loving another woman. The one sour note in the lovely-mother theme is the impression that she is narcissistically involved with herself, and is lacking in understanding. However, these traits are in no way resented by the daughter in her attempt to keep intact the idealized image. Indeed she regards herself as an unworthy and unlovable child who has been a disappointment to her mother.

All my patients, as the analysis proceeded, revealed and explored quite different aspects of the mother image of which two seemed particularly important: the first concerns their own ambivalent feelings towards her, and the second gives some indication of the mother's ambivalence. The first, already hinted at, was a constant concern for the mother's health and safety. Obsessive images of her falling fatally ill, of finding her dead, or cut to pieces were frequent. This was often expressed through a compulsive need to phone her constantly when separated, or rush back to her during vacations. Often these identical fears were transferred globally onto female partners. The need to stay very close, to control the mother's movements to the best of their abilities, and to smother her with solicitude, thinly veiled the underlying aggressive content. The emphasis was on mother's indispensability to the child. It was only much later that the patients were able to discover that this was felt to be a demand *stemming from the mother;* to be independent of her would have been both disloyal and dangerous. The fantasies that the mother, or the sexual partner, might fall victim to a fatal catastrophe were consciously considered a total threat to the patient's personal safety and her object world, but as time went on she could not avoid becoming aware of these were magical means of preventing dangerous impulses in herself from *destroying the maternal object.*

The second theme that turned up with unfailing regularity was that of a rigidly controlling mother wielding omnipotent power over the body of her child, meticulously preoccupied with order, health, and cleanliness. The underlying feelings to which this particular relationship to the mother gave rise are typified in a remark of Karen's: "My mother hated everything to do with my body. She used to smell my clothes all the time to see if they were dirty. When I defecated she treated it like poison. For years I believed my mother did not defecate. In fact I still find it hard to believe!" The examples are legion. One patient was forbidden to mention her excretory needs. She was taught at an early age to cough politely to draw attention to such things. She always felt dirty and ashamed because of her body functions. Another mother referred to constipation as "back trouble" and forbade her daughter to look at her feces. These aspects of the "anal" mother who rejected all that may be attached to the concept of "anal eroticism" had a markedly inhibiting effect on the integration of the anal components of the lidibo, as we have seen. The displacement of these components onto the phallic image of the father have also been noted.

The controlling and physically rejecting aspects of the maternal imago came slowly to consciousness and stirred up considerable resistance, since this was felt to be an attack on the internalized mother, and involved the risk of being separated from an almost symbiotic relationship in the inner object world (Mahler and Gosliner, 1955). The feeling that their bodies, and their whole physical selves, had been severely rejected by the mother was most painfully brought to light by these patients, although their own often violent rejection of their bodies was conscious from the beginning. "My body is repugnant to me, especially my breasts. Everything about me that is flabby is disgusting. I have always tried to have hard strong hands. My hands resemble my father's and help to cover up all that is moist or wrong with my body. I still get terribly anxious concerning urine and shit — I cannot accept these functions; they are somehow disgustingly feminine." Thus did Sophie express her feelings toward her despised bodily self. When she was younger, she used to tear at her skin with a razor blade in order to "purify" herself, but this compulsive behavior was no longer necessary after her first homosexual experiences. The reverse side of this maternal rejection and hatred of their physical selves was expressed by all these patients through fantasies of loving *another woman's body*. They would lavish on a female partner caresses, minute explorations, tenderness, and all the loving that they unconsciously demanded for their own bodies — believed to be ugly and deformed, physically weak, or unhealthy. One patient described the "recovery" of her own body through her female partner in these terms: "Until I met Sarah I had no body, only a head. I always worked well at school to please my mother. Going into the street was a nightmare; I felt awkward, unstable and monstrous, yet I was not aware of the individual parts of my body. Sarah brought my hands and feet, and my skin to life. But I still don't have much. I cannot bear to have my breasts touched. I love her genitals but cannot let her touch mine." Similar intense bodily conflict was manifested by another patient, in that the dangerous fantasies attached to her own body and genitals were projected onto her partner as well. This patient proclaimed a total lack of both clitoral and vaginal sensation, and indeed was confused about where her vagina was located. She would imagine it constricting or cutting like a knife. She had a recurrent fantasy in which she gave birth to a child in broken segments; it later became evident that she attributed to her vagina both oral-devouring and anal-constricting functions. In her first homosexual experience, when she was eighteen years old, she became excited when her partner demanded clitoral stimulation and was happy to administer these caresses to her friend. But when the friend asked her one day to put her fingers into her vagina she drew back in horror, "I was sure my fingers would get stuck inside her and that it would require

the services of a surgeon to separate us. I was so terrified. I just could not comply with her request." This
fear of "getting stuck" was connected to an unconscious
aspect of her relation with her mother. Her mother's
vagina would demand that she remained perpetually
attached, like a phallic organ, and nothing short of a
surgeon's knife could separate them. That this patient's
father was a noted surgeon made her reflection pertinent and rich in symbolic meaning. Only an effective
father could protect her from the maternal wish to
make her into a permanent phallus.

These fragments from sessions shed further light on
the tenacious, yet frightening, tie to the negative
aspects of the internalized mother. The patients all unconsciously regarded themselves as an indispensable
part or function of the mother (Lichtenstein, 1961).
The feeling of being mother's phallus was a narcissistically enhancing aspect, but it was inevitably accompanied by the idea that one was a fecal object, despised yet omnipotently controlled by her. The
daughter invariably came to feel that she existed to
enhance the maternal ego; one is tempted to believe
that these patients served as counterphobic objects
with regard to deep anxieties on the mother's part
(Winnicott, 1948, 1960).

Two further remarks express vividly the complex
and primitive tie to the mother, and the danger involved in wishing to dissolve it, terrifying and crippling though its maintenance might be. "The feelings I
have about you [the analyst, at a moment of intense
maternal transference] are insupportable. I have never
loved nor hated anyone so much in my life. If I love
you you will destroy me; if I hate you you will cast me

out forever." Loving meant devouring. For long periods of time it was important to this patient to believe that I hated her. This made her feel safer and also enabled her better to support her strongly sadistic and hateful feelings toward me. "If you love me I am lost, for then you will destroy me and throw me out like shit — or else you will tie me up to you forever — like my mother did."

Another patient expressed the same ideas in the following fantasy: "My mother and I are fused together. At one end we are sealed by our mouths, and at the other by our vaginas. We make up a circle bound by cold steel bands. If it breaks we shall both be torn." This fantasy, which continued through several sessions, underwent the following transformation: "I broke that circle when I first loved another woman. But there was only one vagina — and my mother got it! With her icy fingers she closed mine up forever." The same patient often felt that if anything worked well in her life (she was an artist), or if she had success or pleasure with her work, her mother was liable to fall dangerously ill and die. Identical terror in the symbiotic relationship is vividly expressed by Mary Barnes whose account in *Two Accounts of a Journey through Madness* (Barnes and Berke, 1971) lay strikingly bare the force of an attachment to this kind of internalized mother image. Mary writes: "It was difficult for my mother to be loved and she didn't understand about unconscious motives. . . . Once I told her, 'Mother, it seemed to me that I caused all Peter's illness and all your sickness!'. . . Feeling happy, enjoying myself, instinctively I would wonder, is mother ill? . . . It's only safe to be dead, in a false state, or hidden away, shut up somewhere, mad Mary." The patients I

am discussing chose other solutions (which we shall examine in detail later) than that chosen by Mary
Barnes; for them, it was heterosexuality and the world
of men that had to be "kept dead, hidden away, shut
up somewhere," while mother was constantly repaired
and reassured. The fear of becoming separate and independent led, in many of my patients, to an inability
to work or to create. If ambitions of this kind were pursued with success, it was invariably at the price of considerable anxiety and fantasies of the mother becoming
ill or dying. It was perhaps no accident that two of the
mothers of my patients did fall gravely ill, at times
when their daughters were beginning to create successful careers for themselves; another suffered from inexplicable hemorrhages when her daughter married.
The latter patient, during this upheaval, dreamed that
her mother had lost her legs and that she was condemned to walk underneath her mother, taking the
place of the legs. How can a leg separate from its body?
And what sort of independent existence could it hope
for? And again how can the mother-body function if its
legs decide to leave it? Such are the dilemmas facing
the homosexual patient when she begins to desire a
loosening of the bonds which tie her to the internalized
mother. Either she will become nothing more than an
amputated limb, or her mother will seek revenge or
die. In most cases these desperate feelings are transferred onto the sexual partner. Said Sophie: "Since my
friend has come to live with me I feel sure I exist. It
was like that when I was a child. I only existed in my
mother's eyes; without her I was never quite sure who I
really was."

To sum up the salient features of the maternal

imago, we might say: The mother, felt to have de-stroyed the phallic image of the father, acts as a forbid-ding barrier between father and daughter. Behind this image, stands the mother-with-the-enema who takes possession of the child's body and its contents. This usually results in very early control over bodily func-tions which, far from liberating the little girl, renders her even more dependent on the mother. Finally, there is the fantasy that the daughter is part of mother's very essence and vice versa — a symbiotic fantasy in which each keeps the other alive. There can never be two women; to separate from the mother (or later substi-tutes) means to lose one's identity (Lichtenstein, 1961).

Apart from the homosexual object choice, one other outcome of this particularly lopsided family constella-tion is a nexus of character traits which affected most of my patients, and which I have also noted in clinical writings by other analysts. Unless compensated by meticulous reaction formations these patients tend to display an inability to organize their lives in even the smallest details. Some of them seemed to live in the midst of disorder and confusion to a punitive degree. The inability to work constructively, or even in some cases to arrange papers, pack a suitcase, or make a de-cision, exemplified the fear that independent ego ac-tivity is dangerous. The feeling of being incomplete, ill-defined, incapable, vulnerable, is the inevitable result of the unconscious symbiotic relationship. The nonintegration of the anal components of the libido, in such a way as to be useful to the ego, further weakens the personality structure. Nothing can be achieved or, if achieved, retained. One had the feeling that these patients were forced to prove that they could accomplish nothing without the constant aid of the mother or mother substitute. The mother who fosters precocious bodily and ego controls in her little girl, with the desire that the child perform for her, deprives the girl of the right to perform for her own pleasure.

Penis envy and the phallus concept

Before summarizing the oedipal constellation and the specific type of unconscious structure it gives rise to, we should first examine the role of penis envy in homosexuality, as compared with heterosexually oriented women. I should like to recall the elements of this concept in Freudian theory, and the theoretical distinction between "penis" and "phallus" since it is important to any understanding of the symbolic structure which contributes to the formation of sexual deviation.

Freud regarded penis envy as a fundamental element in the organization of feminine sexuality; this envy is considered to arise as a result of the discovery of the difference between the sexes, the little girl feeling deprived as a consequence (Freud, 1925). This feeling of deprivation, involving as it does ignorance of the existence of the vagina, leads to the feminine castration complex (Freud, 1908). During the oedipal phase, penis envy is expected to give way to two transformations of the basic wish to have a penis of one's own: the wish to acquire a penis inside the body, usually in the form of the wish for a child, and the desire to receive pleasure from the man's penis in the sexual relationship (Freud, 1920, 1933). Failure to achieve these transformations may result in neurotic symptoms and character problems. The same wishes may also find sublimatory expression.

The term "phallus" has a symbolic significance. As his research progressed Freud became increasingly interested in what he designated as "the phallic phase" of libidinal development, in children of both sexes. The term *penis* came to be reserved for the male organ in its anatomical reality, while *phallus* referred to all that the penis might symbolize in psychic reality—power, plentitude, fertility, and so on. A phallic significance may thus be conferred on any part-object such as breast, feces, urine, child, or an adult person used as a part-object. In recent analytic writings (Grunberger, 1971), the phallus is taken to be the symbol of narcissistic integrity, or again as the fundamental signifier of desire (Lacan, 1966) for either sex. Most analysts today would agree that the penis envy concept, with its symbolic phallic overtones, applies to both sexes; if the little girl is envious of her brother's sexual organ, the little boy is equally envious of the large paternal penis. But over and beyond this envy, interest is centered on the symbolic significance of the penis: the importance of the phallic organization in the libidinal development of boy and girl, and its structuring effect in the oedipal situation (Kurth and Patterson, 1968). This phase of development marks a turning point in psychic life, with lasting consequences for the acquisition of sexual identity and the unconscious structuring of sexual desire. The *phallus*, as the psychic representative of desire and narcissistic completion, plays the same role for both sexes, but the atittude to the *anatomical penis* is necessarily different. The fact that the penis is a visible sexual organ, and that in our phallocentric society the male is regarded as the more privileged, gives women specific problems to overcome, and it is less than likely that these are simply resolved, as Freud claimed, by her eventually having a child. Indeed should she regard her child as the equivalent of a penis, or even as her *phallus*, that is the object of her desire and the means of being sexually and narcissistically complete, she has resolved little of her basic sexual and object relations problems, and can scarcely avoid creating graver ones for her child. To understand the girl's specific conflicts regarding phallic wishes, we must add that these have their prototypes in the earliest mother-child relationship. The first phallic object, in the symbolic sense, the earliest object of narcissistic completion and libidinal desire, is the breast. This particular connotation of the "phallic mother" as the omnipotent mother of the nursing situation — object not only of the baby's needs, but primordial object of erotic desire — was first noted by Brunswick (1940): "The term 'phallic mother'. . . best designates the all-powerful mother, the mother who is capable of everything and who possesses every valuable attribute" (p. 304).

With regard then to phallic envy and its specific development in the little girl, we may trace its origins to the desire to possess for oneself the breast-mother, object of desire, of pleasure, and of need, and thus trace penis envy from oral-sadistic breast envy, through its various anal representations, to its investment in the penis. From this point of view, penis envy, in the form of wishing to have a penis and envy of those who possess one, is only one manifestation, in a continuum, of possible objects of desire in their manifold pregenital, genital, and sublimated forms. Either sex, in the attempt to find a solution to infantile sexual and narcissistic longings, might come to the erroneous conclusion that the secret to all fulfillment is to possess a penis, but, for the reasons already stated, this is more likely to be the little girl's fantasy.

Clinical findings and observations of children all confirm the importance of penis envy in women, but rarely explore its many roots. It cannot be explained by the simple megalomanic wish to possess everything one does not have. Reference has been made to the fact that it conceals early oral longings. We must add to these dimensions all the thoughts the little girl has about her father's penis. Father usually comes to represent authority, order, and the outside world; his penis comes to symbolize these qualities in the unconscious. But over and beyond this, he is also seen as the object of mother's narcissistic enhancement to be desired as such, a symbol of power and protection, and object of mother's desire. It is evident that this powerfully cathected phallic symbol will inevitably represent, in the eyes of the little girl, the principal object needed to guarantee mother's love and sexual interest, as well as an important possession with which to earn respect from the world in general. In consequence, boys are considered to hold an extremely favored position.

There is yet another dimension to the little girl's phallic envy. For both sexes, the wish to be the exclusive object of the mother's love and desire is coupled with a fear of the pregenital mother image, the controlling and demanding mother of the anal-sadistic phase of development, and the equally terrifying devouring mother of oral fantasy. The little girl tends to feel that the possession of a penis would protect her from enthralment and submission to these omnipotent aspects of the mother imago; the boy would not only have more to offer but also run no risk of being a rival to the mother.

It is understandable therefore that an overwhelming number of women find difficulty in resolving the problems of penis envy, the more so since on attaining motherhood they tend to transmit their neurotic solutions to their daughters — for the woman must be held responsible in large part for "solutions" to the problems of penis envy and castration anxiety, since she herself plays a considerable role in the idealization of the penis and the depreciation of femininity.

"We are right when we suppose that this age-old inequality requires woman's complicity, in spite of her apparent protest shown by penis envy. Men and women must be exposed to specific, complementary affective conflicts to have established a *modus vivendi* which could last through many civilizations. . . . At the end of the anal stage the little girl should be able to achieve in masturbatory fantasy a simultaneous identification with both parents in terms of their genital functioning. But there are two obstacles: first, the one originating in the anal period, namely that autonomy in masturbatory satisfaction necessarily means a sadistic dispossession of the Mother and her prerogatives; second, the Oedipal obstacle, according to which the recreation of the primal scene, by identification with both parents, also implies supplanting the Mother, an exacting, jealous and castrated Mother, and an envied, depreciated, and at the same time overvalued Father. The only way out of this impasse to identification is the establishment of an inaccessible phallic ideal. . . . When women holding such imagoes have to deal with married life, they suddenly find themselves confronted with their latent genital desires, even though their affective life is immature for want of heterosexual identification, as they are still dominated by problems of the anal stage. Thus the fleeting Oedipal hopes will soon give way to a repetition, this time with the husbands, of the anal relationship to the Mother, a relation which is then confirmed by penis envy. The advantage of this situation consists in avoiding a frontal attack on the maternal imago and also in avoiding the feeling of deep anxiety at the idea of detaching oneself from her domination and superiority" (Torok, 1964, pp. 167–168).

The homosexual woman and the penis

The above passage delineates subtly the background to a *neurotic* solution to the problems of the sexual difference, the frustrations of the oedipal situation, and the ideals of present-day society. What of the homosexual woman and her particular solution? To begin with, her wish for a penis of her own and all it represents is not, as with the heterosexually oriented, totally unconscious. The homosexual's desire for a penis is frequently conscious, intense, and detached from the man. Many homosexual women recount dreams in which they have a penis, and devise sexual games with a fabricated penis. One of my patients refused to go out of her home during adolescence unless she first tied a fictitious penis around her genital area. Although terrified that this might be discovered, she was equally terrified to leave the house without it. A colleague discussed with me a similar patient, who binds her breasts and ties on a false penis in order to face the world. This patient took hormones which she hoped would produce male secondary sexual characteristics, and was investigating the possibility of having her breasts removed: "My breasts have been bound for two years now...everybody thinks I am a man. I shave every second day. When I flirt with girls I satisfy them sexually, but I always remain dressed. I cannot bear to be touched."

The wish to have an anatomical penis sometimes reaches hallucinatory proportions. Certain of my patients described the impression of actually possessing a male genital. One referred to this "penis" as her "phantom organ" and likened it to the illusions of amputated patients who can still "feel" the missing limb. This patient also thought of having her breasts removed and, like the patient who took hormones, she could not bear to be touched by her partners. As with many of these women, her sexual pleasure was to produce pleasure for the partner. The penis wish is extremely complicated in homosexual women; not only does it exist to repair a fantasied castration but it is also intended *to keep dormant any feminine sexual desires*. The patient who always wore a fabricated penis in adolescence reached a point in her analysis where she began to explore her overwhelming guilt about this behavior. She suddenly wished to make herself a penis once more; it no longer seemed such a hideous crime: "Last night I made myself a penis out of some bits of material. I tried it on and carressed it, and I felt flushed and excited. Then suddenly I had a strange urge to push it inside my body. It nearly frightened me to death." The vaginal sensations and feeling of desire filled her with anxiety, and the thought came to mind that if she were to give in to such feelings she would go crazy, explode, or die. That night she dreamed that her mother was dying. In fact the cruel and prohibiting part of the internalized imago was about to die as the daughter became sexually alive. We were later to discover that this toy penis also had served to block clitoral and vaginal sensation, and thus reinforced the blocking of genital desire.

As we have seen, the deep sense of prohibition and of being threatened by the mother is not the only reason for the wish for a penis. The father's penis has been divested of its symbolic phallic function and significance. To the extent to which the penis is a penis-attached-to-a-man, it is a dangerous image, endowed with violent and destructive qualities. Since, at the same time, the primal scene is envisaged in anal-sadistic terms, men are believed to harbor sadistic or humiliating desires toward women. There is no image of a "good penis"; the penis is never envisioned as a pleasure-giving, healing, or narcissistically enhancing possession when offered to the woman in a heterosexual relationship. In addition, the father's penis was denied by these analysands; much of their own sexual activity was a protest designed to prove that the mother had never desired the father or his penis, and that in fact a penis was quite unnecessary to the sexual act with a woman.

Behind the "bad penis" images, analysis reveals equally dangerous breast fantasies in which the breast is felt to be a poisoning and persecutory object. The equation of breast and penis in the unconscious is inevitably linked to oral-sadistic fears of a paranoid or schizoid kind and, of course, is not limited to a homosexual organization. The tragedy of the homosexual girl's psychosexual development is rooted in the fact that the penis has become detached from the father, the part-object taking the place of the total object. It is introduced as such, to prevent further regression to the traumatic prephallic phase, in which the mother is felt to contain the phallus — not only the father's penis, but the power of life and death over her child. According to the possible variations in the unconscious family constellation, the penis image and its phallic symbolic meaning will vary for different homosexual women. We might say that there are two main poles, one in which depressive anxiety is uppermost, and the other in which persecutory anxiety dominates. In the first case the aim of *repairing* the partner is uppermost and may include a measure of self-reparation, the split in the self-image being repaired narcissistically through a sexual object who is *like oneself*. At the other end of the scale the *fear of the homosexual object* leads, because of paranoid projection, to an overwhelming need to dominate the object erotically, the orgasm of the partner carrying the meaning both of possession and castration. Such women frequently seek no orgastic pleasure for themselves and, if their terror of total loss of self is strong, they will assume a delusional male identity, leading in certain cases to operations intended to "transsexualize" their bodies. The women dominated by such deep anxiety frequently claim that they are *not homosexual*. Their unconscious identity image tends to uphold that they are really men imprisoned in female forms. In practice, they avoid any personal orgastic pleasure while seeking to procure sexual pleasure for their partners. Desire centered only on the climax of the partner characterizes a number of homosexual women. To seek direct erotic pleasure jeopardizes the deep feeling of masculine identity. This in turn is vitally necessary to ward off anxiety of psychotic dimensions concerning the body image and the feeling of identity; both are felt to be threatened by the internalized mother, and carry a danger of fusion with her.

This brings me to the crucial role of castration anxiety in homosexual women. It is perhaps evident from the clinical fragments quoted here that the fantasy of being castrated is more profound, more globally disturbing, than in the case of women who have developed neurotic symptoms or neurotic character traits to cope with castration anxiety at its different levels. It is clear that castration anxiety is not limited to phallic anxiety, stemming from the phase in which the sexual difference becomes significant; nor is it limited to the "narcissistic castration" resulting from the oedipal crises, when the little girl discovers that she is forever outside the sexual bond of the parents, and that her incestuous longings will never reach fulfillment. The anxiety felt by these patients concerns *not only their sexuality but their feeling of subjective identity as separate beings.* This might well be named "primary castration," the prototype of later castration anxiety. If unresolved, that is, if the small girl fails to accept and compensate adequately for the recognition of otherness, then she risks the loss of her ego boundaries, aphanisis, and psychic death.

Castration in this global sense is actually the equivalent of accepting reality, and has to be symbolized in the same way that phallic castration anxiety has to be elaborated psychically for the establishment of *sexual reality* and gender reality. Homosexual relations avoid the many-sided problem of classical phallic castration anxiety by the simple exclusion of one of the sexes; but homosexual activity and its ensuing relationships also aid the ego in dealing with the overwhelming anxiety concerning separateness and fear of disintegration. However, the homosexual way of life is inadequate to cope with all of these problems. Much anxiety is left over, and thus we find in homosexual patients many poorly structured neurotic symptoms — phobic formations concerning oral anxiety (anorexia, bulimia, addictions, and vomiting phobias are frequent), phobic-obsessional symptoms concerning anal and urinary functions, masochistic body rituals, and persecutory fears. Hypochondriacal anxiety and somatizations are also common (Sperling, 1955). All of these symptoms are deeply rooted in the early mother-child relationship, at which time the stage is set for many of the acting-out symptoms, including homosexual resolution of oedipal stress at a later period. The latter solution is more apt to arise when the father has unresolved homosexual problems and feelings of envy and hatred for women.

The homosexual relationship

In his comprehensive book, *The Overt Homosexual* (1968), Socarides writes: "Most overtly homosexual women will in treatment acknowledge the mother-child relationship which they have with the love object.... The homosexual woman is in flight from the man. The source of this flight is her childhood feeling of guilt toward her mother, the fear of merging with her and the fear of disappointment and rejection at the hands of her father if she dared to turn to him for love and support. If she expected that her father would fulfill her infantile sexual wishes there is a masochistic danger present, too. Or she may feel that her father would refuse her and then she would suffer the danger of narcissistic injury. The end result is to turn to the earlier love object again — the mother — more ardently than before. However she cannot return to the real mother due to her fear of merging and being engulfed" (pp. 174–175).

My own clinical experience confirms the extensive research of this author. But I would like to add to his summary a brief examination of the dynamic changes in the psychic economy consequent on the establishment of overt homosexual relationships. Most of my patients were conscious of an intense feeling of having triumphed over the mother, and a wish that she would feel abandoned and punished. Their wish was usually covered by a thin veneer of concern about her feelings, and a fear that she might take revenge of some kind. "Somehow I deliberately let my mother find out about my love affair with Susan. She was absolutely furious, of course — and I was secretly glad, as though I wanted to punish her for something. When she learns I'm in analysis with a *woman*, it'll just kill her!" remarked one of my patients pointedly. There is a large measure of triumph over the father also, since the homosexual solution implies the denial of the father's phallic role and genital existence, and the proof that a woman does not need either a man or a penis for sexual completion. The homosexual triumphs finally over the primal scene and sexual reality.

A further source of gratification lies in the fact that the new relationship is an overtly erotic one. Masturbation and sexual desire, always felt to have been forbidden by the mother, are welcomed by the partner, and guilt feelings are thus diminished. Many old conflicts between mother and daughter are also eclipsed in the relation with the mother substitute. In general, the real mother has always complained about the unfeminine daughter who refused to dress in pretty clothes, was not interested in boys or parties, behaved in ways that seemed irresponsible, unusual, disorderly, and secretive. Now all these same character traits are accepted and even highly valued by the homosexual partner. The unconscious significance of this acceptance is far-reaching, for hidden under the surface of the ruthless, nonconforming, anal-erotic child is the internalized father, and in consequence an anguished fear of losing the identification with him which guarantees ego identity. This the mother has never accepted, while the father has frequently reinforced this outcome by his own conflict with femininity.

One of my patients recounted a poignant moment with her lover which epitomizes the "reparative" dimension of the homosexual love relation. She lived with an older woman on whom she was extremely dependent. Although she had much proof of her friend's devotion to her, she always feared that one day she might vomit and her friend would then throw her out.

She suffered in fact from a severe vomiting phobia. One evening she had a genuine digestive upset and, knowing that she was about to vomit, she called to her friend to do something to stop it happening. In answer to her plea, the friend held out her hands so that the young woman might vomit into them. She did so, exclaiming, "Now you will never love me again!" But her lover deposed a kiss on the regurgitated meal as a sign of total acceptance. This unusual exchange had a profound meaning, and an equally profound effect on the young woman. She was able to analyze, in the months that followed, the unconscious significance of her phobia, and to understand that her friend's gesture meant acceptance of, and forgiveness for, all her forbidden erotic fantasies concerning the father's penis as well as repressed sadistic wishes. Her body image, until then experienced as a fecal object which should be discarded, became an object of value.

The many-sided importance and structuring aspects of anal-erotic and anal-sadistic fantasy have already been stressed; the patient just mentioned presents a crystalline example of a fantasy common to most homosexual women, namely that being a woman is equivalent to being a pile of feces. "She imagined herself as a very aggressive, unattractive, destructive and 'smelly' object. She 'gave off smells' and was filled with bad things. She had deep feelings of guilt for her agression toward both her father and her mother. 'If I show my evilness everyone will abandon me....' This aggression was turned against the self in dreams and made her feel bad as if she were 'a piece of smeared feces'" (Socarides, 1968, p. 184). Such deeply destructive feelings, along with the damaged self-image, are partially healed by the homosexual relationship, where each partner may play the "holding function" of the "good enough mother" of Winnicott's writings (1960). "She is less cruel to me than I am to mysef," said Sophie one day when talking of her lover. These women are often incapable of being "good mothers" to themselves, and can only bestow love on another woman. Something which is missing in the inner object world is thus sought in the partner: through identification with her, instinctual satisfactions and lost parts of the self are recovered.

The aggressive wishes that seek to be contained in the homosexual act and object relation go further back than the phallic-genital frustrations of the oedipal situation, further back than the anal phase of integration, back, as we have seen, to archaic sexual objects, long before the conscious differentiation of the sexes (Klein, 1932, 1950). If the homosexual girl's secret desire at the phallic-genital level is to obtain the sexual emblems of the other sex — the symbolic unattainable phallus, with which to attract the mother's desire — the underlying wishes are those of the baby, all that the infant self unconsciously still demands. This might be summarized as the wish to obtain for oneself, and forever remain in possession of, the breast-mother. Not only is the difference between the sexes disavowed, but also the difference between one person and another, one body and another, the baby and the breast. Such satisfactions and gratifications are hoped for within the erotic homosexual bond. But since this is built upon the greedy oral love of the earliest relationship, it includes the aim of possessing the object to its own destruction. The underlying fantasy, not only of having castrated but also of having lost or destroyed the object, gives rise to intense depressive feeling.

We have up till now been examining the positive aspects of the homosexual relationship; it is evident, however, that few of the basic conflicts are resolved, and that the new relationship contains the seeds of its own destruction. Analysis invariably reveals the greedy, destructive, and manipulatory anal-controlling aspects of the relationship. The need to idealize the partner, the sexual act, and the relationship as a whole is present in order to protect the love object from the fantasied attacks that the individual would like to make upon it. The homosexual needs to believe that her relationship to her partner is reparative and healing. While it is true that concern for the object mitigates greedy oral destructiveness, this unconscious content contributes to the evanescent quality of many homosexual affairs. "I realize more and more that I am crazy to go on caring for her so much. I admit I grabbed at her to live with me because my last friend left me so suddenly and I just can't live alone. Nor can she [the present friend]; but where I really care a lot about her—her failures, her insomnia—she doesn't even know who I really am! My professional problems bore her to tears. I'm sure if I suddenly stopped bringing home money she would leave me immediately for another woman." This remark from one of my partients is one I have heard in different versions from other homosexuals.

Such insights are extremely painful to the persons concerned, and in fact they are only uncovered in analysis when the patient discovers to her astonishment that history is repeating itself; not only does she perceive this with respect to her various lovers, she also comes to realize that a piece of infantile history is being re-enacted: she is once again the little girl performing solely for the narcissistic enhancement and the emotional security of the mother. Thus the tendency to reduce the love partner to a part-object, to victimize her, and to control her every movement is only equaled in intensity by the fear of becoming oneself the part-object, magnetically fixed on the partner. Such patients seek to play an essential and irreplaceable role for the partner, and sometimes end up doing many things for the other woman to the detriment of their own interests or of their work. Here the wheel has come full circle to the childhood relation with the mother; the ego thus continues to pursue its instinctual aims and to maintain its fragile identity along the lines traced out in childhood.

Oedipal structure and ego defenses

The oedipal organization as an unconscious nuclear and structural model of the personality should serve as a starting point for our summary of the findings in this chapter. As we have seen, the homosexual girl has regressed in face of the oedipal situation and restructured her sexual desires in terms of the dyadic mother relationship; thus the father's penis no longer symbolizes the phallus and she herself embodies the phallic object. Through unconscious identification with the father, and by investing her whole body with the significance of the penis, she is now able in fantasy to fulfill a woman sexually. Instinctual regression from phallic-genital to anal-erotic and anal-sadistic expression has left its mark on the object-relationship and has also been invested in character traits. Oral-erotic and oral-sadistic wishes, because of their frightening nature, are kept in check in large part by the homosexual relationship and the sexual act itself. Addictions and compulsions, such as kleptomania (McDougall, 1970; Schmideberg, 1956), are frequent secondary symptoms to deal with these primitive, repressed impulses. There is no dissolution of the oedipal conflict. With regard to the heterosexual object, narcissistic mortification has led to complete conscious withdrawal from the father. Insofar as homosexual oedipal wishes are concerned, the homosexual woman has failed to integrate these into her personality structure, for their normal resolution would have led to identification with the genital mother. Instead, the primal scene is denied, and then reinvented with the exclusion of the male and the penis. Following Bion (1970) we might say that these children have refuted the oedipal myth and created a private one instead. The homosexual solution to id wishes and object relations problems has its counterpart in the ego structure. From the standpoint of clinical categories we are dealing with an unconscious organization that is neither a classical neurotic nor a psychotic one. There are neurotic defense mechanisms at work, but they are not sufficiently organized to protect sexual identity; in addition, there are a number of psychotic defenses that have gone into the homosexual solution and the maintenance of its basic illusions. In fact, we find here the splitting of the ego's defensive shield, as described by Freud (1940). This would seem to provide the nodal point for the conception of a "third structure." Although this identical oedipal and ego structure is found to underlie all sexual deviations (Rosen, 1964), it seems to me inaccurate to refer to this as a "perverse" structure since it is not limited to the sexual perversions. The defensive splitting and the continual acting out to compensate for what is missing in the inner psychic world can also be found in many severe character neuroses, in patients with addictions and antisocial symptoms, as well as in psychosomatic patients (Sperling, 1968). What is more specific for homosexual women is the pathological introjection of the father figure and the erotization of defenses against the depressive and persecutory anxieties that result from these distorted structures.

Splitting mechanisms play a particularly important role in the ego organization. Not only is there a split in the defense mechanisms, but there is also a split in the inner object world (Gillespie, 1956a, 1956b). The image of womanhood is divided into a highly idealized and a totally castrated one—so idealized that it is felt to be inaccessible, and so castrated that such women must disguise their femininity by all the psychic means at their disposal. As long as this type of splitting process can be maintained—and it requires constant projection and disavowal of reality to do so—the ego can protect its identity. Further extension to the splitting tendencies may be seen in the redistribution of the split-off fragments. Although the failure of early splitting into good and bad (which if unhealed leads to a psychotic resolution) has been avoided, there is nevertheless a specific splitting along sexual lines—a "good" sex and a "bad" sex. This is similar to the "false splitting" described by Meltzer (1967). "Bad parts" of the self along with bad feelings attached to the internalized mother are projected onto the father, and subsequently onto men in general, and may lead to a paranoid attitude toward men. But this ensures the "good" which is invested in fantasies of reparation of self and partner, and the hope of recovering lost parts of the self. However, if the female object, which unconsciously contains so much hatred and so many "bad" parts of the infantile self, comes too dangerously close to being a *conscious* container of hatred, then the fear of the partner may triumph over the eroticized defenses, and this would lead — outside of an analytic situation — to the risk of psychotic episodes of a paranoid type. At this point the loved and the hated person coalesce; not only sexual desire, but all desire, the desire to live, is threatened.

Mary Barnes (1971) described the feeling that all instinctual movement on her part was forbidden: "The 'right' thing had always been what someone else wanted of me. . . .Not separate, my desire had to go through someone else. As if I was a tiny baby, I could only be satisfied through 'Mother' gauging my needs. In her womb, the food of blood from her, to me. The trouble with me had been my real *Mother* hadn't really wanted me to have it, food. She had never had any milk in her breasts. She couldn't; she hated me. Yet she told me she loved me, and wanted me to eat. . . .I had to starve to death to satisfy my Mother." Mary Barnes had found no protective halt, such as the creation of homosexual relations to live out sexual desire and to protect her, as she "went down" in the depths of her tortured relation to her inner objects.

The harsh pregenitalized superego of the homosexual is quadrupled in psychotic dissolution. If the neurotic may be said to fight for his sexuality and the psychotic for his very life, the homosexual (and all "third-structure" people) might be said to have found a half-way station between these two aims, in which psychic death is avoided and only one's sexual self is denied. The homosexual girl's unconscious identification with the father gives her a separate identity and enables her to enact the reparative role in the guise of sexual partner, thus repairing all the fantasied attacks contained in her intense demand for possession of the sexual and autonomous self of her partner. This of course is not genuine reparation, and comes within the scope of all that is included in the term manic defense as defined by Klein, Heimann, Isaacs, and Riviere (1952) and Winnicott (1935). It is nevertheless a powerful and protective structure within the ego.

Reference has already been made to the fantasies of the maternal breast as a bad and poisoning object, and to the way in which the homosexual act may keep fears of being destroyed (because of one's incorporative desires) at bay. But to the extent to which such fears dominate the picture and come close to consciousness, we are moving nearer to a psychotic structure than to a deviant sexual one. The same basic fears may also be elaborated through other forms of compulsive behavior such as alcoholism, bulimia, and so on. Since the father symbolically embodies acute paranoid fears, and since persecutory anxiety arises from contact with him, this psychic split gives the homosexual girl the chance to preserve her ego from dissolution; but if such fears return to the *maternal image* there is little chance of a satisfactory homosexual solution. She is also compelled to maintain her ego identity on another front, by keeping her distance from men, for any close affective contact with them will make her lose the internalized penis, the fantasy on which her identity is built. She is constantly and compulsively driven, in her dilemma, to endless repetition in her erotic relationships. Over and beyond the masochistic danger of self-surrender, she is menaced by the potential upsurge of her violently ambivalent feelings toward her partners. Homosexual relationships move continually between two poles: the fear of losing the other, which results in a catastrophic loss of self-esteem — leading to loss-of-identity feelings or suicidal impulses, and the arousal of cruel and aggressive feelings toward the partner which give rise to intolerable anguish. As a consequence of excessive idealization of the partner, homosexual relations contain, to a greater extent than heterosexual ones, a hidden dimension of envy. Thus, in spite of its reparative aspects, the homosexual situation is inevitably precarious. A sexual identity that disavows sexual reality and masks inner feelings of deadness can only be maintained at a costly premium. The homosexual pays dearly for this fragile identity, heavily weighted as it is with frustrated libidinal, sadistic, and narcissistic significance. But the alternative is the death of the ego.

What may psychoanalysis hope to achieve for the homosexual woman? The analyst, whatever his personal wishes may be, can only dedicate himself to leading his patient as far as possible on the road to self-discovery, which may or may not lead to her giving up her homosexual life. The important aim is to bring to her consciousness the varied aspects of her internal drama which until now have escaped her, along with the conflictual roles played by the internalized parents, and the intense feelings of love and hate attached to them. She will then be in a position to retrace what she understood to be her place and role in the family constellation. Only in this way may she come to recognize her own conflicts and contradictory pursuits, and the intricate network of defenses constructed since infancy to deal with confusion and mental pain.

Among other factors, the analytic harvest includes a transformation of the body image. Where she once conceived of herself as ill-made, disorganized, dirty, or sick, she now is able to make a truer appreciation of her physical self. The old hypochondriacal anxieties become less, and often disappear entirely. More solidly "embodied," the patient comes to a different appreciation of herself and her capacities in professional and other social fields.

For many, there is an equally important change in the feeling of sexual identity. In spite of the fact that these patients rarely come into analysis in order to become heterosexual, many do in fact give up their homosexual pursuits and become wives and mothers. Others are not drawn to the heterosexual arena. In spite of its pitfalls, the homosexual solution offers a certain security. However the conviction of having chosen and consciously assumed one's homosexuality is in itself a positive factor in comparison with the former feeling of compulsion. Thus these patients are often able to create more stable, less ambivalent relationships with their parents, and find themselves better armed to face homosexual conflict.

Chapter IV

Masturbation and the Hermaphroditic Ideal

Hermaphrodite, the perfect ephebe, child of Aphrodite and Hermes and gifted with the attributes of both these godly parents, found himself transformed one day into a bisexual being through the love of a nymph enamored of his beauty. Though Hermaphrodite may well have cursed his cruel destiny, simple human monosexuals cling avidly to the fantasy of bisexuality. The bisexual illusion is as old as man's history and culture. Whether we reflect upon the significance of the ancient oriental gods, or Plato's myth of the origin of the sexes, or, coming closer to our own epoch, Freud's science-fiction attempt to credit the female of the species with a tiny penis (in the very place where she thought she had discovered a secret organ of her own), we are tempted to believe that we are faced here with one of man's *urphantasien*. The fantasy of being both male and female, of possessing the white and black magic of both sexes, of being father and mother, or even of being self-engendered — who in his child's heart might not long for this?

The prehistoric truth imputed to these primal fantasies is less convincing and less striking than the universal discovery of their traces in the unconscious of mankind, and the discernment of their nostalgic and reparative function in relation to the inevitable wounds that reality inflicts on human narcissism. The fact that authentic hermaphrodites are so rarely produced among humans and that even those animals so endowed are of a rather humble variety, such as snails and earthworms, in no way weakens the strength of the myth or the fascination of monosexual man wounded in his narcissistic and megalomanic desire by the discovery that he is condemned for life to be but one half of the sexual tandem.

If the idea of bisexuality is a significant one for psychoanalysis, its value is not to be sought in the realm of biology nor in the notion of a phylogenetic heritage such as Freud proposed. It would seem more probable that bisexuality is a wishful fantasy, an ideal, a dream (perhaps for certain people a nightmare), but in each case a product of the imagination of the incestuous child as he gazes in distress upon his vision of the primal scene, in vain search for some godlike defense of his omnipotence before the Fall. From a certain point of view his recourse to a bisexual ideal is a retreat from castration anxiety that is linked as much with forbidden homosexual wishes as forbidden heterosexual desires. It is also a retreat from narcissistic castration fears mobilized by feelings of exclusion, helplessness, and lack of self-esteem. As with the oedipal desires and phallic castration anxiety, this narcissistic fantasy has much earlier roots. What lays the groundwork for

man's later bisexual fantasies? To understand the pro-
fundity of the bisexual dream, whether as an ideal
state or as a forbidden and dangerous desire, we must
go back to the beginnings of psychic life, to the dawning awareness not of sexual identity, but of subjective
identity — the quality of "otherness." I would like to
suggest that the hermaphroditic ideal has its roots in
the fusional illusion that links the child to the primordial breast-mother. The search for an ideal state in
which no lack would exist is in itself witness to the fact
that the breast is already "lost," that is to say it is
already perceived as *the essence of Another*. Although
the bisexual illusion in its various manifestations has
been built on the ramparts of the sexual difference, its
foundations begin with the difference between two
bodies, and the underlying desire to annihilate all
thought of separation with that Other, a perpetually
present desire whose goal is to deny the impossible
otherness and to put an end to all desire.

The breast-mother and sexuality

Following the path that leads backward from sexual
identity to subjective identity, we come to that mythical moment, the psychic dawning of an individual,
and with it the first trace of an object and the first
shadow of a wish. To the nursling, in the beginning,
his mother and he are but one person. Not only does his
biological survival depend on her, but his psychic existence as well. Not yet an object for him, she is already
far more than this, his *Umwelt*, mother-universe of
which he is an essential part. That primary experience

in which the infant is but a small fragment of a greater whole forms the individual's earliest identity (Lichtenstein, 1961; Winnicott, 1960). The child is that *whole*, rendered magically strong by his mother's strength. But in truth it is a relationship of absolute dependence wherein the child is solely what he represents for his mother. All that is growing within him cannot reach light nor find form without her. His mobility, his first affective impulses, his intelligence, his sexuality, are in the first instance all aided or stifled by her. In addition to her care-taking functions, each mother, following her own needs and wishes, will solicit in her baby wishes she alone will have the pleasure of fulfilling (Lichtenstein, 1961). Thus the child, even before its birth but more particularly afterwards, comes to represent a special object for the satisfaction of the different conscious and unconscious longings of the mother. In that first sensual encounter between the two, each one is, or should be, an instrument of gratification for the other. This libidinal imprint on each individual's subjective identity leaves an indelible mark on his psychosexual and narcissistic evolution and structure. *Thus from the dawn of psychic life some part of every subject's identity is, and will forever be, that which it represents for another.* With regard to sexual identity, there is much important research to show that the mother's attitude varies according to whether she has a girl or a boy child (Stoller, 1968) and precociously influences the infant's future psychosexual identity even to the extent of inducing transsexual interventions in adult life (Montgrain, 1975) if her own unconscious problems do not permit her to accept her infant's biological sex. Nevertheless, the child's eventual discovery of the difference between the sexes and his recognition of the fact that his own sexual identity can only be confirmed in relation to that of the opposite sex, demands the renunciation of narcissistic wishes and the loss of an illusion — already foreshadowed in the loss of the breast. What is the significance of this loss?

For the sake of precision I would point out that I am using the word "breast" not to indicate a corporal part-object, but as a concept, in the sense elaborated by Melanie Klein of the mother in her totality: her skin, her voice, her odor, and indeed her whole being as the source of gratification and identity, as well as her essential function of being able to contain and render bearable to her infant the entire gamut of his intense love-hate feelings. In this way the loss of the breast as a part of oneself does not signify the process of weaning and the change to solid foods, but rather the slow and vital discovery on the infant's part that the breast does not belong to him, that it never will be his, and indeed represents the essence of the Other; moreover, that Other may offer this marvelous essence or refuse it. The child will ever after seek that breast-mother, trying by all the means in his power to discover how to bring her to him, not only to satisfy his needs but also and above all to refind, to relive the miraculous relationship he has come to know with her. Reinforced by the maternal ego, the child's ego at this time is very strong, but a prolonged break in the relationship, or failure on the mother's part to function as a protective shield against overwhelming stimulation of any kind, may at this early stage give rise to specific anxieties. These do not refer to the castration anxiety of the phallic phase nor to its prototype which we might call the threat of disintegration, but rather to what might more properly be named the threat of annihilation. The child runs the risk of losing not only his object but his entire identity, and this experience of psychic death may even lead in certain instances to death itself (Kreisler, Fain, and Soulé, 1974).

The loss of the object can only be rendered tolerable and the capacity to distinguish oneself from it made possible by a creative psychic act, the introjection of the lost object within the self, there to become the embryo of an "internal" object and eventually a part of the self. If the infant is unable to confront this primary "castration" by recreating the missing object psychically, the loss, inevitable in the prehistory of every individual, can only be dealt with through delusion or death. Inasmuch as this primordial loss is the essential condition for the construction of personal identity, it is evident that any tendency on the part of the subject to seek to return to primitive nondifferentiation brings with it a serious risk either for the subject's psychic health (psychotic states) or for his life (addictions, psychosomatic illness, suicide). Yet the return to the undifferentiated state remains a perennial desire in everyone, and indeed in adults who are not too psychically perturbed finds a certain narcissistic investment in sleep and libidinal investment in adult sexual relations. The mastery of separation-individuation experiences gives place to more elaborate psychic structures and pleasures, but the renunciation implicit in the process of introjection and identification creates an enduring nostalgia for return to the fusional world wherein one was protected from all frustration.

From the beginning of the separation-individuation

process (Mahler, 1970) consequent to the loss of the breast-mother universe and its illusions, the baby's instinctual life will have a double aim: one part of his libido will seek throughout his life to undo the separation and to create in its place a total corporal union with the object that would be as little symbolic as possible (Stone, 1961), whereas the second instinctual current will attempt at all costs to maintain the subject's independence from the object so that his feeling of psychic vitality and identity may not be once again absorbed into the mother-universe. On this foundation the early oedipal structure will be built. The complex problem of otherness progressively infiltrates the difficulties inherent in the acquiring of one's psychosexual identity, not only in view of the oedipal situation, but also from the point of view of narcissistic integrity. Once again man must discover that what he wants and seeks is the very essence of *Another*, and he will inevitably bring to his sexual desire the intensity, pain, and paradox of the earlier situation.

To have psychic possession of one's sex and a feeling of sexual identity it is necessary to first have psychic possession of one's own body and a feeling of individual existence. *Otherwise sexuality runs the risk of becoming merely an instrument for repairing rifts in the feeling of identity* (see Chapters II and III). This sense of subjective identity, as we know, is liable to multiple attacks which run from complete annihilation ("primary" castration) and disintegration anxieties ("pregenital" castration) to the anguish of oedipal-phallic castration conflicts.

It is not my intention to examine here the various obstacles involved in the creative process of identification with the lost object and its implications in respect to adult sexuality. But I should like nevertheless to recall that the earliest introjection, that of the breast-universe, enables it to become split into a "good" and a "bad" object, thus assuring its unity and eventual continuity. This primordial splitting is essential in that it insures the psychic capacity of the infant to maintain a creative relationship with the Other. Should it be defective, the tiny child will be subjected to serious disorders in his psychic structure and in his growing relation to the external world. The same failure will also endanger his development at the phallic phase in that he may find himself unable, without fear, to identify with the opposite sex and therefore to be confident of his own sexual role and identity. There is a concomitant risk in that he may also create a *false splitting* (Meltzer, 1967) in the representation of the differentiation of the sexes in such a way that the "bad" or denigrated object falls on one side of the sexual demarcation while idealization becomes the lot of the other. Such splitting bears witness to a failure in the integration of bisexual drives, that is, the multiple desires directed toward the two parents. This is patent in many homosexuals of both sexes where there is a manifest phobic avoidance of the opposite sex. The homosexual "solution" is not a direct result of the hermaphroditic illusion. *Narcissus is not Hermaphrodite.* "I do not like women! Nor hermaphrodites either! My need is for those who resemble me," sighs Lautréamont's Maldoror.

The most powerful impediment to the integration of psychic bisexuality is *oral greed.* The greediness for the mother-breast is the raw material of love, but the dangers that may interfere with the development of love and sexual desire are numerous. Let us take for example the much bandied-about notion of penis envy in girls. The banal wish of the little girl to possess a penis of her own, and if need be to take one away from someone else in order to become like her father, becomes transformed into the desire for erotic pleasure through the penis in the sexual relationship. However, if the breast-object has never been internalized as a basic representation and support for the earliest libidinal impulses, if it has *failed to signify the mother's desire* (in other words, *to be the breast* for her baby), then the penis may elicit destructive envy that would block any possibility of a love relationship or feeling of desire. The projection of such instinctual greed makes of the penis, or the male himself, a persecutory object to the girl and in her fantasy she becomes an equally dangerous object for him. In the same way the oral greed of the boy child to possess the attributes of the mother, to take from her that which is necessary to excite his father's desire, must also follow the route that will permit the transformation of these envious wishes into the desire to give the woman his penis in the sex act, which implies at the same time his identification with her pleasure in receiving it.

I shall leave aside the question of penis envy in men as well as the equally important wish of the woman to possess the sexual secrets of the mother. These wishes and their integration form the other pole of sexual identity and normally find their investment in secondary identifications with the parent of the same sex. My interest here is centered on *the capacity to identify with the opposite sex as a fundamental element in the mobilization of sexual desire.* This implies the ability to depend on the Other without fear, for it is the dependent part of the personality that allows recognition of one's own limits and limitations as well as those of the Other. This includes acceptance of the fundamental inability of man to be sufficient unto himself and of man's reliance on Another for satisfaction of all need and desire. To recognize one's need of the object's need or desire is a condition of life, and any attempt to deny this dependence tends in the direction of death.

The drama of subjective otherness is therefore strengthened by the discovery of genital otherness and the forbidden incestuous wishes that this entails. This series of painful blows that reality inflicts on the small child's omnipotent narcissism must find compensation. The child finds many threads of different color and quality with which to mend the holes torn by external reality; with these he weaves his own identity pattern. This pattern will alway have two motifs, one relating to everything that makes the individual *different* from others, and one relating to everything that makes him *similar* to others. A lack in either of these identity dimensions endangers the continuing feeling of identity, whether individual or sexual. In other words, any recognition of identity is first and foremost a recognition of separateness.

This brings us back to our starting point, the hermaphroditic ideal, grounded in an earlier ideal of fusional existence and the illusion of being one with the breast-mother — an essential step in the constitution of primary identity on the way to achieving true identity status. In the two ideals we find the same basic psychic process at work: *disavowal of the difference* in the attempt to maintain an illusory ideal state and to ward off disintegration anxieties, and integration of the difference by *identification* with and *introjection* of the lost object, creative psychic acts by means of which the subject becomes subject and object at the same time in order to span the space that separates him from the Other, without fear of destroying or of being destroyed. If this psychic creation of an inner world of identifications and introjections — many times lost and as often recreated — fails to become established, all sexual desire and indeed any wish for narcissistic fulfillment and achievement, runs the risk of being experienced as a dispossession of oneself or of the Other, drawing the subject into a precarious object world in which there is only one sex for two, perhaps even only one body for two persons.

If, as I have suggested, the hermaphroditic wish to be the other sex while at the same time keeping one's own sex is an unconscious and universal longing, then we would expect to find in adults some sign of its existence that is not pathological (in the sense suggested of one sex or one body for two). As we have seen from a psychological point of view, people are basically and profoundly "bisexual." The double face of identity construction leads to an identification with the parent of the same sex while taking the other sex as its object. The genital sexual relationship cannot alone absorb and satisfy this deep bisexual longing in mankind. The question might then be raised as to where bisexual wishes are to find sublimatory or substitute satisfaction. While I have no complete answer to this question, to my mind there are two quasi-universal expressions of psychic bisexuality: one is clinically evident in

creative acts and processes which permit people to produce magically, through coalescence and the assumption of what they conceive to be their masculine
and feminine wishes, so that they may alone engender
their "product"; many work inhibitions and intellectual and artistic blocks are rooted in the unconscious
refusal to accept bisexual wishes and conflicts. The second quasi-universal activity, one that *par excellence*
carries out the hermaphroditic illusion in the individual's erotic life, is *masturbation.* I shall discuss
masturbation as a creative psychic activity whose aim,
over and beyond its instinctual roots, serves narcissistic
wishes of a bisexual nature and as such plays a role of
considerable psychic importance.

Man and masturbation

Masturbation, normal in childhood, and a banal
manifestation among adults who are deprived of sexual relations, is also relatively frequent among adults
who have satisfactory sexual relations. Yet the frequency of masturbation is rarely discussed in the
analytic literature. My aim here is to explore the role
of narcissistic fulfillment and bisexual illusion in the
masturbation process. I would emphasize the idea of
"process" to indicate that masturbation is an act as well
as a fantasy; as such, these two dimensions may become
separated and find different destinies within the psychic
structure. As for the bisexual illusion, even if the
masturbation fantasy totally forbids a scenario involving characters of both sexes, even if there are no people in the fantasy — or even no fantasy — it is neverthe-

less certain that the masturbatory act recreates within the erotic play a two-way relationship wherein the hand (or its substitute) plays the role of the other person's sex. The fantasy may, however, have repressed all representation of the other sex, perhaps by limiting the roles to people of the same sex as the subject, or limiting the sexual representations to part-objects such as body products, and to organs and orifices other than genitals. The fantasies may also put on stage non-human partners such as animals or a host of mysterious and inanimate objects drawn from the sexual daydreams of childhood. As in the world of dreams, in the autoerotic fantasy world all is possible, provided the fantasy creation, like a dream, meets the requirements of primary-process representability and of instinctual demands. Transformed by repression, condensation, and displacement, the fantasies can combine within their microcosm an invented drama that satisfies not only the pressure stemming from libidinal wishes, but also the stern interdictions of the internalized objects, and the demands of external reality. From this standpoint, certain masturbation fantasies are veritable masterpieces, although of totally narcissistic orientation, and like dreams, they prove to be unusually enriching for the advancement of psychoanalytic understanding. (In fact it may be said that the absence of masturbation fantasies, for whatever reason, in the analytic discourse of patients, is regrettable.) However, these fantasies are compact dramas in which certain essential elements are invariably missing, so that their significance can never be fully comprehensible in terms of the manifest content alone.

It would be interesting to study the phenomenon of

masturbation as the realization of a bisexual desire and unconscious wish inscribed within the somatic self and the psyche from the dawn of psychic existence in the individual. In the *Three Essays* Freud (1905) observes that there are three age phases of masturbation, the first occurring in early infancy. Freud had already guessed at the various links between masturbation and other autoerotic activities, as well as its relation to the parental imagos and the narcissistic self-image. The research work of Spitz and his collaborators has further demonstrated the intimate connection between masturbation and the earliest object relations.[1] In his papers on autoerotism, Spitz (1949, 1962) formulated hypotheses and drew some empirical conclusions concerning three different autoerotic patterns that could be observed during the first year of life. These are described as *rocking, fecal games,* and *genital play.* This observational research distinguished three groups of infant-mother relationship: babies who enjoyed a good relationship with the caretaking mother; those whose relationship was unstable, sometimes good, sometimes deficient; a third group who developed in a total absence of maternal affective relations although enjoying consistent and appropriate physical care from competent adults. The infants of group one (good mother relationship) all demonstrated spontaneous autoerotic behavior in the form of frequent genital play. In the second group (inconsistent relationship) half of the infants studied showed a total absence of autoerotic play while the others engaged in rocking and fecal play.

---

[1]See, in this connection, Chapters X, XI, XII dealing with psychosomatic phenomena and the lack of investment of body limits.

With the third group (competent care but lack of affective ties) there was a total absence of autoerotic activities in all the children studied. (We might note that this latter observation runs counter to Freud's supposition that it is maternal toileting and bodily care that first induce autoerotic activity. The affective relationship and unconscious attitude of the caretaking adult to the infant's body and self would appear to be considerably more important in the libidinal investment that the baby makes of its own body and erogenic zones.) Spitz concluded his study by proposing that autoerotic activity is a function invariably connected with the object relations of the first year of life. When such relations are not established on a positive affective basis, there will be no autoerotism. When the contact with the first object is unstable, substitutes for genital play will be found. Finally, a "normal" mother-nursling relationship favors the development of genital play.

Subsequent studies have confirmed these findings with children of kindergarten age (Miller, 1969). A study made of white American children in New York whose socioeconomic situation deprived them of normal maternal care demonstrated a striking lack of masturbatory play as compared with others having closer maternal contact. Where the latter would fall back upon autoerotic activity for relief when faced with situations of anxiety or frustration, the deprived children would seek immediate action such as caressing or attacking objects or persons in the environment, as though unable to establish some psychic equilibrium through the use of their own bodies.

Studies made on kibbutz children, where the infants

are separated from the parents between the ages of six to nine months, also revealed lack of normal genital play and later, a prolongation of pregenital autoerotic manifestations — finger-sucking or fecal games accompanied by urinary and fecal incontinence, up to six or seven years of age. The form taken by masturbatory activity was concomitantly altered with a predominance of anal masturbation and more interest focused on excretory functions than on the genital organs.

A "good-enough" maternal relationship in the earliest months seems to be a prerequisite in order to ensure adequate libidinal cathexes of the body and the genitals. Additional research has pointed up that children who show a lack of genital autoerotism have a greater tendency to scratch themselves, to indulge in head-banging on floor or bed, or to bite themselves. Such observations might lead us to question whether these *autoaggressions* should normally be contained within the activity of infantile genital masturbation. We might also wonder whether the maternal relationship that facilitates spontaneous genital play is at the same time one in which the mother is capable of receiving and containing her infant's aggressive attacks with patience and understanding. Winnicott (1971b) underlines the importance of the maternal object's ability to "survive" the baby's fantasied attacks on her. The infant's realization that the object survives notwithstanding his states of rage and violence allows him to use the breast-mother creatively.

Thus the creative role that autoerotic activities and later genital masturbation should fulfill is to a certain extent predetermined by the events of the first months of life. The form and fantasies of masturbation will be colored by the early breast-relation. If the mother has been able to permit it, part of the aggressive drives will also be integrated into autoerotic activity, thus protecting the child against self-destructive tendencies. If the infant's wish to be physically united with the breast is registered in his psychic functioning even before he has a stable mental representation of the breast-mother, the same may be said to be true with regard to the desire for sexual union.

The baby's very early discovery of the role of the hand and its link with the future elaboration of fantasy life merits a moment's reflection. It is the hand that is destined to repair the first rupture in narcissistic integrity and the feeling of completion created by the absence of the breast. It is likewise the hand that caresses the genital long before the infant can conceive of the difference between the sexes, and later will play the role of the sexual partner's genital in an imaginary erotic relation. To achieve the latter it is of course necessary that the child introject his fantasy of the primal scene (an image which may be an archaic fusion or destruction, a pregenital infantile sexual fantasy or a truly genital one). From this point of view infantile masturbation at the phallic phase has much in common with the spool game of small children. The latter is a game intended to master the pain of the mother's absence so that the child, instead of being the passive victim of the lost object, is now in control of the appearance and disappearance of some substitute object. But in order for this movement of liberation from the presence of the object to take place, it is necessary that the child be capable of a mental representation of his mother in her absence. This is an indication that the object has already been given up as a part of the self and implies that the internal object has resisted destruction despite the implied destruction of the external one. The infant that sucks its thumb or caresses its genitals is already beginning to recreate within its internal world the first vague representation of a "good mother," thus laying the first cornerstone for the eventual capacity to play a maternal function for itself. This in turn gives the child a certain independence from the external object, a psychic independence that is destined to grow continually unless thwarted by those who care for him. In similar fashion, the child who later will masturbate with fantasies based on his image of the parents and their sexual relationship (from which he knows he is excluded) has likewise introjected this image and can thus — like the thumb-sucking infant who recreates the mother-nursling relation, or who plays the spool game at a later stage — enact the roles of both father and mother in his sexual play. The "success" of the child's masturbatory discovery and fantasy will depend to a large extent on the nature of his daydream and the significance he attributes to the parents' sexual relations. Does he imagine parents who love and care for each other in a coitus that is mutually gratifying? Or is it a relationship without love, even without genital organs? Or of a pregenital and sadistic order? Or again does he imagine the parents enclosed in a loving and narcissistic union from which he is to be forever excluded, forever condemned to be a child spectator? (Perhaps the therapy of the sexologists inspired by Masters and Johnson owes some of its success to the fact that this approach does indeed fulfill in reality one of the most commonplace wishes and hopeless dreams of children, namely that the parents should assure them of their right to sexual life and teach them how to make love. The sexological mother and father are initiating you kindly and willingly into all the secrets of adult sexuality.)

Behind the incestuous child of the oedipal stage hides the greedy and avaricious infant of the oral and anal phases. The fantasies associated with these phases tend also to be integrated within the introjected primal scene created by the child, and in this way the various zones and functions acquire bisexual significance. Zones and functions that follow the container-content model are particularly apt to become endowed with unconscious bisexual meaning.

In many ways the young masturbator denies, through his fantasy act, his patent exclusion from the primal scene along with its accompanying narcissistic injury. At the same time he magically controls the parents by substituting himself for both of them. Finally the masturbatory scenario seeks to contain or to resolve all the various conflicts involved, including fantasies of envious attack and narcissistic mortification. In these manifold ways the hermaphroditic ideal englobes that which preceded it, the illusory breast-universe. It encompasses disavowal of the difference between the sexes, and, at the same time, denial of the first separation from the breast-mother, that is, of the original difference between the two bodies. Thus we may perceive that man's masturbation is as much concerned with his narcissistic integrity as it is with his sexuality.

What does the child achieve through his erotic invention? When his unconscious desire is to be joined to the object in the least abstract and most corporal way possible, all transitional objects will fail him. Whatever the role of need in autoerotic gratification (whether thumb-sucking or genital play), it is evident that the illusion will bring about transitory satisfaction. In addition, the act can be gratifying only to the extent that it is linked with an object in fantasied union. The infant who sucks his thumb certainly wishes to be fed, but he longs above all to rediscover the joy of being one with the breast-mother. As to the act of masturbation, it is its fantasy foundation that gives it psychic weight and importance. Because of the succession of "castrations" induced by reality, and the impossibility of satisfying fusional, narcissistic, and sexual wishes, the child triumphs both over the parents and the external world. The situations and imagined acts that feed the succession of erotic fantasies are fabricated from megalomanic wishes and partial drives, and in particular, those partial impulses which are felt to be most forbidden by the parents. And what greater triumph in putting on stage this masturbatory theater than to use the parents themselves as leading actors — thinly disguised as highly honored, famous or religious figures, to be the seducers and initiators into forbidden erotic relations! Should the idealized characters come too close to conscious recognition they may just as readily be transposed into personages of a different race or a different social class from that of the forbidden parents. Blended with the satisfaction of libidinal wishes are the inevitable aggressive and sado-masochistic themes stemming from the archaic sexuality of early infancy. But these fantasies, like the others, have the merit of causing no damage either to the child or to the objects of his desire.

Over and beyond the oedipal conflict and the anxieties aroused by sexual difference lie the cathexes of prephallic bisexuality, all of which are inevitably woven into the primal scene story, including in particular the transformation of the primordial envy of the tiny child in relation to the breast-universe. Among the overflowing harvest of possible masturbatory fantasies, many of course are destined to be repressed; but they survive in the unconscious and there become a storehouse of dream elements.

As for the "technique" of masturbation, also capable of many a variation, it is perhaps worth emphasizing that "true" masturbation is effected with the hands and nothing else. However if the ability to create erotic fantasies has been profoundly inhibited by the mother's unconscious anxieties (an accident in psychosexual development that takes us back to the first year of life) or if there have been unusually severe bodily prohibitions visited upon the infant in the spontaneous use of his hand, and therefore interference with its linking role, the child may be obliged to invent other objects to replace hands as the first substitutes, and later as the genital substitutes, for the lacking objects of his libidinal drives. The hand, which replaces the breast before replacing the other sex, becomes the fantasy support for all the illusions that will be created to replace the child's lost omnipotence. Between the narcissistically ideal being who lacks nothing, who is fusionally and bisexually complete, and the being who has lost these illusions with their consequent threat of psychic death, there should come into existence the imaginative space for another world of fantasy, along with the magic hand, a borrowed magic that may be used to extend reality and in parallel fashion create a new psychic reality in imagination. Similar creations may become dreams or nightmares, may be transformed into neurotic, psychotic, or psychosomatic symptoms, may become sexual perversions or works of art, but all will bear witness to the eternal attempts of every child to effect some form of self-cure for the inevitable psychic conflicts that will assail him.

Masturbation and psychoanalysis

Interest in the phenomena of masturbation shown in early psychoanalytic writings is confined mainly to infantile autoerotism. Yet masturbation is a familiar theme in the discourse of adults in analysis, even if rarely a spontaneous one. Clinically speaking, adult masturbation assumes many forms, from the complicated staging of fetishist-sadomasochist scenarios to the banal and sporadic masturbation of patients who consider their heterosexual relations to be quite satisfactory. Masturbation may also present itself as a neurotic symptom which the patient would like to lose when it is experienced as a compulsion that dominates — or even replaces — all other sexual relations. In the libidinal economy such compulsive masturbation becomes similar to that found in the sexual perversions, and dynamically it may have little to do with the sporadic masturbation of others in situations of privation or of narcissistic hurt.

At the other end of the clinical ladder we find a certain number of analysands for whom masturbation, even as a childhood memory, seems to be totally nonexistent. The struggle against infantile masturbation has been so desperately fought — and won — that it has undergone profound transformations. The latency child frequently carries such a battle forward on two fronts: against the act itself and against the associated fantasies. If he manages firmly and severely to suppress the *act*, substitutes will be found (perhaps eventual obsessional symptoms) which will then be grafted onto earlier anal-erotic and sadistic conflicts). If it is the *fantasy* that is forced into the unconscious, it may in turn find expression in the form of hysterical symptoms, thereby blocking certain ego functions that have become unconsciously eroticized (intellectual inhibitions, etc.). From this point of view masturbation and symptom formation have something in common in that both are the result of a long process and the attempt to find solutions to conflicting demands. Nevertheless there is a fundamental difference: the symptom is invariably experienced as ego-alien, whereas masturbation is always syntonic with the conscious "I" and confirms the sense of identity. Even though the individual may feel guilty about his masturbation, he nevertheless assumes it is a conscious wish and a deliberate act. The analysis of the fantasies and techniques accompanying masturbation will often reveal the infantile roots of the autoerotic invention and permit us to reconstruct the infantile sexual theories whose essential fragments have been lost to consciousness (Miller, 1969). However it will usually require many months or even years of patient analytic work before such psychic speleology becomes possible.

With regard to the theme of adults who masturbate, sporadically or frequently, while enjoying apparently satisfactory heterosexual relations, little time or space is allotted in analytic writings and at congresses to any discussion of their masturbation and its underlying significance. Yet its incidence is relatively high, as any analyst has occasion to discover in his everyday clinical work. In particular, it is the patients whose sexual relations are the most stable who have the greatest difficulty in talking about sporadic masturbation — as though they sense a profound antinomy between the two sexual expressions. And indeed it may well be that autoerotic and heterosexual activity serve different purposes in the psychic economy. In analysis it is an observable fact that the associations are nearly always accompanied by disagreeable or painful affect. At most the analysand tends to bring small fragments of his fantasies or his fashion of masturbating, as though he could only permit these to emerge when not accompanied by too much emotion. Significant details are thus eclipsed or diminished in importance and may not be accessible to analysis for months or years. Certain patients — and this is no rarity — admit to having avoided masturbation for long periods, even though tempted, because they did not wish to have to discuss it in their analytic sessions! This extreme difficulty that so many analysands display with regard to talking about masturbation activities deserves our attention, the more so since this very reticence is often displayed by patients who handle with ease psychoanalytic theories and interpretations relating to sexuality — analysts in analysis, psychiatrists, teachers, psychologists. This seems to suggest that *masturbation is not regarded as an admissible erotic expression, nor comparable to other sexual manifestations.* Why is such opprobrium attached to man's inclination to make love to himself, to take flight, if only on rare occasions, into erotic self-sufficiency?

One might reply that the answer is perfectly obvious: the masturbatory act, which from early infancy has been firmly forbidden as a public manifestation, is of necessity a secret affair; the accompanying fantasies are stereotyped, childish, impregnated with pregenitality and colored with narcissistic illusions. To this may be added the fact that they reveal both passive and active wishes frequently unacceptable to the rest of the personality. Moreover these same fantasies were linked originally with early incestuous homosexual and heterosexual wishes. Above all, *the masturbator may feel accused of proclaiming an apparent liberation from the constraint of his monosexual state, and his dependence upon Another with respect to all other expressions of sexual desire.* The child who has overcome the downfall caused by the discovery of the difference between the sexes and the interdiction concerning the difference between the generations struggles at the same time with the more primitive wish to be freed from his continual unconscious longing for the breast-mother-universe, and thus to recreate, for himself alone, the closed circle, both magic and narcissistic, where no other person may penetrate.

Added to this procession of fantasies that are apt to feed man's conspicuous guilt concerning his masturbation comes the *analyst's* request that he should say all that comes to his mind! To reveal his secret fantasy creation to another simply because he is called an analyst is rather like taking the risk of an irreparable tear. Such an implicit demand will inevitably revive all the threats of retribution which man's imagination has left to its offspring with regard to the supposed dangers of masturbation: the loss of one's vital substance, of one's intelligence, of one's health, of the love of God, etc., etc. Is this secret triumph that has managed to escape so many maledictions at last to be wrenched from him?

There may be certain historical roots that contribute to the reticence of analysts to discuss more openly the topic of masturbation — if not in their personal analyses, at least in their publications. Freud himself had an ambiguous attitude to the theme. During the celebrated 1911–1912 colloquim on masturbation (Nunberg and Federn, 1974) which was intended to further analytic understanding of its phenomena, Freud appeared to uphold the idea that masturbation in itself was a pathological manifestation, much as he had done in 1893, when he maintained that masturbation was the principal cause of that mysterious illness of the last century called neurasthenia. Five years later, still fascinated and worried by the problem of masturbation, he wrote to his friend Fliess (22nd December, 1897):

"It has occurred to me that masturbation is the one great habit that is a 'primary addiction,' and that the other addictions, for alcohol, morphine, tobacco, etc., only enter into life as a substitute and replacement for it. Its part in hysteria is prodigious, and perhaps my great outstanding obstacle is, wholly or in part, to be found in it. The doubt of course arises whether such an addiction is curable, or whether analysis and therapy must stop short at this point and remain content with transforming a hysteria into a neurasthenia" (pp. 238–239). (With regard to addictions, it seems to me that a more plausible explanation of their etiology is to be found in a pathological development of transitional phenomena and the use of transitional objects; that is, addictive behavior, including part of the etiology of compulsive masturbation, represents an attempt to replace the mother-universe of early infancy.)

Finally, to the heavy pressures that weigh upon all discourse that treats of masturbation must be added the sociocultural pressure exerted against it, even if at present that censure is more implicit than it used to be. A nineteenth-century French encyclopedia (*Larousse*, Vol. 10) informs us firmly that "it is more particularly the children, of both sexes, who are known to give themselves up to this vice thus striking society in the bud since these are the elements destined to perpetuate it; this will therefore exercise a fatal influence both upon the individual and the species. . . . How many children have died because of masturbation? Others are predisposed to numerous diseases and especially to the development of consumption and various troubles of the nervous system. The digestive functions also soon become disturbed in individuals who abuse venereal pleasures. . . . The masturbator will rapidly see his strength diminish, the colors of health fade away, he loses weight and if he is still young his organism is forever arrested in its development. His eyes become dark and sunken and his skin discolored. Such individuals grow weak and lazy and with ease fall into fainting fits. Their muscular strength steadily declines, their walk becomes jerky and their backs stooped. . . . Such a person resembles less a living being than a corpse, scarcely more than a brute, a spectacle that one contemplates with horror when one considers that this unfortunate creature once belonged to the human race" (translation mine).

The cohort of castration fantasies mobilized by the repressive sexual mores of the nineteenth century are still active in man's unconscious. This eloquent piece of Victorianism demonstrates graphically the fate that awaits all those who hope to repair through masturbation the narcissistic wounds for which the human race is a target: a fitting punishment for all who dare to entertain the illusion of hermaphroditic gifts — the privilege of gods and earthworms.

Chapter V

Creation and Sexual Deviation

The possible relation from a dynamic point of view between sublimation and perversion has often aroused a question in my mind. Both terms are used to connote activities in which component sexual impulses are deflected from the original aim or object. In addition my observations in clinical work have led me to reflect on the innovative and creative aspects of perverse sexuality and to see in what ways these inventions differ from authentic artistic creations.

It is a common finding that sexual innovators not only recreate the sexual relationship according to an eccentric pattern of their own, but also give much time to writing scripts, making drawings, or taking photos, invariably centered on their privileged erotic objects, scenarios, or behavior; this activity becomes an important part of the sexual ritual. Two of my analysands spent many hours each week writing stories, letters, paragraphs dealing with a fetishistic scene that was to be played out in the near future. An exhibitionist patient trod many times the path he was to follow and took photographs of the spots where he planned to exhibit himself a week or so before the event was to take place. A female homosexual patient constantly rewrote an erotic stage play in which a couple found themselves forced to have intercourse, and then would actually seek out people to play this scene in the bars and clubs that lent themselves to her quest. Why did these various and passionately invested activities not become genuinely "sublimated"? To what extent do such creations differ from those of the writer, artist, photographer or film-maker? A connected question concerns the eventual distinction that might be made between *pornographic* and *erotic* works of art. Perhaps one might say that the more directly the picture, object, scenario, etc. takes as its goal an orgastic denouement, the more it comes under the category of pornography. Erotica has been well accepted in almost all civilizations and cultures, whereas pornography tends to be looked down upon. It seems to me that one important differentiating factor is to be found in the extent of imaginative space that the artist leaves to the public. Erotica, if it is to be judged as art, should stimulate the fantasy of the onlooker, whereas pornographic inventions leave next to nothing to the imagination, whence their lack of artistic merit. In this case, it seems to me that fetishistic, voyeuristic, and other scenarios are pornographic rather than artistically erotic, which sheds some light on the psychic economy of those who invent sexual perversions. There is a conspicuous lack of fantasy and imaginative freedom in most perverse inventions; once created they tend to be stereotyped and to maintain their central theme and detail for decades as though the person were not permitted to imagine anything else. Analytic exploration of such inventions suggests that the inventor feels that to change or extend his ritualistic pattern would not only be risking castration, but would pose a threat to his feeling of identity. Perhaps the success of many pornographic films, objects, and pictures rests to some extent on the fact that they become "permissible" fantasies to stimulate erotic desire in people who would not otherwise have freedom to imagine their own erotica, and thus rely on socially provided masturbation material instead?

Let us reconsider briefly the notions of sublimation and perversion as Freud presents them in the *Three Essays* (1905b). I have come to the reflection that the two terms are defined in identical fashion: both are conceptualized as activities in which partial sexual drives are deflected from their original instinctual aim, or directed to an object other than the original object of the impulse. Both are concerned with aggressive as well as libidinal components. Doubtless the criteria commonly proclaimed to distinguish perverse inventions from artistic or intellectual creations are sufficiently familiar to dispense with a lengthy discussion of this notion—that is to say the idea that a so-called "sublimated" activity is described as "desexualized" with regard to its goals and is also considered to be possessed of some socially recognized value. Such criteria quite clearly do not apply to sexual deviations since these are neither desexualized with regard to their long-range aim, nor are they possessed of any social value. On the contrary, the man-in-the-street usually gives to the term "perverse" a pejorative connotation. Let us trust that such is not the case with those who consider themselves to be analysts, for the analyst has ample opportunity to observe, in himself as well as in his analysands, that all men hide within themselves a polymorphous-perverse child. Let us add that they also contain a polymorphous nexus of creative resources. But most people are as unaware of their potentially perverse core as they are of their creative potential. The former is usually hidden in their character traits and ways of relating to people; the latter is confined as often as not to the world of dreams. Both are relegated to that "other stage" that Freud named the unconscious. When perverse and sublimatory activities are conscious and manifest, their common primitive origin is readily perceived: for example, the links between the voyeur and the graphic artist, the sadomasochist and the surgeon, the exhibitionist and the actor, the fetishist and the philosopher. Yet people with common sense will nevertheless protest and claim that the differences are surely greater and more important than these supposed unconscious similarities. But it is the destiny of psychoanalysis to turn its back on common sense in order to frame uncommon questions and to seek another sense behind the commonly admitted one. In the same vein we might also ask ourselves what potentially perverse wishes (sublimated in time) might be lurking behind the choice of psychoanalysis as a career — for the analyst is no more exempt from this probing question concerning his professional choice and practice than any other intellectual or artistic worker. (The desire to *know* in place of the wish voyeuristically to *look;* to *understand* in place of the wish to *take;* to *repair* in order to heal feelings of *guilt* — these may be some of the possible elements involved.)

Before leaving the well-tilled field of the pregenital links between sexual deviations and sublimations, one further question requires asking: from the standpoint of psychoanalytic language, what exactly do we mean by "perversion"? The term implies that there is an available definition of what might be considered "normal" sexuality. What would such a term include? Can it even be satisfactorily defined for any given age or culture? The question is too vast to be dealt with in this chapter.[1] I shall content myself here with reminding readers that Freud drew attention some seventy years ago to the fact that the boundary between "normal" and "perverse" sexuality was ill-defined and that many sexual practices usually described as perverse — voyeurism, fetishism, exhibitionism, interest in a variety of zones that have become secondarily "erogenic" — may all at one time or another play an important role in normal heterosexual love relations.

It is nevertheless often observed that perverse sexual relations are devoid of the dimension of love, although this is far from being always so. Other than this lack, perhaps the most striking characteristic of perverse sexual activity is that the individual feels he has no freedom in the matter; he is not aware of having chosen the particular form taken by his perversion. It would be closer to his psychic reality to say that his erotic invention represents an attempt at *self-cure,* an attempt to deal with the immense anxiety aroused in him by his inner model of the sexual relation, a model presented to him by his early objects which is not only restrictive but often lacking in coherence.

[1]For a more detailed discussion of "normality," see Chapter XIII.

His erotic discovery becomes an essential part of his psychic equilibrium from both a libidinal and a narcissistic point of view. But this erotic expression is so narrow and so weighted with multiple conditions that the inventor might find himself at any moment threatened in the maintenance of his identity feeling and his narcissistic economy. The ineluctable feeling of compulsion that accompanies sexual perversions is one manifestation of his dynamic conflict. Take the example of the homosexual and his feverish hunt for partners; being a homosexual is often a way of life, practically a profession (and in fact it is this aspect of homosexuality that is sometimes experienced as painful and symptomatic by certain homosexual patients who seek analytic help). Other sexual deviations such as fetishistic, sadomasochistic, or transvestite productions are imbued with the same obligatory insistence, a compulsive pattern that has frequently persisted since childhood. Such analysands often describe the way in which their erotic fantasies and preparations occupy their waking lives, sometimes taking up several hours each day, to the extent that the ostensible reason for seeking therapeutic help is frequently connected with *work inhibitions*. These hours of ritualistic preparation, the daydreams consigned in writing, the complicated geographic planning of voyeur and exhibitionist, the nights devoted to tracking down homosexual partners, may leave little space for work or leisure, and in some cases, *little desire to escape from the erotic kingdom* in which the individual is king. Drained of libidinal investment, everyone and everything that exists outside the endlessly reiterated stage-play may be experienced as dull, useless, or even incomprehensible.

We should note at this point that intensity of interest and a tendency to exclusive investment is also the hallmark of the intellectual and the artist; but with regard to their productions one essential difference is in *the role played by the public.* The "public" of the sexual deviant, although as powerful for his fantasy life as is the real public for the artist, is reduced to a minimum — as often as not to the subject's own image in the mirror. Nevertheless it may be said that both creative worker and perverse script-writer seek some form of narcissistic recuperation and recompense for their labors; and both have to cope with internal objects they hope to influence or appease through their diverse creations. But it is evident that the intense involvement of the artist in his love affair with the public is not an orgastic ecstasy, whereas the perverse exploit always has as its eventual aim the denouement of orgasm — either of the subject or of his partner. As already noted, the pleasure of the partner is frequently more important to the pervert than his own orgastic pleasure — at which moment he reveals his own propensity as artist! The creative worker, whether in an artistic or a scientific field, also seeks to produce pleasure or excitement and interest, thus invading and affecting his partner — the public. Like the sexual innovator, he wishes to impose upon the other his invention, hoping to inspire the public with *his personal vision,* to pervade it with *his illusion of reality,* in parallel fashion to that of the neosexual inventor who seeks to impose sexual pleasure according to his personal vision or illusion of the sexual act. However, the two activities play a different role in the psychic economy. In the transformation of instinctual expression out of which sublimatory activity grows, the artist is freed — not only from the exigency of orgastic end-pleasure, but also with regard to the form and the content of his inventions. The fundamental themes will usually demonstrate a certain continuity — and this is in fact one essential characteristic of the outstanding creative personality (a Picasso can be recognized at a glance from the farthest end of the gallery, so strong is the personal imprint of the master on his work). The artistic production, though stamped with the personality of its creator, is free from the element of compulsion that marks perverse productions, and the created themes are never identical to the preceding ones. The inventor of a perverse sexual scenario seeks always to reproduce an identical performance; in this sense we might think of his activity as "operational" sexuality, similar to the mode of "operational" thinking described by psychosomaticians. Perverse sexual scenes are created once and for all, and prove little modifiable with regard to their fantasy content or their form of expression.

I would like at this point to dispel a possible misunderstanding. To oppose *perversion* and *creation* may give the mistaken impression that the two forms of invention could not co-exist in the same individual. This is false in that different sectors of the personality may be organized in different ways. Many an analysand reveals manifestly aberrant sexuality, and in other areas of his life demonstrates his capacity for genuinely creative work. And indeed our cultural history contains many famous examples of this dual coexistence. But the reverse propositon is not true, that is, the fact of being homosexual, fetishist, sadomasochist, or voyeur in his erotic life confers no particular creative gifts on the individual. On the contrary, it would be more exact to say that certain gifted persons are capable of authentic creative work *in spite of* their disturbed sexual organizations and deviations, for it is frequently the case that the specific problems which have facilitated perverse solutions to mental conflict, thus blocking any other access to sexual fulfillment, exert the same restrictive and inhibitory influence on the rest of the subject's life — his everyday social relations or his sublimatory capacities in general. Whether the neo-sexual deviant possesses creative ability or not, his erotic creations display a singular poverty of invention and fantasy. The static force that maintains this rigid pattern in place equals that which ordains the rigidity and persistence of neurotic symptoms — an economic factor that concurs with Freud's conviction that perversion and neuroses have a common basis. However the celebrated dictum which decrees that "neurosis is the negative of perversion," while possessing a certain truth, has revealed itself, as clinical and theoretical research has advanced, to be an inadequate description of the unconscious structure behind perverse sexuality.

Freud never returned to the *Three Essays* (1905b) except to add a few footnotes, whereas his theory of the structure of the personality evolved continually and occupied his mind for thirty subsequent years. Thus it could be argued in terms of the so-called "structural" model of the mind that the superego structure of the sexual deviant does not allow him to conceive of sexual relations for himself in other than the most limited perspectives. As with neurosis, it is a question of a surface manifestation that gives little insight into its vast underlying structure. It becomes evident in clinical work that for such patients genital heterosexual relations have been rendered dangerous and forbidden and are perhaps countercathected in consequence. Homosexuality provides one of the clearest examples of this. The phobic investment of people of the opposite sex evidenced by both male and female homosexuals is constructed as much on denigrated and terrifying images of the other sex provided by the parental discourse as it is on oedipal castration anxiety.

Studies of homosexual adolescents of both sexes suggest that everything in the family-transmitted cultural heritage that contributes to discouraging heterosexual interest aids in strengthening homosexual cathexes. Analytic work reveals similar taboos arising from the unconscious sexual conflicts of the parents of other sexual deviants. Patients who are fetishists may remember parental tolerance of childhood games that were manifestly erotic and compulsive; many a transvestite patient recalls the maternal complicity displayed toward the theft of underclothes. The child destined to find a devious path around the oedipal interdictions is often in search of a solution to the sexual and narcissistic problems of his parents. His psychic identity is constructed to a large extent in accordance with their conscious and unconscious specifications. In this respect we might say that *the creation of a sexual perversion is a triumph over the sexual impulses.* As such, it shows some structural similarity to sublimatory transformations. But it is probable that perverse constructions are acquired much earlier in life; this no doubt contributes to their compulsive and relatively enduring nature. The psychic economy underlying sublimatory expressions, however, makes possible infinite displacement and variety. I would hold that the "perverse creation" as a response to oedipal stress and an apparent "solution" to its impasse is also a solution to the conflicts and problems of identity and otherness; it cannot be apprehended simply in the light of oedipal castration anxiety, nor regarded as a mere repository for the safeguarding of pregenital sexuality. Perversions demonstrate that their creator is using sexual capacity to deal with deeper narcissistic dangers.

The homosexual dilemma provides much insight into the dynamic and economic factors that maintain the perverse sexual structure. It was in the wake of a study of the unconscious significance of female homosexuality (McDougall, 1964, 1970), added to the experience of analytic work with male homosexuals, that I first perceived certain important elements concerning the unconscious role of the sexual relationship in the psychic economy and came to a deeper understanding of specific features in the oedipal organization of these analysands. The importance of the homosexual act for the maintenance of identity feeling and self-esteem is only matched by the extreme ambivalence and violence which saturates, sometimes even consciously, the relation to objects. These factors exist in many a heterosexual relationship also, but the narcissistic lesions that lead to homosexual object choice are such that the unconscious demand, directed to the partner called upon to repair these, gives a more compulsive and more destructive aspect to the homosexual exchange.

The "family portraits" drawn by these patients, male or female, are strangely alike (as described in the preceding chapters of this book). The maternal imago dominates the scene in all directions; her highly ideal-ized image remains nonconflictual since the split-off hatred is in most cases projected onto the father. The latter image is endowed with negative qualities of one kind or another, the father being remembered in ana-lytic associations as absent, cold, stupid, brutal, of in-ferior descent, and so on. As such the paternal image occupies little psychic space in the inner object world, at least from a positive point of view. This repre-sentation thus fails to fulfill the normal symbolic role of the father in the oedipal structure. His symbolic phallic value is so reduced that this image is rendered inapt either as an object of identification for the son or as an object of desire for the daughter. The model of the primal scene distilled by this couple: unattainable, ideal mother and despised or distant father, and the nature of the oedipal organization to which these im-ages give rise in the child's psychic world is obviously a distorted one from a sociocultural viewpoint. The situation is further complicated by the fact that the im-ages are brutally and unrealistically split: the con-sciously denigrated or missing father hides an uncon-scious image of a male being possessed of an ideal and unassailable phallus (a role often attributed to the maternal grandfather or to God, incontestable phallic figure). The venerated maternal image in turn conceals a darker side — a primitive destructive imago created from the fantasies of the "anal" mother who controls, drains, and crushes her offspring, or the "oral" mother who stifles, sucks in, and devours her infant. The homosexual, male or female, unconsciously seeks pro-tection from these terrifying pregenital and archaic parental images by erecting a "phallic barrier" against them. For the girl this becomes an *identification with the idealized phallus* and for the boy an *incessant quest for an ideal phallus in his choice of object*. Both have created an external narcissistic object to take the place of the damaged paternal imago, and attempt in this way to repair a fundamental *symbolic* lack in their internal psychic world. The ego ideal, also projected outward, produces a continual psychic hemorrhage of the self-image which the individual seeks to heal through the magical sexual act.

The attempt to give meaning to a lacunary sexual model created on the basis of a distorted oedipal structure, and the disturbances of libidinal and narcissistic economy have been explored in nonhomosexual deviants in Chapters I and II. The study of a fetishistic perversion was taken to illustrate the fact that the sexual act invariably includes the wish to gain, conserve, or control an external representation of the idealized (and unconsciously terrifying) phallus. The fetishistic object is created through splitting, projection, and displacement mechanisms to repair the symbolic failure and to ward off the threatening unconscious fantasy image. The repressed violence of most homosexual patients noted above (see also Chapter III) is also manifest in nonhomosexual aberrations. In either case, the erotic game represents the unconscious enactment of a castration drama. The scenario and its acting out are required to heal the breach in the internal psychic world at the point at which the castration complex has failed to become meaningful through the symbolic significance of the phallus (symbol of desire, fertility, complementarity) for the two sexes. These sexual games do not therefore fulfill the same function as the *jeux amoureux* of love, since their primary aim is the mastery of castration and disintegration anxieties, and only secondarily the fulfillment of a sexual longing. The fetishistic construction, in this as in other respects, seems to be paradigmatic of all perverse organizations.

The distinguishing features of the sexual structure of homosexuals and fetishists would appear to me today to apply also to all nonhomosexual deviations of an organized kind, and to allow for their differentiation from neurotic and psychotic sexual structures. I do not wish to suggest that these are rigidly delimited categories or that neurotic, psychotic, and perverse symptomatology may not be found in the same individual. It would be more accurate to suggest that most personalities are created from a mixture of neurotic and psychotic defenses combined with sublimatory and perverse solutions to psychic conflict at different times. The ego has many ways of defending against dangers that may threaten its integrity. But with regard to specific sexual patterns, I would suggest that the perverse organization is composed of both neurotic and psychotic defenses — the well-known "splitting of the ego" with regard to its defensive network was first pointed out by Freud in connection with certain perversions. It should also be noted, although I have not dealt with this aspect of the question here, that the choice of perversion is of considerable importance in the unconscious structure — the difference for example between homosexual and nonhomosexual perversions, or between feminine and masculine manifestations of perverse inventions are all highly significant. But my present goal is limited to delineating specific elements that might be found to underlie all perverse structure and to arrive at a better appreciation of the creative function of perverse sexuality as a whole in the psychic economy. I shall review briefly certain aspects of the oedipal constellation in order to link it with the role of transitional phenomena, and then discuss the innovative dimension of perversion phenomena.

The oedipal structure is striking in its homogeneity: a mystical couple rather like the parents of the infant Jesus — an idealized virginal and asexual mother and an evanescent and impalpable father, vaporous as the Holy Ghost. Concealed within these ostensible portraits we discover their unconscious counterparts: a maternal imago felt to be mortally dangerous to her child, and a paternal imago endowed with an ideal but death-dealing phallus. Divorced from the conscious paternal image, the phallus is thus incapable of assuming its normative symbolic function, namely as the essential signifier for the understanding and structuring of sexual and social realities, that is, the acquisition of one's sexual identity and the comprehension of one's place as a member of a given society. Instead of an inner confirmation of one's narcissistic, sexual, and social value, there is a feverish and anxious search for any or all of these confirmations in the external world. This relentless pursuit bears witness to the severity of the symbolic failure which may vary in gravity from one individual to another, and may therefore spread beyond the sexual plane to that subjective identity. Sexual activity thus becomes a perpetual quest for self-confirmation on these different planes and tends to be utilized to ward off the overwhelming panic or depression that arises with the threat of narcissistic pain or loss. The groundwork for this symbolic failure,

however, antedates the oedipal crisis and the associated problems of the sexual difference, and leads us
inevitably back to an early failure concerning the
difference between one body and another, and that
earliest lack from which grows the feeling of otherness
and the beginning capacity to represent such a lack
psychically. Here the first illusions are created to fill
the empty space left by the recognition, however nebulous, of the absence of the Other. To this psychic activity in the human infant, Winnicott has given the name
of *primary creativity* (1951, 1971a). This is the raw
material from which *illusion* and *psychic reality* are
fabricated. In speaking of the coming into existence of
the transitional object, Winnicott emphasizes that its
principal interest from the point of view of psychic
functioning is not that this object takes the place of another object (mother, breast) but that instead of being
the original, corporal object, it is a thing-object whose
significance has been entirely created by the infant
himself. It seems evident that in order to be able to create such an object the infant most possess a mother who
is able to allow him to invent such a substitute for her.
A child who has not been enabled to find his own psychic inventions to support his mother's absence or her
other normal moments of maternal failure runs the risk
of finding the renouncements of the oedipal situation,
and the creation of psychic defenses to palliate these,
unduly difficult.

Like transitional objects, perverse objects are invested with symbolic magic though they are but
"transitional" symbols, and we might question the
possible similitude between them. Let us take the objects of fetishistic perversions. The fetish, like the tran-

sitional object, represents a real object, and it too draws its specific value from the fact that it is *not* the real corporal object but a *creation of the subject*, similar to the first "not-me" possession of the infant. And in the perverse scenario, even the partner may well represent an inanimate "not-me" possession. However, the transitional object is in no way a perverse one, and has little possibility of ever becoming a fetish. Transitional phenomena, whether objects or activities, are a normal stage in infant maturation and indicate the growing capacity of the child to interiorize an object and symbolize its relationship to the external world. The fetishistic object, on the other hand, indicates a failure in symbolization, and in particular, an incapacity to render symbolic the difference between the sexes in the adult sexual relationship, along with the renouncing of omnipotent wishes that this entails. It is evident that the two—transitional object and fetish—belong to two distinctly different periods in maturation. But they may be said to have in common their symbolic construction and reparative function, and are both intimately connected with the maternal image and its missing or absent qualities. It is probable that the kind of mother who cannot allow her infant to find and invest his transitional objects or activities (because of her own fragility and urgent psychic "need" of her child, perhaps even as a substitute transitional object for her own infantile self) is like the mother who, because of her inner problems, facilitates a perverse solution to the oedipal impasse (this difficulty being linked to her own unresolved oedipal conflicts). The child, refusing to give up his incestuous attachment, is unable to achieve a secondary identification with the object of the same sex and finds himself condemned instead to endlessly seeking narcissistic recovery of his damaged sexual identity.

In this connection I would like to quote from Chasseguet-Smirgel's (1971) article on the hierarchy of creative acts: "...the privileged activity of creation allows the individual to effect a narcissistic reparation without the need of external intervention. Indeed many patients who have fallen ill through an impoverishment in narcissistic supplies in early infancy, manage, by means of creative activity, to make up for their narcissistic deficiency in *autonomous* fashion. From this point of view creativity is autocreation, the creative act drawing the intensity of its drive from the desire to palliate, *by the subject's own efforts*, the gaps left or provoked by others" (pp. 102–103, my translation; italics added). The idea here expressed is in accordance with my own conception of *deviant sexuality as a creative effort to deal with important gaps stemming from the early maternal relationship*. I do not propose to develop further the narcissistic aspects of the psychic structure that may give rise to perverse sexuality, more particularly since these narcissistic lesions are not specific to perverse sexual pathology; innumerable other forms of acting-out symptoms are fed by a similar psychic economy (for example: addictions, delinquent acts, repetitive character pathology). I shall limit myself here to exploring the creative aspect of perverse sexuality and its specific mode of mental functioning.

If the sexual system of the pervert furnishes his psychic structure with a solid rampart against the infiltration of psychotic anxieties, it is nevertheless intrinsically fragile in that this restraining wall could be constructed only by erasing associative links between psychic representations and external reality. Thus the person's hold on reality may be somewhat tenuous, or at least his capacity for reality testing in regard to human sexuality. To fill the gap left by the elision of the phallus as symbolic of sexual union for both sexes, and in response to castration anxiety, the subject has found himself obliged from childhood to create new signposts and symbols, to invent new knowledge, and to have recourse to illusion.

I trust I have made clear the nature of this illusory *savoir* and the fantasies on which the perverse scenario is built and on which the adherent's belief and secret are founded, for this allows him to uphold his sexual solution as a precious piece of esoteric wisdom, perhaps proclaiming it as the "true" secret of sexual desire. Normality, the pervert declares, is the castration of Eros. From a certain point of view this is true, for perversion triumphs over the oedipal situation as it does over genital sexuality. The latter, by definition, always depends on Another, and on this Other's complementary desire. Even where there exists a "perverse couple" perversion remains the "System D" of human sexuality, the very essence of independence from others and of self-sufficiency. This creates loneliness and the need to make sexuality into a desperate game, for such is the price exacted from the child who must maintain the illusion of being the true object of maternal desire, having the right to castrate the father and invent an idiosyncratic sexual pattern.

In the analytic situation the depression that lies behind this feverish erotic activity comes rapidly to the surface and gives to the affective expression a tonality reminiscent of "manic defense" in the Kleinian sense. In the course of reconstructing their personal past history and its relation to their inner psychic world, these analysands frequently recover memories of fatal disillusionment with regard to what they truly represent for their mothers. The child who can find no other source of identificatory support for his sense of self and of personal esteem may be able to recreate the shattered illusions through erotic inventions — and at the same time mend the tatters so brutally torn in the fabric of his identity. ("If I am not the unique object of my mother's desire, then who am I for whom?" And finally: "Who am I?") From this point the perverse scenario and its enactment may serve as a mask to disguise sexual truth as well as being a container for the rage, mortification, and violently destructive impulses aroused by the child's discovery of parental "treachery." Nevertheless it must be remembered that incestuous longings and the realization of their improbable fulfillment is part of the human lot, and is not a sufficient explanation of the perverse sexual choice and organization.

The weight of important life events and also of certain incisive remarks on the part of parents are frequently brought to light in the course of analysis, and give further clues to the urgent necessity for the child to create new identification points to compensate for the collapse of the incestuous dream. Sometimes the last straw has been added by the birth of a sibling, by a remarriage, or again by denigrating remarks on the part of the parents concerning the child's sexual interest or sexual characteristics. Certain parents also exercise a castrative effect on their growing children by behaving as though they had no sexual impulses, interests, or feelings. Common examples are the parents who laugh at the pubescent child's growing modesty and his wish to be alone in bathroom or bedroom when he is unclothed, or those who parade in the nude before their children as though it were unthinkable that this might mobilize any erotic desires in the children. By their apparent denial of the existence of sexual drives, particularly when this denial has been accompanied by highly seductive behavior of a close bodily kind, such parents create internal images that by their very ambiguity facilitate perverse sexual inventions.

The French novelist, Violette Leduc, in her autobiographical story *Thérèse and Isabelle* (1966) gives a cystalline account of her awakening to homosexual relationships following a traumatic family event. An illegitimate child who has always lived alone with her mother, she learns suddenly that her mother has found a husband and in consequence she is to be sent to boarding school. There she is sexually seduced by her friend Isabelle. The following excerpt poignantly expresses the young girl's feelings:

"So mother is getting married! For how long are we to remain separated? To think of all those years I dug the earth for her, climbed through the barbed wire, stole potatoes from the fields. . . . I used to say I was her little fiancé and she would smile. . . now I shall never be her man, never be the factory worker who brings home the pay. Mademoiselle is married! She has smashed everything; she has all she needs—a married woman. She has put a man between us. Yet we were sufficient to each other; I was always warm in her bed. She called me her little beggar. Climb into my arms she would say...but Monsieur is there. She wants a daughter and a husband. My mother is a greedy woman....She has someone and I have met Isabelle. I have someone; I am Isabelle's; I no longer belong to my mother" (pp. 20–22, my translation).

Thus the mother-tied child makes a determined effort to free himself from his erotic and incestuous bonds with the aid of a neosexual invention. The relationships, scenarios, and fundamental symbols that give it meaning are of course predetermined in their essentials long before adolescence, and are frequently well established as conscious fantasies during the latency period. Negation, disavowal, and displacement come to the child's aid when he can no longer maintain the fiction of the castrated male image and of being mother's sole phallic object; but he is still unable to discover the true objects of her desire. Since neither the father nor any other available man has ever been signaled as her true sexual counterpart, the child rarely dreams of turning to the father or seeking a father substitute to identify with, or in the case of the girl, of choosing a man as a sexual object. In addition, the exclusion of the father — to which unconscious conflicts in both parents have frequently contributed — is in accordance with infantile wishes that seek to maintain the myth of an ineffectual, denigrated, or useless father and of a mother whose sole wish is to be completed by the existence of her child. Thus the oedipal situation tends to be circumvented rather than resolved. Maternal complicity and paternal failure are the fundamental elements on which the inner object world is structured and out of which a heterodox sexual model will be created. Similar imago patterns have been observed and reflected upon by a number of analytic writers, but the child's part in the neosexual invention has received less attention. Among the many unknown factors in this respect one important question is directed toward understanding how a private sexual myth may be maintained in spite of its illusory quality and without its partaking of psychotic sexual explanations.

Freud many years ago pointed out that man's sexual instinct is not, at birth, attached to any given object — desire must find and in a sense create its objects. The links thus created between instinct and object will reveal themselves, from an economic point of view, to be extemely resistant. When the objects of desire seem far removed from those recognized by the society to which the individual belongs, we may then regard the structure of these deviant scenarios and the psychic mechanisms that underlie them as comparable to the way in which dreams are constructed. A patient pays a prostitute to wear a specific type of shoe with high heels; she must then stamp on his penis while calling out humiliating phrases to him. The patient watches this scene in the mirror until his mounting excitement results in an ejaculation. Another wears a black apron that hides his genitals but reveals his buttocks; he whips himself in front of a mirror, and the sight of the whip lashes leads to a climax without ejaculation which the analysand describes as "other-worldly." A homosexual patient licks the anus of his partner and must extract a modicum of his fecal matter in order to achieve orgasm.

Such erotic plays are founded on esotric and complicated scripts, but, like dreams, they are theatrical productions in which certain elements, essential to rendering the plot comprehensible, are missing. We are, of course, dealing with a *manifest content* constructed by means of primary-process thinking: condensation, displacement, and symbolic equivalents are the basic psychic elements involved. And the principal actor himself finds his creation, to which he has lost the key, to be a sexual enigma. He attempts with determination to convince himself and others that he possesses the key to adult sexuality, and tries to validate this secret knowledge in his erotic invention and through the "proof," which frequently becomes a compulsive demand, of orgasm. But the *latent content* continues to escape him. What is this sexual plot trying to prove or to fulfill? Whence are derived the unusual objects, zones, and aims which to the uninitiated seem so unlikely to stimulate erotic desire? These new primal scenes are worthy of our attention. Although the players, the props, and the stage-sets are as infinitely variable as man's imagination, the theme is invariable. As already discussed in the preceding chapters, the plot concerns essentially the drama of castration. This theme is presented as an exciting game, a playful castration whose script and characters are carefully controlled by the actor-producer and so contrived that the anxiety inherent to the plot remains hidden.

Several "classical" perverse scenarios have already been recalled in Chapter II: that of the sadomasochist who seeks to inflict or endure pain, sometimes even directed at his genitals or those of his partner, in order to play out the castration theme; that of the fetishist who reduces the make-believe castration to a bout of beaten buttocks, or to painful bindings, in which the traces left on the skin become the symbolic equivalents of castration, yet are so readily effaced; the disguise of the transvestite who plays at making his genital disappear as he glides into his mother's clothing in a simulated attempt to purloin her identity while still protecting his own sex; or again the drama of the homosexual in his incessant search for the penises he wishes to incorporate — orally or anally — thus repairing his fantasy of self-castration while at the same time castrating — and repairing — his partner.

But there are other "castrations" than those belonging to the phallic-oedipal constellation, castration-disintegration anxieties that form part of the affective experience of the infant. These too often demand to be script-written and played out in the magical erotic scene. When the traumatic past concerns the archaic sexuality of early infancy, the threat to be mastered is not aimed at the sexual organs but at the whole body. In an article on a case of perverse masochism, de M'Uzan (1972) describes one such scene: "The patient, stifling between the mattress and the bedsprings, would thus partake in the sexual relations of his wife with another man; this other man was first requested to slap the patient, require him to kiss his hands and feet, and then order him to ingest some of his excrement." In this scenario, written and directed by the patient, we can detect the need to master pregenital traumas and primitive fantasies such as an infant might experience in his early relationship to his mother, where breathing, skin, excrements, and the whole body are sensually involved. If we attempt imaginatively to verbalize the archaic drama being enacted by this patient, we might suppose he has first submitted to chastisement by the father-figure and may now share in the parents' sexual relationship while being hidden in his mother's body. Although he cannot see what is happening, he nevertheless participates in the primal scene through kinesthetic and auditory sensations — as well as being the master of ceremonies and directing the whole production!

In spite of the marked difference in the level of regression between this scenario and others already quoted, we may notice that the plot still turns around the same theme and delivers the same message: *Castration, at whatever level, is harmless and indeed is the very means of achieving erotic excitement without danger.* Thus the person comes to terms with his overwhelming anxiety through the aid of his erotic theater, rather like the child with the spool playing the peek-aboo game in order to overcome the trauma of separation by putting on his own show and controlling the dangerous elements himself. By means of massive disavowal of castration and disintegration anxieties and of the realities of the primal scene, along with the denial of archaic aggressive impulses, the neosexual inventor is able to maintain the unconscious fantasy that the genital organs of his parents are not complementary to each other, and that he is in no way excluded from their eventual sexual relationship. In other words, the child has exchanged the oedipal myth, rooted in the sociobiological structure, for a private sexual mythology running counter to the cultural discourse. From this point on, his psychosexual life will develop in conformity with this new model of sexuality, even though he will recognize intellectually that his is a fictitious primal scene. It is evident also that the creator of this fiction will find himself engaged in a continual battle with external reality. To realize that "one and one makes two" is not in itself a profound intellectual acquisition, but he who, in spite of evidence to the contrary, calculates on some other numerical system, is going to encounter difficulties wherever he goes; he will have to make constant personal adjustments. The false arithmetic of perverse sexuality is not always entirely limited to the sexual relationship; it may color the understanding of human relations in general with the concomitant risk of precipating moments of psychotic confusion.

How are we to understand this neosexuality from a dynamic and a developmental point of view? How does one manage to contain — and maintain — the image of a dead phallic father along with an abysmally unlimited and nondesiring mother in one's inner object world? And how does one manage to maintain the disavowal of the primal scene and its significance at the same time making light of castration anxiety on all levels? What psychic mechanisms make this possible, and where are the probable fixation points?

In order to make a more concise comparison between the "perverse solution" and the "neurotic solution" to psychic pain and human conflict I shall once again refer to the Freudian conception of the evolving fantasies of the young child in his attempt to come to terms with the inacceptable realities of sexual difference and subjective otherness:

1. At first the child believes there is only one sexual organ — the penis. A simplified *unisex* theory.

2. Sooner or later he will make the inevitable observation that women do not have penises. Thereupon the child attacks his own perceptions. "There was a penis

there; I saw it." *Disavowal* wins the day. This is a drastic form of "denial through word and act."

3. As the ego evolves, external reality takes on an inexorable thrust that renders the simple solution of disavowal difficult to uphold. The child begins to create *imaginary events* in order to deal logically with the problem. *Denial through fantasy* takes the place of disavowal ("mother has been castrated by father"; "her penis is hidden inside her"; etc.). This step is a considerable advance in psychic elaboration.

4. The progressive acceptance of the difference between the sexes and the progressive understanding of the interdiction concerning the difference between the generations leads *children of both sexes to countercathect the disquieting maternal genital.* The female sex organ becomes invested as disgusting, dangerous, ugly, or uninteresting, and femininity is equated with derogatory qualities. Thus, in one fashion or another, the mother's open genital ceases to be an object of interest and fascination. At this point the child appears to have "resolved" his oedipal crisis. Most often, however, he has simply managed to repress in a global way the whole gamut of his infantile sexual theories and fantasies, thus laying in store the material for future neurotic creations.

5. The childhood phase that results from the above constitutes what is known as the *latency period* — marked by libidinal regression and the clinging to pair-groups in which youngsters of both sexes seek homosexual reinforcement against the adult world. This group reinforcement is notably lacking in fact among those who are destined to find a homosexual or other deviant solution to oedipal conflict and pregenital cas-

tration fears. At this stage such children are frequently solitary little beings who are already aware that they are "different from the others."

6. In the best of all possible words, the oedipal drama is "resolved" — although this idea is probably part and parcel of *psychoanalytic* mythology! The child who achieves this transformation must *accept* that what he wishes were so shall never be; *he must admit that the secret of sexual desire is signified by the very fact that his mother does not have a penis;* he must further accept that it is *the unique privilege of his father and of his penis to complete her sexual organ, and that this is also his mother's desire.* In short, the child must renounce forever his earliest erotic desires and his narcissistic magical wishes. Small wonder that few achieve this without some psychic perturbation! In any case, this step leads to the concept of *secondary identification* to which most "normal neurotics" have access, though at the cost of unresolved longings which continue to flourish in the unconscious.

The child who fails to achieve the profound reorganization in his feeling of sexual identity brought about by this "resolution" of the oedipal crisis may find himself obliged to invent a deviant sexual pattern so as to circumvent the oedipal problem with its unpalatable truths. (It might be added that there is little doubt that these very truths were never clearly formulated for him by those who brought him up.) Such a child is blocked between what I have described as stage 2 and stage 3 of the Freudian developmental schema. Having destroyed his own perceptions, the child now finds himself obliged to create a *neo-reality* to fill the void left by his disavowal of sensory perception. The difference between the neurotic solution and the perverse illusion is situated at precisely this juncture. Although reaction formations, phobic countercathexes, and other neurotic defense work will contribute to the fantasy elaboration of the painful conflicts in both neurotic and perverse symptomatology, in the latter the neurotic aspects are based on the fundamental *disavowal* of sexual reality, and therefore do not become organized into true neurotic symptoms.

Freud's concept of disavowal (*Verleugnung*) includes, if one examines it closely, the two types of defense already indicated: the first, the denial or disavowal of reality *through word and act*, and the second, the denial or disavowal of reality through *fantasy construction*. As already mentioned in Chapter I, I find that the term *disavowal*, chosen to translate *Verleugnung* in the *Standard Edition*, suggests "denial through word and act." It seems to me, however, that the term *denial* might usefully be reserved for "denial through fantasy," and thus maintain the distinction emphasized by Anna Freud (1936). The child who is able to declare, following his perception of female genitalia, that he *saw* a penis is not distinguishing clearly between inner and outer reality. He is using a far more radical and primitive form of defense than the child who admits there was no penis but seeks to work on the dilemma mentally and comes to the conclusion that the penis will grow later on. The latter has agreed to *think about the affectively disturbing situation.*

This capacity to contain and elaborate painful affect and frightening ideas bears witness to an important internal transformation which will be of cardinal value to the child in his later psychosexual development and sense of sexual identity. Even though he may conserve his fantasies in repressed form as the nodal point for eventual neurotic symptoms, he will nevertheless have protected his relation to external reality and acquired some independence from it. "Reality" might indeed be equated with the recognition of the mother's genital and the existence of the vagina, as Lewin (1948) so aptly remarked many years ago. Lewin advances the idea that "thinking of nothing" frequently refers to repressed throughts about the female genital. To this notion I would add that the "nothing" which so astonishes the child and mobilizes such anxiety in him does so for a double reason: it brings him not only the disquieting knowledge of the difference between the sexes, but also of the underlying *significance* to be attached to this difference. In discovering that his mother has no penis, the child of either sex has surprised the sexual secret of the parents. Over and beyond the common and indeed ineluctable fantasies of castration — as something that may befall little boys or that has already befallen little girls — this discovery reveals to the child the place where a real penis comes to fulfill its true phallic function. Sexual knowledge, gained to a certain degree through sensory perception and intuitive deduction, now receives external and incontrovertible proof. The mother's sexual space furnishes the unavoidable evidence of the role of the father's penis. To the interdiction of incestuous wishes is now added narcissistic mortification, following on the knowledge that not only is one excluded from the parents' sexual relationship, but one is not and never has been the desired sexual object of either parent. But the children with whom this chapter is concerned want nothing to do with this unwelcome knowledge. They choose instead to deny the difference, to hallucinate a penis, eventually to put some inanimate object in the place of the penis as the source of desire, or in numerous other ways to create a new sexual order. The invention enables the child at one sweep to elude the incest taboo, castration anxiety, and narcissistic mortification — an all-over victory, but one that must be dearly paid for by the relinquishing of certain links with external reality and the loss of a part of one's psychic identity. The father's penis loses its symbolic and structuring function for the personality, and at the same time important fragments of knowledge are effaced. The inner elaboration and intricate defense work that gives rise to neurotic creations is, on the whole, less damaging to individual integrity. As already pointed out, however, the two forms of psychic management may well co-exist in the same individual.

Two dreams from different analysands illustrate these diverse modes of facing castration fear and narcissistic pain. One patient had a complicated fetishistic construction that enabled him to have a restricted though anxious sexual life, whereas the other suffered from severe sexual impotence due to neurotic anxiety. Each recounted his dream in the same day — the two dreams having been mobilized, insofar as the day residues were concerned, by an incident that stimulated transference affect. On the previous day both analysands had remarked that a door in my apartment, which was usually closed, had been wide open. Through the open door both were able to observe that plumbers were at work on my central heating system.

The fetishist: "I dreamed that I was lying beside a

woman and was asked to look at her legs. I stared for quite some time, but couldn't make out what I was supposed to reply. It seemed to be a problem in logic. Finally I admitted that I would never find the answer because I had never been good at mathematics." In his associations to this dream the patient mentioned the open door, but added that he was not at all sure what the workmen were doing inside my house. From there he went on to remember his long hours of erotic day-dreaming during his lonely childhood.

The other dream, also linked by the dreamer to his glimpse, on the preceding day, of the open door, went as follows: "I am trying to penetrate a woman, but something stops me and I become flaccid; suddenly I find myself inside your house. I am told I may not go further along a certain corridor because those are your husband's private quarters. Then I find myself trans-ported into your garden. There are rare animals around, and a man explains to me that they are half cat and half serpent. They rise up from the ground, cross one another, and fly everywhere. The man asks if I am afraid of being touched by them, and I say that I'm not, but I'd like to understand how they manage to stay up in the air like that."

I leave my readers to make their own free associa-tions around the multiple metaphorical meanings con-tained in the dream. It is evident that a flourishing fan-tasy life in repression is seeking pictorial expression. The many symbolic and associative connections delin-eate, among others, the questions of a young child con-cerning parental intercourse, the father's penis and the inside of the mother's body. The first dreamer, in con-trast, shows that such fantasy formation has been stifled in the bud, leaving a denuded impression of meaninglessness, and a poverty of psychic representations that demands recuperative action. The dream carries the patient back to the memory of solitary games of his childhood. In the space where fantasy-denial and elaboration might have helped to deal with the *unthinkable* anguish occasioned by what he had perceived and by what he had been told, he had invented a new system. His information on the nature of human sexuality was backed by no symbolic significance to render it understandable. Instead, there was a *blank*, an unknowable reality, a question to which he could find no answer. The little boy, unable to make the necessary "mathematical deductions," was destined to evolve for himself a factitious, fetishistic explanation to the enigma of sexual desire. He had been able only to *disavow external reality* as a means of defending himself against mental pain. It was nevertheless true that he had had the inventiveness and the courage to replace the missing knowledge by a new logic and a neosexual creation; but it was a "crazy" courage, equal, within its circumscribed area, to the monumental challenge that the psychotic flings at external human realities. The latter, more concerned with protecting his psychic existence than his sexuality, reinvents an identity and his own system of thinking and communicating, ignoring or misunderstanding most of the identity signs and symbols provided by his own sociocultural environment.

We are here at the crossroads of perverse and psychotic formations, where disavowal becomes the abolition of psychic representation, or at the very least the destruction of the significance that should be attached to perceptions and to words. It then reveals *rejection from the psyche*, which has followed the ego's inability to contain and work through knowledge that is painful and threatening to its cohesion, consequently putting the representations out of the ego's reach and judgment. This is the concept of *Verwerfung* postulated by Freud as the fundamental mechanism underlying psychotic psychic structure. In attempting to untangle Schreber's psychic functioning, Freud came to the conclusion that what had been "abolished" from the inner psychic world would be recovered from the external world in delusional form. Bion (1967, 1970) has described such phenomena in the concept of "K-minus," and Lacan (1966) in his concept of "foreclosure." Such mechanisms, while blocking access to the truth, allow some recovery in psychotic organizations of what is lost in the form of hallucination or delusion. In perverse organizations, we find a similar form of psychic functioning. In order to construct perverse sexual theories and acts which to the inventor seem more "real" than ordinary sexual assumptions and activity, a fragment of psychic truth has to be thrown out, leaving, as Bion puts it, a "denuded" representation; the mental representation has lost its underlying significance in the order of things. The neosexual inventor must in turn recover from the external world something of what has been foreclosed from psychic awareness, if he wishes to safeguard some sexual expression. It is of course a recuperative venture on a much smaller scale than that underlying psychotic thought processes, since it deals mainly with the crumbling of psychic truth regarding sexuality, and not with a global unstable self-representation and representation of the place one occupies in the eyes of others. In place of delusion there is created an *illusion* that will permit some form of sexual relationship to be rebuilt from the shattered fragments. This illusion is not experienced as a created solution to a confusing and painful problem; it is more often lived as an exigency imposed from outer space, just as the delusions created by psychotic thinking and use of words appear to the ego to represent reality. The unreality of perverse sexual theory is confined to a limited sector. The delusional quality of psychotic sexual theory (delusions of influence, the psychotic "homosexuality" of Schreber, etc.) is reduced, in deviant sexual theory and practice, to partial or inanimate objects. These miniature "influencing machines," which permit the circulation of desire as well as its rigorous control, are perhaps a form of "focal psychosis," but they represent for the individual a guarantee concerning the continuity of sexual desire, and the integrity of personal identity. Equally important, these same partial or inanimate objects are also a container for the subject's destructive wishes toward the objects of his desire. No one is castrated; no one is killed.

I have spoken much more about the desire than the violence and aggression woven into the construction of sexual deviations. This aspect of our exploration requires a chapter apart, particularly since the capacity of a neosexual creation *to contain and harmlessly discharge hatred and violence through erotization of these affects delimits perverse organizations from psychotic ones* (see McDougall, 1980). The psychotic elements that lie behind deviant sexuality may seek two different forms of psychic expression in the sexual relationship: the erotic act may include the fantasy of *repairing the partner* for imagined castrative or other attacks, following a *depressive* mode; or the fantasy may reveal the need to *control and master the partner erotically* in order to *protect oneself* against attack, that is in accordance with a *persecutory* mode of thought. The orgasm of the partner is then felt to be equivalent to his castration, and the subject thus escapes the danger of finding himself the object and victim, able to be manipulated and "influenced" by sexual desire.

It should be noted that these two fundamental fantasies are also included in genuine creative acts: in the relationship between the artist and his public there is the wish to *dominate* the Other in order to project upon him, and thus combat, one's own fears, anxieties, and excitements, and the fantasy of *repairing* Another (projected onto the public) in order to assuage feelings of guilt.

As already noted the perverse sexual scene may often be interpreted somewhat like a dream, and this leads us, after a rather long detour, to its innovative and creative aspects. It is worth emphasizing that it is precisely the *nonsexual elements* that reveal its creative dimension — and indeed that occupy much of the psychic space and time devoted to planning and dreaming around the scenario, that is to say, all the factors that fill the space between the subject's desire and the final outcome that puts an end to the venture. With certain sexual innovators, such as fetishistic and voyeuristic patients, one discovers that this space-time may occupy as much as several weeks, during which the place, the props, and the project will be ruminated about, written down, or planned in detail. Something similar takes place with certain homosexuals who spend hours "cruising" for a variety of partners, often with the illusory script in mind that they will discover the mythically "perfect" body, penis, or person. In all these erotic realizations the denouement is frequently felt to be disappointing, depressing, or even disagreeable—*for it is the end of the illusion.* The desperate game is over—until the next time. It may of course be held that the quality of illusion-disillusion and the perennial return of desire are just as marked in normal heterosexual lovers. It is true that illusion plays an essential role in all lovemaking and that the finality of sexual ecstasy tends to bring in its wake a nuance of banality. For the sexual deviant it would be on the whole true to say that there are more illusions at stake and that there is the risk of much greater narcissistic loss. One patient expressed this in simple terms while describing his nightly search for homosexual partners: "The only thing that interests me is their ejaculation, since this is the acme of my pleasure. I cause it and control it; afterwards I go home and masturbate, but as often as not I avoid it, because that puts an end to my desire. There's nothing left to live for and I am nothing either. I hardly exist."

I come finally to the question with which this chapter opened: the construction of a perverse scenario is a creative act, but something is lacking to give it the quality of an artistic production. Although the answer may appear simple, there are many analytic questions that need to be asked in order to understand it psychologically. What has prevented its transformation into a genuine creation capable of being freed from its compulsive quality, its static rigidity, and its orgastic conclusion, thus allowing these various factors to be invested differently in the psychic economy? In what dynamic respects does the perverse invention differ from that which results in an artistic or an intellectual production? This question becomes increasingly complicated when we consider that frequently the two areas of invention exist side by side in the same individual. The creative personality, or creative parts of the personality, have an inner mobility of a specific kind; everything that attracts the subject's attention becomes dynamically important — to the point that such interest often appears naïve to other less sensitive onlookers. If all that surrounds him is capable of mobilizing his awareness so that he looks with new eyes, listens with open ears, and questions what to others may seem obvious and banal, it is in part due to the fact that any object — even the most commonplace — becomes fecund because it is immediately linked with an infinity of other representations, impressions, perceptions, and reflections, in a to-and-fro movement between primary and secondary processes. This is in marked contrast to the immutable quality of the perverse inventions.

Also, creative minds question the conventional, connect disparate ideas, and dare to imagine that which does not exist. In this respect the erotic creations of perverse sexuality are similar, for they too bring unusual elements into juxtaposition; they too question the accepted order and dare to invent that which is not already in existence; this process too follows the laws of primary process and infiltrates secondary process thought. Subsequently, these different dimensions are, as with the creative act, crystallized into an act that seeks outward expression for its specific public. Like the fever that feeds artistic activity, aberrant sexuality was in its beginnings also brought forth under pressure; the continuing production brings intense narcissistic pleasure and satisfaction as does the act of creation in the artist. At this juncture it should be remarked that *the pleasure of creating* far exceeds the contemplation of the created object. To a truly creative individual, the production is always more important than the final product. (To Picasso is attributed the saying that the only work that counts is the work that has not yet been accomplished.) The analogy with deviant sexuality is evident. This dimension has its roots in the anal erotism of early infancy. At this stage of his life the little child experiences an immense delight in the eliminatory acts that give birth to his first visible creations—his own body products; these are secondary to his pleasure in producing. The products in themselves only become objects of particular interest *insofar as his mother gives them special importance.* She is the essential "public" who in the first instance gives to these partial objects *their signifying function as objects of exchange.* This aspect is important for our present query concerning the differentiation between perverse and artistic activity. It is evident that many transformations are required for the pleasure in bodily production to become pleasure in eventual creative production. One of the first pitfalls is that this pleasure-in-producing becomes forbidden because it is so intimately associated in the unconscious with anal-sadistic and anal-erotic sexuality, as well as pregenital love fantasies of an incestuous kind. Infantile love combined with destructive impulses is a difficult mixture to assume. If the large majority of human beings are neither artistic nor neosexual creators, this is partly because such impulses are strongly countercathected; most people are not prepared to assume the transgressions inherent in any production of an innovative kind, nor the anxiety which accompanies such production.

The pervert, like the creative artist and intellectual, has the courage to transgress in creating that which does not already exist, and also is prepared to deal with the intense anxiety that is so often aroused. But his aim and his relation to the objects of his exchange are different. Who is destined to receive this product? In a sense it is for no one, which is certainly not the case with regard to sublimated creativeness. It has already been emphasized that pleasure in production takes precedence over the undoubted pleasure in the contemplation of the product; but it should be noted that added to the pleasure in the product is the all-important dimension for the artist of *offering his product to the judgment and contemplation of the public.* (Should this double narcissistic and libidinal aim be lacking, we are not dealing with an artistic or intellectual *vocation.*) The anxious waiting for some reflecting echo from the chosen public is linked in the unconscious to the need for approbation and confirmation that the production — experienced unconsciously as a forbidden erotic and aggressive act — is in fact an approved and admired activity. In addition, the product always runs the risk of being regarded as a partial object of anal or phallic quality that should not be revealed publicly; thus there is the corresponding need for reassurance that this gift is acceptable, desired, of value, and a source of pleasure to the public in question. The affective involvement of any artistic or intellectual worker with his public — his *public*-ation — marks one of the most significant differences with perverse productions. The fantasy of a public (as I tried to show in Chapter I) is an essential element in any perverse scenario, and contributes to its erotic effect, but it is limited to a secret relationship, basically an analerotic and anal-sadistic one between mother and child in the unconscious inner world. It aims at recovering, in its very defiance, the third dimension of the "spectator" who will confirm the individual in his sexual *identity* whereas the dimension of true "publication" seeks narcissistic confirmation of sexual and subjective *value* in the eyes of others. If the path carved out and followed by the sexually deviant has been carefully traced to avoid crossing the paths of others, this solitary route has been "chosen" in part so that the individual in his sexual pursuit will never meet the Other who might impose an interdiction to his earliest sexual aims and objects and their symbolic significance. Since by reason of this detour the subject loses an important confirmation of his own identity, he is obliged to search out and constantly recreate his erotic theater. The pervert (or the perverse sector of the personality) has a still greater need than the artist (or artistic and creative part of the personality) of this narcissistic confirmation and validation of his innovation, for the dynamic motor of perverse sexuality is more closely linked with anxiety than with desire. This is not to say that the transgressions involved in creating a work of art or making a scientific discovery fail to mobilize anxiety; but *this creative activity is offered to the judgment of the Other* whereas *the perverse creation is only secretly offered to an invisible public whose role is not to judge but to be duped.* We might say that the perverse sexual creation, a precocious childlike venture, has been almost too brilliantly successful. The molten stream whose source lies in infant sexuality and infantile megalomania has thence been channeled into a mold in which it has solidified, and must from there on serve as the magic response to all narcissistic wounds and to all nascent desire — gesture of defiance, of despair, petrified for the rest of time.

In conclusion, we might say that the neosexual innovator, like the artist, is also a *master of illusion*, but with one essential difference: *art is the illusion of reality*, an illusion that the artist creates for himself and for others in the hope that he may communicate, and finally *impose his illusion on others and have it accepted as such*. The perverse scenario, with its specific plot and action, is *the illusion that has imposed itself on the creator*, but which he then, for the rest of his life, attempts to impose on others in the hope that they will accept this illusion *as a reality*.

Chapter VI

The Anti-Analysand in Analysis

In this chapter I shall trace the portrait of a certain kind of analytic patient who is becoming more frequent in today's practice. I hope to delineate characteristic features which may be recognized by other analysts as belonging to a specific clinical "family." The patient I have in mind appears well motivated to undertake an analysis. Filled with good intentions, he adapts readily to the analytic *situation* — in contradistinction to the analytic *process* — and accepts with apparent ease the formal aspects of the analytic protocol. This patient comes to sessions regularly, fills the silent spaces of the analytic hour with clear and continuous associations, pays the fees at the end of the month — and that is all. After several weeks of listening to him, you begin to realize that nothing is happening, either in the context of his discourse or between him and yourself. No transference feelings are expressed with regard to the present; as to the past, his stock of childhood memories remains static, divorced from present-day reference, and lacking in affect. Such a patient shows a preference for recounting daily events in

213

which, though irritation may be expressed, there is little trace of anxiety or depression. Limited tenderness toward others is displayed, and one often has the impression that "love is just a four-letter word." This analysand rarely seeks within himself the factors that might contribute to his conflicts with others, yet he is far from happy and totally unsatisfied with his life. In spite of his diligence — and your own — the analytic process never quite gets started.

You may have noticed in this description that this patient in no way resembles those considered as "counterindications" for a classical analysis: that is, patients who do not tolerate the frustration imposed by the analytic situation with its customary austerity, who take flight at the first awakening of transference feelings, who act out in ways that may be disastrous for themselves or others, or who lose contact with reality and seek escape in psychotic fantasies. The analytic experience makes an overwhelming impact on the psychic equilibrium of such patients, and one must be careful not to engage them too rapidly in full-scale analysis. In contrast, the patients I am trying to describe appear unmoved by the impact of the analytic relationship, do not regard it as frustrating, do not lose for one moment their firm grip on reality, do not act out either within or outside the analysis (unless one considers their whole way of life as a continual acting out). Finally, it is important to emphasize that these analysands do not in any large measure display that particular form of acting out manifested in psychosomatic illness. That unexpressed emotional conflict is not somatized is of specific interest in that these patients reveal many of the characteristics of the mental functioning of so-called "psychosomatic" patients, and in particular, the phenomenon which Marty and de M'Uzan (1963) have named "operational thinking." I shall return to this point later.

It is tempting to name the subjects of my study the "robot analysands." Indeed I shall sometimes refer to them in this way since they give the impression of moving through the world of people and things like automatons, their thoughts appearing to be programmed along accepted channels. For many this also affects their manner of speaking, a robot language impregnated with clichés. However, the term "robot" carries with it a suggestion of passivity which would be erroneous. By choosing instead the term "anti-analysand" I hope to convey the impression of force as implied in the concept of anti-matter, a massive strength that is only revealed through its negative effect, its opposition to the functions of cohesion and liaison. In the psychic economy, such a force mitigates against the formation of all the creative links that allow a psychoanalytic treatment to become what Strachey (1934) called a "mutative" experience. In a certain sense these patients might be said to be engaged in "anti-analysis" which requires a measure of forceful and continued activity, but whose effects are only discernible through the absence of psychic change: a negative force of anti-liaison which at the same time petrifies all that has been split, foreclosed, or otherwise ejected from inner psychic reality. Such a patient does not speak in an incomprehensible or distorted fashion. He talks of people, and of things, but rarely of *the relation between people or between things.* In listening to his analytic discourse we do not clearly detect behind the manifest communication a vitally important latent one. Nor do we have any inkling of who we are or what we represent for the patient at different moments in the session. Nor do we witness that interpenetration of primary- and secondary-process thinking, the intermingling of dream imagery, fantasy and conscious thought that so often opens the way to an intuitive understanding of what the patient is struggling to communicate. The unconscious inner theater never reveals itself. We slowly come to realize that certain essential linking thoughts, which normally give depth of meaning to the analytic discourse, are missing. These may be links in time between past and present events, links in the content of associations, or affective links with others having libidinal or narcissistic importance for the patient — and last but not least, there is little evidence of transference ties to the analyst or to the analytic adventure. The primordial tendency of human beings toward object-relating which gives to the transference relationship its blind instinctual quality (and makes life itself a worthwhile adventure) is perhaps the most conspicuous lack. What phenomena are we engaged in observing?

The outstanding scientific observer Konrad Lorenz once remarked that the most difficult and often the most important observations are those that detect that an object is *missing*, that an action *fails to occur*, that an anticipated phenomenon is absent. In psychoanalysis, which is also an observational science, it is equally essential, and difficult, to "see" what is missing from the analytic scene or from the patient's communications. We owe to the French psychoanalysts, Marty and de M'Uzan (1963), a series of observations of this kind, which I would readily compare with those of Lorenz, that led to the discovery of a missing dimension in the recorded verbal communications of patients with psychosomatic illness in an interview situation. As with these patients, the style of speech of the anti-analysands tends to be flat, lacking in nuance, meagre in the use of metaphor. As to content, there is in both cases an apparent poverty of imagination and a difficulty in understanding other people. Added to the restriction in the content of thought and the quality of communicating is a noticeable lack of affect. An impoverishment in the communication of ideas as well as of emotion cannot but limit severely the field of analytic observation. But since the analyst is also a trained observer of his own thoughts and emotions, he is usually quick to detect his countertransference affects and to turn them to account in order to understand more profoundly what is occurring in the analytic relationship. It is largely through studying my countertransference feelings (insofar as they are conscious) that I have become aware of the clinical picture I am describing and have arrived at certain theoretical deductions regarding the psychic structure and functioning of these patients.

Although interesting and different from normal-neurotic patients, these analysands do not always afford us much pleasure in the exercise of our analytic function. Not only do they engender in us a feeling of helplessness; in addition, they make us feel guilty! So they are something of a challenge. After all, it seems inadmissible to say of a patient who comes regularly to his sessions month after month, who follows as best he can the basic rule of saying all that comes to his mind during the session, and who clings tenaciously to the belief that psychoanalysis is a valuable experience and one that he wishes to possess, that this diligent patient is unanalyzable! Unless we ourselves, like him, are insulated against self-criticism, we can scarcely avoid feeling that something must be wrong with our analytic work. Before blaming him for his incapacity to profit from what we are offering him we must first question our decision that led to his being in analysis. Are we in the wrong for having judged him to be analyzable and having thus accepted him? Is his true symptom the fact that he continues to be in analysis? These and other harassing questions form the basis of a searching inner dialogue.

I am also beset, as time goes on, by the countertransference queries that graft themselves onto those already mentioned. The patient lying on my couch is offering me today a series of associations that in no way differ from those he brought to his first analytic sessions some four years ago! Is it a resistance on my part to grasp the underlying significance of what he recounts? Over the years, in my seminars for young analysts on the phenomena of transference and countertransference, I have steadily maintained that everything the analysand says has some reference to the analytic situation or relationship; that no thought, no fantasy, is ever entirely gratuitous. If I have been unable, in spite of my concern and my varied attempts to communicate something which would produce some change in this analysis, have I been unimaginative with him? Should I have made more "Kleinian" interpretations of increasingly archaic material, overlooking his constant refusal to accept any interpretation as worthy of attention? Should I have adopted an aggressive "Reichian" approach and attacked with force his characterological "armor-planting"? Yet, when I come to think of it, over the four years I have elaborated many hypotheses, tried many an innovation, made interpretations of Kleinian, Reichian, Winnicottian and Lacanian inspiration, as well as some special ones of my own — to no avail. Experience has taught me that to remark on the feelings of emptiness and dissatisfaction (for the analysand is quite as unhappy as the analyst in these situations), or to propose fantasies of one's own, which might be linked to the endlessly factual narrative, can only lead such a patient to the conclusion that *his analyst has a problem.* "But I say everything that comes into my head and you are not satisfied. What do *you* want me to talk about?" Should I throw away the structured analytic situation? Have him sit up and face me? Invite him for a drink? Anything to shake him up. I become aware that, even if my analysand shows no trace of conscious fantasy, I on the contrary am filled with odd ideas, with a wish to act out, change something, anything to get us out of the rut. But then if I were to act upon these ideas I in turn would become an *anti-analyst!* The structured protocol that protects my patient from my violence toward him also keeps me in my role of analyst. Thus I resist the temptation to throw away the analytic relationship — but what next? I must also resist the temptation to fall asleep!

At this point, I admit that most of what I have written above was noted down during a recent session of Mr. X. He is a typical robot analysand. I consider my work with this patient as a complete and spectacular failure. And he is no more satisfied than I with this fruitless partnership. Architect, forty-four years old, married, with two children, Mr. X comes from a milieu in which analysis is highly esteemed, wherein many friends and even family members have had analysis. These latter details are also typical features of my anti-analysands; they are not specific to Mr. X.

In the beginning I saw X four times a week. After two years of seeming stalemate, I tactfully reduced him to three, then to two weekly sessions. X was not fooled. He told me he was well aware that his analysis was not progressing. This opinion was further supported by the fact that a friend told him an analysis lasts four years — and here we were in the fifth! He wondered whether I might have bungled his case. I seized the occasion to tell him that I had been asking myself the same question, and suggested we might consider a change of analyst. But Mr. X would not hear of it. Denying my intervention to the effect that he felt rejected, he requested I return the two sessions that had been taken away. He seemed prepared to settle in for another four-year siege, as though he were not truly suffering from the sense of stagnation. I was and could not feel optimistic about the value of continuing. These countertransference feelings should have been useful to me and should have provided the basis for future interpretations, but I did not hold such expectations in this case. Even though my affective reactions have given me valuable insight into the psychic functioning of patients like Mr. X, this did not produce any significant change.

I could take at random any of X's sessions to demonstrate the atmosphere generated by his associations. On the day on which these lines were written he was complaining, as he had often in the past, of his children's constant and inexplicable demand to be always at his side. He loved them, naturally, but enough was enough! Without transition, he went on to describe a sort of cupboard he was building in his country cottage. He complained bitterly of his wife's lack of interest in the cupboard. After twenty minutes, like his wife, I too lost interest in it. The sole difference was that I felt guilty about it. Yet I knew in advance that for X a cupboard would never be accepted as a symbol; there was no significance to be found in this choice of topic. I could, of course, suggest that he was trying to find out if I was more interested in his cupboard than his wife. He would most certainly reply: "Do you think so?" and proceed to give me the measurements. Refusing to let slip my analytic mask of benevolent neutrality — which otherwise might have led me to say, "Ah, how you bore me, you and your cupboard" — I beat a narcissistic retreat. Embedded in my own thoughts and fantasies, I suddenly realized I had stopped listening.

What went on in Mr. X that led him to cling so tenaciously to this nonanalysis we were doing together? And *why* did nothing ever happen between us that might turn this laborious partnership into a truly constructive analytic experience?

Before attempting to answer these questions I should first comment on my reasons for having accepted X as an analytic patient. I had no lack of patients; indeed, he was obliged to wait nearly a year before beginning his analysis — a delay he accepted cheerfully, although he expressed considerable disappointment at not beginning immediately. X had been referred to me by a senior colleague who knew the family well and, having talked with X about his analytic prospects, considered him a "good analytic case." But this did not in any way make me feel I had to take him. The truth of the matter was, having interviewed X myself and having weighed his reasons for wanting analysis, I too was convinced that he was an excellent "case." Like the other patients who resemble him, he was intelligent, showed a cultural acquaintance with psychoanalytic ideas, knew several people (including his own wife) whom he considered to have benefited considerably from analysis. Among the different reasons he advanced for seeking analysis the first was that his wife had brought up the question of divorce, an eventuality to which he was bitterly opposed. He was to tell me many months later that he was opposed to divorce as such because it was not consistent with moral standards. "Normal" people did not divorce and that was that. The fact that his wife might have been unhappy in the marriage, or that he himself might have felt emotionally attached to her, did not enter into his approach to the problem. In this initial interview, however, he offered a more promising insight into his wife's demand. He confided that all his relationships seemed unsatisfactory, in particular that which he maintained with his wife. He even went so far as to question whether something in his own character might have led his wife to wish to leave him. In saying this he was trying to give me what he considered to be a good "analytic" explanation for the inexplicable; this in no way meant that he believed it or intended to explore such an idea. X then went on to offer, as others like him had done, a sprinkling of neurotic symptoms: a hindering phobia, some professional inhibitions, and a recurrent sexual symptom. I was to discover to my dismay that these symptoms did not interest him in the slightest. He talked to me also about the early death of his brother when he was ten, of his weak and philandering father, and of his pious and stern mother — promising internal objects such as a "good neurotic" might be expected to harbor. Not only was he in search of self-knowledge, he was convinced that analysis could help him to find it, and was prepared to devote time and money to this end. What more could I want? Alas, I did not know that Mr. X had never failed an examination in his life — and that he was little likely to fail his initial interviews with the psychoanalyst. I am tempted to say that X "fooled" me, which in fact he did, but this would imply that he acted in bad faith, which was not the case. He revealed everything he considered it his duty to show me in order to justify his request for analysis. In the bottom of his heart he held his wife responsible for all that was wrong between them, and where she could not be held to blame the world in general was considered at fault. These were articles of faith that could neither be put in question nor modified; they formed an integral part of his character and were essential to the maintenance of his feeling of identity.

Patients like Mr. X have all developed such pivotal keys to explain their problems and dissatisfaction with life. If for Mr. X the cause of his discontent was the existence of his wife, his children, and his colleagues, for Mrs. O, a young professor in her thirties, married, with two little girls, all misery stemmed from the fact that she was a woman. The following fragment of her analysis comes from a session in the third year of our work. "You say I never talk about my childhood. Well now I was born in L.... and my cousin also, the boy who was two years younger than I was. We lived there until my mother's death. My father preferred my cousin, that was only normal. My mother tried to show no preference, but of course she was pretty disappointed to have had a girl. But I've told you all this before." "Yes, but you have never explored the question of how painful this must have been for you." "Nonsense. I won't buy that. Why those were the happiest years of my life." "It might not have been easy feeling that both your parents preferred the boy. You may have wondered why?" "Naturally I would have preferred to be a boy — but who wouldn't?" Having gone into this question with Mrs. O from every conceivable point of view, I tried on this occasion to elicit a new fantasy. I told her that some men envied women because of their ability to create children, or to attract the father sexually. "Then they must be nuts!" replied Mrs. O vehemently. The implication once more was that my continuing attempts to find an underlying meaning to her pain and fury about being a woman obviously meant I had a problem, since her position was the only sane one. Perhaps she was right in considering this to be my problem, since I could clearly remember that one of my principal reasons for accepting her in analysis was that she had sobbed bitterly when I told her that from all she said I felt she had problems about being a woman. Through her tears she had whispered she "lacked femininity." What I had not grasped was that she felt convinced I would see the dilemma of being a woman in the same light. My effort to find an explanation for her intense bitterness only served to exasperate her. If I had not had the courage to point out that, even after analysis, she would still be a woman, it was because I truly believed she wanted to understand her pain and find a creative solution to it. Instead she wanted to convince me of the grave injustice she had suffered from birth, and stick to her simplified solution. There is no doubt she had suffered from hurtful parental words concerning her sexuality and her femininity, but the neurotic symptoms to which these had given rise evoked no interest in her. Her total frigidity, a severe phobia about being touched, even by her husband and children, seemed to her to warrant no exploration. "It's like that and that's all there is to it!" Later she confided to me that her therapeutic goal was to have completed "a thousand analytic hours." This figure had been proffered by a psychoanalyst friend as being the right number.

Here briefly are the clinical features of my anti-analysands:

— This type of patient presents himself with a convincing and acceptable set of problems from the usual analytic point of view with regard to suitability for analysis. His robotlike character structure enables him somehow to be correctly "programmed" in advance for his project.

— Once installed in the analytic situation (whose conditions he accepts without ado) he begins a detailed and intelligible recital but the language he employs is striking by reason of its lack of imagery and affectivity. In spite of better than average intelligence, the patient is capable of displaying a banality of thought akin to mental retardation. The affectless quality of his object relations recalls those of children who have suffered early object loss. Where events of loss or abandonment have actually existed, these are recalled without emotion, and treated like inevitable injustices. There is no reliving of such events in the transference, nor interest in exploring the loss.

— His neurotic problems, as well as those of others, arouse no curiosity in him.

— With the exception of a few fixed memories, he lives firmly rooted in the present; like journalists, he seems to live for the events of a single day. Though his past or present be filled with dramatic events, he seems to devitalize these, making them appear banal.

— His emotional links to the people important to his life are presented as flattened, lacking in warmth. He nevertheless frequently expresses dissatisfaction rising sometimes to heights of considerable anger against his close friends and family, or directed to the human condition in general. In spite of this the patient maintains stable object relations and in no way seeks to be separated from the objects of his wrath and rancor.

— The transference carries the same feeling of affective emptiness; even the aggressive feelings readily expressed against the entourage are stifled in the analytic context. The analyst may have the impression of being *a condition rather than an object for the analysand.* I would readily describe this as an "operational" transference. It in no way resembles the *transference resistance* noted by Bouvet (1967) as characteristic of obsessional patients. The anti-analysand does not maintain an optimal safe distance from the analyst as does the obsessional neurotic: instead, he appears to deny that any distance exists, thus denying the analyst any individual psychic reality. This way of apprehending the analyst is repeated with people in the everyday world. To this extent, it may be considered a sort of "transference" from an habitual relationship pattern, but its roots in the infantile past are difficult to discern since the world of internal objects is also somewhat delibidinized.

The course of the analysis does not reveal massive repression—which otherwise might have found some transference expression or revealed itself in dreams, symptoms, and sublimations. Rare dreams do, however, reveal evidence of primitive psychic conflict. A vast chasm seems to separate the anti-analysand from his instinctual roots, giving the impression that he is also out of contact with *himself*, that this is not restricted to his inner and outer objects. There is thus an overall impression of an ill-defined transference from the past in which the small child of former times urgently had to create a void between himself and others, wiping out their psychic existence and so stifling intolerable mental pain. The distance between subject and object is then reduced to nothing, but *without any recovery of the decathected object in either its loved or hated aspects*. Where the object should have found a place either as part of the subject's own ego or as an object of his ego, there is a blank. Such patients do not therefore get lost in their contact with others or merge in psychotic fashion with parts of other people. It would be more exact to say that others have become lost somewhere inside them. These are children who have never mastered the spool and the peekaboo games which inspired such profound reflection in Freud. Refusing to admit other people's psychic reality, refuting the trauma of separation, these patients dispense with many aspects of identification because Others have become exact copies of themselves. Instead of seeking to know their psychic reality they offer their own. It is no doubt for this reason that the analyst's interventions and interpretations elicit only marginal interest and have little impact. When the patient finds himself forced to recognize difference and separate existence, whether this becomes evident through serious differences of opinion or a mere difference in matters of taste, he is quite likely to react with excessive hostility. But in general Otherness does not threaten him in that he disavows its possible influence.

Since the same phenomena appear in the transference, with consequent denial of the analyst's separate psychic reality, little affect is projected into this psychic space. As a result, hypotheses and anxiety about what the analyst thinks of him do not unduly preoccupy the analysand and do not propel him to fear criticism or to seek approval or to question his desires and relationships, nor even his symptoms. If the analyst persists in trying to *analyze* different aspects of the patient's associations, thoughts, and feelings, or to interpret fleeting transference manifestations — in other words if through these means the analyst reveals himself as *Another* by searching for underlying meanings in his analysand's discourse — the patient is liable to feel persecuted, unless he comes to the conclusion that the analyst is disturbed in some way.

What holds this psychic structure together? Such denial of certain cardinal aspects of the external world would suggest the danger of psychotic symptoms. This disavowal of difference more closely resembles a radical rejection from the psyche of all that threatens the individual than it does a fantasy construction that has simply been repressed from consciousness. There is thus created a sterile void between the subject and others, across which no threatening feelings or ideas risk to invade him. Yet disavowal and denial of reality form part of the fundamental mechanisms that structure the human psyche from babyhood onward, and thus continue to function in limited areas in everybody. The important factor is the way in which such eliminations from the psychic sphere are recovered or otherwise compensated for. The denial of reality and difference is more simple to follow at the level of the phallic phase and the denial of the difference between the sexes than at this more global level of the difference between one human being and another. In previous chapters I traced the successive variations that might result from the disavowal of the primal scene and from attempts to deal with all the fears that are subsumed under the concept of the castration complex such as neuroses, perversions, and sublimations, which are different ways of recovering what is lost from psychic content through repression and denial. However, the defense mechanisms I am attempting to delineate here are of an all-encompassing kind. They correspond to what Freud called "repudiation from the ego" (*Verwerfung*). This might no doubt be considered as a prototypic form of castration anxiety — centered around archaic fears of separation, disintegration, and death — and which no doubt underlies the more sophisticated problems of sexual identity, oedipal rivalry, and forbidden sexual wishes. The prototypic anxiety concerns the dawning of psychic life and the beginning of subjective identity.

Our robot analysands, faced with what one might presume to have been overwhelming psychic trauma in early childhood have been unable to fill the gap left by the absence of the Other, a gap that might otherwise have been constructed by lively inner object fantasy or identification (in the service of maintaining ego identity and autonomy), by fantasies of a forbidden nature destined to be repressed (nuclei for future neuroses), or by the creation of a delusional system to compensate for the violent "repudiation" (such as Freud described in the Schreber case). Neither repression nor pathological projective identification predominate in this defensive system. Instead, these patients would appear to have constructed a sort of reinforced concrete wall to mask the primary separation on which human subjectivity is founded — an opaque structure that impedes free circulation both in inner psychic reality and between the internal and the external world. This approaches what Winnicott called the *false self* construction, in which an attempt is made to keep alive a sensitive inner self that dares not move, while an outer shell is maintained to adapt to all that the world is felt to demand. The patients I am describing maintain their existence in the world of others by following a set of strict conduct rules in an immutable system. This system appears to be detached from any inner object reference of either a superego or ego-ideal kind, and reflects a dimension of what Abraham called "sphincter morality." In settling problems, these analysands appear to know the "rules" without understanding the "law" that underlies them, and thus tend to make their own laws while being careful not to break rules that might lead to sanction. An example comes to mind.

Mrs. O, of whom I spoke earlier, believed that all men despised women and that all motorists despised pedestrians. One day she arrived in a triumphant mood for her session, having just killed two birds with one stone: A few minutes earlier she had been preparing to cross a little-frequented street, when a man in a sportscar passed right in front of her. Without a second's thought she brandished her umbrella, like a vengeful phallus, in such a way as to score a deep scratch the whole length of the little red car. The man, enraged, sprang from his seat and threatened to call the police. Mrs. O disappeared in panic, delighted nevertheless that for once justice had been done.

Nothing in these idiosyncratic internal rule-books may ever be called into question, for if doubted the system runs the risk of falling apart, leaving emptiness in its wake and terror at the threatened loss of identity feeling. The character trait that leads the person to blot out other people's psychic reality also makes it difficult for him to grasp his own, and can give rise to veritable thinking difficulties; it is as though he lacks the elements necessary to further reflect on his many predicaments in the way that Bion (1963, 1970) conceptualizes the thinking process in terms of *alpha* functioning. Thus such a patient has difficulty in grasping and thinking through a problem such as the question of otherness and all it implies. Although this gives rise to considerable irritation with others, especially those who manifestly threaten the person's inner system of weights and balances, he is on the whole *unaware of his own suffering*, unaware of his psychic fragility and his loneliness. In consequence, he can neither think nor talk about these problems. As the years go by, there is no relief from the accumulated pressure. In order to render more clearly the incipient danger of remaining out of touch with one's personal psychic pain I shall choose an analogous image from another field.

There exists a rare physical illness in which the person afflicted suffers from his *inability to suffer* in that he is incapable, for physiological reasons, of registering and thus feeling sensations of pain. This is potentially a very grave illness in that it endangers physical survival — unless of course the sufferer is able to learn *certain basic rules* that he must follow to the letter since they replace the normal biological alarm signals. If he should perceive that blood is flowing from a wound in his body, he must learn to bind it rapidly. Should he accidentally place his hand in the fire or on a burning surface, or run a sharp instrument through his hand, he must remember to withdraw his hand or to pull out the damaging instrument immediately and then deal with the resulting wounds. In addition he must constantly be on the look-out for such physical hazards since he has no in-built warning systems, and must therefore follow a careful set of rules which would seem incomprehensible to other people. Otherwise he runs the risk of burning, or bleeding to death, without warning. To stay alive he must learn to act like an *automaton.* Because of his disability he will tend to seem unsympathetic to other people's physical suffering, and perhaps even deny that it exists. Our robot analysands have developed a psychic insulation of this order. The analytic process has little chance of acting upon this impermeable protective layer, since the person concerned senses that his psychic life may be endangered should he change any one of the rules by which his affective and objectal life, and indeed his philosophy of life in general, is governed. Like the subjects of the above-mentioned physical illness, these patients give the impression of being in excellent health. Their seeming normality may be a danger signal, a problem I shall deal with extensively in the final chapter of this book. Afflicted with inner wounds whose pain they do not feel, they run the risk that their psychic hemorrhages may continue unrecognized and unabated.

The construction of such an infallible psychic system gives to the ego the strength of a computerized robot which in turn becomes the invincible guardian of the subject's psychic life — but at the price of a certain inner deadness. Vital contact with others must be avoided, and they will tend to be held at distance through the system of denial and repudiation we have been examining, as though death emanated from the Other. The dilemma of the analyst is twofold with the anti-analysand: not only must he realize that his very presence, his otherness, the very reason for which the patient came to see him in the first instance, is itself felt as a dangerous situation; he must also accept that he is struggling with anti-life forces in his patient, forces that will strive to reduce to zero every movement susceptible of awakening instinctual desires, of reanimating hope — all of which may draw the individual into libidinal relationship. Freud's concept of the *death instinct* finds its place here. Might we conceive of certain people whose only means of survival is to employ the forces that eventually lead to death?

At this juncture I should like to explore the question of psychosomatic potentiality with patients of this kind. Clinically they display many similarities to the gravely ill patients studied by Marty, de M'Uzan, and David (1963). In their book, *L'investigation psychosomatique*, the authors stress the following characteristics: a detached form of object relating; marked poverty of verbal expression, and concern with things and events rather than people; absence of neurotic symptoms; gestures in place of emotional expression of a verbal kind; a notable lack of aggression, even when circumstances seem to call for it; a general climate of inertia that requires vigorous handling on the part of the investigator if a stalemate is to be avoided. Further research by Fain and David (1963) points to the meager fantasy and dream life of psychosomatic patients.

Our anti-analysand demonstrates a similar form of relating to others, the same poverty of verbal expression and absence of emotional response, and a similar lack of conscious fantasy and of dream life. From my reading of the above texts I would add that everything points to a notable lack of unconscious (repressed) fantasy which would tend to deprive an individual of a potential psychic capital to buffer himself (through the formation of sublimations, or indeed of neurotic and psychotic symptoms) against life's inevitable frustrations and occasional catastrophes, while at the same time enabling him to maintain viable contact with others.

The robot analysands differ from the psychosomatic patients in three important respects: they do not suffer from manifest psychosomatic maladies;[1] they do not

---

[1]Since this chapter was written, I have observed that many of these patients suffered in intermittent fashion from various *allergic conditions*, possibly facilitated by similar factors in the psychic structure.

demonstrate the typical inertia in the interview situation observed in psychosomatic investigation; they show no conspicuous lack of aggression and, on the contrary, express aggression in what might often be considered an inappropriate fashion. I shall explore these points of divergence more fully.

The question of the "somatization" of psychic conflict is fraught with complexity. In discussing my anti-analysands with an analytic colleague who played for many years an important part in psychosomatic research in France, I gave a detailed description of their character traits and system of relationships. "These are typical and indubitable psychosomatic patients," my colleague insisted. I protested that the patients in question showed no marked propensity toward psychosomatic afflictions. "Just wait. They'll get them!" he retorted. Although I am prepared to believe that these analysands may well be in danger of falling ill in this way, this does not afford me an explanatory hypothesis, nor define their present status and form of psychic functioning. To make a somewhat rudimentary analogy, let us say I am seeking to define what kind of animal a dog is. If I were told that a dog is an animal that has fleas, I might protest that my dog has none. Even though I am assured that with time he will get them, this still does not tell me what a dog is. What is a "psychosomatic patient"? If this architect, at present in his forties, were to have a myocardial infarction or suffer from essential hypertension at the age of sixty-five, is he a psychosomatic sufferer? And at what point could this be said of him? Perhaps in the long run we all die for psychosomatic reasons. And in the short run it is possible that the apparently "normal" individual, the man-in-the-street, who would not dream of seeking an analysis, is more exposed to psychosomatic hazards than the neurotic.

Coming now to the inertia displayed by the psychosomatically ill in preliminary interviews, it may be said that this in no way characterizes the anti-analysands in their *initial* contact with the analyst. On the contrary they are particularly active in pleading their cause as future analytic patients. However, the inertia appears later in the course of the analysis, and is particularly discernible in the lack of response to interpretative attempts, or when the patient is invited to imagine situations which might be linked to or underlie his daily conflicts. Faced with a conspicuous void in fantasy production with my patients, I have frequently resorted to offering personal fantasies based on the details of family relations and childhood events furnished by the analysand in the course of his associations. Such initiatives, if they are not rejected out of hand as absurd, may bring forth a brief flowering of images and daydreams, but these die rapidly away. This is rather like getting a broken alarm clock to work by shaking it. It will produce momentary ticking sounds only to stop again. To think you have repaired it is mere illusion. In this situation, although the analysand does not display inertia and shows no wish to leave analysis, the *analyst* tends to get discouraged and finally to become inert. His repeated efforts to interpret, to identify, to question, to innovate, in order to set the analytic process in motion are liable in the last resort — and not without reason — to make the patient feel persecuted. Although these feelings of being criticized or otherwise attacked by the analyst are apt to bring forth new material for a short while, the insights thus gained tend to be wiped out and later denied. The analyst who has succeeded in being perceived for a brief period as Other, as possessed of a different psychic space and psychic reality, will eventually be denuded of his otherness and reabsorbed into the patient's psychic world.

One of Mrs. O's sessions provides a limpid example of such a phase. She had fulminated throughout the session, much as she had done for three years, against the injustices inflicted against women, but had finally broken down in tears (which was unusual for her). I suggested that the fact of being a woman was felt as an inarticulate threat and perhaps based on painful and depressing fantasies that were still to come to light. "What rubbish! I won't buy that. This is not a personal problem of mine—it applies to all women," replied Mrs. O. That night, however, she had a nightmare in which she was watching a play. On the stage, two "colossal females" were holding down a young girl in order to force into her throat a large egg without its shell. The egg was disgusting, dripping, and stained with blood. This object of disgust was at the same time a blood-stained sanitary napkin. In her dream Mrs. O remarked to an unidentified and invisible person that the young girl would shortly be having her periods. Among the many possible interpretations of such a dream, certain themes are immediately suggested by the manifest content alone: the overwhelming female figures would appear to effect a castrative attack upon the young girl in order to make her bleed correctly and become a woman. This is a maternal castration of an oral-sadistic and archaic kind, a situation of "force-feeding." At the same time, the accession to adult female sexuality is depicted as a brutal and disgusting anal incorporation. There is in the awesome threesome a hint of a telescoped primal scene. Finally, it might be presumed that at one level the unknown listener to whom Mrs. O explains the horror that is occurring on stage is the analyst, whom she has tried hard to convince with regard to the miserable situation of womanhood. All this and much more is potentially inscribed in the condensed dream scene. Mrs. O had no associations to this strange dream, so with extreme caution I suggested that perhaps it depicted the painful fashion in which she might have experienced getting her periods and becoming a woman. "Well I certainly remember nothing of the sort. So you won't get me to *swallow* that!" replied Mrs. O firmly. I then proffered the only interpretation I felt she could accept, namely that the overbearing women of the dream represented myself with my analytic interpretations, trying to get her to "swallow" (to reintroject) many thoughts and feelings she did not consider to be true. In my mind there was no doubt that Mrs. O had in fact suffered great emotional pain, perhaps from early childhood, over being a girl, and perhaps over having to "swallow" many other unpalatable ideas as well, but that she did not wish to re-experience this pain nor even think about it. Her rule-book said that in talking of the difficulties of being a woman she was simply commenting on universally acknowledged facts. What right did I have to thrust my analytic "insights" down her throat? Mrs. O considered with interest the idea that she might feel I was thrusting interpretations down her throat like the forceful dream women, but then dismissed it as preposterous.

The defensive psychic structure of these analysands aims at keeping the destroyed affects out of reach, at maintaining the paralyzed sectors of their inner lives, and the hampered wishes, where they are. A definitive solution to mental pain has been found, so why suffer needlessly. The palpitating center of all that may happen in the exchange with others, whether for good or bad, has been extracted leaving only an outer shell, impervious to pain. Thereafter the external world will tend to be peopled with those who fulfill well-defined functions, and if necessary each object will be replaceable.

What occurs within the analyst who finds himself the helpless witness of this paralyzing process? He suffers of course by being reduced to impotence with regard to his analytic function, but the fact that a patient by reason of his psychic structure prevents our doing constructive and creative work with him does not seem sufficient explanation for the specifically painful feeling these patients arouse in the majority of analysts. After all, many analysands are not able to make extensive use of their analytical adventure. In addition, we are accustomed to protecting our patients from our own therapeutic ambitions, which we know from experience may be harmful rather than helpful to the analysis. Our distress with the anti-analysands goes beyond the question of professional failure and narcissistic injury. It is true that our interpretative work, far from promoting the analytic process, falls into a bottomless pit, leaving us bereft of an echo and therefore threatened in our analytic identity. But again this is a familiar problem; many patients put up forceful resistance to the analytic work and the analyst's endeavors for long periods of time. With the patients I am discussing here I suspect that something more specific is involved. Although our attempts to identify with the different dimensions of their obscure enigma and their throttled psychic pain are vigorously rejected or rendered insignificant, this still does not prevent us from identifying introjectively with both the ego and the inner objects of our analysands. Since the analyst's work always has as its goal the observation and understanding of psychic reality—his own as well as that of his patients—he is obliged to capture certain objects of analytic observation, namely the love, hate, rage, anguish, and other kindred emotions that lie behind the words, largely through his countertransference reactions, if these important affects have been detached from their original objects and representations. In Chapter VII, I refer to this type of transmission of experience in analysis as "primitive communication" to indicate that the analyst's function is similar in this respect to that of the mother's with her as yet nonverbal child. Faced with the robot analysand, out of touch with his own suffering, the analyst will point out sooner or later his observation that the patient is cutting himself off from his affective and instinctual roots. But with these particular patients such interventions go unheeded. The analyst must stand helplessly by watching his analysand psychically hemorrhaging, allowing himself to be crushed to death for an unknown cause. This unequal struggle with a deathlike force brings to the countertransference a measure of intense anxiety, and a wish to protect oneself from it. Thus one is tempted in such a situation to shrug one's shoulders and say of the patient that it is his problem, we have done our best and that's that. But whether we want it or not, it is also our problem. Not only does the enigma require understanding, but this death-bearing force must exist somewhere within us all.

Thus we are left with that which is legitimately ours to work with — our countertransference affect of pain and anxiety — as the sole means for furthering our understanding of these patients' psychic reality, other than our theoretical sources of information from other fields.

In reflecting on the impression of intolerable pain and bereavement that these analysands, in spite of themselves, communicate (and it might be noted that several, though by no means all, had known early loss of parental figures) I found myself thinking of the children studied by Spitz and also by Bowlby, who at a very early age lost contact with a parental object, whether through death, abandonment, or hospitalization. Bowlby and his research team have recorded their observations of a repeating pattern of behavior demonstrated by such traumatized children. Following a period of protest and anger, they become depressed and withdraw into themselves for a variable length of time. Once this period of detachment is over, they appear to have completely *forgotten* the loved or essential object which has failed them. In the most serious cases, the child from then on will invest solely inanimate objects, and henceforth only people who give him concrete *things* may be allowed to count. Unfortunately for our purposes, Bowlby, who describes so sensitively the conduct of these children, does not investigate the intrapsychic processes implied in the maturation of object relations. His "attachment" model, fruit of meticulous observation, gives little insight into the libidinal economy involved. It is evident that the small child, because of his psychic immaturity, can with difficulty, if at all, accomplish the work of mourning. His urgent *need of the object* does not permit of his introjecting it in its absence and thus securing inwardly an object that otherwise is constantly disappearing or definitively lost. Instead massive denial and displacement will occur, and this must inevitably distort the identification processes. In addition to the elimination from the inner world of well-elaborated whole objects of a living kind, there is the subsequent danger that all aggressive impulses will be turned against the self and set in motion a potentially destructive process. At the same time the cutting of the outer object ties and their affective links further impoverishes the inner object world with consequent diminution of imagination and fantasy life. The anti-analysands resemble these bereaved children. Like them, they appear to have mummified their internal objects (whether good or bad), and attach themselves predominantly to factual and concrete aspects of interchange with others. Experiences coming from the "outside," including the experience of analysis, find no symbolic resting place in the inner world and as a result rapidly lose their affective charge.

At this point I come to the third area of divergence with the typically psychosomatic patients — the absence of aggressivity. In this respect, the anti-analysands are more like the grieving children in the first phase of their detachment cycle. The robot analysands possess a considerable fund of hostility that can, and in general is, projected onto others, thus creating a solid, if ill-tempered link. The extensive irritation so often expressed toward the important others in the patients' lives reveals that, to this extent at least, the Other may be envisaged as a valuable *container*, even though somewhat of a garbage pail. This recalls the analytic function that Meltzer (1967) has named the "toilet-breast," with the exception that these patients seem unable to establish a "nourishing" exchange; their deep and, in a certain sense, positive attachment to their hate objects is unconscious. The consciously vented anger maintains an affective link with its object, and this may be one of the reasons why these patients appear to strive toward a chronically angry relation with their entourage. It is important to emphasize that this constant feeling of being ill-used and the reiterated hostility may be regarded mistakenly as an indication of *psychic suffering*. It may be more accurate to consider this way of relating to the world as a bulwark against self-destruction and a safeguard against terrifying emptiness and the shadow of psychic death. It might even be that this aggressive screen serves as a protection against psychosomatic explosion.

Be that as it may, the constant activity of these analysands in the service of their negative feelings does give many signs of being a manic defense, though poorly structured, against an unelaborated depression stemming from early psychic trauma and of which the subject is unaware. The early break between the self and its important objects would seem to have destroyed not only the continuing capacity for libidinal investment but also the desire to explore, to question, to know more. *This is the death of curiosity.* The ravaged child will no longer seek to know what is happening within himself, nor what takes place inside the others. The "dark continent" of woman is no longer peopled with fabled monsters or fairylike creatures, and the *passion for knowledge* which finds its earliest source in the small child's wish to burrow inside, to take possession of the mother's body and all its contents, suffers a paralyzing blow. The magic book of fantasies about all that links one human being to another has been firmly closed — and in its place come the rules of conduct and an operational relation to the external world.

Two theoretical approaches seem to me germane to this type of psychic functioning. The violent splitting off from the inner object world and the instinctual roots of feeling, whose damaging effects we have been following in these patients, recalls what Bion (1963) describes as "minus-K phenomena," and what he also refers to as "ego-castration" or the "castration of meaning." The representations are there, undistorted, but denuded of their significance, and thus cannot be used as elements of conceptual thought. Another approach to similar phenomena is that of Lacan (1966) in his concept of "foreclosure," following on the Freudian concept of "repudiation" from consciousness, which unlike repression, treats the psychic events in question as though they had never existed. Such events or representations are thus excluded from their place in the symbolic chain. Freud considered that this defense mechanism was predominant in psychotic structures, and the work of Bion and of Lacan would support this point of view.

However our anti-analysands are not psychotic. The denial of psychic separateness is not compensated through delusional formations; instead these patients remain, if anything, excessively attached to external reality but on the condition that affective links with others remain severed and the interpenetration of ideas severely controlled. By these means the patient may hope to protect himself from intolerable hurt, but at the price of cutting any tie that might draw him within the circuits of desire and the orbit of other people's wishes, fears, and refusals. It is not surprising that in the analytic situation the transference is destined to be still-born.

But the anger and irritation and the reiterative search for fictive enemies who may be held to blame for the treachery and abandonment of the earliest objects remains. The analyst becomes in his turn a fictive enemy to be warded off. Are we within our rights in attempting to decipher and pull apart this precious rage? The question is difficult to answer since in the majority of cases the analysand does not give us the opportunity to do so. The cancellation of libidinal investment, and even of the vital anger, in the relation to the analyst, and the recurring elimination of the attempts to find meaning to his deep unsatisfaction, tend to create a cold and sterile space between the two partners to the analytic relationship, which eventually extinguishes the analyst's ardent desire to know more. It is indeed sad to note that the analyst risks becoming, like the patients themselves, indifferent, even to their psychic pain.

Perhaps this tragic result has dynamic significance for the patient nevertheless, in that he may implicitly ask to be allowed to protect his angry tie with the external world. The persecutory objects contain a part of himself and are thus a living receptacle for a vital dimension of his personal identity. As for his unrecognized suffering, does he not ask us to contain this without reacting and, to the extent that we identify with it, to keep it to ourselves? Is this finally the successful realization of his analytic project?

Yet this facile explanation is not a satisfactory one, for it is obvious that these analysands cling tenaciously to *their* analytical adventure, more than many a normal-neurotic patient does—and this in spite of obvious stagnation. It has sometimes seemed to me that they cling to the analysis like a drowning man to a lifebelt, even though he no longer believes he will ever reach the shore. I would suggest as a hypothesis that such patients hold to the hope that somewhere inside them there *is* a hidden universe, an unconscious mind, another way of thinking and feeling about themselves and about others. Even if the patient does not himself believe this, he knows that his analyst believes it, and he thus clings to this faint source of hope.

Chapter VII

Countertransference and Primitive Communication

Certain patients recount or reconstruct in analysis traumatic events that have occurred in their childhood. The question has sometimes been raised as to whether we treat this type of material differently from other analytic associations furnished by the patient. And if so what are the differences? Ever since Freud's discovery that the traumatic sexual seductions of his hysterical patients revealed themselves to be fantasies based on infantile sexual wishes, analysts have been wary of mistaking fantasy for reality. Nevertheless there are many "real" events that leave a traumatic scar on our patients — such as the early death of a father, having a psychotic mother, or a childhood handicapped by illness. When these events are within conscious recall they inevitably present us with special problems because of the varied use the patient will make of them, and in particular because he will so frequently advance the argument that there is nothing to analyze in this material since the events "really happened." They have, however, become part of the patient's psychic reality, and must therefore be listened to with particular attention.

With regard to traumatic events stemming from even earlier periods, before the acquisition of *verbal* communication, the detection of their existence becomes considerably more complicated — to the point that we may only become aware of the traumatic dimension through the unconscious pressure it exerts on the analysand's way of being and speaking, and thus may eventually only be accessible if captured through our *countertransference reactions.*

Before proceeding further, it is necessary to define what constitutes a psychic trauma for any given individual, since it is evident that events which may have exercised a deleterious effect on one patient appear to have left another unscathed. The appreciation of "traumatic" sequelae is further complicated by the need to distinguish these from the universal "traumas" inherent to the human psyche, namely the drama of separating oneself off from the Other, the traumatic implications of sexual difference with the interdictions and frustrations it engenders, and finally, the inexorable reality of death. Human beings must come to terms with each of these traumatic realities or they will fall psychically ill. My contention is that a catastrophic event may in general be considered traumatic to the extent that it has impeded the confrontation and resolution of these ineluctable catastrophes that structure man's psychic reality.

Before coming to the question of *early* psychic trauma in adult patients, it is pertinent to the aim of this chapter to consider briefly the role played in analysis by catastrophic events which have occurred after the acquisition of language and the capacity for verbal thought. Such events when recounted in the course of the analysis often present themselves as unshakable facts, rather than as thoughts and free associations which can be explored psychically, and as such serve the function of resistance to the unfolding of the analytic process.

Such was the case with a male patient whose mother had been killed in a road accident while driving her car, when he was only six years old. The father, warm-hearted and attentive to his little boy, was also represented as being somewhat alcoholic and at such times, irresponsible. In the early months of his analysis the analysand attributed the totality of his neurotic character problems to his mother's premature death, thus using the tragedy as an alibi which became a resistance to further questioning. Later his associations revealed the fantasy that the accident was in fact a suicide. In the mind of the bereaved child his father's drinking problem and irresponsibility (representing, in the unconscious, a form of sadistic primal scene) had pushed his mother to this act of despair; the father was therefore responsible for his loss of his mother. However, under the impact of the ongoing analytic process, yet another fantasy came to light: it was he himself who was responsible for this crime. He wished to take his mother's place with his father and be the only one to share in his warm sensuous way of relating. By dint of magical thinking he had caused the death of his mother. Whatever the facts of her accidental death may have been, the only reality with which our analytic work was concerned was this inner reality, a childhood fantasy based on a repressed homosexual wish and a repressed death wish toward the mother. These unconscious wishes weighed heavily upon the psychic functioning and the libidinal economy of the patient. An external event had accidentally become an accomplice to the little boy's fantasy life at a time when he was already struggling with homosexual and heterosexual oedipal desires, thus presenting him with a doubly traumatic experience that was to render the solution to his oedipal conflict more than usually difficult. In the process of the analysis it became possible to interpret the tragic happening *as though it were a projection*, the result of omnipotent childlike thinking. From this point onward the mourning and identification processes, blocked by the patient's repressed infantile fantasies, were able to resume their course. In place of a constant feeling of living fraudulently, of inner deadness, of terror in the face of any fantasy wishes, the patient was now able to construct an inner world peopled with living events and objects, and thus confront the world of others on a more adequate basis.

Although it is important to distinguish between real and fantasy events, it is nevertheless true on the whole that psychoanalysis can do nothing to modify the effects of catastrophic events if they cannot also be experienced as omnipotent fantasies; only then can the analysand truly possess these events as an integral part of his *psychic capital*, a treasure trove that he alone can control and render fruitful. In other words — no one can be held responsible for the tragedies or traumatic relationships that the external objects and the world have brought into the small child's ken, but every individual is uniquely responsible for his *internal objects and his inner world.* The important thing is to discover to what use he puts this inner treasury with its full quota of pain and loss.

It is admissible on this basis to hold that traumatic events often function as screen memories and as such may yield much valuable analytic material. Neurotic symptoms may be conceived of in general as springing from parental words and attitudes, more precisely, from the child's *interpretation* of his parents' silent and verbal communications; they may likewise arise from his interpretation and psychic elaboration of traumatic happenings as in the case cited above. In the long run, the analyst's way of handling material stemming from traumatic events, although more complicated, is not markedly different from his way of dealing with neurotic intrapsychic conflict. From the point of view of countertransference, he has only to be aware of the danger of complaisant confusion with the patient, since the tragic event, or crippling accident, did actually take place.

Can the same be true for traumatic experiences which have occurred before the acquisition of verbal thought and communication through the symbolic use of speech? In the first years of life the child communicates through signs, chiefly cries and gestures, rather than through language. And in fact he can only be said to *communicate* by means of these signs to the extent that they are understood by Another who treats them as communications. From this point of view it may be said that *a baby's earliest reality is his mother's unconscious.* The traces of this early relationship are not inscribed in the preconscious as are those elements that have become part of the symbolic verbal chain; they have a different psychic position from representations contained in the form of *repressed* fantasies, and thus have little chance of seeking partial expression through neurotic symptoms. The traumatic phenomena of infancy (*in-fans*: nonspeaking) belong to the area of primal repression. When subjected to mental pain, the baby can only re-establish his narcissistic equilibrium through primitive defenses such as projection-introjection and splitting mechanisms, hallucination and repudiation, and these are only effective to the extent that the relationship with the mother allows them to operate through her attempts to understand her infant and her capacity for introjective identification with him. It should be noted in passing, that psychic suffering at this presymbolic phase is indistinguishable from physical suffering, a fact that is evident in psychotic communications as well as in many psychosomatic manifestations. If the verbal child may be said to *interpret* his parents' communications in his own way, the infant makes, so to speak, a *simultaneous translation* of the parents' conscious and unconscious messages. Since the capacity to capture another's affect precedes the acquisition of language, the nursling cannot but *react* to his mother's emotional experience and her unconscious transmission of it in her way of relating to her baby. The mother's ability to capture and respond to her infant's needs will depend on her willingness *to give meaning* to his cries and movements, allowing him eventually to introject this meaning and be in communication with his own needs. Outside of what he represents for his mother, the baby has no psychic existence. Not only is she the assurance of his biological and psychological continuity, she is also his *thinking apparatus* (Bion, 1970).

This digression concerning the mother-baby relationship may serve to elucidate two of the main themes of this chapter, namely the nature of our analytic approach to those analysands who would seem to be marked by a breakdown in communication with the mother in babyhood, and second the way in which such breakdown may express itself in the analytic relationship. The burden of this lack may then fall to the analyst who will find himself in the position of the mother, obliged to decode or to give meaning to his patient's babylike, inarticulate messages. It is of course true that this primitive form of communication and archaic link is always present in the relation between analyst and analysand. We might call it the original, or *fundamental transference*. But this basic dimension does not require particular emphasis when the analytic discourse is freely associative, and when its manifest aim is to communicate thoughts and feeling states to the analyst. We are then listening to a manifest communication which contains rich latent meaning to the analytic ear. The patients I have in mind use speech in a way that has little in common with the language of free association. In listening to them the analyst may have a feeling that it is a meaningless communication at all levels, or he may be aware of being invaded with affect which does not seem directly attributable to the content of the patient's communication. The question is how to understand and use such countertransference affect. I hope to show that these analysands frequently use language as an *act* rather than a symbolic means of communication of ideas or affect. At such times, unknown to analyst and patient alike, the latter is re-

vealing the effect of a catastrophic failure in communication that has occurred at a time when he was
unable to contain or to work through, psychically,
what he was experiencing. The traces of these early
failures are confined either to somatic expression,
which may be considered as an archaic mode of
thought, or may give a hint of their presence by the in-
coherences and blanks they produce in the patient's
way of thinking and feeling about what happens to
him or concerns him. Such experiences may leave some
verbal traces or find symbolic expression, but the attempt to elaborate or interpret these stops short. One
may discover that with such patients any feeling or
fleeting thought that risks reanimating the original
catastrophic situation is immediately stifled, or ejected
from the mind, with such force that the individual will
suffer from authentic disturbance in his thinking processes or may appear to function like a robot. He is
unable to allow sufficient psychic space or sufficient
time for the unconscious remnants to become available
to conscious processes. Once the nascent thought or
feeling has been ejected, he will frequently plunge into
action of some kind in an attempt to ward off the
return of the unwelcome representation and mask the
void left by the ejected material. Economically speaking such action assures a certain discharge of tension,
and might thus be termed an "action-symptom." In this
way talking itself may be a symptomatic *act* and therefore an "anti-communication." The analyst might thus
capture in negative what has been up till then an inexpressible drama. The lost material behind such action-
symptoms will often reach symbolic expression, for example, in dreams, but then fail to stimulate associa-

tions or mobilize affect.

Here is an example of one such dream from a patient whose problems led one to suspect that his inner world contained many areas of desolation and destruction of meaning:

"I dreamed I was back in the town where I was born. It's a small village but in my dream it was vast. And empty. There wasn't a living soul. Empty houses, empty streets. Even the trees were dead. . . . I woke up suddenly. There was more to the dream, but I can't remember what. And all because of my wife! We had a violent dispute at that moment over some silly thing. And I don't remember that either."

No associations were given, and the patient's interest in his dream seemed to vanish with the telling of it. The dream theme, which awakened in the analyst a feeling of desolation and of something uncanny, gave rise to no such sentiments in the analysand. On the other hand his quarrel with his wife, a familiar theme with this patient, continued to fill him with rage, even though he had forgotten what the quarrel was about. His intensity over the incident was in marked contrast to the deadness of the dream theme and mood. An unconscious link between the two "forgotten" items clearly provides a clue to the dynamics of the patient's psychic situation. We had already discovered that he only felt "fully alive" when he was engaged in hostile exchanges with those around him. The quarrel was a form of "manic defense" against dead or depressing inner experiences, the latter having failed to find representation in either thought or feeling. There was little doubt in my mind and indeed in the mind of this patient that he had suffered early psychic catastrophe in his relation to those who cared for him, but there were no memory traces, and such remnants as were able to arise from unconscious sources led to no further associations. They appeared to seek expression solely in action. The repressed elements from which we might hope to reconstruct the infantile past are nonexistent here. The "catastrophe" has affected the patient's capacity to think about himself and to contain painful affect, and can thus only be guessed at through his acts — acts not yet capable of translation into communicable thought.

For certain analysands, *speech itself becomes this act* in the analytic relationship. Rather than seeking to communicate ideas, moods, and free associations, the patient seems to aim at making the analyst *feel* something, or stimulating him to *do* something: this "something" is incapable of being named, and the patient himself is totally unaware of this aim. Such an analysand will often put questions to his analyst or say things like "Well, after all the things I've told you, isn't it time you said something? Can't you tell me what's wrong with my life?" Or: "How do I know there's someone there if you don't speak? I might as well talk to a wall!" Obviously all patients are apt to express such feelings, but the usual neurotic patient will accept that his turning to the analyst and addressing him in this way has some meaning, and will try to cooperate with the analyst when he seeks to interpret the feelings that prompt such remarks. With luck he will recognize readily that a childlike part of him demands reassurance or feels frustrated by the rigors of the analytic relationship, and he may then use this insight to further his understanding of his personal history and his forgotten past. But the patients I have in mind are not able to maintain sufficient distance to observe these phenomena in themselves, and so are unable to examine the underlying significance of their transference. They feel constantly angry or depressed with the analysis and yet desperate about the feeling of stagnation. The demand that the analyst interpret in a context in which there is no apparent interpretable material is a sign that the analysand is in the throes of an experience that cannot be expressed, giving way instead to a feeling of uneasiness. This in turn makes him want to call upon the analyst to show signs of his existence in order to stifle the rising tide of emotion, or to put a stop to the continuation of the analytic process. One discovers later that at such moments the patient is inundated by feelings of rage, or anxiety, to a degree that prevents him from *thinking further* in this context. In his distress he is no longer sure that he is accompanied by a live person who is listening, and following him, in his difficult analytic adventure.

The analyst, who tends to feel constantly questioned or pushed to take action, will at the same time find himself blocked whenever he attempts to interpret. That is, he will become aware *that he is no longer functioning adequately as an analyst.* In fact he is receiving what I am calling a *primitive communication* — in the same way in which we may conceive of an infant who is gesticulating wildly, or screaming, as *communicating* something to someone.

I am making two propositions here:
— In these cases it is permissible to deduce the existence of sequelae to early psychic trauma which will require specific handling in the analytic situation.
— This "screen discourse," impregnated with messages

that have never been elaborated verbally, can in the first instance only be captured by the arousal of countertransference affect.

To better illustrate what I am describing I shall take a clinical example. This analytic fragment, which dates back over fifteen years, is not one of the most incisive to throw light on this type of analytic problem, but it is the only case on which I took lengthy notes at the time, and indeed was prompted to do so because I did not understand what was happening between my patient and myself. Since that time I have often been able to capture such oblique communications, and this has enabled me to establish better contact with an archaic dimension of the patient's psychic structure—thanks to what I was able to learn from the analysand about whom I am going to tell you.

Annabelle Borne was forty-four years old and had eleven years of analysis behind her when she was first sent to me by a male colleague. After a single interview with this colleague, she asked him for the name of a woman analyst. In our initial interview she told me she had already had three analysts. The first analysis had been terminated on her own initiative because the analyst became pregnant during the third year of the analysis, and this fact was intolerable to her. She continued for five more years with a male analyst, a valuable experience in her opinion since she was able for the first time in her life to have a sexual relationship, after many years of painful solitude, and to get married at the age of forty to a man with whom she shared many intellectual interests. Although not frigid, she was uninterested in the sexual side of their relationship.

Partly because of this loss of sexual interest, but also because of a persistent feeling of dissatisfaction with all her relationships, a feeling of not understanding people, of being an outsider, badly treated by others, decided her to continue with a third analyst. The latter, after three years, advised her to discontinue on the grounds that she was "unanalyzable."

Perhaps because I showed surprise at this apparently forthright prognosis, Mrs. Borne asked the analyst to write to me, which he did, saying that he did not advocate analysis but that the patient might benefit from a modified form of psychotherapy. In spite of this gloomy verdict, Annabelle Borne wanted to continue with analysis. Life seemed so hard and she had already been greatly helped by her former analytic experience. At our second meeting she told me something of her initial reasons for seeking help. She did not feel "real" and had little contact with people of her own sex and none whatever with men. At the age of nine she had been sexually attacked by a brother six years older than she. For many years she believed that this event had permanently damaged her and was responsible for most of the painful aspects of her life. She no longer felt this to be a sufficient explanation of her difficulties, but that the answer to her problems probably lay within herself, although she could not see why. She added that she had little hope of finding an analyst who would suit her. She had not cared for Dr. X who sent her to me and she didn't care for me much either. Nevertheless she had decided to ask me to accept her as a patient in spite of this mistrust. I, on the other hand, found her likable. Her story intrigued me, and her frankness also. Several months later we began our work together, and this continued for four years.

Our first year together was trying for both of us. Nothing about me suited my patient. My silence exasperated her and my interpretations even more so. My consulting room, my clothes, my furniture, my flowers incited constant criticism. As for her life outside analysis, it seemed that everyone in her entourage lacked tact, thoughtfulness, and understanding in their dealings with her. At the nursery school attended by her little boy, no one gave her the cooperation she expected. We searched in vain for some insight into this endless repetition both within and without the analytic situation. Interpretations which one day seemed fruitful proved the day after to be sterile, or would give rise to a flood of denigrating remarks from my unhappy analysand. She considered me indifferent to her painful experiences or, if not, incompetent to understand and help her. When, one day, I remarked that she felt me to be a disastrous mother who would not, or could not, help her child to understand what life and living was all about, she replied that I was exactly like one of Harlowe's cloth monkeys — a reference to H. Harlowe's famous research experiments on infant rhesus monkeys brought up by a surrogate cloth mother. (These monkeys, incidentally, were noted for their incapacity for contact with other monkeys, and for their inappropriate expressions of rage.)

Annabelle also accused me of ridiculous optimism in continuing my persistent efforts to understand her distress. I myself began to feel that I was about as useful as a cloth monkey for all the good she was able to get out of our analytic work together. A couple of days later this pessimistic opinion became a certitude.

On this occasion Annabelle Borne found yet another metaphor apt for expressing her discontent and irritation with her analyst. She had recently read of Konrad Lorenz's experiments with ducklings who have lost their mother in the first days of life. If presented with an old boot, they will follow it just as readily, and will show to this grotesque maternal substitute the same attachment as they would have shown toward a real mother. I was this old boot — and she, presumably, was the bereaved duckling. I suggested she was waiting for me to become a *real* mother to her. "Not at all," she replied. "I've never expected anything from anybody. But you're worse than nothing! This analysis is making no progress...if anything, my problems are getting worse...it costs money so that all the family must suffer because of you. Otherwise we could have long holidays in the sun. But I keep coming here, no matter how bad the weather....Impossible to park my car in this wretched Latin Quarter. I'm sick of analysts... sick of you...your blond hair, your consulting room, your flowers! You don't care about me — and you haven't the guts to tell me that this analysis is a waste of time!" And so on, till the end of the session. As she was leaving, Annabelle cast a withering glance at a pot of flowers on my desk and spat out one last furious remark: "People who like flowers should be florists — not analysts!"

This session was not markedly different from many which had preceded it, yet on this occasion I felt discouraged and depressed. Up to this point my patient's negativism although fatiguing had given me food for thought and led me to question the efficacy of a classical analytic approach with an analysand so devoid of insight and of willingness to examine anything at all. Yet she obviously suffered greatly, so I was prepared to carry on in the hope that one day we would discover the true object of her immense rage and frustration. But it now seemed to me that what little therapeutic alliance existed had finally fallen apart. She was clearly unwilling to continue in analysis, so why should I bother to encourage her in such a fruitless endeavor? The more I thought about it, the more I became convinced she was right, though I was aware of stifling an uneasy feeling that I was simply slipping out of a disagreeable task and letting down a patient in distress. To get rid of this uneasiness I decided to take notes on the session, and to make a summary of our year's work together — a final attempt to see more clearly into her impalpable psychic world.

Her parents as she presented them were a typical middle-class couple, father much admired but very involved with his professional activities; mother represented as somewhat vague, artistic, narcissistic. Then there was the brother at whose hands she had suffered sexual assault when she was nine. She had never dared tell her mother about it because he was the mother's favorite child; nor could she tell her father because she felt too guilty about the whole incident. Her many years of analysis had led her to understand that she had experienced the sexual relation as an incestuous one with her father. In spite of its traumatizing quality it had also represented the fulfillment of an infantile oedipal desire. From her earlier analyses there had been many interpretations relating to penis envy as the basic reason for her bitterness and dissatisfaction with life. She had complained often of her mother's preference for the older brother, and of the supposed facility of his life as compared with her "hard" existence, but other than this had furnished little material that warranted further interpretations of her envious attitude to her brother or his penis. Her associations tended to be centered on the feeling that her mother was more gifted, more feminine, more loved by the father and that she herself could never equal her mother. There was a recurring screen memory relating to her mother which dated from the time when she was four or five years old. She had a clear vision of gazing at her mother's breasts which were overflowing with "green sap." This fantasy-memory filled her with anguish. My attempts to link this green sap — sap of life? cadaverous death? with other associations such as her feelings about the analysis and all she hoped or feared from her mother, or from me as an analytic nursing mother, had led us nowhere. My attempts to uncover the underlying significance of her manifest thoughts and feelings were rebuffed as a refusal to admit the daily injustices from which she suffered.

Apart from the vivid screen memory there was little other evidence of fantasy activity, and a paucity of dreams. My interventions had failed to set in motion that interplay of primary and secondary processes which is the hallmark of a functioning analysis. As for the transference, all attempts to find meaning in it were given short shrift. I had little doubt that she experienced me as a bad, almost a dead mother, and that I and the whole environment which treated her so badly also occupied the place of the envied brother, nourished with the green sap of maternal love — of which Annabelle so clearly felt herself deprived. But a year's work had shown me that Annabelle wanted nothing of this, rather as though she clung to feeling angry and ill-treated and wanted to prove that nothing could be done about it.

Having thus collated and reflected on the many harassing questions this analysis raised in me, I took the decision — not without a twinge of guilt — to tell Annabelle that she was right to wish to terminate her analysis with me. After all, I said to myself, I would not be the first analyst to find her "unanalyzable."

Right on time as always, Annabelle arrived with an expression almost of gaiety on her face. She began speaking the moment she stretched out on the divan.

"I don't remember a thing about yesterday's session — I only know it was a *good* one. I did lots of things afterwards."

I heard myself reply "You don't remember anything about yesterday's session?"

"Absolutely nothing!"

"What makes you feel it was a 'good' session?"

"Well. . .I remember that I was humming a song as I went down the stairs, straight after I left here. And goodness knows I don't often feel that happy!"

Still acutely aware of my distinctly *unhappy* feeling, and anxious searching, after this same session, I asked her, thinking it might provide a clue, if she remembered the song she was humming.

"Let's see. . .um. . .oh yes, that children's song 'Auprès de ma blonde, qu'il fait bon, fait bon. . .dormir'" (How good it is to sleep beside my blond girl).

Her angry vituperation of the previous day in marked contrast with the euphoric aftermath, her irritated reference to my blond hair, in equally marked contrast with the revelation of a libidinal wish in the song, and other incongruities, decided me to tell her that I remembered yesterday's session very clearly; she had expressed strong feelings of anger, disappointment, and irritation with me and the analysis. There had been no trace of a feeling that it could be "good to sleep" beside a blond analyst. Annabelle was very struck by this recall of the material of her session and began to wonder herself what all these contradictory expressions might mean. I suggested — following my own counter-transference affect of the day before — that perhaps she went off so light-heartedly with the hope that *I* would feel disappointed, irritated, and angry in her place.

"How strange! I think you're right. I've often thought to myself that I'd like to see you cry."

"Would they be *your* tears that I am to weep?"

For the rest of this session Annabelle gave much thought to this new idea — in striking contrast to her familiar attitude of disdain or dissatisfaction. At the same time I began to realize that she rarely ever expressed any *depressive affect.* Indeed in thinking back I was also aware, for the first time, that in spite of the virulent content of her analytic discourse I had the impression that much of what she said was *devoid* of affect. Her apparent anger was perhaps hiding inexpressible sadness.

The following night she brought a dream: "They were taking me to a police station in a sort of tumbril. A huge poster announced that 'Mrs. Moon was wanted for murder.' I am wheeled down a long corridor, like a big hospital. I'm very small and the tumbril has turned into a cot. As we go along I throw pieces of cotton in a furious way onto the floor."

In her associations to the dream, "Mrs. Moon" suggests the analyst "who is supposed to throw light on what is dark and murky." Then she went on to realize that this dream name was also an anagram of her own mother's name. The cotton recalled something she had been told about her babyhood. She was a baby who "never cried"; her mother, who was often occupied for long periods of time, would give the baby pieces of cotton in her cot, and she would suck these frenetically until her mother returned. "But where was she?" cried Annabelle. "I never had a mother!" And she began to sob. The little "child who never cried" was to cry in her analysis for many months to come.

"To survive is easy. The hard thing is to know how to live." — *Annabelle Borne*

I shall leave aside all the associative links, forgotten images and fantasies, which enabled us to reveal in Annabelle the small abandoned baby-self, catastrophically searching for an omnipotent yet absent mother. All she could find was a surrogate cloth mother with breasts of cotton, and for which, apparently, no true transitional object had ever been created. Any introjection of, or identification with a loving, caretaking mother stopped at this point, depriving Annabelle of any possibility of being in contact with her own needs, or in any way fulfilling a maternal role toward herself. As in the analytic situation, she made magic, megalomanic demands on people at the same time treating them like cloth monkeys and punishing them accordingly. In moments of tension she could neither contain, nor psychically elaborate upon her distress.

The next three years were spent in recognizing this dilemma and in studying the moments when the lonely, rage-filled baby occupied the whole of her inner psychic world; then, in putting this traumatized infant into communication with Annabelle Borne the adult. Although these two sessions allowed me considerable insight into the way in which my patient thought about herself and her relation to the world — or rather the way in which she *prevented* herself from being able to think and feel about her involvement with internal or external objects — she found no immediate relief in our analytic work. Later she was able to tell me that the two years that followed this phase of the analysis had brought her more suffering than she had ever known. Nevertheless the working through of this psychic pain wrought a profound change in her which she herself called her "rebirth." I should add that she did not suffer alone. My own countertransference was sorely tried, but I was better able to put it to use. I had constantly to be on the lookout for her tendency to pulverize any nascent thoughts or feeling states of which she became aware; and she would frequently evacuate these by trying (unconsciously) to get me to feel them instead. Further, I was in no way free from feelings of exasperation when she would systematically decry or destroy the meaning of any interpretation that promised to modify her stony feeling of anger and incomprehensible solitude. It was through analyzing my own perplexity that I discovered she felt *humiliated* by each discovery and each new turning in her analytic adventure. My compensation was that I no longer felt lost with her on this difficult journey. Even though my words often angered her, I knew she needed to hear them. For without my realizing it, my somewhat silent and expectant attitude during our first year of work together had reproduced the original situation which she carried inside her, of an evanescent maternal imago that was out of reach and persecutory at the same time. Thus Annabelle did not treat me like a real person. She accorded me as much individual status as a voracious nursling might; she could not conceive of my having any independent thoughts or wishes which were not controlled by her; nor could she accept that I be occupied with any other peson or thing than herself without feeling that this would be damaging to her. The painstaking exploration of her struggle allowed us to analyze her constant use of projective identification, and the inhibiting effect this exercised on her constantly painful existence. Instead of immediately getting rid of any hurtful thoughts or depressed feelings which came to consciousness during the sessions, she would now try to hold on to them, and to put into words the unexpressed, at times inexpressible, fantasy and affect they aroused in her. Three years of patient work allowed us to (re-)construct and explore the contours of the empty desert of baby Annabelle's psychic world. The old-boot-analyst that one was unwillingly but compulsively bound to follow, the cloth-monkey-analyst with cotton breasts that one was obliged to accept as nourishment, slowly became a *transference object* whose existence was recognized, and toward whom infantile needs and primitive wishes could now be attached, and talked about. Every object in my waiting room or consulting room, the slightest sign of the existence of any other people in my life (particularly other analysands), any change of clothing or furniture, my pots of flowers, all brought forth torrents of anger which seemed to Annabelle not only painful, but impossible to contain and to reflect upon. We needed many sessions to plumb the wells of hatred and despair that lay behind her earlier provocations. "You will never be able to imagine how much I hate you and envy you; how much I want to tear you apart and make you suffer."

Despite the fact that my existence as a separate person having needs, wishes, and rights which did not necessarily coincide with hers was a source of constant pain, and the fact that the idealized object she projected upon me engendered a continuing narcissistic wound, at least I was also now part of her analytic process, no longer a simple receptacle destined to contain all that was too heavy for her to carry alone, no longer a mummified mask for all the objects who had failed her in the past. We came to understand that she felt constantly persecuted by me, as she did by everyone in her entourage, but neither she nor I had been aware of this. Her despair, so long a part of her, had become virtually painless.

The most important conflictual material at this stage of her analysis could be summed up under all that is included in the Kleinian concept of *Envy.* Instead of being caught in the toils of jealousy and in conflict with the desire to triumph over the rivals for her mother's or father's love, she sought total *destruction* of any object belonging to the Other. In the light of this understanding, her sexually traumatic relationship with her brother took on a new significance. Through the sexual act, she now possessed her mother's adored object — and in her fantasy she possessed it *in order to destroy it.* She had created an illusory solution which was not a psychotic but an erotic one, and thus could feel she had triumphed over the traumatic event. She was able for the first time to reveal the elements of her erotic scene, and this enabled us eventually to be able to analyze its significance. Her childhood and adult masturbation fantasies all turned around her brother. She would imagine him immobilized against a wall, while different kinds of "tortures" were carried out on his penis; these were fantasied as being orgastically satisfying to the brother, and were highly exciting to her. Thus she controlled, in imagination, her brother's sexual response. Under the guise of giving him pleasure, his image was also protected against feelings of destructive hatred. As with many sexual deviations, her sexual game served several contradictory purposes: she was able to show and deny at the same time her incestuous wish; and more important, she was able to master actively what she had passively experienced, for she was now both author and actor of her fantasy film, and no longer the victim of the rape which had been lived as a castration. She was the all-powerful castrator. The disavowals included in her erotic fantasy also allowed her to triumph over the primal scene — by inventing a new one — and provided her with fantasied revenge for the mother-son relationship. But it gave her no adequate resolution of her oedipal conflicts and also left her with a damaged image of her own body and sexuality. One part of her had never assumed her feminine gender reality. When, for example, adolescent classmates talked about waiting to get their periods, she would mock them in her mind "because I was convinced that this would never happen to me. I was somehow different from all other girls in my imagination. When I finally discovered my own menstrual blood I didn't recognize it. I thought it was something due to masturbation. I kept it a secret for two months."

With regard to this nexus of sexual fantasy and the torture game on her brother's penis, it is evident that "penis envy" is not an adequate explanation. The destructive elements of the fantasy went far beyond the traumatic experience, and also had primitive roots which were concerned with more archaic sexuality than the discovery and understanding of sexual differences. These roots led us back to the green sap of the mother's inaccessible breasts. The manifest "game" of her brother's castration, rendered ego-syntonic through erotization, hid a deeper fantasy, namely of controlling and destroying the breast-mother in order to possess for herself the magical green sap. Father and brother, symbolically represented as phallic appendages of the omnipotent mother, were regressively fantasied as being the contents of her breasts.

Without sex, without sap, without knowledge about how to live, Annabelle lived out defensively an unelaborated depression, poorly compensated by her particular form of relationship to others, more an act than an exchange, contact rather than communication, but nevertheless a living link.

In an effort to transmit her continuing experience that each day presented her with insurmountable problems, Annabelle would often talk of the "hardness" of life. The word recurred incessantly, attached at one time or another to each relationship, to all the part-objects...the mother's stony breast, the brother's dangerous penis, the analyst's rigorous time-table. "I have come to realize that I have never for one minute felt comfortable — either in my body or in the presence of others. It's so hard, hard to feel good, hard to do the simplest things. Eating, walking, defecating, making love. So hard, so complicated. Why do I not have the secret? Why don't you give it to me, you mean, hard creature!" The analyst-breast, omnipotent idealized image had survived as an inner object in spite of the three years of "hard" blows dealt out to it by the suffering analysand-child, who occupied most of Annabelle's inner psychic space. There was no doubt that I now existed as a separate person and also as an analyst, so that she could "use" me effectively to understand different aspects of the intersystemic war within her (Winnicott, 1971b). But she refused all approach to the idealized, hard, omnipotent being who was supposed to contain the secret of life and of *her* life. I had to be patient while waiting for the possibility of interpreting this idealization. I was able eventually to make an intervention born in part out of my exasperation at not being able to get further on this question. "Why are you so hard? Why do you not tell me *how to live?* You stand there mocking me, waiting for me to discover everything all by myself." I replied that she asked me for a secret to which she alone held the key, that I did not know the answer, nor why she stopped the sap of life from running through her veins. I understood how much she was suffering, but I too was discouraged by my own failure to be able to interpret better what she was experiencing. "I know you are trying to communicate this hard and terrible feeling," I said, "and it is a failure on my part somewhere to catch your message; I do realize that we are both going through a hard moment, and I feel I have let you down." This intervention produced an unexpected and explosive reaction — of joy. Could it be possible that an *analyst* did not understand? That an *analyst* could feel baffled, discouraged? That analysts were not *omniscient* had never once crossed Annabelle's mind in fifteen years of analysis. I was eventually able to show her that she needed to believe in this fetishlike magical "knowledge" in order that she too, at the end of her analysis, might come into possession of it. Her discovery that no one was endowed with this ineffable quality inaugurated the final phase of her analysis with me. The exploration of her idealizing projection enabled her to mourn for its loss and to relinquish her own omnipotent demands: the demand to be spared every frustration, to triumph effortlessly over every "hard" reality, whether internal or external.

Annabelle was at last able to take care of the confused and desperate child within her, and to understand that there were other solutions than destructive elimination whenever she was faced with envious rage and voracious wishes. Construction began to replace destruction in ways which she alone could discover. For the first time she began to care genuinely about her body, her health, her appearance, her love life, her work life, all of which had been left untended, as though growth and change were impossible. She confided these changes shyly to me. In one of our final sessions she said, significantly, that she had sown flower seeds in the spring without telling anyone, in case they died. To her astonishment they had all borne flowers.

Some years later Annabelle sent me a beautiful book dealing with the artistic domain she had made her own, and of which she was the author. In a hand-written dedication she attributed to analysis the discovery of the essence of creativity—that *living was creating*.

Primitive communication

I have given the name of primitive communication to this kind of analytic discourse in order to emphasize its positive aspects, since in general we are much more aware of its negative effects. Patients who tell us many things as a way of not saying anything, of not revealing, even to themselves, what lies behind their communication, or who talk in order to keep the analyst at a distance, are of course maintaining strong resistance to the analytic relationship and mustering powerful forces against the analytic process itself. And they may even be quite conscious that this way of communicating with the analyst (and often with their whole entourage) is defensive, and in some way is eluding what they really would like to say. Nevertheless to the extent that the analyst reacts to the patient's words, some form of communication is taking place. This latent communication is not a truly symbolic one and cannot be compared with the repressed thoughts which lie behind normal-neurotic analytic associations. Here instead we find words being used in place of action—as weapons, as camouflage, as a desperate cry for help, a cry of rage or of any other intense emotional state of which the patient is but dimly aware. These feeling states may have no connection with what the patient is recounting.

This kind of analytic material raises a number of questions. We might question the function of such "communication" and then compare it with the free-associative analytic monologue which ordinary neurotic patients produce in response to our invitation to do just that. We might also ask why certain patients are more apt to use verbal channels in this way and what may be inferred from such language "symptoms" with regard to traumatic childhood history and its ensuing effects on ego structure and defenses. Although I shall deal briefly with these questions my main interest is the exploration of the way in which the analyst receives this kind of analytic communication, and how he may best use it to further the analytic process. This process depends to a high degree on language communication, and the particular mode of communication which we call free association allows us to explore the interpenetration of primary and secondary processes. The "basic rule" relies on the verbal expression of thoughts and feelings, and it is hoped that to the extent that the analysand can eventually allow ideas, fantasies, and emotional states free expression in ways in which he would not normally permit himself to function verbally this interpenetration of conscious and unconscious knowledge of himself will set the analytic process in motion. The invitation to "say everything" — along with its implicit counterpart "and do nothing" — not only opens the way to transference affect but also enables the analysand in hearing his own words, to get to know his thoughts and feelings in an entirely new way. However, this expectation becomes questionable with people who use language in ways that alter its essential function, and more particularly in the analytic situation with its intimate dependence on language and communication.

What indeed are the aims of what I am calling primitive communication, and in what major ways does it differ from other verbal communications? What role does it play in psychic economy? To what system of internal object relations is it entailed?

Although the efficacy of *words* in the communication of thoughts and emotions is considerably more limited than we like to admit, nevertheless the primary aim of verbal exchange among adults is the desire to communicate information to those to whom one chooses to address oneself. But this is far from being its only aim. Communicate — from the Latin *communicare:* to render common, to be in relationship with, to be connected — reveals its underlying etymological and affective meaning. All people in certain situations, and some people much of the time, use verbal communication literally as a way of maintaining a contact, being in relation with, or even being part of, "common to," another person. This vital link with the Other may override in importance the symbolic function which consists of the desire to *inform* someone of something. From such a viewpoint verbal communication might be considered an approximation to crying, calling out, screaming, growling, rather than to *telling* something. To this extent such communication would be a means not only of remaining in intimate contact but also a way of conveying and discharging emotion in direct fashion, with the intent to affect and arouse reactions in the Other.

The analytic situation, since it dispenses with the usual conventions of verbal exchange, is particularly apt to reveal unusual features in verbalization which might pass unnoticed in everyday conversation (Rosen, 1967). The austerity of the analytic protocol tends to highlight such differences. In Annabelle Borne's analytic associations it was noted that her words had partially lost their communicative aim. In addition this use of verbalization impeded the free association of ideas. The fact that we were able to discover together the wide gap between what she *said* and what she *felt*, between the content and its accompanying affect, finally allowed her discourse to become meaningful to both of us, and the patient to recover many lost feelings. At the same time we were able to understand that she frequently spoke with the main intention of arousing feeling in the *analyst* without knowing why this was so important, or what this feeling represented to her. Her need to induce feeling states in others was in fact connected with early traumatic situations in which she had been unable to deal with intense emotion and did not know how to communicate her need for help; instead of containing and elaborating her emotional pain and using it to think further, she had effaced all knowledge of its existence or meaning. Thus past events and affective experience had been simply ejected from consciousness as though they had never existed. For the first time many of these emotional states were able to achieve psychical representation. Communications like those of Annabelle Borne differ in an essential way from those found in an ordinary neurotic associative process, even when these are directed toward arousing feeling in the analyst. In the latter, the attempt to let one's thought and fantasy roam freely tends to reveal, behind the patent communication, a latent theme to which the analyst is "listening." The person unknown to himself is communicating another story, revealing himself an actor upon another stage, but for which the script, once conscious, has been forgotten. Such secret scripts and dissimulated scenes are of course present in patients who use language to penetrate the listener and provoke reaction from him, but from the standpoint of analytic work vitiate the aim of laying bare this latent underlying meaning and render the capturing of repressed ideas and memories peculiarly difficult. Meanwhile the analyst is likely to feel bewildered and invaded by affects that hinder his analytic functioning — *unless he pays attention to them.*

The depressive and frustrating feelings which Annabelle Borne aroused in me had little to do with repressed ideas in her analytic material. The primary aim of her words might well have been described as an attempt to discharge, through the very act of talking, pent-up and painful tension, whose content and causes were unknown to her. The secret aim of which she was able to become conscious was to *share* a pain which could not yet be expressed through the medium of language and was not capable of being thought about. It was a demand to be *heard rather than listened to*, a need for communion rather than communication. In the months to come we were able to pinpoint the moments at which such communication became imperative. Faced with the slightest hint of a painful thought or feeling, Annabelle would immediately manage to pulverize its psychic representation. As a consequence she had no true awareness of the existence of the idea or affect in question. But the debris of this psychic elimination had the effect of altering her perception of others, and in consequence her manner of feeling about them and communicating with them. The same thing occurred in the analytic transference.

Of course the various themes that Annabelle Borne used to fill up the essential silence left in the wake of all that had been repudiated from consciousness were not devoid of significance in themselves, nor of any reference to repressed material. It was for example patent that lurking behind the persecutory images and ideas, the problem of *Envy* loomed large, but it remained out of interpretable reach as long as the ejected feelings of depression, abandonment, and deprivation — along with their inevitable corollary, intense feelings of hatred — remained blocked from access to psychic expression, blocked therefore to verbal reflection and expression. In a sense many of Annabelle's remarks and observations were devoid of interest for her; she was relatively unaware that they might have a potential effect on her analyst, her friends, and family, or any others with whom she maintained communicative links. The unconscious benefit thus procured was the protection of her inner object world from destruction due to her envious rage and narcissistic mortification. At the same time it permitted her to maintain contact with the external object world in spite of the continual feeling of dissatisfaction which her relationships afforded her. Perhaps too, her aggressive contact strengthened her feeling of identity. But all this was obtained at a high price. Not only did she feel overwhelmed by the "hardness" of existence in all its aspects, she suffered a veritable impairment of her capacity to *think*, in particular with regard to the causes of her mental suffering. With her defensive, almost brutal elimination of awareness of affective pain she was in fact hampered in dealing with her genuine *needs*, and not only with the fulfillment of wishes. At the beginning of our analytic work together she was relatively unaware of having any personal desires other than the wish to be "comfortable," and was equally unaware of what she demanded and expected from others.

This way of experiencing raises the question of the space occupied in psychic life by the external objects. Implicitly the Other is called upon to capture and deal with an inexpressible appeal. In a sense it is a demand to be understood without passing by the normal verbal channels, to be understood by mere signs. *Infans*, the infant unable as yet to talk, must have his needs heard and dealt with in this way, since he has no other means of communication. When he is capable of *asking* it is no longer a question of vital need, but until this time he is totally dependent on his mother's interpretation of his cries and gestures. To the extent that an infant can conceive of Another who will respond to his cry, he may be said to be "communicating" in this primitive way. At this point he has already reached a certain stage of psychic growth in regard to the object; he no longer feels that the Other is a hallucinatory part of himself (which might be equated with a psychotic form of object relation) but instead believes the Other to be *all-powerful*, in which case the response of the object to the signs emitted is interpreted as positive because the object wants the infant to be gratified, or in the case of a negative response, as a refusal because he wants the infant to suffer. That is to say, this type of relationship is under the sway of primary-process thinking: if good things or bad things occur, in either case they are felt to derive from the omnipotent desire of the all-powerful Other. This Other automatically understands and responds as he wishes! (This type of thinking prevails in what we might call narcissistic character pathology.) With regard to this projected idealization and expectation of the external world we are sometimes inclined, as Bion (1970) has pointed out, to overlook the fact that, in spite of the satisfaction which symbolic communication eventually brings to the growing person, to be *obliged* to speak in order to be understood, and to have wishes granted, is a continuing narcissistic wound in everyone's unconscious. For certain people, fusion and communion, rather than separateness and communication, are the only authentic means of relating to another person. (One patient who regarded separateness as a calamity, used to say that if she had to *tell* her husband what she needed or wished for in any field, then his complying with her wish no longer had any significance. It was indeed a proof that he did not love her.)

Fusional communion, that archaic form of loving which is the nursling's right, is still implicitly awaited by certain adults. Any threat of separation, or reminder of subjective difference such as having to convey one's wishes through verbalization, can only spell punishment and rejection. We are dealing here with the "infant" inside the adult, who has never truly understood the role of verbal communication as a symbolic means of making one's desires known. No doubt these are the babies who were not sensitively "listened to" and "interpreted" by those who brought them up. My own clinical experience with patients who live out this inarticulate drama leads me to believe that their childhoods were marked by incoherent relationships with the earliest objects, and in a context in which the inevitable frustrations of human growing and development were not tempered with sufficient gratification to make them bearable, so that the supreme reward of individuation and subjective identity was not acquired with pleasure, but instead continues to be lived as a rejection and an insult. The fact that one's wishes can be both communicated and responded to is scarcely believed to be true. Such was the case with Annabelle.

One further factor: the demand to be understood without words implies also a terror of facing disappointment or refusal of any kind. This is felt not only as a narcissistic wound, but as an unbearable pain that cannot be contained and psychically elaborated, and which may destroy one. Thus the ineluctable factors that structure human reality — otherness, sexual difference, the impossibility of magic fulfillment of wishes, the inevitability of death — have not become meaningful. Otherness with its reward of personal identity and privacy; sexual difference with the reward of sexual desire; the refinding of magic fulfillments in creativity; the acceptance of death itself as the inevitable end which gives urgent and important significance to life — all may be lacking for these patients. Life then runs the risk of being "meaningless" and "hard." Other people tend to be seen as vehicles for *externalizing* this painful inner drama of living. It is in fact the creation of a system of *survival*. At least contact with others is assured and something is communicated. Many people with this way of relating find themselves pushed to manipulate others, although unaware that this is what they are doing, in order to bring about the catastrophes they already anticipate. Thus relationships are often directed toward proving the inevitability of preconceived conclusions concerning them. This is another way of "communicating" one's distress and of combating one's feeling of utter impotence in the face of overwhelming forces. There are many ways in which such a system of interpersonal relations may be expressed theoretically: in terms of persecutory anxiety and projective identification (Klein, Grinberg); of the need of the subject to use others as containers (Bion); of the urgent necessity to recover lost parts of oneself, the "self-objects" (Kohut); the tendency to deny the independent existence of others as a defense against pathological forms of object-relating (Kernberg); the "false-self" concept (Winnicott); the use of others as "transitional objects" (Modell).

Out of touch with important aspects of themselves, these patients have difficulty in accepting that others are also prone to anxiety, depression, frustration, and irritation. Thus the struggle against archaic fantasies and emotions is reinforced by the struggle against outer reality and the pain of others. Like nurslings forced to become autonomous before their time, they must be prepared to stave off all sources of conflict and psychic suffering, whether these come from inner or outer psychic space. Unknown to themselves, they are working with a model of human relations in which separate identity must be vigorously denied since absence and difference have not been compensated by a well-constructed inner object-world; thus the patients' own feeling of identity is unstable. Nor is it easy then to grasp what others are trying to communicate, and assumptions about human motives run the risk of being erroneous. Separateness is rejected as a postulate and in its stead we find the constant externalization of conflict in an attempt to keep everything in its place, and in this way exercise an illusory control over other people's reactions. These are the "wise babies" described by Ferenczi, who must control everything with the babylike means at their disposal. We must of course admit that such an imperious nursling slumbers inside all of us, but he is usually confined to the omnipotent world of dreams. Neurotic patients discover this megalomanic child within themselves, with astonishment; others, like Annabelle, discover that throughout their lives they have been striving to reinstate the rights of this demanding infant and, most of all, his right to be heard and his need to be in meaningful communication with others. Although the adult ego is unaware of his existence, the angry and desperate child is screaming to be allowed to breathe. Only thus is there any hope that this inarticulate infant may have access to a more elaborated form of self-expression.

It is evident that the analyst who receives such communications in analysis finds himself listening to a discourse which will not make sense if he consistently treated it as a normal-neurotic transmission of ideas and affects under the sway of free association. He will seek in vain for repressed ideas pushing their way into consciousness, and will be forced to realize that he is observing a part of the personality dominated by primitive mechanisms of defense: disavowal, splitting, fore-closure, all of which serve to exclude psychic events from the symbolic chain, particularly those that are apt to produce psychic pain. We might well ask ourselves to what extent it is possible to penetrate the barriers of primal repression and explore the basic layers of the personality structure. Can we hope to "hear" that which has never been formulated in ways in which it might form part of preconscious ideas, that which has never been encoded as thought and thus not preserved in a form accessible to recall and to symbolic elaboration? Here the limits of the analytic process must be called into question.

I would suggest, however, that to the extent that areas of experience have been repudiated from the psychic world to be projected into the external world, these ejected fragments of experiencing are expressed in behavior, or constantly enacted in the form of primitive exchange. In certain privileged situations and moments we can "hear" at least the distress signals; we come to know that these signs are an indication of profound pain which cannot yet be fully recognized by the individual as personal suffering. He feels blocked, hampered, hamstrung, and furious with the world. This is the basic message.

The role of countertransference

How does this message strike the analyst? In the first place the analytic ear may be rapidly alerted by the particular *use of words*. In the case of Annabelle Borne there was a notable discordance between content and affect, so that much angry and discontented feeling was in fact hiding inexpressible depression; with other patients, in a similar inner drama, we find ourselves listening to an interminable monologue recounting daily facts which seem to have no further echo beyond the mere words, either for the analysand or the analyst; others again use words in ways that make us feel confused, that is to say, the ordinary associative links such as we find in everyday conversation and everyday analytic communications may be lacking. Rosen speaks of subtle disturbances in the encoding of thought processes which emerge in the analytic situation, and of the fact that the analyst must sometimes become aware of the latent content through media other than words—signal systems such as gestures, posture, facial expression, intonation, pictograms, etc. I think that we are often attuned to such subliminal messages well in advance of being able ourselves to encode and verbalize what we have understood. Modell (1973) suggests that the capturing of affect may well precede the acquisition of language. On the basis of personal experience with very young babies (who often react in striking fashion to the affective states of those who are looking after them) and also deductions drawn from my analytic observations, I would go further and say that the transmission of affect unquestionably takes place earlier than symbolic communication. Modell's further observation that an analytic discourse that lacks affect is a sign that the analytic process has come to a halt, seems to me highly pertinent to analytic research into the nature of communication.

A further observation concerning "primitive communication" is that veritable "free association" (with all the limitations and filtering systems that normally accompany it) is lacking. There is no *Einfall* (which means, literally, a sudden upsurge or breakthrough of a thought, fantasy, or image from some inner but hitherto unrecognized source). This interpenetration of primary and secondary processes, hallmark of a functioning psychoanalytic process, is not taking place, and thus tends to give a featureless aspect to the analytic monologue. Although it may seem like an "empty" communication, it will often produce a feeling of "fullness" in the analyst, a frustrating feeling to which he must turn his attention. In the analysand's desire to be intimately "linked" with the analyst through his verbalization, he may take little heed of the fact that the analyst is apt to respond emotionally to the content, especially if it is depressive, aggressive, or anxiety-arousing, and there is correspondingly little questioning of the supposition that the analyst will be equally pleased to be linked through this verbal stream — even though it be, for example, a vituperative monologue which takes the analyst as its target, or a confused discourse which takes no account of the difficulty in seizing its meaning. In their efforts to remain plugged in, as it were, to the analyst's mind, these patients are appealing for help and pushing the analyst away at the same time. The patient may be said to be under the sway of a condensation — not of thought, but of aim. He seeks to obtain love and attention which will reassure him that he is being heard and being held, that he exists, and at the same time must punish the Other for all the bad and hard things he has had to endure. It could be conceived of as a demand upon an idealized breast, the maternal function, such as a nursling might experience it were he able to express it.

If these patients do not talk about what really concerns them — their contradictory seeking, their pain in living, their difficulty in feeling understood or truly alive — it is because *they do not know it.* Unaware of the impact of their words, they are equally unaware that they too occupy a psychic space in the minds of others. The others are considered to be alive, existent, and therefore need little else, whereas the subject of this distress is screaming out his right to become alive too, with the underlying assumption that the world owes him this. For many patients the discovery of this dilemma may be an inaugural experience encountered in the analytic situation. The analysand may for the first time make a conscious distinction between himself and Another, with the recognition that both exist, each with his individual and separate psychic reality. People with no clear representation of their own psychic space and their own identity tend otherwise to relate to others in ways that elude *their* psychic reality too; that is to say, they tend to perceive only what accords with their preconceived notion of the Other, and of the world in general, and to eliminate perceptions and observations that do not fit in with the existing idea.

This way of relating has a marked effect on the transference relationship. Much of the force of transference comes from the interplay between the analyst as a figure of imagination and projection and the analyst as a real being. As an imaginary object, he becomes the eventual target for all the investments attached to the original inner objects, whereas his qualities as a real person remain largely unknown to the analysand. Patients who operate within the relational framework described in this chapter maintain only a minimal distance between the imaginary and the real analyst, so that transference projections are rarely perceived as such. Neither partner to the analytic tandem will be endowed with any clearly delineated identity. This sort of analytic relationship might be included in the concept of an idealized narcissistic transference as described by Kohut, or as an attempt at fusional denial of separateness, or again as an attempt to establish a pathological form of archaic object relations as envisaged by Kernberg.

Such patients will tend to use a model of human relationships based on the postulates that belong to primary-process thinking — that is to say, all things bad or good which happen to the subject are due to another person's wish, and indeed his good, or bad will. There is little questioning of the important events in his life as far as his own participation is concerned. In analysis, if the patient feels bad, he is quite likely to believe that the analyst is indifferent because deep down he *wishes his analysand to suffer.* If and when these analysands become conscious of their own projected aggressive and destructive wishes, they are more than likely to stifle such feelings and rapidly eject their associated ideas from consciousness. Thus they often do not know when they are angry, frightened, or unhappy.

As already emphasized, we are not dealing with mechanisms of repression or isolation, but of repudiation from the psychic world, splitting, and projective identification. In consequence the principal anxieties to be faced are more concerned with the self and the maintenance of identity than with sexuality and the fulfillment of desire; "psychotic" anxiety mobilized by fear of disintegration and dedifferentiation, takes a larger place than "neurotic" anxiety attached to all that is included in the classical concept of the castration complex. If the latter runs the risk of producing sexual and work inhibitions or symptoms, the former disturbs the whole pattern of relationship with others. There will be a tendency to use others as parts of oneself, or in the place of transitional objects where they are destined to play a protective role and to be used to filter hostile impulses. Within the analytic relationship this tends to create the type of fundamental transference to which Stone (1961) referred in his classic work on the analytic situation, that is transference affect which is more concerned with Otherness and the fear of (wish for) fusion than with the transferences typical of the neurotic structure.

The symptomatic kind of analytic discourse that ensues may be a manifestation of a number of psychic ills. In a sense the "signs" discerned here as being the unformulated but true communication might be regarded as minimal elements of psychotic thought and expression; nevertheless there is no contamination of thought, nor do we find the surrealistic use of words so markedly present in psychotic verbalization. Annabelle Borne had not created a personal grammar; there was no confusion between the signifier and the thing signified. But she had a similar fragility in her idea of herself and her relations to others, in which the limits were ill-defined, suggesting a lack of early structurization of a stable self-image, and consequently an unclear picture of others. This kind of relationship may well give rise to a form of personal esperanto whose communicative aim might have psychotic overtones.

The idiosyncratic use of language which may pass un-noticed as such in the everyday world, since it respects syntax and symbolic reference, seeks nevertheless, in the way that psychotic communications do, to restore the primary mother-child unity, to be understood through and in spite of one's way of communicating. The distinction may be said to lie here: patients like Annabelle Borne do not use words in accordance with primary-process functioning, but their way of relating to others follows the primary-process model, namely, of total dependence on the omnipotent will of the Other. Thus language is used in the service of this form of relationship. Perhaps in this way psychotic disorgan-ization is prevented, for these patients are not detached from outer reality; they do not dream up situations, causes, and perceptions which exist only in their inner world. Instead they utilize others, in accordance with what they find, who are apt to take in and give back to the subject something that is offered and something else that is demanded. Nevertheless the patient may be said to be "creating" the meaning that the other person has for him without taking too much account of the Other's reality, while at the same time submitting him-self to this Other and suffering accordingly. I would add that such relationships are by no means rare in the world at large, and that relatively few such people seek analytic help.

My contention is that when we find this way of com-municating and relating reproduced in the analytic setting, we have indications of early psychic suffering, presumably rooted in the period when the small child tries to use the mother as a subsidiary part of himself and so deals with vital needs and conflicts through the "language" at his disposal. We might say that part of the patient is "outside himself," in analysis as in everyday life, and he therefore treats others, or the analyst, as vagrant segments of himself, which he naturally attempts to control.

It is evident that this will give rise to countertransference phenomena that are different from those that arise with the normal-neurotic analysand. For the latter, equipped as he is with the familiar neurotic forms of defense against psychic pain and conflict, the analyst becomes a figure of projection for his own inner objects, since his mental conflict stems in large part from intrapsychic struggles. Such a patient introjects a representation of the analyst who thus becomes an object of the analysand's ego, although constituted differently from the genuine inhabitants of his inner universe. The analyst is, so to speak, an immigrant with a temporary visa who draws upon himself forbidden desires, idealized representations, threats, fear, anger, etc., belonging to the original objects. The analyst's unique position in this psychic world provides the transference relationship with considerable force, and as already emphasized, permits the patient to measure and explore the distance that separates the analyst as an imaginary person from the analyst as a real being with an individual identity. It is in this space between the visions of the analyst that the most fruitful interpretative and reconstructive work is accomplished. Countertransference interference if present stems mainly from unresolved personal problems of the analyst — and it is not an uncommon occurrence for a "good neurotic analysand" to become aware of these, see clearly that they are not a matter of his own projections, and point them out!

But in the case where the distinction between transference projection and reality observation is blurred, the way in which the analyst receives the patient's transference expression is likely to differ. Hidden in the shape of "pseudo communication" that seeks less to inform (literally: to give form to) the analyst of his thoughts and feelings than to get rid of painful intrapsychic conflict and arouse reaction in the analyst, we must wonder how the latter may best capture and interpret this "language." In the beginning he does not "hear" the message, nor does he immediately become aware of its emotional impact. It is difficult to detect what is missing, particularly since its ejection leaves no unconscious trace, and no neoreality has been invented to take its place as with psychotic patients. Gradually affect is mobilized and indeed accumulates in the analyst; while the analysand flattens or distorts his affective experience, the analyst becomes literally "affected." The patient's associations have a penetrating or impregnating effect which is missing in the usual neurotic transference and analytic monologue. What has been foreclosed from the world of psychic representation cannot be "heard" as a latent communication. It is the emotional infiltration that contains the seeds of future interpretations, but in order to be able to formulate these the analyst must first understand why his patient's discourse affects him in the way it does. I would agree fully with Giovacchini (1977) when he points out with regard to delusional patients that to view them as unanalyzable on the basis of an insufficiently self-observing ego is too glib a dismissal of a complex problem. With the kind of patients I am describing the analyst is apt to feel in the first instance that he has somewhere along the line *ceased functioning adequately as an analyst* with this particular analysand.

Although the analogy cannot be carried too far, the analyst is at these moments in the situation of the mother who is trying to understand why her baby is crying in an angry or distressed fashion. At this stage it is evident that the baby can have no identity over and beyond what he represents for his mother, and it is she who must *interpret* his signs and give them meaning — that is convert them into communication. In Bion's terminology she must fulfill the role of being her child's thinking apparatus until such time as he is able to think for himself. The analyst, of course, has more modest aims than those which would imply becoming his patient's thinking apparatus! It is not his role to teach his analysand how to perceive the world and how to react to it. At most he hopes to lead his patient to discover who he is — and for whom. But to do so he must be prepared to decode the sounds of distress that lie behind the angry or confused associations.

One is tempted to surmise that these analysands had mothers who were unable to "listen" to their infants and to give meaning to their primitive communications. Perhaps the mother herself reacted with resentment and rejection to her baby's unformulated demands, as though they were a personal attack on her, or reflected a narcissistic failure on her own part; in such cases she would fail in her role of "interpreter" who must teach her baby to express his needs, to discover his desires, finally to be able to *think* for himself. But then this also requires a mother who grants her child the *right to in-*

dependent thoughts even if these run counter to her own at many points. We have here another seed to the creating of communication disorders.

Whatever the reasons may have been, the analyst who inherits this psychic puzzle will feel himself "manipulated" by his analysand in the latter's attempt to protect himself from psychic pain, and avoid, forever after, becoming the plaything of another's desire. By writing the script in advance he lays out the scene in such a way that little is left to chance — other than the capacity of the chosen actors to fulfill their roles. Traumatic thoughts and feelings are in this manner controlled through immediate evacuation from the subject's own psyche, to be played out in the external world, an attempt at magic fulfillment and narcissistic reparation.

The analyst must be prepared to capture the patient's difficulty in thinking about himself through the blockage he experiences in his own thinking, in order eventually to recover the expelled representations and the stifled affects. These may then be rendered into archaic fantasy, capable of being expressed verbally, and the associated feelings contained and explored within the analytic relationship. The durability of this relationship functions as a guarantee that such powerful affects may be safely experienced and expressed without damage to either analyst or patient. I think this is what Winnicott means when he says that "the reliability of the analyst is the most important factor (or more important than the interpretations) because the patient did not experience such reliability in the maternal care of infancy, and if the patient is to make use of such reliability he will need to find it for the first time in the analyst's behavior" (Winnicott, 1960, p. 38).

It is probable that what has been submitted to primal repression cannot be communicated except through "signs" such as those described here, and that these signs will be registered through countertransference feelings. The inadequate functioning of the analyst at these times will manifest itself in many subtle ways. In addition to feeling manipulated he may find himself reacting to the sessions with boredom or irritation, or catch himself giving aggressive interpretations, maintaining a stubborn silence, or wandering in his mind along paths which have no relation to the patient's associations. In spite of all the well-known pitfalls of countertransference affect, I am obliged to suppose here that these "signs" in the analyst are more than the unique reflection of his own inner emotional state or his unconscious reactions to the patient's monologue, and that we are dealing not with a repressed, but with a primitive communication, not decodable in the usual way. If at such times the analyst persists in seeking repressed content, in giving interpretations as though to neurotic material, in replying aggressively, or turning away in silence, then the *analyst is acting out.* He is now obstructing the analytic process by his *countertransference resistance.* Like all other human beings, we as analysts have difficulty in hearing or perceiving what does not fit into our pre-established codes. Our own unresolved transference feelings play a role role here, since the garnering of analytic knowledge has been accomplished through and deeply impregnated with transference affect and thus tends to carry a built-in resistance of its own, making it difficult for us to "hear" all that is being transmitted. We tend to resent the patient who does not progress in accordance with our expectations, or who reacts to our efforts to understand as though they were hostile attacks. These problems, added to our personal weaknesses, provide us with a delicate task.

Annabelle Borne's analysis had come to a standstill due to my own inability to catch the meaning of and to examine my countertransference expectations and irritations — up until the moment when I told her she sought not so much to communicate her ideas and emotions as to make me feel sad and helpless. When she was, so to speak, able to take back and possess her own tears, we could then listen together to the paralyzed, unhappy child entrapped within her. From that time forward we could permit this child to grow and to express herself for the first time.

The way in which we normally listen to our analysands, a free-floating attention similar to that asked of them, might better be described as free-floating theorization, and it is notable that with the patients under consideration here, it is difficult to utilize our various "floating theories" about the patient and the nature of his analytic tie to us. Such floating hypotheses take much longer to organize themselves. This is due in part to the analysand's particular way of communicating and in part to the difficult roles he implicitly needs us to assume on his behalf. The attitude of "expectant silence" which to the neurotic spells hope, and opens a psychic space wherein long-buried desires may once more come to light, offers little but desolation and death to patients like Annabelle. Their need to feel they exist in other people's eyes, to feel truly alive, to a large extent dominates all other wishes and invades almost totally the territory of desire. The unsure limits between one and the other makes the analysis of the relationship between the two partners hazardous and the mourning for lost objects difficult. It is impossible to mourn the loss of an object one has never possessed, or whose existence has never been truly recognized as distinct from one's own, or as an integral part of one's inner world. On this shifting sand, "transference" interpretations are not constructive, and indeed run the risk of perpetuating the misunderstandings and mutual distortions of the first communications between mother and child. Silence, or the so-called "good analytic interpretation," instead of creating a potentially vital space for feelings and thoughts to come into being, or stimulating further associations and memories through which a new way of experiencing may come to life, run the risk of opening instead onto the silence of the primal unconscious, psychic death, nothingness.

Nevertheless all that has been stifled by the force of primal repression remains potentially active, and indeed actual, since it is inevitably ejected into the outer world. All that has been silenced becomes a message-in-action, and it is this action-communication language that may install itself within the analytic situation, there to express itself through signs and secret codes. It is then possible for the analyst to aid his patients to stop the psychic hemorrhage created through continual acting out and direct discharge of tension, pain, and confusion; to render the action-symptoms expressible through language, and to enable the patient to undertake his analytic adventure. In the next chapter, we shall examine the role played by the narcissistic economy in such personality structures.

Chapter VIII

Narcissus in Search
of a Reflection

Leaning over a pool one day in order to quench his thirst, Narcissus for the first time in his life perceived his own image reflected in the water. Its beauty was such, so goes the myth, that Narcissus became enamored of it. Unable to detach himself from this illusory love, he pined away leaving a flower behind him, and an echoing nymph. We might nevertheless wonder whether this bewitching image was not a long-awaited one and so thirsted for that Narcissus feared losing, should he tear himself away from his reflection, not only his amorous illusion, but his very existence.

Was it truly a love experience? The fascination that human beings constantly display for themselves contributes, as Freud so well demonstrated (1914), a dimension of estrangement to the *state of being in love*, because of the tendency to project our own "ideal" ego upon the Other. Nevertheless the fact that Freud planted the love relationship in pathological soil raises a number of unanswered questions with regard to human narcissism. We might assume that Narcissus was endowed with a fragile and fragmentary psychic structure, and that this would inevitably affect his amorous destiny. In a thought-provoking book on being in love David (1971) makes a profound study of analytic concepts of the love relationship. "There can be no truly amorous goal," writes David, "without the recognition of an irremediable narcissistic insufficiency, or more precisely, of an *inevitable and urgent demand that the Other be Other, that his essence is his Otherness.* It is because of its difference that the object is essentially and dynamically a sexual one. Similitude lies in the shared lack, and the reciprocity of the desire to repair it" (my translation; author's italics).

What then might be lacking to Narcissus, lover of his own image?

In his *Metamorphosis 111* Ovid taxes Narcissus with his credulity and the vanity of his exploit since "the object of his desire is inexistent." But can we fully accept that Narcissus's effort to seize this fleeting and transparent reflection is completely vain and has no meaning? That there is no object to his search? It is possible that the circle he draws around himself encloses a space filled with longing and despair, that the apparent self-satisfaction that emanates from the picture of Narcissus is the illusion of the *observer.* Might we not also suppose that this fragile flower-child gazing upon his own image is seeking a lost object in the pool that is not himself, but the *recognition of himself in the eyes of Another?* This recognition of oneself as a separate and unique being is sought by the infant's avid gazing at his reflection in his mother's eyes — a reflection destined to give him not only his mirror image, but also what he represents for his mother (Winnicott, 1971b). Only thus may he hope to recognize himself as having a privileged place and a personal value in the eyes of this Other who looks at him and talks to him.

It may happen, however, that the mother's attention and intensity of feeling are diverted from her child toward some painful situation that excludes him; if that be the case, her gaze will reflect nothing, like un-mirrored glass. Or again, she may seek in her child her own reflection and a confirmation of her own identity.[1] This image of oneself captured in the dawning of psychic life might well be called *narcissistic;* should it be a fragile and fleeting reflection, it will give rise to an equally fragile and fleeting feeling of narcissistic integrity and self-esteem.

Whatever may have occurred in the early relationship as a consequence of the frailty of either partner, the creation of a self-representation is ineludibly linked to the necessity for man's young to come to terms with the reality trauma of otherness. This requires the psyche to take into itself something that can only be found in the first instance in the outside world. I suggest that only the *illusion of a personal identity* is capable eventually of healing this wound. This feeling of identity, though founded in illusion, is nevertheless an essential element in the psychic economy. I would furthermore propose that the maintenance of this feeling of personal identity might be considered as a primordial need in the individual's psychic life — equal in intensity and importance to the instinct of self-

---

[1]This would seem to have been the fate of Narcissus, mirror for his mother Liriope, nymph of the waters, reflecting pool where Narcissus could only discover the death of himself as a separate entity.

preservation in relation to biological life — an unending struggle against psychic death. The self-representation is based on an intricate interpenetration of the libidinal investments of the self with those of the inner and outer objects, intricate intermingling of the narcissistic and the libidinal economy, a mutual pact which is ceaselessly renewed.

This perpetual oscillation, the systole and dyastole of psychic life, destined to maintain the feeling of identity, can nevertheless be seriously impaired, with grave psychological and even biological consequences for the individual. Narcissus plays a more important role than Oedipus in the elucidation of certain of man's graver psychic ills. Psychic survival occupies a more fundamental place in the unconscious than the oedipal crisis, to the extent that for some people, suffering occasioned by the question of sexual rights and desires takes on the appearance of a luxury. Of course the struggle to maintain one's narcissistic integrity and feeling of self-esteem is incumbent on every human being; and it should also be mentioned that perturbations in the narcissistic equilibrium may well produce symptoms that are more readily analyzable than many deeply entrenched neurotic problems. For others, however, the maintenance of their narcissistic homeostasis demands the setting up of innumerable defenses or protective relationships which play a truly vital role. Narcissus, faced with the danger of losing sight of his reflection in the water might choose instead to allow life to drain away from him, or plunge into the bottomless pool toward a deathlike fusion, rather than face the void within himself — void not only of his sexual identity, but also of himself as separate from the Other.

Subjective identity, like sexual identity, can only come into being through Another, while at the same time the Other acquires also his status as a separate and a sexed individual. Constructed around name and gender, personal identity must be maintained by a constant movement in psychic space between the self-image and the image of the objects of the ego; this structure will in turn determine the relation of the self to the outer world.

Taking as a starting point the narcissistic image as an *intersubjective phenomenon*, I should like to examine clinically the role of the Other, in the economy of identity, in patients fraught with a particularly sensitive narcissistic fragility. People who must constantly struggle to maintain their narcissistic homeostasis may do this in two different ways: they may keep a prudent distance from others felt to be a threat to their equilibrium, or, on the contrary, they may grasp on to others, displaying unquenchable need of the person chosen to reflect the image that is missing in the inner psychic world. Sometimes the sexual partner is asked to fulfill this function. In both cases it is frequently a question of psychic survival. The nature of the request made of analysis and the complexity of countertransference affect are evident in the first meeting with the future analysand.

Preliminary interview: Sabine is trying to explain what she is seeking. "I can't go on like this. How shall I explain? It's as though nothing was worthwhile. Can you see what I mean?" She casts a fleeting glance in my direction as though to say she has little hope of being understood. "It's as though I'm not truly alive. Not real. I need to be alone a great deal of the time, be-

cause when others are around I'm never altogether
present. People empty me out. It's particularly bad
right now. Sometimes I think of killing myself. I've
thought about it — I would kill the children first and
then myself." This death-dealing project is described
with little perceptible affect. "When I met X I thought
I'd found the ideal life companion — so many interests
and friends of his own that I could be alone whenever I
needed it. But he has become horribly dependent on
me. It's quite unbearable. He never leaves me alone. I
ask myself. . . what is the good of going on." A long
pause. "Do you think a psychoanalysis could help me?"

Friends and colleagues — what would you reply? No
good telling me we do not know anything about
Sabine. With a few supplementary interviews you
would not know more. She cannot word her quest
differently. Does she suffer from depression?

Not really. Obviously she is expressing depressive
affect, but there is no trace of sadness, and, clinically
speaking, she is not depressed. She manages to keep
working, to see friends; she lives with the man of her
choice, expresses considerable maternal concern for
her two little boys. And yet she is tied up in her dilemma like a bird caught in a net. She needs "many long
hours alone in order to feel whole."

Perhaps it is something of a dramatic display? Hysterical structure? But what is she displaying? Everything that typifies the hysteric is lacking here. We
might say she is a case of anorexia nervosa with regard
to living, but this would be stretching the definition of
hysteria unduly. Even her fantasy of suicide is totally
lacking in drama and erotization.

Maybe she is one of those vague hysterical characters where everything is inhibited rather than converted. What pleasure does she get from her body? From her sex life?

She eats, she eliminates, she sleeps. Not very much, it must be admitted, and with little expressed pleasure. She is not frigid, but rarely desires sexual relations. In a way she is almost without desires of any kind.

Perhaps everything libidinal is confined to her mental functioning. What does she do in those long hours of solitude?

She says she needs many hours to think; she prefers writers to other people. An intellectual.

Borderline? She claims she does not feel "real." Withdrawn? Schizoid?

This description does not satisfy me. Her self-created solitude does not enclose a psychotic emptiness. Her inner world is on the contrary varied and rich. She is a keen observer of life around her. Conversations, countryside, the world of theater and art are all passionately interesting to her. But she is an observer rather than a participant; the important aftermath of each experience is to carry away with her to her personal hideouts all that has moved her and to gaze upon it — like a collector of trophies. But it is a totally private "collection"; the presence of others spoils her enjoyment of it. It is only among the others that she feels unreal.

Her relationships seem pragmatic, operational; perhaps her fantasy life and her affects are blocked? Psychosomatic?

Not that I know of. She is not an "alexithymic" person nor does she have the "operational" decathected kind of relation to others that is ascribed to the so-called psychosomatic personality. On the contrary, she feels constantly threatened by invasion from others, and has to keep a prudent distance from them in order to "recover and to renew herself" as she puts it. She will go so far as to say that she has no vital need of others in order to feel content with life. Of course she is not duped by this illusion, or she would not be here, in an analyst's consulting room! But in spite of her appeal to analysis to help her, she believes quite sincerely that she is totally sufficient unto herself.

A narcissistic personality disorder! It's not a neurosis — it's the "self-illness"! But what does that mean? We are all narcissists at heart, with a fragile "self" that has to be kept going in the world of others. I am tempted to reply with a quip that has been attributed to Winnicott: "Neurotic or narcissistic? But this has nothing to do with the analysands. It is the analysts who are either neurotic or narcissistic!" A polemic remark, but one that raises some interesting speculations. My own analytic patients can with difficulty be categorized in such fashion. The majority of them have a mixture of hysterical, obsessional, and phobic characteristics; they have moments of perversion and delinquency; some go through transient psychotic episodes and all of them "somatize" at one time or another when under stress. Over and beyond that, they are all struggling to keep their narcissistic image on an even keel! What is the symptom of the self? Is it not the task of every human being to maintain his feeling of self-identity and self-esteem? Admittedly it is more difficult at certain moments than others, and more difficult for certain people than for others, at all times. But terms such as "narcissistically" cathected self, and "narcissistically" cathected objects do not suffice to advance our understanding of the immense complexity of the narcissistic libido and its interrelation with object libido nor of why a patient like Sabine must make such colossal efforts to protect her intimate "self." Can we truly assume that narcissism follows a separate line of development from that of object love?

My esteemed colleagues, I thank you for having lent me your voices in order to help me elucidate my own perplexities; this has led me to put into question the heuristic value of this relatively new diagnostic category of "narcissistic personality disorder," whose most prominent exponent is Heinz Kohut (1971).

In spite of the richness and acuity of Kohut's clinical observations, his theoretical conceptions create perplexity. Are there two libidos — one for the self and another for the object? Although Freud constantly strove to maintain the distinction between object libido and ego libido, this distinction often became blurred in his writings. Moreover, from a conceptual point of view, Freud did not at any point envisage a double source of libidinal energy. The comments of Laplanche and Pontalis in *The Language of Psycho-Analysis* (1973) on this point are pertinent to our reflection. They demonstrate concisely that throughout Freud's writings the terms referring to either object or ego libido do not refer to the differential origin of libidinal energy, but to its differential placement: Freud clearly indicates two modes of *investment* and not two *sources* of libido.

Kohut's research creates a striking impression that the "self" is in some way cut off from its instinctual basis. My personal clinical experience points, on the contrary, to the immense importance of archaic instinctual and fusional conflict with the early objects as a powerful source of perturbation in the structure of the narcissistic self-image.

Certain of our conceptual difficulties no doubt arise from the fact that many different clinical pictures are subsumed under the category of "narcissistic disorder." Indubitably, an increasing number of today's analysands give more importance to suffering arising from disturbance in their narcissistic equilibrium than to neurotic suffering concerning object relations. This predominance of a phenomenological order leads us to wish that such patients might form a cohesive clinical entity. However, a perusal of the vast literature dealing with an infinite variety of psychic organizations with rich and varied symptomatology inevitably creates confusion in our attempts to conceptualize this clinical richness.

It is possible that the clinical confusion reflects an already existing theoretical one contained in the Freudian concept of narcissism. This concept, according to Freud (1914), no doubt suffers from its metaphors, drawn from the physiological and biological research of his time. This gives rise specifically to the notion of a source of energy capable of cathecting the ego as well as an object in the external world. To this energy is attributed the property of being able to pass from one to the other of these two poles in such fashion that as one is diminished, the other automatically will be increased. This apparently logical idea is less satisfactory from certain clinical standpoints. Freud, for example, presumes that the state of being in love causes a loss of narcissistic supply to the benefit of the loved object. But it might also be maintained that the fact of being in love may be felt by many as a narcissistic gain, and that loss of narcissistic value may ensue following the loss of a loved object. The case of Sandra, cited further on in this chapter, demonstrates this in striking fashion. In other cases the loss of the love object may even eventuate in such drastic diminution of narcissistic libido as to precipitate serious depressive or psychosomatic crises (see Chapter IX).

It is not my intention to explore here the complexity of narcissistic homeostasis in its relation to libidinal objects — whether these be internal or external ones, or the ego itself taken as a love object. My aim is more simply a wish to convey, through the medium of a few clinical vignettes, a clearer view of the complexities involved.

Let us come back for a moment to Sabine. Her past history reveals that while she was still very young she had to bear the sudden disappearance and finally the death of both parents. But unlike most children bereaved when very small, she had kept alive many vivid memories of her parents' appearance, words, foibles, and acts — memories which extended back to the age of fifteen months. Family reports confirm what I was able to deduce from her adult personality traits, namely that Sabine had become precociously independent of her parents, indeed of her whole entourage, from a surprisingly young age. Remembering certain exploits from the age of two and a half, she would say, "My parents hardly noticed what was going on, so deeply engrossed were they in their personal problems. Even then I felt I was quite different from them, and I did not depend on them to any great extent" — a disavowal certainly, but at the same time acknowledgment of her early attempts to deny her basic needs. There were already two younger siblings, and one is tempted to surmise that Sabine's early independence was partly constructed to contain intense feelings of narcissistic mortification or overwhelming anxiety (such as is also aroused in children with psychotic mothers, who in consequence become prematurely self-sufficient). In Sabine's case reality confirmed her illusion of autonomy. Her parents were killed when she was five, although she did not know this as a certainty until some three years later. She was told they were "traveling." She knew this to be untrue, but carefully hid her knowledge "in order not to upset the adults and the younger children." She believed herself to be uniquely responsible for the two little ones, but she had created a family romance—another important disavowal for her young narcissistic image—in which all three had the same mother, but she alone was the child of the father. She went so far as to tell this story to many schoolteachers and family friends as an indubitable truth.

The important element here, however, is not the extent to which Sabine's historical reality contributed to the construction of her system of psychic survival, but the way in which this system functioned, in particular her own representation of herself and others. This psychic structure might well be described as a practically unshakable series of narcissistic defenses, protective barriers such as I have found in many patients who suffered early object loss—though certainly not limited to these particular cases. Such analysands frequently display character organizations marked by poorly elaborated depressive or anxiety states, or strong psychosomatic potential. This system, which might be described as the illusion of self-sufficiency and of invulnerability, will frequently include ego ideals of a most varied kind, moving from the Christlike to the criminal.

"I create my own laws," explains Sabine, "but luckily I am usually in agreement with society on most important points." Among her many struggles with the constraints of external reality, the following is typical: "I'm not dissatisfied to be a woman, but I can never accept that I had no choice"—defiance in the face of reality which might have resulted in a homosexual object choice or in a delusional solution. One further protective device consisted in warding off sexual desires. "I shall never be a slave to my sexuality. If a man claims to be in love with me, and this does happen from time to time, I flee him like the pest. I can only enjoy sex with men who are not particularly concerned with sexual conquest. Each time I make love without premeditation it has been a great pleasure. But this could never be the basis of my relationship with a man. The idea of being tied up by sexual wishes is horrendous. . . . When I was adolescent and heard the others talking about sexual relations, I wondered how I was ever going to survive such an experience. I imagined that I might not even know who I was afterwards, or even that I might die. After my first sexual experience, I drew a great sigh of relief. 'Good heavens—I'm still here!'"

Such anxious fantasy has little in common with typical oedipal guilt; it is closer to a threat of a primitive kind in which disintegration fears are projected on the feeling of self, and in which feared punishment is not the loss of sexual rights and fulfillment, but the loss of subjective identity. Sexual identity and sexual wishes, instead of reinforcing the feeling of personal identity, threaten the self-image with dissolution. The hand of Another makes the mirror of Narcissus tremble; this Other may be allowed to remain, but on condition that he confine himself to the role of Echo.

The sexual reation is not the only one that threatens the self-image and the narcissistic equilibrium of this young patient. "I have such trouble with people... it is always difficult for me to master situations in which I meet others. I can't take in what people are telling me. I'm completely overwhelmed by my perception of everything that surrounds them — their mouths, their gestures, the colors they wear... their closeness. All of this is torture to me." While she is talking, Sabine wrings her hands and speaks in a small strangled voice. "And yet I so desperately try to understand, but the effort I make exhausts me. The proximity makes it impossible for me to listen." I asked: "As though you were afraid of being invaded by the others?" "Exactly! A fear of *becoming the other person*. In order to understand them I find myself in their place... because... well it's so difficult to explain... I make such an effort to show that I have truly understood but I get lost in the process. If only people would *write* to me, there would be no danger and I would understand everything they said. In their presence everything gets scattered. Even on the telephone it's difficult... I should make tape recordings to play back afterwards."

Everything Sabine describes gives the impression that she does not feel protected from psychic invasion, as though her "psychic skin" had huge holes in it through which others could penetrate and take possession of her. At the same time she has an urgent need for the threatening world of others. "I get worn out by listening to people for hours on end. All my life people have confided in me. The idea that they are suffering obliges me to make an incredible sacrifice because I cannot bear their misery — even when the things they recount do not interest me in the slightest." In other words, Sabine projects onto her vision of the "suffering others" the predicament of a small child who has neither been heeded nor understood.

She will move mountains to satisfy their demands; otherwise she is unable to bear the pain of identifying with their supposed (fantasied) frustration. Yet she cannot, will not, accept anything in return; instead she exhausts herself in the endless attempt to gratify an unrecognized part of herself, the ideal ego, the megalomanic child toward whom she is pitiless.

Her ego is thus constructed as a bulwark against this need, and gives rise to the compulsion to be a mirror for the others always ready to reflect the longed-for image, mother earth struggling to nourish her imaginary children. "As for myself, I reduce my needs to the merest limit; I rarely know when I am hungry; there are few material objects that hold any value for me . . . and I suppose you are right when you tell me that I derive satisfaction from feeling so different from others . . . they all are waiting for things, for words, for gifts of time, and attention. You say I am afraid of wanting anything from the world of those others. But what could they possibly bring me anyway? With their view of the world they could never see mine!" Later Sabine was nevertheless able to discover the importance of the "others"; she counted intensely on this "other world" to provide her with treasures of memory which she took back with her into her private kingdom. The following fragment of her discourse is rich with meaning:

"I never know at the moment that I am experiencing something, what I think or feel about it. . . a play, conversation, a mountain view, . . . It is only afterwards when I am alone that I can contemplate these precious things and find them for myself. Also I *have* to recover something, otherwise I feel ill with grief and solitude." At such moments Sabine would find herself totally cut off from the rest of humanity and suffused with feelings of depression and irreality. But her ways of recovering contact merit our attention. "After having seen an overwhelmingly beautiful landscape, a moving film, or had an enlightening conversation with a friend, I am able to live and relive those moments; *but I myself am no longer there* — I watch and listen." From being "contained" within the experience with the concomitant risk of being emptied out, Sabine has now become the container. She is no longer involved; she contemplates. The narcissistic hemorrhage has been stopped.

In order to better understand the survival system of patients like Sabine, let us consider those whose survival tactics appear to be in total opposition. For Sabine (and others like her) the only way to preserve her feeling of identity and to maintain narcissistic homeostasis is to flee into solitude "in order to recover her self"; she clung to herself and closed the door against others, against the terror of being swallowed up by them and losing her individuality and volition. Some equally fragile people flee instead to the world of others in order to cling to them, to create the illusion of being one with them, with the hope of achieving a more stable narcissistic image and economy. Such people invest soli-

tude with fantasies of dying, and avoid any autonomous activity for fear that it may separate them from
the Other, or others, who serve as mirrors to confirm
that they exist and have personal value. The object of
such a demand is often but not always a sexual object.
Here there is no fear of losing oneself in the Other; on
the contrary, this illusion of fusion is sought in the
same avid way that a baby drinks in its mother's visage
and voice with her milk. Once again oedipal conflict
and the problem of desire take second place — or at
very most find expression in an archaic register which
borrows from and hides behind genitality, to confirm
narcissistic integrity.

Long before Sandra came to Paris I had received a
series of letters from a colleague, friend of the family,
recounting her numerous psychological problems.
Nineteen years old, daughter of a powerful French
family, she had, from babyhood, been constantly in
the hands of pediatricians and psychiatrists for "psychosomatic problems." As a nursling she was only able
to sleep in her mother's arms; later she suffered severely
from anorexia. Until four years of age she was fed
almost exclusively by bottle, and it was many years
before she would eat meat. She appeared equally lacking in appetite with regard to learning, to the extent
that special schools were advocated because she was
considered unsuited for the schools attended by the
other members of the family. My colleague's reports
stated further that "Sandra never reads for pleasure
and still plays with her food like a child. She does
everything very slowly, chews on her hands, and even
while playing the guitar will stop from time to time to
chew her knuckles. She cannot sleep alone at night

without overwhelming terror; believes herself to be ugly and incapable of attracting boyfriends; has few girl friends." The violence of the quarrels between mother and daughter led the consulting psychiatrists and friends to advise separation from the family. It was thus that Sandra came to Paris for an undetermined period, during which she was to continue certain cultural pursuits in an unstructured setting, and was to live in a private guesthouse which accepted responsibility for several young girls of "good family."

Sandra herself telephoned for her first appointment. A tall, slender, very pretty girl, she nevertheless slunk along the walls as though trying not to be noticed. She was able to tell me later that she had to avoid drawing attention to her thin legs. It seemed to her that people commented on them all the time. "As everyone knows, the only feature that really counts for a girl is her legs. I am plain, skeletal, and sexless." Here Sandra revealed an illusion concerning her body image that had psychotic overtones. She went on to complain bitterly of her mother who criticized mercilessly her refusal to use make-up, to go to the hairdresser, denigrated her choice of clothes, incited her continuously to eat more, to sleep alone, to be less "nervous," and so on. This recital took up most of the hour. At the end she asked me in a somewhat defensive and hostile voice what *I* wanted from her. She added that she had come to see me solely to please her mother and her doctors. "But what your mother and the doctors want doesn't interest me. I would like to know what *you* want." "What I want?" she replied as though to say, "But who am I?"

I told her that if she wanted nothing, that was up to her. After a short silence Sandra said, "Well I never thought of it as something for me. Maybe I'd better see you again." At our second meeting a month later she told me with both pride and misgiving that she had a lover; she had announced this provocatively to her mother who had ordered her to take oral contraceptives without delay. "My boyfriend is so good-looking, and so unlike my family. The only problem is that he often keeps me waiting, and I can't stand it." Here for the first time Sandra proffered an authentic request for psychoanalytic understanding: "This problem with A is more than I can cope with alone — I am so terrified he's going to leave me. Every night I have nightmares; my roommate says she hears me crying out in my sleep." The state of "being in love" and the vicissitudes of transference love such as Freud described them from the standpoint of illusion, projection, and blind idealization, were perfectly illustrated in Sandra's overwhelming attachment to her friend A. It required nearly a year of analysis, four times a week, for Sandra to be able to reveal to me, or even admit to herself, that her lover, out of work, on the border of delinquency, took time off to see Sandra solely to make love and to ask for money; to this end Sandra would wait for hours in the local bistros or in his room. She also avoided all mention of her frigidity in their sexual relationship. Her whole discourse was centered on her immense joy, her amorous passion, and her extreme distress when A made her wait. Several friends warned her against this doubtful acquaintance; she brushed their words aside as indications of envy. Only in his arms was she free from her torturous doubts about her worth.

How may I describe the climate of this difficult

analysis? In the depths of her despair about A's failings, Sandra would rock back and forth on the couch,
moaning (much as she had done when she was a small
child and could not sleep "for fear of becoming blind").
She lost weight in an alarming way; talked endlessly
and incoherently about the tragedy of her thin legs;
dreamed that she was an animal without legs, attacked
by a snake, lost in a forest, pursued by wolves, torn
apart by tigers — nightmares that somehow failed to
contain the themes of castration, abandonment, and
sadistic terror in their manifest content. However, as
the months went by, Sandra was able to find connections between the dream themes and her devastating
relation with A, and could perceive the underlying relationship with her mother. With little interpretative
help, she discovered her fantasies of female castration
and of oedipal jealousy. These discoveries astonished
and delighted her, and no doubt helped her eventually
to question her passion for A. But she remained painfully dependent on her next love. B was not delinquent; he was a simple workman who did not ask her
for money. She lived with him for eighteen months.
During this period we were able to analyze her fantasies of her vagina as a devouring and dangerous
mouth; this led to the disappearance of her sexual anes-
thesia. She was plunged into crises of suicidal despair
most of the time, convinced that B planned to abandon
her. "When he leaves the house I stop living. He has
agreed to work less so that he can spend more time
with me, but it's not enough. My sex now belongs to
me; we make love all the time, but it is not enough. It's
as though I want him inside me all the time — inside my
body. Or perhaps I want to be in his — I cannot bear to

be physically separated from him. When I am alone I don't dare look in the mirror. My thin body, my skinny legs. How could B love me? He is my only mirror — and he isn't big enough!"

Not until the reign of lover C could Sandra admit B's alcoholic problem, nor the fact that outside their sexual passion they shared no cultural or other common interests. Of C she would say, "He is my drug and I cannot tolerate life without it. When he has to go away for a few days, I am in constant terror that he will never come back. When there is the slightest difference between what I expect from him and what he actually does, I no longer exist and want to kill myself. But I do manage to keep eating. I don't lose weight any more."

In other words, Sandra demanded a *perfect reply* to every wish that linked her to her lover; and these wishes were treated like urgent needs. If they were unfulfilled, she could only hope to die. Such a relationship is that of the babe in arms and, like the nursling, Sandra attempted to obtain magical control of her need-dispensing object. Every gratification confirmed her feeling of existence and of self-esteem. Each disappointment exposed her to narcissistic mortification and the threat of psychic death. "I only live for him, do everything he wants so that he will listen to my needs. Why does he always let me down? How can he not understand that when I am depressed...have a cold ...it is desperately important that he be there?"

Sandra began to see more clearly into the nature of her love relationships, but this knowledge was gained slowly and painfully. "The other day my girl friend criticized D. I was in such a rage I could have slapped her. I couldn't sleep for hours that night." Her living mirror: if a shadow fell upon it her whole image was threatened — the slightest defect in this glass, and her reflection was broken to pieces.

After six years of analysis, Sandra was able to live — and sleep — alone, without anguish, in her own small studio. She was no longer painfully thin; she no longer slunk along the sidewalk trying not to be seen. She had begun to study and even had gained entrance to the university. But her deep narcissistic demands continued, and intense narcissistic problems still remained to be analyzed. Her present man friend she described as "less handsome than all my other beaux, but much more intelligent; and we have so many things in common. I sometimes dream of having a child of my own, but I'm still too much of a child myself. X has many problems in his life at this moment. I haven't seen him for three days — and I had a horrible nightmare as a consequence. A monster was swimming after me to tear me to pieces. The night before I saw that film "Jaws" (in French, *Les dents de la mer* [teeth of the sea]). Of course the first thing he took was her leg. X cuts off my legs when he forgets to phone me...he's my shark and I'm so furious with him for it...I cannot bear the disappointment. There I go again carrying on like a child. The other day I was in the cinema and I saw a girl eating an ice cream. I felt I needed it more than she did, and I trembled with irritation and desire to get it for myself." I reminded her that she had described her need for her lover and of the image he gave her of herself as a state of starvation: reflection and nourishment were somehow superimposed.

"That's perfectly true — I never leave him in peace. Am I too greedy? When I was a teenager I used to vomit while waiting for the boys to come and take us to the cinema. With my lovers it's the same thing. I no longer vomit — but I want to eat them up, like ice cream. It is so painful to be so starved." After a short silence, *"But the shark — is myself!"*

This was in fact the first time that Sandra had been able to grasp that behind her constant search for an echoing reflection lay a primitive dimension to her sexual relations — the voracious love of the tiny infant who throws himself upon the maternal breast in order to assuage his thirst at the same time that he seeks to find in his mother's eyes the confirmation of his own existence. At the end of this session Sandra said, "But really I don't understand why I am like this. No one ever pursued me with such avidity. Where did I ever meet a living soul who was as greedy as myself? Of course — *my mother.* She wanted perfect children. She nourished herself with us. Her sharklike teeth are in us" (*les dents de la mère* [teeth of the mother]).[1] But from this time on, my young patient was able to recognize that it was with the Sandra-shark inside her that she now had to contend.

Rather than be exposed to such devouring love and such object dependence, as Sandra displayed, my self-sufficient patient, Sabine, protected herself by becoming anoretic in her relation to the world at large.

In the clinical excerpts presented here, I have left out all reference to homosexual and heterosexual oedipal material, as well as much *anal*[2] material, in

---

[1]Sandra's reference to the film *Jaws* in French led to this recognition.

[2]This dimension of the libidinal structure deserves special study in view of its privileged position with regard to the first exchanges that the infant understands — hence its importance in consolidating the feeling of personal identity and the developing representation of the self in relation to the external world, and its implication for Winnicott's concept of transitional phenomena.

order to concentrate on the purely narcissistic aspects. I have also excluded any discussion of the "neurotic fringe" which, though not too thick, was nevertheless important in both patients: Sabine's obsessional phobia concerning touching and being touched that found an echo in her style of narcissistic defense, and Sandra's hysterical preoccupation with her masculine mirror objects which concealed important homosexual implications.

These two narcissistic organizations, which appear from a phenomenological point of view to be in complete opposition, are nevertheless concerned with a basic proposition I wish to discuss.[3]

A further point relates to the cross-currents of "sex" and "self." Sandra's narcissistic object was at the same time a sexual one — but such is not necessarily the case. Sabine's protective narcissistic isolation was not an autoerotic solution, but it could well be so in people with a similar kind of defensive structure.

The mirror object, such as Sandra's, is not necessarily a *love* object; it just as frequently appears as an object of hatred, and the necessity to cling to it reveals itself to be equally compulsive — to the extent that there is little doubt that we are observing the vital role of a *narcissistic* object. Each meeting with such an object brings to the subject the feeling that he is "alive" and "real." In the preceding chapter, centering on the role of countertransference with patients involved in this kind of narcissistic quest, the case was cited of a woman who tended to create continuing and passion-

---

[3]In fact, it is not difficult to find in our analytic practice patients who present a mixture of both the narcissistic defense and narcissistic relationships, but both forms are more easily studied through extreme examples.

ate drama with those who were close to her; these scenes were the reflection of an inner drama which she could neither contain affectively, nor think about to any marked degree. But the very fact of being able to recreate its content with objects of her external world brought her a feeling of being alive and the reassurance that those important to her life truly existed (that they had not been damaged or destroyed by her hatred and her immense demands). Unconscious dramas of this kind take a heavy toll on the psychic economy. In the long run, they contribute to the narcissistic hemorrhage, leaving in its wake feelings of emptiness, of confusion about the role of others in one's life, of not knowing how to live or what life is about.

For certain people the whole world, without distinction, may be the potential narcissistic mirror. "A bad-tempered taxi driver, an insolent salesgirl, a difficult colleague, and so on all have the power to ruin my whole day. I cannot get the thought of the incident out of my mind, and am filled with rage for hours on end," complained one patient whose image of himself was exposed to continual and extreme oscillations. Thus his feeling of self-esteem was threatened by any passerby who was capable of reflecting back to him the image of an unloved being. He was constantly on the watch for signs in the external world that might *repair* a feeling of inner narcissistic damage, but once found, these were immediately lost again, and only the constant externalization of his self-hatred, followed by days of rage and mortification, could ward off feelings of intense depression.

For others like Sabine, who cling to their own being and to a carefully preserved solitude in order to strengthen a fragile feeling of identity, this may take the form of an autoerotic recovery of self-feeling. A man who had come to analysis for acute anxiety states and depersonalization phenomena, which arose whenever he encountered work impediments or was obliged to spend more than a few minutes in a crowd, recounted a typical incident: "Everything went wrong all day at work, my boss, my colleagues, the work itself...out in the street I felt as though the crowd were invading me; they wished me no harm, but I felt as though my body was becoming vague and dissolving away...I was drowning, exactly as I had been all day at work...but it was now dangerous. I had to get protection urgently...something around me which would isolate me from others and put a stop to this feeling of dissolving. It is difficult to communicate this terror." Subsequently the patient dived into a taxi with a single thought in mind — that he must go home immediately and masturbate. "I rolled myself into a ball, nude, at the bottom of my bed under the blankets. At the moment of ejaculation it was as though I had come out of a dense fog. I found myself again." Much later this same patient found the courage to discuss in his session the fact that he would on occasion swallow his sperm after such incidents of dramatic "recovery" of his sense of self. Behind his fantasies of imagining in his onanistic activity that he was both man and woman, we can detect the more primitive fantasy of being both mother and child, of taking himself into maternal arms and of nourishing himself with his own substance in order to feel narcissistically whole. Although all masturbation fantasies may be held to contain and to enact a narcissistic and hermaphroditic illusion (see Chapter IV) we see here a particularly striking picture of an adult version of the ruminating babies who have had to create premature defense mechanisms when faced with a psychically irrepresentable danger in the earliest relationship (see Chapter XI).

I do not propose to explore fully the various paths of research which abound in the field of narcissism; I wish only to indicate two such directions before concluding with some comments on specific aspects of the analytic situation when dealing with the psychic structure's narcissistic economy.

The first theoretical perspective concerns the nature of the psychic functioning in analysands whose self-representation is highly unstable and whose narcissistic economy is unusually fragile. Such observation can only be made within the analytic situation. It is evident that such analysands are faced with an *inability to represent psychically and render significant situations involving the absence of an object or the recognition of a lack in themselves.* Either the self-image becomes vague, or the image of the Other fades. This blank where there should be a mental representation[4] can be widespread and yet pass unnoticed for a considerable time in the course of an analysis. A woman patient who experienced an intense need of the presence of her women friends as well as of her lovers in order to assure herself that she was truly alive and appreciated, never questioned this urgent demand on her entourage. I once drew attention to her unusual way of referring to

[4]This can also be expressed in terms of fragile inner objects, which are attacked or destroyed; as a basic fault in the process of introjection and identification; as a symbolic lack in the structure of signifiers, etc.

friends and love objects, and to her inability to stand solitude: "But the people and things which prove to me that life continues and that I too am still alive are all *placed around me — they are not inside me!* If my friends or my lover are not physically present it is as though they no longer exist. An inexplicable pain... alone I am surrounded by a void and I have to take care that this does not empty me out completely... when it is particularly bad I manage to keep hold of people in an abstract way. I wander round my studio for hours *repeating their names.* That takes the place of their faces and helps me to bear the emptiness." The difficulty of course resides in the fact that the name without its corresponding inner object representation loses its vitality and psychic function. This leaves the person with a feeling of deadness, of being out of communication with the world.

This same dilemma was expressed by another patient in the context of the transference relationship. He expressed violent anger before each weekend break, and said: "You must understand that I need you constantly there beside me; otherwise I am incapable of bearing this anguish. I cannot even imagine that in two days' time I can continue to talk to you. I am forced to double my dose of sleeping tablets." It was as though he could keep no inner image of the analyst without her physical presence. Thus there was no continuing relationship, no inner dialogue which might have permitted further elaboration. "But no one can imagine someone who isn't actually present," replied this patient. "You are talking arrant nonsense. How could I possibly carry an idea of you inside me? You aren't there, so it's pointless to think about it."

This inner void calls to mind Winnicott's work on the creation of potential "space," and on the capacity or incapacity of the small child to be alone *in the presence of the mother*, that is, make use of an inner representation of her in order to play without having to keep going to her. It is possible that the patients I am describing here have never truly acquired the "capacity to be alone" in this sense. This leads to a consideration of the concept of *transitional objects and transitional phenomena.* It is tempting to surmise that as children, these patients never created a transitional object capable of fulfilling its function and permitting gradual internalization of the object so that its absence could eventually be tolerated without catastrophic loss. It might be said that Sandra's lovers held the role of a transitional object in her psychic economy, rather like the "security blanket" of the small child which represents the mother and at the same time the child's own discovery and creation. When a person is used in the place of a transitional object, he is perceived in projective fashion which may have little to do with his actual reality. Sandra's love objects, at least in the early years of her analysis, were indeed her "creation," her security blanket which permitted her to dream and to sleep peacefully. Sabine, on the other hand, could only think clearly and sleep well when she was alone; in a sense she was her own transitional object. The most condensed image of this particular solution to early psychic trauma is that furnished by the patient who made love to himself while rolled up in a ball, and who afterward fed himself with his own secretion. We see here a short-circuiting of all transitional phenomena, a breast-penis fantasy in which the patient attempted to be both nursling and feeding mother in an autoerotic act, but lacked the inner psychic capital necessary to allow him to survive without danger in the world of human relations.

Going further back in ontogenetic development, this predicament seems linked to certain observations in the field of psychosomatic research, particularly those of Fain (1971) on the dawning of psychic life and its relation to the psychosomatic maladies of infants such as merycism and grave insomnia. Many years of observational research on these babies and their mothers seem to point to the existence of disturbed object relations from the beginning of life. As a consequence, in place of what would normally be the beginning of an inner object representation, there is a *psychic blank.* For example, Sabine, mental merycist, nourishing herself with her own psychic content rather than risking dangerous relations with others, resembled these tragic infants. When listening to others or enjoying a new experience, she was invaded by a confusion of perceptual impressions of shapes, sounds, and colors, as though she had not internalized the mother's function as a sheltering screen to protect her baby from overwhelming impingement from internal or external stimuli. The same is true of Sandra, infant insomniac, who in adulthood was still unable to sleep without a mother substitute. It is noteworthy, however, that *these patients did not show any marked psychosomatic disorganization.* Although it cannot be asserted that these analysands are protected from such an eventuality, I think it probable that *the creation of narcissistic defenses or of narcissistic object relations serves as a protection against psychosomatic explosion.* It is permissible to suppose that Sandra was able to evade the deathlike aspects of her relationship to a "tranquilizing" mother[5] by becoming gravely anoretic. This rudimentary form of defense bears witness to the existence of larval fantasies of a dangerous internal representation that must be kept at a distance through the refusal of food, taken as a symbolic equivalent of the invasive mother. The anoretic barrier is notably lacking in certain patients (in particular analysands with a history of gastric ulcer) who reconstruct in analysis an early maternal relationship of this kind. One is tempted to ask whether the psychic functioning of the future ulcer patient would have allowed him to become anoretic, as though there were a lack of narcissistic defense.

The psychoanalytic adventure with patients whose suffering and conflict are largely expressed in terms of their fragile narcissistic libidinal investments is bound to be reflected in the transference relationship. This is invariably an archaic expression of the kind denoted by Stone (1961) as "basic" or "fundamental"[6] with certain fusional aspects to it. There are not two people but one in the analyst's consulting room: either the analyst is felt to be a narcissistic extension of the analysand, or the analysand feels that he is a mere extension of his analyst! In the first eventuality, anxiety aroused by the threat of separation is entirely disavowed and wiped from consciousness. Outside of the analytic session, the analyst is eclipsed in the psychic world of the analy-

---

[5]The question of the "tranquilizing mother" will be taken up in the next chapter.

[6]It is of course true that all analyses tend to pass through stages of such narcissistic fusion and confusion, but the transference is not totally dominated by the obliteration of one of the partners to the analytic relation.

sand. His nonexistence as a psychic object is frequently accompanied by the conviction that the patient is an equally nonexistent psychic object for the analyst. One patient who frequently missed a session never thought to make the slightest mention of the fact: she believed that I would scarcely notice her absence. It was only in her fourth year of analysis that she felt compelled to phone me and say she was going to be absent. "I'm beginning to believe that when I am not present I nevertheless continue to exist for other people," she said, "and so you too are beginning to exist for me."

For my patient Sabine, separation from me was equivalent to my death. Incapable of experiencing and elaborating anxiety around events such as holiday breaks led her to leave one or two sessions in advance of my vacations. "Since we're going to stop, I'm no longer here in my thoughts. I've already left." Like the child with the spool, she had constituted herself as the agent of the break and not the victim of it. During the long summer vacation she was totally convinced that I must be dead, and made elaborate plans for continuing her analysis alone. The effect of finding me on her return was somewhat traumatic, and she found herself unable to utter a word. We were able to understand that she was much more at ease with a dead than a living image of me. The unavoidable evidence that we were two separate people had the effect of reawakening the recognition of her dependency, felt not only as a painful wound, but as a threat to her carefully protected feeling of narcissistic integrity.

When, on the contrary, the analysand feels himself to be a mere segment of the analyst, every separation conjures up fears of loss and death. Sandra, who clung as tightly to her transference image as she did to her mirror objects, constantly feared that I would disappear because she was "fated to lose all that was valuable to her," and she expressed feelings of pain at the injustice of such an abandonment.

It is evident that in spite of the diametrically different form of transference, the basic fantasy is the same: in a relation between two people, there is only place for one; the other must die.

The transference with such fragile patients cannot fail to evoke countertransference reactions different from those aroused by patients with a more solid sense of self. There is also the paradoxical fact that these analysands whom I describe as "fragile" have nevertheless created unusually strong and effective defenses. These forms of psychic conservation might be thought of as techniques of survival by the creation of a fortress against mortal danger. It is possible that this danger, rooted in the presymbolic period of psychic life, corresponds to what Bion has described as "nameless dread"; the baby whose mother is incapable of containing her infant's anguish and rage, and eventually rendering it both tolerable and meaningful, runs the risk of *introjecting an object felt to be hostile to his wish to live.*

It is clear that bastions built against such terror are not constructed to give way readily. In addition, such defense work deserves our respect in view of the essential role it plays in the maintenance of the personality structure and its psychic economy. The risk that analysis may attack such protective bastions, exposing the analysand to psychotic danger, is nevertheless slight. There is a greater risk that the analytic experience will prove fruitless in uncovering the dangers of the archaic sexual universe and terror of psychic death that underlie such perturbed narcissistic states. Certain patients leave analysis with the continuing impression of inner deadness and the conviction that they then lack the secret of living. Perhaps the most important threat they will have to overcome is contained in the fact of *aging* — with its potentiality for depleting man's narcissistic reserves.

The analyses of patients who attempt to repair their fleeting feeling of personal identity in the ways described in this chapter are clearly fraught with problems of a technical order. How can one communicate with Narcissus, who only hears with his eyes, in his attempt to obliterate either his own image or that of his analayst. The analyst who accepts this challenge must be prepared to leave his classical silence interspersed with judicious interpretation intended to further the analytic process to put the patient in better contact with himself, to enable him to listen to his instinctual desires and to become acquainted with his feelings of love and hate. But how can we expect Narcissus, who is fighting a constant battle against nonexistence and the feeling that he is under threat of death, to listen to the messages coming from his own unconscious?

The analyst in these circumstances will serve no purpose if he allows himself to be reduced to the role of Echo, as sometimes happens. He must invent some other mode of intervention, forcing himself to speak when he would rather keep silent, or to remain silent when tempted to give vent to countertransference reactions. Whatever course he chooses, he is bound to make mistakes, and these will be less lightly pardoned by these patients than by an analysand who has created a "normal-neurotic" transference. The analyst must be prepared to assume the nonexistence so feared by his patient, while identifying with the other's need to fend the analyst off as dangerous and intrusive. He must recognize that this defensive wall hides a contrary demand, namely that the analyst become him and live for him. The situation is further complicated by the fact that many such patients consider the obligation to *speak* in order to communicate their distress as an additional narcissistic affront. During the relatively long periods before the analysand is able to feel more solidly entrenched in his own identity and sense of worth, the analyst is called upon to fulfill the function described by Winnicott as "holding the situation in time and space." In terms of the analytic situation, this implies holding and containing the different elements of thought and feeling that the analysand displays until such time as he is able to experience them in the transference.

If for some of these patients the analyst is feared as a destructive and death-bearing object, for others he is endowed with the magic power of knowing the secret of life, a secret that has been denied to the analysand and which he has a right to possess. This "secret" often refers to the person's inability to conceptualize his own place and value for his parents.

Those who seek to nourish themselves with the analyst's substance as well as those who flee him like the pest tend to induce subtle forms of acting out in the analyst. He may become complaisantly silent or again respond readily to questions and demands for a confirming echo when the patient's anxiety is at its height.

A further pitfall has to do with the analyst's own Narcissus.

It sometimes happens that while listening to certain of my patients I am reminded of a distant memory, of a little boy of seven called Patrick. Third child in a family of five, Patrick was brought to therapy because he was always stealing the toys, money, and candies of other members of the family. One day the mother insisted on recounting Patrick's latest misdeed: when no one was looking, Patrick had stolen into the kitchen and eaten the Sunday cake intended for the whole family. I asked Patrick when we were alone what he thought about this incident, and he replied: "Well it's like this—food is more important to me than the others." This verdict was pronounced in a tone of serious certitude. Perhaps a glimpse of what Kohut has so tellingly called "the grandiose self"? When our adult patients allow us a glimpse of the small voracious and intransigent Narcissus within themselves, when they ask to be protected, repaired, and compensated for the real and imaginary blows fate has dealt them, when they ask to be spared the inevitable pain of universal human realities, I sometimes say to myself: "But who does not want all this? Why does this one think. . .that food is more necessary to him than to others?" Any attempt to analyze this kind of analytic material must be carefully filtered by close examination of our own transference attitudes to our patients' narcissistic pain; otherwise our interventions run the risk of being over- or underindulgent, or even hostile and moralizing. There are certain psychic hungers that are capable of killing the human spirit—and the analysand is usually right!

The fact that we may understand the psychic functioning of these patients, follow the logic of their quest, and be able to identify with their suffering does not necessarily mean that we are going to make this discourse and our understanding of it apt for analysis. Each time I find myself working with an analysand who presents such a problem, I am well aware of the fact that I might find myself faced with an impenetrable fortress.

If, on the contrary, the patient allows us to enter his stronghold, if he can gain sufficient confidence in us to reveal the uneasy linking of the life and death forces within him, and if we are then able to recognize the violence of these same forces within ourselves, this analytic voyage taken together has a chance of permitting both participants to come through it enriched — the patient with a new dimension of his sense of self, and the analyst with the discovery that those who expect most of him are often those who also teach him the most.

Chapter IX

The Psychosoma
and the Psychoanalytic Process

The difficulties of being human oblige us to create an infinity of psychic structures to bind or in some way cope with the inevitable physical and mental pain we are going to encounter. We have to start doing this shortly after birth and are only able to do it because of a unique phylogenetic heritage: the capacity for symbolic functioning. Most of our psychic pain is occasioned on the path to acquiring individual status and personal identity followed by the acquisition of our sexual identity. Freud was the first to emphasize the essentially traumatic nature of human sexuality, while Klein and her disciples have thrown light on the earlier traumas inherent in the process of separating one's image from that of the primordial Other in order to become a person. We must find answers early on to the conflicting claims of instinctual life and reality demands these processes bring in their wake, and for the rest of our lives much of our psychic energy will be directed toward maintaining the solutions we have found. Some of these solutions make life a creative adventure; others are maintained at the expense of psychic, and eventually somatic, well-being.

Anthropologists such as Lévi-Strauss postulate that sexual laws of some kind are inherent in any social structure in that they are the minimal requirement for distinguishing a social group from a herd, such as may be found in brute nature. In psychoanalytic theory, insight into the complexities of social and sexual integration is attained through the concept of the Oedipus complex, of castration anxiety, and of the symbolic structures to which they refer. These relatively sophisticated structures are intricately bound up with language and indeed could not exist without it. Beyond them lies the darker, infraverbal and pregenital area, less weighted semantically (leading Freud to designate this the *prehistoric* part of the individual's psychic story). In this early phase, psyche and soma might appear to coincide, although the extensive charting of these laboriously mapped areas of the mind (the principal cartographers after Klein being Winnicott and Bion) tend to show that the psyche grows out of the soma almost from birth. To attain the primitive psychosomatic level of existence is rather like trying to recreate the experience of original awareness, as mystics do. Any research into psychosomatic pathology must struggle with the unknowns of this early phase of psychic functioning. The psychic material that enters into the primordial fusion of mother and nursling is composed of smells, sounds, and visual and tactile sensations. These are in themselves despatializing factors, and this no doubt favors the setting in motion of one of the earliest of psychic mechanisms, subsumed under the concept of *projective identification*. These mechanisms will dominate until such time as language spatializes and limits the psychic structure, thus delimiting the inner and the outer world, while at the same time the infant begins to inhabit his *soma*. He becomes embodied. Little Oedipus comes to terms relatively late with the problems caused by the difference between the sexes, the narcissistic mortification of the primal scene, and the relinquishment of his erotic and aggressive incestuous wishes. We are concerned here with the much smaller Narcissus who must come to terms with the definitive loss of the magical breast-mother and with the ineluctable demand to create psychic objects that will compensate for his loss. His capacity to create the symbolic structures necessary for this achievement will be circumscribed in large part by the limits of his parents' unconscious fears and desires. The mythical moment in which the fusional identity with the mother is relinquished requires a mother who herself is prepared to accept the loss of the magical union. This loss might be considered as the primordial castration in an individual's life. Many parents, through intense narcissistic identification with their young, tend to spare them the inevitable confrontation with reality beyond the point demanded by their immaturity. The anxieties to which this primal separation give rise are usually qualified by terms such as annihilation and disintegration, and in turn might be conceived of as the prototype of castration anxiety proper. Once again it is a global menace. Frustration, anxiety, and conflict have not yet become symbolically attached to the sexual organs.

The inherent difficulty facing the infant in his task

of becoming an individual is of a more global, more "psychosomatic" nature than the problems encountered in coming to terms with sexual realities. Failure to sort oneself out from the "not-me" environment and so to create a sense of personal identity produces more catastrophic results than does a similar failure in the acquisition of sexual identity and the rights that belong with it. Yet such catastrophic failure does not necessarily result in a startling psychosis. It may go unnoticed while its insidious effects continue, silently, like the Freudian death instinct. When this occurs, body and mind have somehow lost their connecting links.

In the earliest attempt to deal with physical pain, frustration, and absence psychically, we have the first "mysterious leap" from body to mind. We know very little about it. Considerably more knowledge has been garnered by psychoanalysis about that still more mysterious leap in the other direction, the leap from mind to body which underlies hysterical conversion and the various inhibitions of bodily functioning. Long before such complicated psychic creations are absorbed, the baby must first have been seduced to life by his mother, for herein lies the initial movement that stirs the first glimmerings of psychic life. This much we know: the structuring of the psyche is a creative process destined to give each individual his unique identity. It provides a bulwark against psychic loss in traumatic circumstances and, in the long run, *in man's psychic creativity may well lie an essential element of protection against his biological destruction.*

This brings me to the first point of this chapter: the importance of man's innate capacity for symbolic activity and psychic creation, in particular, the *hetero-geneous character* of these creations. In the attempt to maintain some form of psychic equilibrium under all circumstances, every human being is capable of creating a neurosis, a psychosis, a pathological charac-ter pattern, a sexual perversion, a work of art, a dream, or a psychosomatic malady. In spite of our hu-man tendency to maintain a relatively stable psychic economy and thus guarantee a more or less enduring personality pattern, we are liable to produce any or all of these diverse creations at different periods in our lives. Although the results of our psychic productions do not have the same psychological, nor indeed the same social value, they all have something in common in that they are the product of man's mind and their form is determined by the way his psyche has been structured. They all have inherent meaning in relation to his wish to live and to get along as best he can with what life has dealt out to him. From this point of view it is evident that the *psychosomatic creations* appear the most mysterious since they are the least appropriate to the over-all desire to live. If their psychological function is conspicuous by its absence, their biological meaning also eludes us. In many respects they are the antithesis of neurotic or psychotic manifestations. In-deed it is frequently when the latter cease to function that psychosomatic (as opposed to psychological) illness declares itself. My reflections on this particular phe-nomenon have been much enriched by the extensive re-search into psychosomatic illness carried out by my col-leagues in the Paris Psychoanalytical Society. I refer in particular to the works of Marty, Fain, David and de M'Uzan. My personal interest in psychosomatic symptoms and their relation to symbolic processes has come from a different direction, which I hope will become clear.

My second point is that man's irrepressible psychic fertility of whatever order is coexistent with life itself. If we admit that something like *psychic death* may occur, then it is possible that when psychic creation falters or comes to a halt man may be threatened with biological death. The psychic processes that create and maintain psychic health *as well as those responsible for maintaining psychic ill-health* are nevertheless on the side of life. When we, for any reason, fail to create some form of mental management to deal with psychic pain, psychosomatic processes may take over.

This brings me to my final point. The psychoanalytic process is itself a creative one in that it re-establishes separated links and also forges new ones. Like our psychological creations, these links too are of a heterogeneous nature: liaisons between past and present, conscious, preconscious, and unconscious, affect and representation, thought and action, primary and secondary processes, body and mind. I would suggest *that psychoanalytic processes are the antithesis of psychosomatic processes.* Psychosomatic transformations pose special problems in the course of an analysis, and it may be that they demand a different approach from that required to understand the neurotic parts of the personality. I do not wish to suggest that there are special "techniques" for dealing with man's different psychic manifestations, but simply that further insight into the processes at work may alter our way of listening to our patients. Itten, in his remarkable book on color and painting (1961), writes of artists in words that might apply equally to the intuitively creative aspects of the analyst's task: "Doctrines and theories are best for weaker moments. In moments of strength problems are solved intuitively, as if of themselves." So is it with analytic work. Itten goes on to say, "If you, unknowing, are able to create masterpieces in color, then un-knowledge is your way. But if you are unable to create masterpieces out of your un-knowledge, then you ought to look for knowledge."

The rest of this chapter will be concerned with background material, theoretical and clinical, to elucidate the above points. My hope is to contribute to our knowledge of the silent messages of the body and to stimulate reflection on our intuitive understanding of the psychosoma, so that we may come to know better what we have done, unknowing.

Psychosomatic man

Research into the meaning and treatment of psychosomatic illness is at the crossroads of various scientific disciplines. Although I shall give a bird's-eye view of the psychosoma and the use of the term *psychosomatic*, I can describe only that picture which may be obtained through the psychoanalytic microscope. This instrument is a highly specific one, concerned with psychical and symbolic functioning rather than somatic transformations; in addition, the latter are objects of study for which it was not originally conceived. Furthermore, from a research point of view, psychoanalytic case sampling can scarcely be called unselected. In the first place, people suffering from disorders of psychosomatic origin seek a physician rather than an analyst for their somatic ills — unless of course they consider they have psychological problems as well. Sometimes, however, patients who are unaware of suffering from psychological symptoms do turn up in the analyst's consulting room, complaining, for example, of gastric symptoms or cardiopathology, because a psychoanalytic or psychiatric consultation has been suggested by the physician. In these cases opinion among analysts would be sharply divided as to whether such a request should be met with an offer of psychoanalytic help. Some would consider full-scale analysis to be the best available treatment if allied to appropriate medical care. Others would advocate a modified form of analytic psychotherapy. Others again would consider the project to be fraught with danger and would regard the presenting symptoms, if unaccompanied by any neurotic manifestations, as a counterindication for analysis.

The fact of the matter is that the analyst is rarely given the choice. Not only will he find himself constantly confronted with psychosomatic behavior of a general kind in all his analysands, he will also discover that a considerable number of his patients, whether he wishes it or not, suffer from authentic psychosomatic disorders. These may range from allergic skin disorders, bronchial asthma, hyperthermic states, and hypertension to peptic ulcers and ulcerative colitis. This frequency is in no way due to a preponderance of psychosomatic pathology among psychoanalytic patients. Psychosomatic manifestations affect analysts as well, and indeed must be regarded as a common phenomenon in the population at large. If we include in our considerations the psychosomatic aspect of increased sensitivity to infectious diseases and the psychological problems of the accident-prone, we shall be obliged to recognize that most of our patients, as well as our friends and colleagues, suffer at one time or another from psychosomatic manifestations. In my own analytic practice, although no patient has ever come to me specifically for his psychosomatic troubles, I have had, over the years, twelve analysands who at some time in their adult lives had contracted plumonary tuberculosis, in circumstances which left little doubt as to the important part played by psychological factors. I have had many patients with gastric dysfunctions of varying severity, including two with a serious history of peptic ulcers. Bronchial asthma has been the lot of several others, and I have had the usual run of patients suffering chronically or intermittently from urticaria, hay fever, eczema, and the like. The psychological problems raised by the somatic symptoms of these patients have given me much food for thought, particularly when I felt I had uncovered certain features in common among them. The analyst cannot but feel that psychosomatic man is a challenge to his understanding of the psychological determinants of physiological symptoms.

In addition to the ubiquitous nature of psychosomatic disorders, it should be added that they are often resistant to cure, whether approached from the physiological or the psychological direction. Yet, psychosomatic patients suffering from grave symptoms *do* get better, and frequently as a result of psychoanalytic help when all else has failed. Let us add in passing the common clinical observation that people who have had several years of analysis find their susceptibility to colds, influenza, headaches, stomach aches and such like, dramatically reduced as the analytic work progresses. Why this should be so, and whether it is our treatment that cures them, is another matter!

Psyche and soma in psychoanalytic theory

The uses and abuses of man's body by his mind are so varied and so extensive that it is well to define what we mean by the term "psychosomatic," and to delineate in particular the distinction between psychosomatic disorders and hysterical or other somatic manifestations. We might recall that Freud designated two types of somatization: *conversion hysteria* and *actual neurosis*. In a sense one was the antithesis of the other. Whereas in hysterical conversion we witness the "mysterious leap" from mind to body, in the concept of the actual neuroses there is a leap in the opposite direction, from the somatic to the psychic sphere. In either case an invisible barrier is crossed. The problems raised by this transition have, to this day, lost little of their mystery.

Although "actual neurosis" as a nosographic entity is little used nowadays, it is pertinent to our inquiry to note, as Laplanche and Pontalis (1973) have pointed out, that in Freud's conception the "actual" symptoms (neurasthenia and anxiety neurosis) were principally somatic ones. Being of a physiological order, they were considered by Freud to be devoid of symbolic meaning and therefore not truly within the scope of psychoanalytic treatment. Freud's belief that the actual neuroses are brought about as a reaction to actual everyday tension, and in particular to the blockage of libidinal satisfactions, is closely related to certain modern conceptions of psychosomatic reactions, though today the notion of psychic "pressure" would lay equal emphasis on the blockage of aggressive impulses and on all that might be subsumed under the term of environmental stress. Freud considered that conversion hysteria and actual neurosis both arose from sexual sources, but whereas the latter was related to present-day sexual problems, the former stemmed from the sexual conflicts of early childhood, and the physical symptoms retained their symbolic significance, i.e., they appeared in the place of instinctual satisfaction and were in essence a symbolic solution to an unconscious conflict and not a reaction to frustration. It is evident that the "somatic" symptoms of conversion hysteria are symbolic in that they refer to a *fantastic* body in the literal sense of the word, a body functioning as a small child might imagine, or a fantasy body such as might be contrived by primary-process thinking.

After the construction of his topographical model, Freud also came to consider hysterical conversion and hysterical identification as *ego defenses.* In this way were added to the well-known list of hysterical symptoms those that use the body to translate inhibitions of id impulses as a reaction to the repressive forces of ego and superego. Thus inhibitions of bodily functioning such as constipation, impotence, frigidity, psychogenic sterility, anorexia, insomnia, and so on have come to be considered as closely allied to classical conversion symptoms. In every case *the symptom tells a story.* Once decoded, the story always reveals the hero to be a guilty victim of forbidden wishes who has met setbacks on the pathways of desire. His symptoms might be said to result from the combined effects of his unconscious fantasy life and the structure of his ego defenses. These symptoms, of indubitable psychogenic origin, do not form part of what is denoted by the term *psychosomatic*. We might say that in hysteria the body lends itself and its functions to the mind to use as the mind wills, whereas in psychosomatic illness the body does its own "thinking." The drama being expressed is a more archaic one, and its elements have been stored differently. The symptoms are signs, not symbols, and follow somatic and not psychic laws. Unlike the hysterical dramatizations, the thinking of the soma is carried out with, sometimes literally, deadly precision. The recurring character of science fiction, the mechanized robot who takes over, without a shred of emotion or identification with human wishes and conflicts, is a pristine image of the workings of the psychosomatic symptom. The soma is no longer concerned to translate the wishes of the psyche as in neurotic illness. If we attempt to define the area covered in today's terminology by the word *psychosomatic* we might say that this term is reserved for organic disorders of demonstrable physiological dysfunction. Although they have no apparent symbolic significance, they appear nevertheless to be linked with the patient's personality structure, life circumstances, and history, i.e., they declare themselves in connection with situations of stress arising either from within the individual or from his immediate environment. The psychosomatic sufferer, however, is rarely aware of any such connections and is frequently *unaware* of being under any particular stress. This definition, though extremely vague, serves to distinguish such disorders from hysterical manifestations in which there is neither physiological lesion nor infection, and also from organic illness in which no links with the personality or to environmental stress are apparent.

At this point we come back to the fact that the mental and the physical are indissolubly linked, yet essentially different. The psychosoma functions as an entity. There is little doubt that every psychological event has its effect on the physiological body just as every somatic event has repercussions on the mind, even if these are not consciously registered. Industrial research has produced convincing statistics to demonstrate that people are more apt to fall ill, need operations, or have accidents when they are feeling depressed or anxious than when they feel fulfilled or optimistic about their lives. Indeed one does not have to be a psychoanalyst to recognize that there is a *relationship of contiguity* between the psychological and the biological events in any given individual's life. This type of intuitive knowledge is within the scope of the porter's wife or somebody's grandmother. "No wonder he had that car accident after all the trouble they've had with the family," and "Naturally she came down with the Hong Kong flu straightaway after the accident," are typical comments from my concierge on the trials of his neighbors.

Freud's position with respect to the psychosoma should be recalled. He grounded the psychoanalytic theory of mind on firm biological territory and constantly emphasized the tendency of the organism to function as a whole. Nevertheless, he chose to concern himself solely with the psychological aspects of the psychosoma and showed a distinct disinclination to cross the frontier between the psychological and the physiological, even in areas where he recognized organic illness as being of psychosomatic origin. At the same time, he was constantly preoccupied with the relations between body and mind and the fact that psychic processes grow out of organic ones. His theory of the instincts and of libidinal development, and the importance he accorded to erogenous zones all witness to this interest. With the expansion of psychoanalytic knowledge and the ever-increasing accumulation of clinical experience and research it was inevitable that analysts would concern themselves with psychosomatic symptoms arising in their analysands and would try to decode their meaning. It was also inevitable that they would at first try to reconstruct the underlying fantasy formations the somatic symptoms might be thought to symbolize, following the well-known pattern of the hysterias. But this did not turn out to be easy. Freud had already made the discovery that such symptoms, unlike hysterical symptoms, yielded no answers under hypnosis. As time went on, other analysts were to discover that with psychosomatic patients presenting few neurotic symptoms, the analytic process did not by any means reveal the clear oedipal and preoedipal structures, with their contingent of fantasy, sexual symbolism, and object relation patterns, which were the fruit of analytic work with patients suffering from hysterical and obsessional neuroses and from sexual perversions. In fact, many of the patients whose reactions to anxiety were almost exclusively psychosomatic, revealed themselves to be refractory to analytical therapy. Others plunged into the analytic adventure wholeheartedly, analyzed many of their neurotic symptoms, and terminated analysis with their psycho-somatic disorders intact. Others again found their symptoms modified, or even lost them completely. The theoretical reasons adduced to explain the effects of psychoanalysis on psychosomatic symptoms did not meet any great measure of agreement among analysts.

We are, today, far from the epic period of Dunbar, Margolin, Alexander and other pioneers in this field. Re-reading their inspired texts, I feel the magic has gone out of the high hopes held at that time for the future of psychosomatic medicine and the role that psycho-analysis might be expected to play therein. Nevertheless, many correlations were found between specific emo-tional conflicts and specific personality traits on the one hand, and specific psychosomatic afflictions on the other. These were studied by psychiatrists using both physiological and psychological techniques. At the same time, analysts, using only their therapeutic skills and in-tuitions drawn from classical psychoanalysis, attempted to reconstruct the unconscious fantasies which might be thought to underlie somatic symptoms. Perhaps the best known of these are the dramatic hypotheses contained in the published papers by Garma (1950). Speaking of pa-tients with gastric ulcers, he would describe the ulcer as a vengeful "bite," which the patient was obliged to give himself as a punishment for his babyhood wishes to bite his mother's breast. Thus, out of unconscious guilt, the future ulcer patient might select food harmful to himself, and procure for himself an introjected bite simultaneously into his stomach and psyche. In addi-tion, the ulcers were ultimately found to carry miscel-laneous symbolic meanings related to the castration complex.

I should mention at this point that I personally see no objection to correlating environmental stress with gastric functions. Nor do I take umbrage at fantasy constructions of the kind created by Garma. But I do not feel they give us much insight into causes. The fact that stress situations cause gastric hyperfunctioning in certain individuals does not tell us why this should occur nor why most people are not affected in this way. The fact that an ulcer patient may get better during analysis, while it can without doubt be attributed to the therapeutic skill of the analyst and the effects of the analytic process, does not in any way indicate that repressed fantasies of the kind described above were the *cause* of the ulcer. We are faced here with a methodological error of some dimension which begs reflection. First, insofar as spontaneous fantasy productions in analysis are concerned, it should be noted that any somatic event will tend to attach to itself ideas dealing with different aspects of the castration complex as well as fantasies concerning the early mother-child relationship. I should like to take two examples of bodily anxiety having nothing to do with psychosomatic causes to illustrate my point. The first concerns a male patient whose mother was black and whose father was white; the second a woman who bore the consequences of polio, contracted in childhood. Both these patients lived their physical problem, black skin and paralyzed limb, as though it were a visible sign of castration in both a sexual and a narcissistic sense. They also attached to the somatic facts fantasies of a dangerous and persecuting mother who was held responsible for their psychic suffering. These fantasy constructions were helpful, yet it would be absurd to hold that the castration anxiety and the early persecutory anxieties were the *cause* of the black skin and the polio *sequelae*. We may be making a similar methodological error if we assume that a peptic ulcer is caused by the fantasy of a devouring-persecuting mother, or that the tubercular bacillus is an introjected part-object with bad intentions. The internalized object, whether total or partial, benevolent or malevolent, is entirely imaginary. Although it plays an important symbolic role, it occupies no physical space and leaves no physical trace, even though our metaphorical use of language may lead us to believe that it does. The somatic event, invasion or explosion, will inevitably tend to attract the fantasy of a malevolent object to it as a result of the analytic process, with its stimulation to link primary and secondary modes of thinking, thus creating new ways of feeling and experiencing. These may provide the analysand with new pathways for dealing with psychic tension. This, as I hope to show, is particularly important for people who have predominantly psychosomatic reactions to instinctual and environmental conflict.

There is further methodological error to be indicated at this point. Since the interaction of psyche and soma are intricate and inevitable, we may easily lose sight of their fundamental difference. A cartesian metaphor like "body is white and mind is black" might yield the idea that psychosomatic manifestations could be considered as an infinite series of greys. But this simplified graphic model would overlook the essential difference between psychic and somatic functions. We might do better to compare the psychosoma to a fusional substance like sea water. In spite of its unity our sea water can be transformed on the one hand into a heap of dried salts and on the other, a cloud of watery vapor. Let us say that the somatic elements are the salts and the psychic dimension the watery cloud. This allows us to conceive the two components as different in substance and subject to different laws. The fact that they combine should not allow us to obliterate their dissimilarity. Following the analogy a little further, one might also emphasize that neither substance quite adds up to a piece of living ocean. So we can readily sympathize with those who find that the somatic approach to the problem resembles a pile of dried salt, drained of its psychic fluid. And we can well understand that the somaticians and the psychobiological experimenters, when faced with the archaic fantasy constructions and hypotheses which the less rigid psychological approach allows, feel they are called upon to take arms against a sea of suppositions — a cloud of watery vapor with no solid matter left. In fact neither tells us much of what is going on in the stormy ocean, an image that is more evocative of man's psychosomatic dramas. Nevertheless, theoretical confusion will result if we overlook the fact that *somatic processes and psychic processes are governed by different laws of functioning.* We cannot apply the laws that structure psychological functions to those that govern physiological functioning. There is not a causal but an analogical relation between the two orders. Konrad Lorenz's brilliant observations and reflections clarify this fact and lead him to say that the movement from soma to psyche will remain forever mysterious. From our psychoanalytic observation post we are constantly made aware of the intricate and ineluctable interdependence of psyche and soma; yet we are confronted with their ineradicable difference.

I may be told at this juncture that this is so much theoretical hair-splitting, that if patients are able to modify their psychosomatic symptoms as a result of psychoanalytic therapy, then it matters little what causes what, or what is or is not authentically *symbolic*. I cannot agree with this approach. Our theories do affect our practice, not only in our way of listening to and understanding our patients' communications, but also in the form and timing of our interventions and interpretations. The fact that psychosomatic patients often show little spontaneous fantasy, whether attached to their somatic afflictions or to other aspects of their lives, is an important note for the attuned ear of the analyst. One may become aware as it were of listening to a song in which the words are present but the melody is missing. I personally feel that such analysands should be helped to an awareness of this lack and to analyzing the reasons underlying the phenomenon.

The objection is sometimes made that somatic illness is not within the domain of psychoanalysis. This is perhaps due to the fact that analysts feel lost without their symbols. We might say that psychosomatic transformations, while partaking of the quality of signs (as symbols might be said to do), are not symbols in the sense that neurotic symptoms may be so considered. They may more readily be assimilated to psychotic objects which are also marked by faulty symbolization. Freud's example drawn from the case of the Wolf Man expresses this clearly. The Wolf Man referred to the dints in his skin as vaginas — which, as Freud points out, is not symbolic usage and can in no way be regarded as a hysterical representation. Signs may represent the body or bring messages from it; they do not symbolize it. The body only becomes symbolic when, taking the place of something repressed, it enters into relationships of meaning with other psychic representations. Faced with the elusive psychic dimension of psychosomatic maladies, there is a risk that the analyst may feel his patient's inexplicable soma to be a narcissistic affront to his interpretative powers (Marty and Fain, 1965). Thus there is a countertransference dimension which may lead many an analyst to a lack of interest in his patient's psychosoma when it behaves in ways that put it beyond the reach of the analyst's sphere of influence, or at least make it appear intractable to methods that succeed so well with the neurotic parts of the personality. As analysts we will always be primarily interested in man's body as a mental representation held through the network of language. Yet we might well question by what mysterious means the psyche is able to make a breach in the body's immunological shield, and might well concern ourselves with the elusive biological purposes of disorders such as bronchial asthma or gastric hyperfunctioning, when such events occur within the analytic situation. We possess a theoretical structure capable of apprehending these questions. Concerned as we are with symbolization and psychic significance, we are particularly well placed to observe the point at which symbolic functioning breaks down or has perhaps never been fully operative. Those who are interested analytically in psychotic states well know to what extent the mind, when it leads an existence detached from the reality of the body that contains it, suffers immeasurable damage. The links that have been destroyed (not repressed as with neurotic formations) between psychic and corporeal reality may have to be recovered through delusional constructions, as Freud (1911) demonstrated in the Schreber case. But there are other alternatives to those used in psychotic creations. The ego, instead of detaching itself from external reality may create another sort of splitting, in which the instinctual body is not hallucinated but *denied existence through psychic impoverishment.* Instead of some form of psychic management of disturbing affect or unwelcome knowledge or fantasies, the ego may achieve complete destruction of the representations or feelings concerned, so that these are not registered. The result then may be a *superadaptation to external reality,* a robotlike adjustment to inner and outer pressure which short-circuits the world of the imaginary. This "pseudo normality" is in fact a widespread character trait and may well be a danger sign pointing to the eventuality of psychosomatic symptoms. The creations of the psychotic ego may often serve to protect the body from destruction and death. A factor of alternation between psychotic and psychosomatic incidents has been clinically observed by Sperling (1955). I would add that the loss of other well-established psychic patterns, such as organized sexual perversions or dominant character patterns, and exposure to events sufficiently traumatic to overthrow well-functioning neurotic defenses, may also expose the individual to psychosomatic attack. Two brief examples may clarify this notion. A patient whose character defenses were of a rigid, uncompromising nature had developed a series of tactics for dealing with sexual anxiety. To begin with, she maintained firmly that sex had no interest for her and that she was pleased to be frigid. Since she did not want her husband to suffer from her lack of interest, she had contrived a system whereby the couple made "appointments" to have sexual relations on a given day. Sometimes she was able to procrastinate or in various ways make her husband forget the appointment. The system worked more or less satisfactorily from my patient's point of view. On one occasion her husband sent a telegram announcing an unexpected return from a two months' business trip and including reference to a "sexual appointment." My patient was unaware of any emotional reaction and had no dreams that night, but the next morning found her body practically covered with urticaria, the first attack she had known. The sudden news had had the effect of a traumatic event in that her habitual defenses were overthrown and rendered inoperative, and no others were available to take their place.

Another patient reported a war experience in which a bomb exploded beside him, killing his companions while he was knocked unconscious. He recovered unhurt except that his skin was covered with great patches of psoriasis, an affliction until then unknown to him. We cannot say that the explosion "caused" the outbreak; it overthrew his usual psychic defenses in the face of danger, laying him open to somatic explosion. No doubt everyone has a threshold beyond which his psychic defense work can no longer cope, at which moment the body bears the brunt.

This brings me to the theoretical model of the Paris psychosomaticians, which comprises an economic theory of psychosomatic transformation and the concept of a psychosomatic personality structure (as opposed to neurotic, psychotic, or perverse structures). The economic concept is closely allied to the early theory of the *actual neurosis*, emphasis being laid upon urgent instinctual discharge which escapes psychic elaboration because of deficient representation and diminished affective response: in short, an impoverishment of the capacity to symbolize instinctual demands and their conflict with reality, and to elaborate fantasy. Instinctual energy, bypassing the psyche, thus affects the soma directly, with catastrophic results. This particular theoretical approach to psychosomatic formations is in complete opposition to the theory of hysterical formation, the latter being the result of repressed fantasy elaborations while the former would result precisely from the lack of such psychic activity. The failure to represent instinctual conflict symbolically leads to a specific mode of mental functioning, and this may in turn determine a "psychosomatic character pattern," as noted by Marty, de M'Uzan, and David (1963). In each case the authors have delineated certain characteristics observed in seriously ill psychosomatic patients, based on several years of research (see Chapter VI).

1. Unusual object relations, notably lacking in libidinal affect. This is also manifest in the interviews in that these patients, compared with others, show little interest in the investigation and practically none in the investigator.

2. An impoverished use of language marked in particular by what the authors call *operational thinking (la pensée opératoire)*. This refers to thoughts that are pragmatic in the extreme; e.g., "What kind of woman is your mother?" Reply: "Well, she's tall and blonde."

"What was your reaction when you learned of the death of your fiancé?" "Well, I thought I'd have to pull myself together." "Were you upset when you ran over this woman with the baby?" "Oh, I was insured against third party accident." In the three cases cited, each patient was being questioned about circumstances that appeared to be closely connected with the onset of serious psychosomatic illness. Listening to recordings of such interviews, one is struck by the flattened affect and an impression of unusual detachment. These have a psychotic resonance, yet there is no resemblance to psychotic ego functioning in other aspects of these patients' lives, nor to any form of psychotic thought disorders. Indeed, "operational thinking" may be highly intellectual and abstract. De M'Uzan has pointed out that the outstanding feature of such thinking is its detachment "from any truly alive internal object representations."

3. A marked lack of neurotic symptoms and neurotic character adaptations.

4. Facial movements, bodily gestures, sensorimotor manifestations, and physical pain will appear where one might expect neurotic manifestations.

5. Preliminary interviews are characterized by a type of inertia that threatens to bring discussion to an end, unless the investigator makes vigorous efforts to stimulate associative material concerning the patient's relationships, life experience, and illness. Dramatic or painful events are recounted with little emotional overtone or are omitted if not directly solicited.

A paper by Fain and David (1963) deals with the cardinal importance of dreaming and of unconscious fantasy in the maintenance of psychic equilibrium.

The work of Despert, Lewin, and French is reviewed and linked to their own research. In their conclusions the authors state that the psychosomatic patient reveals a damaged capacity for creating fantasy to deal with infantile and present-day anxieties. Comparisons are drawn with psychotic patients who, in circumstances similar to those that precipitate psychosomatic illness, will suffer hallucinatory episodes. Unlike the psychotic, the psychosomatic patient remains closely attached to facts and things in external reality. The ego may show impoverishment, but there is no distortion. However, in both cases pathological problems arise in proportion to the inability to use regression or dreams. The comparison calls to mind the clinical findings of Sperling (1955). Although she adduces quite different theoretical conclusions, she notes alternations between psychotic states and psychosomatic illness in the same individuals.

I come now to the important contribution of Fain (1971) concerning the earliest beginnings of fantasy life and their role in the predisposition to psychosomatic illness. This includes findings from earlier research (Fain and Kreisler, 1970) on babies suffering from serious psychosomatic disturbances in the first months of life. One group is comprised of infants who are only able to sleep if rocked continually in their mothers' arms and otherwise suffer from almost total insomnia. Fain's studies suggest that these mothers have failed in their function as a protective shield against exciting stimuli, precisely through overindulging the exercise of this function. Instead of the development of a primitive form of psychic activity akin to dreaming which permits most babies to sleep peacefully after feeding, these babies require the mother herself to be the guardian of sleep. The author links this breakdown of the capacity to recreate symbolically a good internal state of being, to an allied failure to develop autoerotic activity. Fain's observations lead him to the conclusion that these babies do not have a *mère satisfaisante* (satisfying mother) but a *mère calmante* (tranquilizing mother). The latter, because of her own problems, cannot permit her baby to create a primary identification which will enable him to sleep without continual contact with her. Cases of infantile asthma show a similarly disturbed mother-nursling relationship. Analogous observations have been made concerning the mothers of allergic children. These mothers appear to allow no satisfactions which are not obtained in direct contact with themselves. Autoerotic activity and the capacity for psychic development is blocked in these children. "We have postulated that these mothers unconsciously wish to bring their children back to fetal bliss inside their own bodies," writes Fain.[1] In other words, we find here a pathological exaggeration of what is fundamentally a normal instinctual attitude on the mother's part, namely, to create a sheltering womblike world for her new-born until he is able to provide this for himself. But, because of her own unconscious needs, she does not create conditions in which the baby can take over this function. If her libidinal interest in the other aspects of her life, particularly her love life, does not lead her to *disinvest* her baby sufficiently (e.g., wishing it to go peacefully off to sleep leaving her free for other preoccupations) she may overdo her

---

[1]Excerpts from Fain (1971), my translation.

protective role, thus keeping her baby tied to her bodily presence.

Fain describes three types of baby sleep patterns related to early psychic functioning: the first infant makes small sucking movements while sleeping; the second sleeps with his thumb firmly planted in his mouth; the third sucks frenetically and does not sleep. We have here three modes of autoerotism that manifest qualitative differences in the balance between motricity and the capacity for psychic representation. This in turn implies a difference in the distribution of narcissistic libido and that part of the libido which remains attached to the object. The first baby reinforces his capacity to maintain sleep through some form of hallucinatory discharge of excitation; the second requires a real object for a much longer period of time; babies of the third category are thrown into a perilous cycle of endless discharge. The author concludes from his observation of the mothers that "the continual investment of the baby by the mother impedes the development of primary autoerotism and this automatically leads to a most dangerous vicissitude—the exclusion of libidinal activity from the symbolic chain. . . . This type of maternal failure is frequently accompanied by a corresponding failure in the father's role as a figure of authority" (p. 323). This reference to the parental attitudes indicates that the groundwork for eventual ways of reacting to the oedipal crisis is already being laid down.

At the opposite end of the scale of infantile psychosomatic disorders is the strange malady known as *merycism* in which the baby constantly regurgitates and then swallows his stomach contents until dehydration and exhaustion set in. Here the baby has created *prematurely* an autoerotic object that enables him to dispense with his mother. Observations of the mothers reveal that among other unusual restrictions, they impose severe prohibitions on all normal autoerotic activity. "They react to thumb-sucking as though it were a truly oedipal masturbation to be suppressed at all costs." In comparison with the tiny insomniacs, the merycist babies show a significant contrast — they sleep well. The author points out that in order to sleep, a baby must develop the capacity for adequate autoerotic activity as well as the autonomous ability to maintain a protective barrier against stimuli both from within and without. These children succeed in decathecting the sensorium, but there is nevertheless a serious symbolic gap in that the mother's absence is in no way compensated *psychically*; it is totally disavowed through the baby's having precociously created its own protective barrier against her absence, and one which continues to isolate him from her even in her presence. She is the helpless witness of his autoerotic activity. "The external object is first 'perceived' in that part of the body formed by the mouth-esophagus-stomach area. [For these children] there is a total separation between the instinctual world and the somatic area where the oral impulses make themselves felt, and, on the other hand, the sensorium where stimuli from the outer world are captured." Thus we see that a kind of primal chasm may be created at this early stage between the id impulses and their eventual representations drawn from the external world. Instinctual aims and autoerotic activity then run the risk of becoming literally *autonomous*, detached from any *men-*

tal representation of an object. We may have here the foundation for a subsequent dangerous separation between psyche and soma in adult life. Bion's theory of undigested "beta elements" seems to me germane to this line of research.

From a historic-genetic viewpoint, Fain's research suggests that there are two predominant trends in disturbed baby-mother relationships which are apt to create a predisposition to psychosomatic pathology. The first is unusually severe prohibition of every attempt on the baby's part to create autoerotic substitutes for the maternal relationship, thus vitiating the nodal point for the creation of inner object representations and the nascent elements of fantasy life. The second trend is the antithesis of this, namely, a continual offering of herself on the mother's part as the only object of satisfaction and psychic viability. The work of Spitz (1962) on mother-child relationships and the importance of these in creating or hindering the development of autoerotism coincides in many ways with Fain's observational research. One might say that it is a question of leaving the baby too much or too little psychic space in which to be mentally creative on his own. My own clinical experience, derived mainly from analytic work wth adults, has shown that patients with predominantly psychosomatic reactions to anxiety situations tend to reveal parental imagos showing both these tendencies. A tubercular patient with many other psychosomatic symptoms described her mother in these terms:

"She was so demanding, so attached to me, that I had to be constantly beside her. I could never turn to anyone else. She made it impossible. At the same time there was not a trace of warmth in her attitude toward me, as though all she wanted was total power over my *physical* being. Emotionally she did not recognize my existence. . . I know now that my outbreaks of eczema reoccur whenever I feel abandoned by my fiancé. And also during your holidays! But whenever I feel manipulated and controlled I get these crippling back troubles again. Feeling abandoned and being controlled are both ways of bringing my mother back."

I do not think it would be a misrepresentation of Fain's work to describe the mothers of his observational research as performing *an addictive function.* The baby comes to need the mother as an addict needs his drug—i.e., total dependence on an external object —to deal with situations which should be handled by self-regulatory psychological means.[2] In my clinical work I have found similar imagos in patients showing "acting-out" behavior other than addictions and psychosomatic symptoms, notably in perversions and in character patterns marked by discharge reactions. The mother's failure, through being too close or too far away, to fulfill her function as a shield against the stream of stimuli to which her baby is subjected, includes her failure to make sense out of his nonverbal communications. There is then a grave risk that his own capacity to give the rudiments of meaning to what he experiences and to represent psychically his id impulses and their subsequent objects, will be impaired. The differentiation between representation and symbol will also be confused eventually. We are thus

---

[2]It may well be supposed that for the mother in these cases the baby also has fulfilled the function of an addictive object, a *needed* rather than a *desired* object.

dealing with the basic substratum of a wide spectrum of clinical disorders in which individuals are pushed to "action" in place of psychic activity and containment.

Absence and *difference,* the two reality experiences around which identity is construcated, must become significant and also infused with libidinal meaning and value if the individual is to create a viable psychic model of existence and of his own place in the order of human relationships. On the foundation of this early model of Otherness will be constructed the oedipal model, a blueprint to make sense of, and symbolize, sexual and social relationships. Here the significance of the father's role, already communicated in an important way through the mother's psychic economy, comes into full play. This factor may then be decisive for determining which psychological "solutions" will dominate in adult life.

If psychosomatic personalities may be said to be "antineurotics" due to their inability to create neurotic defenses, from another standpoint they may also be considered as "antipsychotics," in that they are "over-adapted" to reality and the difficulties of existence. Although the ego differences are striking from a phenomenological point of view, both states would appear to derive from some breakdown in symbolic functioning, and we might expect similarities at some point. Two have already been indicated — a certain quality of object relationship and a tendency to stifle or to lack affectivity.

Ekstein's work with psychotic children gives an insight into certain features which call to mind aspects of psychosomatic patients. Take for example his study of the preoccupation of psychotic children with monsters, and its connection with their inability to contain and to elaborate internal excitement. This research is summarized by Yahalom (1967) who writes: "The pressure of what he [the psychotic child] wants yet fears, gives ground before his inward drive. *He tries to cling to something concrete, reachable by his immediate senses, so that he can escape being overwhelmed by a flood of archaic matter.* He then calls upon some creature, a delusionary introject, as a kind of substitute superego" (p. 375, italics added). This mechanism is closely allied to the tendency of the psychosomatic personality to cling to the concrete and factual aspects of living and to pursue them with intensity. Yahalom says, "In order to release an impulse with relief there must be a representation of an 'object' that absorbs the release. This can be called a safety element. The original safety element is the 'satiating mother' and the safety explains the insistent search for a 'mothering echo'" (p. 375).

The "satiating mother" recalls in striking fashion the "addictive mother" of infants suffering from psychosomatic illnesses. I hope to show later the ways in which a similar kind of object relationship is revealed clinically by "psychosomatic" analysands. In either case — satiating or addictive mother — the children run the risk of not being genuinely object-related. The little patient described in Yahalom's paper revealed typical distortion of true symbolic functioning in her use of words and her lack of affect. A further remark of this author to the effect that psychotic defenses sometimes block out awareness of sensation, or even deny those elements in the observing ego which are critically affected by threatened loss, comes remarkably close to the concept of "operational thinking," the hallmark of the communications of the psychosomatic sufferer.

The desperate search for facts and things in the external world and the tendency to treat people as things in an attempt "to grasp at some fragment of experiencing" (Rochlin, quoted by Yahalom) recalls de M'Uzan's description of the desperate clinging of the classical psychosomatic patients to what he calls "the factuality of existence." The attempt to cling to unconnected facts, things, and persons makes itself felt in the analytic discourse of certain patients, and the analyst frequently feels at loss to understand why his patient is telling him the facts of his daily existence without a trace of affect or interest in the significance that the facts may have for him. This is also reminiscent of the rituals to which sexual perverts resort when they feel threatened. We have here another example of a failure in symbolization. The ritualistic acts help to overcome castration anxiety which is unduly intense because it has never become truly symbolic of sexual realities and is thus used to ward off threats to narcissistic integrity by external means. It is interesting to note that Yahalom, in order to illustrate this point with regard to psychotic traits, takes the example of a homosexual patient who claimed that he "fell in love with a partner because of the wonderful smell of his hair." It seems to me that we are faced here with a lack of symbolic structures to give meaning to the representations and their allied affects, so that sensations and experiences impinging from without and within are not readily integrated into an elaborated psychic system. In default of a sound psychic model of one's existence as an individual in relation to others, there will of course be a dangerously deficient feeling of inner "safety." If the model does not contain such symbolic and fantasy construction to order, process, and contain all that is experienced, the individual will experience existence as an overwhelming phenomenon fraught with the danger of being submerged and losing his identity. "Safety" must then be sought in the external world. The acquistion of language and other symbolic capabilities should normally enable the child to develop an ever-increasing network of internal representations and permit him in this way to free himself from helpless dependence on the environment and his important objects. He may then be in a position to deal with frustration and excitement through symbolic mediation.

In trying to come to terms with the substructure of all "action disorders," including psychosomatic "acts," we are in the area of transitional phenomena and are witnesses to *the attempt to make substitute objects in the external world do duty for symbolic ones which are absent or damaged in the inner psychic world*. Such attempts are doomed to failure. The victim of this kind of lack is doomed to endless repetition and addictive attachment to the outer world and external objects. To come back then to the striking *differences* between psychosomatic and psychotic creations, we might say that whereas the psychotic child clutches at a delusional "monster" to palliate the lack of the internal object brutally projected outward, the psychosomatic sufferer has precociously laid his monsters to rest. He has *lost* them. I would suggest that there are deeply buried archaic fantasy elements encapsulated somewhere in the unconscious, but that these are unartic-

ulated linguistically and thus have no access to preconscious or conscious thought. Stored at a presymbolic
level, they do not find expression even in dreams (I
would suggest further that we all contain such still-
born monsters). With a psychic substratum in which
the "monsters" have been neither allowed to grow up
nor projected in hallucinatory fashion, but simply
neglected through lack of psychic nourishment, what is
missing is something much more subtle. Perhaps a concept such as *negative hallucination* might be invoked
here. Bion (1962), Green (1973), and Fain (1971) have
each explored in different ways the contours of such a
concept. Such a mode of mental functioning would
lead to an arrest in ego development which would be
markedly different from that found in psychosis. The
split, the schism, is drawn in differently. In psychotic
states the ego is overwhelmed by the imaginary world
once it slips out of its traces, and is then no longer able
to perform its initial function of inhibiting hallucinatory fulfillments (Freud, 1915a). The psychosomatic
ego has choked the archaic elements of fantasy in their
very beginnings and thus becomes split off from its instinctual roots, leaving few elements available for the
creation of psychotic delusions. These may in fact
come into being under the impact of the psychoanalytic process. My own clinical experience with
analysands suffering from psychosomatic disorders of a
serious kind has taught me that they may have to recreate their psychotic monsters, and live with them
even in projected form for a while, until such time as
they can be contained and integrated. This kind of
psychic growth allows patients to feel alive in new
ways, even though they bring with them a measure of

mental suffering. Not only neurotic pain but also many perverse and "crazy" creations come to life. Although there are finer creations of the spirit than perversion and psychosis, in the long run it is better to be mad than dead.

Observations and speculations

When trying to delineate a "psychosomatic personality" solely on the basis of my own clinical experience, I am continually brought up short by the fact that "psychosomatic" analysands display the most varied of personality structures. But then they came into analysis because of neurotic symptoms and character traits. This may differentiate them from those patients who recognize no psychological suffering and seek help solely for their physical symptoms, whose character pattern has been sharply defined by research workers in the field in different countries. However, the apparent dissimilarities may be erroneous. As the analysis of patients with many psychosomatic reactions proceeds, one finds certain analysands who have created strong reactional defenses against anxiety to which others have surrendered. Take for example the hyperactivity patterns noted by many psychosomaticians in their patients. While I frequently find this character trait in patients whose symptoms are predominantly somatic in conflict situations, I have found just as many in similar circumstances who feel depressed and listless and complain of inability to get themselves going. The overactive others may well be using manic defenses against incipient depressive affect and the pull to inertia. With regard to character patterns and specific psychosomatic manifestations, I have again come to feel that my first clinical impressions were erroneous. One example will suffice. For a long time I had clinical evidence that my allergic-skin patients showed an exacerbated sensitivity to the environment and tended to protect themselves physically and psychically from being scratched or bruised. In contrast, it seemed that my respiratory sufferers (mostly tubercular or asthmatic) worked to the point of extreme fatigue while their regard for their physical health was not only hardy, but indeed foolhardy. As time went on, I found tubercular patients who were like sensitive babies with regard to their physical selves, and eczema patients with hardy body ideals. Then I came across analysands afflicted with both types of somatic disturbance. Although future research will undoubtedly bring deeper insights into the structural factors allied with the choice of psychosomatic expression, for the present the most promising approach seems to me to be the exploration of a possible "psychosomatic mechanism," a specific form of functioning which would predispose an individual to psychosomatic, rather than psychic, creations in situations of stress or conflict. I shall therefore refer in this section to "psychosomatic" patients — although I cannot define the limits of such a concept — to indicate analysands who tend to react with either psychosomatic maladies or increased sensitivity to infection and a tendency to bodily accidents, when faced with traumatic events and conflictual situations arising either from the past or the present (including the psychoanalytic situation). Although it is theoretically important to differentiate between a truly psychosomatic illness such as nonspecific ulcerative colitis and the contraction of an illness such as tuberculosis, I am mainly concerned at this point with what might be relevant to a "psychosomatic disposition" and what signs other than somatic illness might reveal its existence. I wish now to give some clinical examples of sexual and relational patterns common to most psychosomatic patients. It will be noticed that these are not specific to people who have declared psychosomatic manifestations. They may nevertheless have a certain prognostic value and make us aware of the threat of eventual somatic transformations under the impact of the analytic process. Because of their nonsymbolic quality such manifestations are totally silent before their somatic realization, and it is therefore necessary to listen to something which is not there, a psychic gap in which a somatic creation might appear instead of a psychological one. I reiterate that the analysands under discussion all utilized a number of neurotic mechanisms (otherwise they would not have been in analysis), and in most cases had not given much importance to, or even mentioned their psychosomatic history.

Sexual and object relations

When psychosomatic analysands talk of their love and sex relations one often finds oneself, once again, listening to a missing dimension. This is in marked contrast to the way in which neurotic patients present love relationships of a neurotic order. Of course neurotic patients seek help primarily for their sexual problems —

or for the symptoms which are an unconscious compromise and "solution" to their conflict. People with psychosomatic reactions to conflict, although they bring problems in the oedipal-genital sector, more often come to analysis because of feelings of hopelessness about all their relationships or because of depressive affect in general. This vague clinical categorization clearly overlaps what are called character neuroses, but does not usually include the same fate and failure patterns that "character problem" patients display. Just as frequently there are no overt sexual problems. Analysis reveals that these analysands, both men and women, speak of their sexual partners, and treat them as though they were feeding mothers upon whom they are desperately dependent. Although sometimes unaware of feelings of emotional attachment, these patients cling avidly to their mates and tend to fall physically ill when threatened with abandonment by them. Just as frequently, however, psychosomatic personalities reveal what appears to be a contrary pattern — their love objects are highly *interchangeable*, the central demand being that someone must be there. This "someone" is cast in the role of a "security blanket" and thus fulfills the function of a transitional object. Both types of object relation are connected with traumatic early mother-baby relationships, and it is evident that both kinds of dependence are reminiscent of the "addictive" mothers of the psychosomatic babies studied by Fain and of the "satiating" mothers of Ekstein's psychotic children.

My attention was drawn first of all to this kind of sexual attachment in analysands who had suffered from pulmonary tuberculosis. With one exception, all had fallen ill at times in their lives when they were facing separation or abandonment by people who, consciously or unconsciously, represented the addictive mother of early babyhood. In each case they had been unable to grasp the extent of their pain or bereavement, frequently because they had no inkling of the ambivalent role of the Other, nor of the fact that they were bereft, and therefore could not work through their loss. Instead of opening their hearts to grief, it seems they opened their lungs to invasion by tubercular bacilli. I have come across two cases of ulcerative colitis in which there was an identical inability to elaborate feelings of rejection or work through a process of mourning. A case presented by Loriod (1969) of a patient with multiple somatic transformations demonstrates in striking fashion this refusal to experience or give in to mental pain.

Analysis of this desperate clinging to the Other — or undifferentiated Others — yields the insight that this is less a sexual dependence than a protection against the loss of identity feeling and the threat of total annihilation. A patient whose dependence on her lover was such that any threat or break in the relationship found immediate discharge in somatic symptoms of various kinds would cry at such occasions yet would invariably add that she *did not know why* she was crying. After four years of analysis she was able to discover that she never felt quite "real" in any relationship. The inevitable urge to establish an equally dependent tie to the analyst led her to continual acting out rather than to the confrontation of the wish and the panic it aroused. "It's embassassing for me to tell you this, but as a matter of fact I'm never wholly *here*," she replied when I once drew her attention to the acting-out aspects of her reaction to the analytic situation. "I go on talking normally, but I'm always somewhere else. I've been like this all my life — as though I didn't live in my own body. Now it begins to frighten me. Yet everyone considers me so normal. I only a feel real, feel that I exist, when I make love. My body somehow comes together around my vagina."

At other times she said that smoking had a similar effect, it "pulled [her] body and mind together so that for a brief moment there is a feeling that one really exists." Her sexual relations fulfilled the role of a drug. Outside these moments she was deeply afraid of depressive feelings and a tendency toward complete inertia. "I would like to lie in bed all day with a bottle, like Mary Barnes, without thinking, until I simply stopped being." This intelligent and apparently well-adjusted analysand also had no apparent sexual problems, and indeed found her sexual experiences highly satisfactory. Like many others with her particular mode of psychic functioning, this outward appearance of "normality" was misleading. In the same way, her sexual relationships were called upon to bear a heavy load. One cannot truly possess one's narcissistic integrity nor one's sexuality if one does not symbolically possess one's body. If the sexual relationship is the only confirmation of individual identity or is felt to be the only protection against the unknown dangers of existence, then sexual relations will be invested with considerable and compulsive intensity. Unusual circumstances led to a rupture in the relationship between this patient and her lover. With the loss of her mate she lost everything: her sexuality, her narcissistic self-image, her capacity to sleep, and her ability to metabolize her food (several of my somatizing patients suffered dramatic loss of weight in times of threatened or actual separation from their "addictive" objects). This patient was threatened with losing her body in every sense of the word. Her concern for her physical health was reduced to nothing, and she became aware, in the light of her past history, that she was exposing herself once more to serious health hazards. What should have been an *internal* conviction — of narcissistic integrity and individual identity — had constantly to be confirmed externally.

Two important discoveries changed the course of her analysis and her whole mode of psychic existence, and these in turn altered her somatic sensitivity. One discovery concerned her very first experience of masturbation. She was then thirty-eight years old. Under the impact of this tardy discovery she exlaimed one day that for the first time in her life *she felt her body belonged to her and had limits.* Her attitude to her corporal self changed. Not only did she give more thought to her physical well-being, she also began to look prettier and to feel more alive in her relations with others, who also began to exist in their own rights. In certain circumstances she became more demanding, and in others she felt she had the permission to refuse tasks and demands she did not welcome. It was as though she were aware for the first time of her feelings and their connections with other people. At the same time she made the discovery of transference feelings; instead of *acting out* to stem a rising tide of panic before any possibility of emotion in the analytic situation, she was able to contain and explore these nascent feeelings: in

particular, strong emotion around separation experiences in the analytic relation and feelings of intense
rage whenever I failed to understand immediately
what she was communicating when it could not yet be
expressed verbally. She demanded continual presence
and understanding without having to pass through the
channels of language. She acted, and felt like, a misun-
derstood baby. Homosexual fantasies made their appearance in her dreams and her associations around
this time, and these served ultimately to strengthen her
own sexual identity. At the same time, her psychosomatic symptoms notably diminished.

I have given this analytic fragment in some detail
because in many ways it is exemplary: from the point
of view of the affective stifling which so often keeps at
bay violent anger and omnipotent demands, and also
with regard to the lost links between the physical self
and sexual desire. The loss of affective reaction renders
object relations pragmatic and decathected, and the
gap between the body and its instinctual impulses has a
deleterious effect on the sense of identity. Further, *the
masturbation history is frequently disturbed in psychosomatic patients*, at least in my clinical experience.
Often masturbation seems to have been discovered
very late in life (anything from twenty to forty years)
or it has been practiced in childhood and adolescence,
but in deviant ways which avoid all contact between
hand and genital, and in many cases is devoid of fantasy content. Deviant attempts to fulfill sexual wishes,
where these existed, have usually been given up
without compensation of any kind. Thus they have
neither developed into organized perverse practices,
nor been repressed to become the raw material of neu-

rotic symptoms, nor projected and recovered in delusional form. Instead there is destruction of affect and a
loss of symbolic representation of sexual desires. This is
a sorry state of affairs, for sexual relations risk becoming pragmatic and compulsive, and the sexual experience itself suffers from its imaginative impoverishment. There seems little doubt that man's most intensely erogenic zone is to be located in his mind! Thus there
is an "operational" dimension to these patients' sexual
lives. In the course of analysis such fantasies as might
be constructed to match affective states of which the
patient is aware (and this may take several years) are
often extremely archaic and disturbing to him. This in
turn may precipitate further flights of acting out, so as
to leave no space for fantasy or the eventuality of
"holding" a sexual desire. One analysand expressed his
dilemma in these terms: "I cannot bear to caress or to
be touched by a girl unless I am going to make love to
her immediately." When asked what would happen if
he could not immediately fulfill such a project, he
found himself at a loss to explain a rising feeling of
panic. "But I have never *imagined* making love to anyone. I always say to myself that I must plan to have a
girl ready to sleep with me each night because I simply
can't be alone. *I have never in my life experienced a
sexual desire.*" This patient was able subsequently to
allow sexual fantasies to flourish in his imagination,
although he felt for a considerable time that he would
have to act them out, even though this would occasion
certain social risks. Another patient in a similar phase
of analysis summed up his feeling in these words: "But
if I become aware of a wish then I have to do everything I can to fulfill it; otherwise what is the good of

imagining anything?" The fear of having to sustain the frustration of a desire is only matched by the fear of going mad. A third psychosomatic patient who was also trying to understand his fear of fantasizing said: "But you don't understand. If I just let myself think no matter what, I'll end up like Don Quixote with a saucepan on my head charging at buses."

These three patients were all able to "resexualize" both their bodies and their minds, so to speak, and to allow sexual relationships of a meaningful kind into their lives. All three displayed terror at the idea of giving their imaginations some freedom and equal if not greater terror at the idea that the thoughts and impulses would be uncontrollable. We enter here into the domain of *retention*, clearly having its roots in the anal phase, and the *inability to give libidinal meaning to the capacity to retain*, originally one's feces and all they symbolize, later one's thoughts, impulses, and inner objects. Fantasies of being poisoned or of risking explosion if one held back discharge impulses was also an important theme, but this leaves the psychosomatic domain and enters into familiar neurotic territory.

This brings me to a clinical fact that entails a certain theoretical confusion. It is my belief that psychosomatic symptoms, which in the first instance arise because of a lack of symbolic representation and affective expression, may often be susceptible to a process of "hystericalization" or "obsessionalization" when the analysand is encouraged to invent situations to accompany his somatic symptoms. The resistance to do this is considerable, but the results are occasionally rewarding, when a somatic manifestation which has attracted little attention slowly becomes meaningful.

The fantasies are often disturbing to the analysand because of their archaic quality or their sadomasochistic content. An ulcer patient, little given to daydreaming, particularly where his sexual relations were concerned produced a fantasy of ingesting his partner's fecal matter. This was accompanied with massive erotic excitement and slowly grew to be a compulsive thought. As his experiments in creating fantasies around fleeting emotional states and bodily sensations continued, he began to invent daydreams whenever he felt the painful sensations he knew to be premonitory of a recurrence of his gastric pathology. These fantasies were usually of an incorporative nature, drinking sperm, eating skin, biting off nipples and heads of penises, etc. Not only did his gastric symptoms disappear for the first time in many years, but the gain from the point of view of the analytic process was considerable. The gastric symptoms and the whole digestive area became an object of psychic interest to my patient and threw much light on other aspects of his life and character structure. This progress was made in the face of considerable resistance since he feared that the fantasies might drive him crazy and force him to act upon what he imagined. He slowly built up a phobic attitude to these thoughts which acquired all the characteristics of obsessional ideas, and he then attempted to repress them. However, with a certain amount of prodding, he allowed them to evolve and to come into connection with other ideas, notably the growth of authentic sexual desire and his first truly libidinal love relationships.

A similar process which took a more "hysterical" direction was that of another patient with gastric pathology who also had many skin allergies. This patient complained bitterly of the frightening quality of the fantasies which crowded his mind when he was in a state of sexual frustration, and of the analysis which permitted such fantasies to exist: "I keep imagining that some men have tied my testicles with wire, then they throw me forcefully into a deep chasm, again and again, until my testicles are torn off. But the most terrible part of it all is the tremendous sexual excitement it gives me. I'm sure I'm going crazy and it's all your fault!"

The daydream symbolizes an archaic primal scene with an oedipal overtone: the young man is forced by the men to enter the "chasmal" woman, and the punishment is castration, although as we can see the daydream starts off as an engulfment of the whole body in the exciting experience. Nevertheless anxiety is slowly becoming attached to the sexual organs. The whole imaginative "creation" was a considerable change for this particular patient in view of his earlier more sterile mode of psychic functioning, devoid of conscious imagining and with little sign of an unconscious fantasy life either. The main sign of psychic conflict had lain until then in his somatic explosions which brought him perilously near to death's door. The point I wish to make, however, is that this patient could not avoid joining the newly created phantasmagoria to the fact that he frequently had outbreaks of eczema around the testicles. Although the eczema continued to occur (notably just before the analyst's holidays) the conjunction of eczema and fantasy allowed a considerable libidinal investment by the patient of his whole genital area. This affected both his erotic experience and the nature of his love relations.

These patients would seem to fit the category of the babies observed by Spitz (1962) who, because of early maternal failure, never indulge in what he describes as "normal genital play," that is, spontaneous hand-genital play of infants who have a harmonious and stable relation with the mother. They recall also the infants of Fain's studies whose early contact with the mother prevented their devising autoerotic means to deal with psychic tension, thus damaging extensively the subsequent development of fantasy life. This failure to make absence significant might also be expressed as a failure to internalize "the breast." Bion (1962) pointed out that the breast, before being capable of symbolization, must first be capable of representation as a state of "no breast"; otherwise it is purely good or bad, and cannot in this state become the nexus of further thought and affective elaboration, and so will fail in its symbolic function. In psychotic states the "good" and the "bad" become projected outward as idealized and persecuting objects. In psychosomatic structures this does not occur. The different "breast" representations are simply excluded from the symbolic chain, and *decathected without compensation.* Thus instinctual impulses, whether aggressive or libidinal, run the risk of not gaining representation. The early fragmented elements of "fantasy" which might be supposed to accompany instinctual impulses are thus not stored in ways that allow them to evolve into the material of neurotic fantasy constructions. In consequence there may be little psychic filtrage or binding through fantasy links and semantic symbols, but a tendency to inappropriate somatic discharge instead.

In Winnicott's (1971a) terminology this would include people who are constantly "impinged upon" by the environment, and in parallel fashion are unable to "use an object" creatively. Winnicott's concept of the use of an object and of people who fail to achieve this relationship with external objects also applies to those who have primarily psychosomatic solutions to tension and anxiety. Rosenfeld's description (1971) of a similar failure to use an internal or external object is in the statement that the healthy part of the personality is that part which is able to *depend on another* without fear. All these different theoretical approaches are coming to grips with the same complicated area of human experience and with similar enigmas in psychic functioning. In each case there is a breakdown in object relations due to the attempt to make an external object behave like a symbolic one and thus repair a *psychic* gap. The object or situation will then be sought addictively. Basically, all addictions, from alcoholism and boulimia to the taking of sleeping tablets and pep pills, are attempts to make an external agent do duty for a missing symbolic dimension. This type of psychic functioning is reminiscent of the role of the *fetish* in the sexual sphere, but is by no means synonymous with it since the latter has succeeded in reducing global primitive anxiety about phallic castration anxiety; it is this anxiety that is then combated by external rather than internal management. The psychosomatic patient has rarely achieved this "genitalization" of anxiety; he keeps at bay terrors of the order of "primary castration." It is not surprising that we find in our psychosomatic analysands oedipal constellations similar to those found in sexual perversions in which the role of the father is much diminished and the importance of his penis as a symbolic phallic object in the psychic world is accordingly weakened. The phallic symbol is still embedded in the mother, and so castration anxiety runs the risk of involving the whole body and the self rather than being restricted to the sexual sphere and sexual relations and identity. Their struggle is to feel whole and alive.

The extent to which larval fantasies (Beta elements), which are excluded from symbolic expression in the preconscious, find, for the first time, verbal expression and affective counterpart, may determine the possibilities of diminishing the risk of somatic discharge which otherwise short-circuits language and with it the capacity to elaborate fantasy. It is possible that constructive (that is protective) fantasy, for dealing with absence and difference, can only be "stored" as a psychic treasure to the extent to which it is held through words and the early elements of "thinking," in the sense of Bion's research. The "attacks on linking" (Bion, 1959) which he ascribes to psychotic states are restricted in psychosomatic personalities to an attack on fantasy life and on the capacity to represent affect. Instead of ego distortions we find a perilously autonomous ego. The absence of neurotic, perverse, and psychotic mechanisms is a danger signal for the soma. These same factors also pose problems in severe cases with regard to the advisibility of psychoanalytic treatment. There are risks to be weighed in both the somatic and the psychological direction.

Somatic versus neurotic defense

The failure to create protective neurotic symptoms

may become clearer with a clinical example. Three patients (two women, one man) came to analysis because of feelings of failure concerning their personal lives. All had suffered from severe bronchial asthma since childhood. Allergies ranging from cats and household dust to grass pollen were held to be responsible for the attacks. As the analysis of these patients proceeded, it became evident that the asthmatic attacks followed certain "geographic laws." Two of these patients suffered attacks of increasing severity as each drew near to the town or suburb *in which the mother lived.* The third suffered increasingly in proportion to the distance that separated her from the parental home. One can scarcely avoid comparing this relation of distance with the neurotic control of geographical space in *phobic* patients, yet the difference is considerable.[3] In order to create a phobic object, or situation, the mind has had to do a lot of work of an intricate symbolic nature. Whether this be revealed in phobias connected with sexual anxiety such as agoraphobia, or whether it is a question of more primitive phobic situations concerning early pregenital conflict, such as food and dirt phobias, or hypochondriacal concerns, the affective charge connected with the phobic situation is available to the patient's consciousness. He has been able to contrive a symbolic displacement of the dangerous object or situation which can be dealt with by avoidance. With the patients I am describing here there was no such displacement, nor any awareness of the rage, grief, and anxiety which later

---

[3]Pankow (1969) gives interesting insight into the relation of asthma to psychotic and neurotic body imagery.

came to be attached to the mother's image. All were aware of strong dependency feelings toward the mother, and each of the three patients had made a supreme effort to leave the parental home, but the original object had never been given up. Although physical separation was achieved, there was a fundamental lack of any identification to a "caretaking mother." Each of these patients was saddled with an impossibly high ego ideal: all worked unceasingly in the service of their professional duties, and whatever blows life dealt them, they did not flinch, as though forbidden to feel emotional pain or in any way bind their psychic wounds. It took many years of analysis for the unshed tears to come to the surface along with the wish to be comforted and cared for.

Sexual love relations, which constantly ended in disappointment, showed somewhat opposite features in that these analysands tended to "mother" their partners to the point of castration. This was true of the man as well as the two women. I came to feel that these patients were establishing smothering relations with their sexual partners (with little regard for the others' wishes), such as they had known in childhood, while unconsciously they desired magical babylike gifts in return for their love. Their behavior was in fact erratic. They desperately wanted to be close to someone, yet they could not bear to be in close contact for long. Any jarring note in the harmony of the relationship was liable to end in immediate rupture. As with my other somatizing patients, there was a familiar history of infantile masturbation in that none had known normal manual masturbation. One had evolved adolescent rituals in which feces played an important role;

one of the women had devised a series of instruments to insert into her anus and vagina, while the other had learned to attain erotic excitement by withholding her urine and pressing on her bladder, and in adolescence would reach orgasm by these means.

Miss L became interested during analysis in the ostensible fact that her mother's proximity coincided with the severity of her asthma attacks. She slowly pieced together her childhood dependence on this mother, the only person capable of calming her sobbing spasms, and later, her asthmatic attacks. Her father was kept rigorously out of the little girl's room because he was said to make the asthma worse. Other outside influences were also kept at bay. Miss L could not run, play, or go to school like other children. Even though she had developed few inner psychic means of coping with the myriad situations calculated to arouse anxiety, she nevertheless left home in her early twenties following a violent altercation with her mother over her right to have a man friend. Apart from statements like "my poor mother's a bit potty," Miss L expressed no strong emotion about her. She was aware of *sensations* rather than sentiments in her mother's presence. Encourged to put these into words, she was finally able to say: "I can't bear to *touch her* — as though her body were covered with filth, almost as though she might poison me." These "sensations" thus slowly evolved into emotions with strong affective content. Miss L discovered that whenever she was angry with her mother, she would avoid physical contact with her. As the severity of her attacks decreased, her *dreams* became more frequent and more colorful.[4] In some of these dreams the mother was drowning, often smothered under symbolic representations of the daughter's feces and urine. It was possible to construct babyhood fantasies in which she wanted to attack her mother with her bodily products in moments of speechless rage; at other times there was the idea that she wanted the mother to suffer and be stifled as she herself was during her asthmatic attacks. In various ways, we arrived at the conviction that she had never quite sorted out her body from that of her mother. It became clear that her particular form of masturbation by withholding her urine and squeezing her thighs together also represented a way of holding an idealized mother inside her in fusional union. This brings to mind Fain's ruminating babies who established precociously an autoerotic substitute for the mother by retention of their stomach contents. As with Miss L, this is a *somatic* compensation and not a psychic *identification*, or true internal object representation. It seems that the maternal object had not survived the attacks made upon it. As Miss L began to experience the same intense rage in the analytic situation, particularly at times of separation, we discovered her fear that such feelings would destroy everyone of importance to her. If others did not explode she herself would burst. At this point she developed for the first time a series of hypochondriacal fears concerning her body—the body to which she had never given much love or consideration. She also traversed a homosexual interlude on the way to the discovery of her sexual

[4]An inverse relationship between dreaming and psychosomatic manifestations has been noted by other analysts—e.g, Berne, (1949, pp. 280–297); Sami-Ali (1969).

body and that of her partner. The penis became for the first time a significant object of desire with phallic meaning. Her past sexual relationships began to seem meaningless, for up till then each man or woman in her life had been a version of the "addictive" mother.

I would like to emphasize at this point that it was not the fantasies of drowning her mother in urine or killing her with fecal matter that caused Miss L's asthma attacks, but her incapacity to tolerate and to elaborate such fantasies in a two-body relationship. It could be proposed that the asthma attacks did in reality carry out the fantasy of a persecuting introject, but this leaves many questions unanswered. Why did such a psychic object fail to arouse elaborated fantasy which might have given rise to the development of a phobia, or even a delusion? At what point did psychic defense work cease to develop or to function and somatic dysfunction arise in its place? The representations and emotions that might well have accompanied her stressful babyhood experiences had neither been projected nor repressed, but totally *rejected* from the ego as though they had never existed. The fantasies in question might indeed be considered to have a universal quality, but an adequate mother-baby relationship is required to absorb them and make them meaningful. Miss L had clearly not been able to "use" the parental objects to help her deal with her lively responses to the world and her lively instinctual demands. She had rendered them lifeless and only her body "remembered."

I have given this outline of Miss L's analysis because it followed a trajectory I have found to be typical with other patients having quite different somatic reactions to inner conflict. The point I am trying to make is that there is an important difference between disorders that are a reaction to unconscious or preconscious ideas, and a disorder that arises in the absence of such fantasy. The dyadic relationship between mother and child has not progressed in certain sectors toward a three-person world, nor has it remained caught in the toils of endless projective identification. Instead there has been retrograde movement from a two-body to *a one-body relationship* which we could perhaps call *psychosomatic regression.* I would like finally, to sum up this "one-body world" and the way in which psychosomatic sufferers tend to regard their bodily selves (compared with patients with other personality structures), and the effect that this unique and primitive type of independence has on the ego ideal.

The body as a psychic object

There is a marked difference between psychosomatic patients and patients who talk about their bodies in neurotic terms. Whether this be the bizarre and imaginative discourse of the hysteric who, all the while talking of his symptoms is drawing our attention to something else, a sexualized element that has been displaced, or the elaborated fears and fantasies of patients suffering from what one might call "castration hypochondria," fears of cancer, tuberculosis, syphilis, which take on the characteristics of compulsive ideas and are often linked to an obsessional structure, we are dealing here principally with repressed fantasies concerning the oedipal drama and with infantile sexual wishes that have undergone regression to pregenital fixation points.

The difference is just as marked if we consider the "organ speech" of the psychotic (Freud, 1915a) which follows the primary mental processes used to make dream thoughts. Freud's examples of "the girl with the twisted eyes" and the Wolf Man "who worked out his castration complex on his skin" demonstrate, as Freud emphasized, that schizophrenic thought is also widely different from neurotic symbolization. In the latter, cathexes remain intact while in the psychoses the attempt to recover one's lost objects results in the patients "having to content themselves with words instead of things."

If we turn now to the psychosomatic patient we must first note that his pathological organic processes, which have nothing imaginary or hallucinatory about them, *will only find mental representation from the time that they inflict physical pain*; otherwise they are obligatorily silent. Once the symptoms break the bonds of silence, they still fail to receive much attention in the analytic discourse. Either they are ignored or are referred to in ways that appear to attach little psychological importance to them. This is frequently accompanied by an attitude of blithe disregard for one's physical welfare as though the body were a decathected object even in the face of evident dysfunction and physical pain. "I had been having these pains for about two years. I didn't know what caused them, but I had contrived a way of walking which made them bearable. This went on up until the ulcer perforated," reported one patient. This is reminiscent of the decathexis of the body achieved by certain patients who indulge in psychotic episodes of self-mutilation and whose massive splitting mechanisms enable them to feel no pain. The ability to stand physical pain when it is highly erotized, as in certain sexual perversions, also comes to mind. Although the aims are very different, there is some common ground in the psychic mechanisms at work which has its roots in the earliest mental functioning of the baby, and which finds expression in psychotic, perverse, and psychosomatic creations.

Allied to the physiological "hardiness" of many a psychosomatic patient is a character trait that has already been alluded to as a frequent manifestation in psychosomatic personalities: the refusal to give in to psychic pain, anguish, or depression. This gives an impression of superhuman emotional control and is allied, I think, with a pathological ego ideal that refuses need and dependency. "I always had to cope alone and I always shall. No one ever helped me to become myself." "I was forced to fly before I had any feathers. Now I must just keep going. Whatever happens I must not stop nor look down." "I never had what they call a 'transitional object.' Mother wouldn't have allowed it. I learned early that I could rely on no one but myself." These three patients, all with marked psychosomatic problems, might well be adult incarnations of the *merycist* babies who had to "cope alone" without the psychic capital to do so. This splendid isolation gives the impression that such people are untouchable and invincible and contributes to the observations made by the Paris psychosomaticians of the operational mode of object relations and the unshakable barrier of "operational thinking." The persons concerned show little libidinal investment in their external objects and appear drastically cut off from their inner ones. In many cases it might be true to say that they are dimly aware of a need, so total and so abject, that to recognize it would destroy the relational mode upon which their ego identity is built. To let disappointment, anger, despair, or any incapacity or failure reveal itself would be tantamount to an insupportable narcissistic wound. The lines of a modern folk song by Simon and Garfunkel epitomize this character trait:

> I touch no one
> And no one touches me.
> I am a rock.
> I am an island.
> And a rock feels no pain
> And an island never cries.

The infant who cannot internalize the breast, who cannot create within himself his mother's image to deal with his pain, is a lonely island. One way out is to turn oneself into a rock. Thus many psychosomatic patients continue on their unwavering tightrope, ignoring the body's signs and the mind's distress signals. This invincibility invades the analytic situation. The stifling of feeling, the breaking of associative chains, the attack on the analyst's attempts to make symbolic links may give the analyst the feeling that his patient is unanalyzable. And it may be so. The upsurge of emotion is often felt like a "crazy" intrusion into the mind, and words may acquire the hypercathectic charge of psychotic objects if they become infused with fantasy.

Much of the success or failure of the analysis of the psychosomatic dimensions of the personality depend on the extent to which the transference is able to bear the coming alive of archaic instinctual impulses, and consequent ego perturbation. Perhaps the limits of the analytic process in these cases are the limits of the analyst. One does not always "survive" as an inner object for one's patients, and then the mother-nursling failure is repeated once more and the psychosomatic defenses hold firm. On the other hand, the analytic process can produce overwhelming change even though to do this it may lead the rock to feel great pain and the island to cry for many years to come.

Chapter X

The Body and Language
and the Language of the Body

Reading a clinical psychoanalytic vignette is rather like examining a tiny fragment of cloth with no knowledge of the garment from which the fabric has been torn. I wish simply to examine certain threads with which a particular piece of analytic tissue was woven — a biopsy if you wish. The fully recorded session that follows is intended solely to illustrate some of the points that have been raised in the preceding chapter. The excerpt provides no account of the course of the analysis (indeed, much of it had little to do with somatic events) and only a fragmentary glimpse of the patient's psychic structure and personality. The session quoted gives no evidence of the patient's sense of humor, his love of music, his capacity to care for those around him, or other creative aspects of his life. At the time he was at grips with the deathlike sectors of his intimate self. One might be tempted to call him a pervert, a borderline psychotic, a character-neurotic, or a grave phobic. Like most people he was capable of being any one of these at certain times, but none of the labels would really fit. His courage and determination to live a new psychic experience enabled him to create a different inner reality and even to find traces of old psychic creations that had long been destroyed.

At the time of this session my analysand had at last been able to imagine things without too much anxiety, and was beginning to capture his thoughts and feelings the moment they came into awareness. He could allow himself to be invaded by the sudden eruption of ideas or strange perceptions and sensations which before would have been forcefully ejected from consciousness. It will be noted that he was aided in this effort by my constant interventions. When our patients can no longer build fantasies or dream, then we must dream for them — until such time as they find the courage to regain contact with their psychic reality and creativity.

As with many of my somatizing patients, this analysand feared his fantasy life as others might fear madness; even in his sleep, he dared not dream. When the dreams began to form, or to be remembered, they were scarcely symbolic, and as is often the case, were littered with themes of corporal damage, blood and body fluids, partial objects and organs. The waking fantasies expressed by my patient during the session quoted here may appear violent, crude, or bizarre, as though the elements of which they are composed had waited many long years in a larval state until the experience of analysis allowed the patient to acquire sufficient freedom (coupled with valiant determination) so that they might surface and find expression — perhaps for the first time — in words.

Paul Z, thirty-nine years old, assistant director in a

branch of an important international company, and an indefatigable worker, sought analysis because of depressive and anxious feelings of an ill-defined nature. He felt people did not like him; he had violent quarrels with his wife; he had been refused an important professional advancement to which he felt entitled. He had also suffered for fifteen years from a severe form of peptic ulcer, but did not mention this in our initial interviews. In the course of the analysis, he related certain incidents relevant to the period just before the ulcer was discovered. "I had come to Paris to study; it was my first time away from home; the pains became severe shortly after that. Sometimes the pain was atrocious, but it never occurred to me to consult a doctor. I had learned to walk in such a way as to lessen the pain. That continued for three years... up until the perforation...."

At the time of the session noted below, Paul was in his fifth year of analysis. For two years he had been free of gastric pathology with certain rare exceptions that I wish to discuss.

Since the reasons that prompt an analyst to take notes invariably affect his way of listening — and even of intervening — I shall first describe the circumstances which led me to record this one so fully. At the time I was giving fortnightly seminars to young analysts and students on the psychoanalytic process, and was currently engaged in exploring the different forms of separation anxiety that occur in the analytic situation. Experience had taught me that announcement of the analyst's holidays falls into the analytic relationship like a lead balloon, and the marks left by its passage vary according to the patient's pattern of psychic functioning. I had therefore taken notes on several sessions from different analysands during the month preceding my summer vacation.

Mr. X, for instance, accused me of irresponsibility. Why was I taking so many weeks? No doubt going off with a lover to some exotic paradise. I would think of nothing but my pleasure and give no thought to his loneliness. Mr. Y, on the other hand, feared I might have a car accident. He presumed I would be driving alone, since I was either a widow or a spinster (he never could decide which suited him best), and thus I ran the risk of being gravely hurt, without help, possibly dying—leaving Y an orphan without an analyst to look after him when the holidays were over.

You will have noticed that Mr. X's associations are consistent with a classical oedipal organization; separation awakens anxious feelings of exclusion from the paradise of the primal scene. For Mr. Y, on the other hand, separation spells death; he is living out a dyadic mother-infant relationship in which the whole self is threatened, and disintegration fears take precedence over castration anxiety; feelings of oedipal rivalry are not yet on the horizon. As for Paul Z, my ulcer patient, the holiday announcement brought forth no affective reaction, nor any spontaneous fantasy constructions around the impending break in our relationship, but as always in the past, a *recrudescence of his gastric symptoms*. Not only did these somatic events occur with a regularity which even Paul could not deny; they were also accompanied by other nonverbal manifestations. For example, he could never remember the vacation dates and on more than one occasion had turned up for his regular session after my departure! This time he had carefully noted that our work for the year would cease on July eleventh, but this did not prevent his announcing, on the second to last session, that to his intense regret he would have to miss the session of July twenty-fifth. The following notes were taken the day after, that is during the final session before the summer vacation.

PZ: No session on the twenty-fifth? Well, well! Madame has decided to take her holidays? Anyway I couldn't care less [pause]. In case you're wondering, I'm thinking about my penis. Large, suntanned, very good-looking, I assure you. [Here Paul takes up a theme which has appeared on several occasions since I announced my vacation dates—elaborate fellatio fantasies in which we are both supposed to participate and to find sublime pleasure. The fantasies are strictly nongenital, nonoedipal, limited to partial objects: mouth-penis.]

JM: Do you think there's some connection between our coming separation and these erotic fantasies that link us together—and maybe deny the separation?

PZ: Perfectly absurd! So you're going on vacation? Fine! I'd be crazy if I made a fuss about so little [pause]. My penis isn't as good-looking as I pretend...a bit misshapen, and dark-colored...in erection it looks like a pick.

        [Paul cannot tolerate the idea (or the affect?) that he would be in any way disturbed about the holiday break. By offering me a flattering view of his penis, he feels he has changed the

PZ: subject under discussion. My intervention suggesting the two themes may be related is received as a narcissistic hurt — which may account for his revising his offer! In any case, the
scene changes subtly into a sadistic one, and the
associations that follow clearly reveal the
counterpart to his erotic fantasy.]

PZ: I see myself attacking your mouth with my sex. It
leaves a brown terrifying stain on your breasts
[pause]. My arms are jumping again, as though
they had electric shocks in them. It's annoying.
[The fantasy of buccal aggression is no doubt
also relevant to my *words*, which Paul feels as
an attack on his phallic narcissism. It is important to note that in the place of *feelings*, Paul
describes physical *sensations;* these would seem
to be the residue of an affect that has been
stifled, or in some way failed to achieve psychic
representation. Since he frequently brings such
"communications," I try to prod him to find a
verbal equivalent for the somatic sensation.]

JM: Do you think of anything that might go with
this sensation of electric shocks in your arms?

PZ: You might tear my penis to pieces with your
mouth. Good God, what have I said now?
[It took Paul (and myself) some time to realize
that he never allowed himself to imagine anything freely; when he does at last permit spontaneous fantasy to arise, its violent nature
shocks him, but by now he is convinced that
this is the only way to get into closer contact
with his unconscious, and he therefore pursues
such fantasies when they surge forth in spite of

the anxiety they sometimes arouse. As we can already see, he has great difficulty in containing and working through any *ambivalent* feelings — whether these be about himself, part objects, or whole objects. Here it is his penis that is "split" into two contrasting images, along with his image of the analyst. From an erotic fantasy in which his sex organ is to awaken fascination and desire, he passes to the opposite in which his penis becomes ugly and dangerous — and the analyst violent and castrative. The *wish to attack* is immediately projected onto the analyst (although the only sign of its existence comes through the sensation of electric shocks in his arms.) From being the attacker, he is now the victim, and must protect himself. Castration anxiety in this phase of Paul's analysis can only be expressed in primitive pregenital terms: penis-breast and mouth-vagina, mutually gratifying and mutually destructive, while the "dark sex" and "brown terrifying stain" foreshadow fantasies of fecal attack. The part objects are neither "good" nor "bad," but idealized and persecutory. The "good-looking" penis, capable of repairing separation, is transformed into a destructive object; the mouth, erotic and incorporative, becomes a castrative organ that tears up what it encounters — briefly, all that is included in the concept of "oral-sadistic love" and archaic oedipal anxiety. Faced with this primitive psychic conflict, Paul does not deal with it by *repression (Verdrängung)*, but by foreclosure *(Verwerfung)*; the whole conflict is thus eliminated from the symbolic chain and will tend toward *reactions other than neurotic symptoms:* delusional projections or somatization.]

PZ: I've had terrible gastric pain the last two weeks — but I don't want to talk about it. So childish that this always happens before the holidays. And eczema between my fingers too! But that's due to sexual frustration. Nadine rejects me totally these days.

[Here Paul unwittingly proposes the Freudian hypothesis of the *actual neuroses* to explain his eczema! In an attempt to render his somatic manifestations more "neurotic," more available to verbal thought, and with the hope of warding off the constant blocking of affect which destroys so much of Paul's psychic reality and hampers the analytic process, I try to link these afflictions to some fantasy content of an affective kind.]

JM: Nadine and I both reject you: she refuses sexual relations; I abandon you for the vacation, and tear your penis with my teeth. Instead of getting aggressive, you present yourself as sick, helpless, totally incapable of harm.

PZ: But I've no aggressive feelings about either of you. Besides, I *adore* women!

JM: Maybe there are two parts of you — one that adores women and another that is afraid of their aggression?

PZ: Somehow that idea upsets me...I feel something shrink in my stomach.

JM: Can you imagine "something" in the place of

this shrinking sensation?

PZ: Nadine! When she won't make love with me I imagine her stuck on a pick—and it's white-hot. She wriggles like a worm—can't get off [pause]. That thought gives me considerable pleasure.

[The "pick-penis"... the castrating mouth... the abdominal attack which in one instance is the pick in Nadine's stomach and at another moment the "something" that shrinks inside his own... the confusion between inner and outer, between self and object, all catch my attention, and I wonder vaguely if this is "ulcer imagery," but I find no adequate interpretation and decide to wait.]

PZ: Your silence frightens me [pause]. I'm thinking of my fear of crowds... July fourteenth, they can celebrate it, I assure you, but you won't find *me* in the streets. I'm always afraid the crowd will turn nasty.

[An interesting example of *projective identification*. Paul now attributes to the anonymous "crowd" hostile feelings of his own which he can neither contain nor elaborate. In place of the attack on "Woman" with his "pick-penis" (perhaps against the content of her abdomen: a "crowd of babies"?) it is Paul himself who is threatened with attack from the crowd. Since it has now become the depository of his own sadism, he can avoid it magically—he only needs to keep away from crowds. This is the first time his phobia of crowds has revealed any fantasy roots, but they are far from consciousness. His next associations show that the defense afforded by projective identification is fragile and tends to break down, leaving somatic sensations and feelings of depersonalization in its wake.

PZ: The other day as I left here there was a crowd of people gathered in the street — a demonstration or something. Gave me a peculiar sensation...I felt dizzy. Said to myself "Now imagine something quickly so you can get across that street." So I thought of my penis, standing up, strong and clean. Like a positive statement.

[A nascent feeling of anxiety, stemming no doubt from an archaic form of castration anxiety linked to the above primitive fantasy, is once more experienced somatically; the affect becomes "peculiar sensation" and "dizziness." Faced with the hostile "crowd-woman," Paul seeks to protect himself once again, apparently with his "pick-penis." This attempt to surmount overwhelming anxiety through erotization recalls his similar attempt to deal with unexpressed feelings of abandonment regarding the vacation break by erotization of the transference — a psychic movement strongly reminiscent of that found in sexual deviations.]

PZ: But my idea didn't work. Right away I saw my penis all brown and horrid and covered with sores. So I wasn't protected...I couldn't think ...I [pause]. Ah, it's a feeling I have; I don't even want to say it. I'm even afraid to say it here...well, I felt as though my head split into two pieces. Such a horror — it made me want to throw up. I tell you, it split in two!

[Submerged by his inarticulable conflict, Paul seems to have suffered a brief moment of depersonalization. His head "split in two" is a thought produced by *primary-process thinking,* just as it might have appeared in a dream. This highly condensed image reflects Paul's ambivalence, his sadomasochistic impulses, his confusion between himself and others, the mixture of libidinal and destructive impulses. He seeks a way out of his dilemma. His highly invested gastric area provides him once more with a somatic metaphor in place of the missing representations and emotions: the psychic conflict presants itself as a wish to vomit. Paul makes a valiant attempt to analyze the incident and put into words the thoughts that have escaped symbolic representation.]

PZ: If you want to throw up it's because you think you're just a lot of vomit. The word "Frankenstein" came into my mouth. That's it — I'm Frankenstein. Attacking people's bodies . . . devouring them . . . it's not the first time I've had this idea . . . fills me up . . . horror. I . . . vomit!

[The image of Frankenstein who tears people apart in order to make perfect beings is here condensed with that of Dracula who lives by sucking his victims' blood. Paul's fellatio fantasies, which disintegrated into images of the torn-apart penis, suggest that he is attempting once more, through erotization, to deal with the archaic terror of having torn up and eaten his love objects (their partial representations), and in consequence risks being torn apart and devoured himself. This oral-sadistic love, projected a few minutes earlier on the "crowd-woman," has been brutally reintrojected in the condensed word image, "Frankenstein." Paul's persecutory anxiety has become depressive; he is no longer the victim but in a flash becomes the greedy oral-castrating infant who loves his objects to their destruction. I am reminded here of a recent session in which Paul claimed that he felt "jumpy and under attack" because my stomach was rumbling (I find my stomach often rumbles when listening to my "gastric" analysands). On this occasion Paul had immediately associated the feeling of "attack" to a recent meal taken with Nadine. The sight of "torn bits of sardine, floating in oil" was so disgusting and frightening to him that he had felt suddenly confused, and did not know what he was doing there. My interpretation at that time — that he felt attacked by my abdominal noises as though my inside resembled the sardines, torn up and in pieces — had been rejected as absurd. Today it seems that in his fantasy world, he (Dracula-Frankenstein) might be held responsible for the torn-up or eaten-out inside of the woman. This might make anyone feel confused, and impel one to want to "vomit up" such an image. I hesitated to communicate these ideas to Paul without being sure that he was ready to accept them as ideas to work over, particularly since he was making an effort to grasp and put into words for the first time the

PZ:

overwhelming feeling of having to "vomit up"
an essential aspect of his being.]
How can I say it...the intense effect of the
word [whispers, "Frankenstein; there, I said
it"]...and the films...and the fascination...
as though, well, I get lost...feel horrible...
falling apart. [From here on Paul's associations
become rapid and somewhat garbled, at times
inaudible. For some minutes I noted nothing of
what he said, but instead wrote some of my
own thoughts about him: that it would be
tempting to imagine that his destructive and
cannibalistic fantasies were in some way the
cause of his gastric pathology, but everything
pointed to the contrary conclusion, namely that
his very inability to allow himself to create such
ideas, to put them into words (or to have been
allowed to play them out as games in his childhood?) left him today with an anonymous
dread about which he was unable to *think*.
Since he seemed to have destroyed or, at the
very least, denied access to large sectors of his
psychic reality, he was under continual
pressure, which no doubt facilitated somatic expression—much as an infant suffering intense
psychic pain for which he has no words might
vomit up his food or in some other way suffer
from gastric hyperfunctioning. Paul's ulcers
could not be considered to have any symbolic
meaning (although as a result of the analysis
they acquired fantasy content), but perhaps this
response could be thought of in terms of a
psychosomatic regression to that early stage of

psychic life in which gastric hyperfunction might be a normal expression of love as well as of hate. I had made rough notes to this effect — perhaps because Paul's confused and excited monologue stirred up in me the need to put some order into *my own* thinking. In any case, I was brought back abruptly to his discourse when he suddenly announced:] Now I'm completely lost — and I wonder if your head isn't as muddled as mine with all these thoughts.

JM: Perhaps you are trying to get rid of the "lost" feeling by putting your muddled thoughts into my head? Is my head "split in two" now?

PZ: Ha! That's truer than you think. All week I said to myself, "there we are, gastric pains are back again, and that could be really serious. And eczema as well! Just wait till I tell her how ill I am and that it's all her fault." I promised myself you'd go off on holiday torn apart with guilt because you've conducted this analysis so badly!
[Paul proceeds to develop at length the pain and anxiety I am to suffer during the vacation. It occurs to me that, for the first time, he is reacting with some trace of affect when faced with a holiday break. It is not Paul who is to suffer, but me, and I am to carry something of *him* away with me — his anxiety and pain.]

JM: So I may go off on holiday on condition that I carry you in my thoughts; but I'm to be "torn apart" inside with anxiety? Do you think this is a way of getting rid of your own inner anxiety, by giving it to me instead?

PZ: Bitch! Oh my God what have I said? I'm sorry

...the word just slipped out you know [pause]. You aren't angry with me, I hope? [pause] Say something! I'm afraid.

JM: Of dangerous words? Thoughts that can kill? [Reference to an earlier session where he was afraid to imagine things in case they came true.]

PZ: Ah...yes! Just now I didn't dare say it, but I was thinking about...well...a fascinating detective novel...the criminal, well he was a strangler. But he only strangled women. Exciting desire. Ah, if only I were crazy! You know there's something special about strangling ...almost a caress [pause]. I say, do I scare you?

[The flourishing fantasies of violence and physical attack on women which have marked this session are in such striking contrast to his statement that he "adores women" and would be incapable of aggressive thoughts about them, that I leave the theme of separation anxiety and its accompanying ambivalence to interpret instead the split in his id impulses. I link this to the fantasy of woman as dangerous. I ask him whether the exciting idea of *strangling* women might not be a way of having erotic contact but keeping the dangerous woman under control. This intervention led to sudden free associations concerning puberty and masturbation fantasies of sadistic intercourse.]

PZ: What you said there gave me a strange feeling —reminds me, when I was about nine, I often used to *strangle my penis*. It hurt terribly, but I got terrific pleasure from it.

[Thus I learn for the first time about Paul's attempts to master castration anxiety through the invention of a sexual deviation in which his fear (that his penis will be "strangled" because of forbidden sexual wishes) becomes the very source of excitement and pleasure (see Chapter II). The repressed fantasies revealed in the masturbation game began to take their place in the chain of archaic primal-scene images: the devouring and castrating mouth...the strangling vagina with oral and anal qualities...the "strangler-strangled" relationship in which Paul would strangle the woman's neck instead of his penis and thus, through the lack of distinction between self and object, could contrive by projective identification to approach and at the same time control the dangerous female and the frightening impulse.]

PZ: Say something! Frankly, I don't feel you're very well-disposed toward me today.

JM: The "bitch-woman" with a sex that strangles?

PZ: Now there's an important idea! [His whole body, which has been taut and rigid throughout the last ten minutes, relaxes visibly. At the same time, other new associations come to the fore—and bring forth a classical symbol of the dangerous female genital.] That makes me think of my terror of *spiders*. Loathe them. There was one in my office the other day, near the ceiling. I was paralyzed with fright... couldn't understand a word my secretary was saying.

[The spider-woman, devouring and strangulating, with her paralyzing effect, now stood out clearly for me behind the "adored" image. The sexual relationship becomes a sort of duel in Paul's unconscious fantasy, in which he is up against terrible odds and there is no sign of a *symbolic paternal object* with which to identify or from whom protection might be sought. Perhaps Paul must "tame" his sexual objects by massive seduction, or else dominate them by fantasies of sadistic attack? There was no protective space between his sexual wishes and the archaic all-powerful maternal imago. Meanwhile Paul is recounting a series of spider memories which would appear to have permeated his whole childhood. He remembers that as a little boy he adored playing with insects, *especially spiders,* and would play with them for hours. This period coincided with the time of the penis-strangling game—latency and early puberty. Paul suddenly noticed his contradictory attitude to spiders: the favorite companions of his childhood and today a source of phobic anxiety.]

PZ: How did I get on to this thing of spiders anyway?

JM: The "spider-woman" who is not "very well disposed toward you today"?

PZ: Wow! I get a picture of my sex positively *mangled* by you.

[A countertransference movement of which I was quite unaware at the moment led me to overlook my identification with the penismangler. Leaving the territory of the split maternal image, I directed my attention to the frightening lack of an internal father-*protector*, and thus to the inevitable fear of finding the *castrative* father somewhere inside the woman — possibly a rich source of many of his fantasies of oral-anal castration by strangulation. The woman and her body would remain a source of hidden terror as long as this condensed primal scene continued within. I also had in mind a recent dream of Paul's in which he stretches out his hand to grasp a ray of light; as his hand closes on it, it turns into a black snake. This dream led him to recall the incident of a man who climbed over a "log" which suddenly reared its head and revealed itself to be a dangerous snake. His thought was fixed on the image of the snake biting the man's genital, and on how one has to be so careful of what appears on the surface to be innocuous. The "spider-genital," in spite of its harmless appearance, may hide a "strangling-biting black snake," an archaic fetishlike construction which is a common enough fantasy element in condensed oedipal organizations such as Paul's: the incestuous child risks being "mangled" by the mordant phallus inside the woman, a dangerous and uncontrollable representation of the father's penis, detached from its true object. I told Paul that he appeared to feel threatened by me as though I hid a mangling black snake-penis which would attack his own. In so doing I abruptly left the terrain of the female genital, endowed with oral and anal sadism, to move into that of a feminine-phallic metaphor which he was in no way ready to accept.]

PZ: I don't understand what you're talking about! A penis inside you? What's that go to do with it? Oh, I can easily imagine you with a penis — but that's not what *frightens* me. A penis penetrates; I'm afraid of being *strangled*! You helped me see this, and I agree with everything you've said up to now, but this penis idea doesn't make sense to me.

[Paul's downright refusal of my ill-timed interpretation set me thinking. He was right — it was precisely the *lack of any symbolic penis representation* that left him helplessly frightened of being devoured, torn up, mangled. The paternal phallus played no structuring symbolic role in Paul's psychic reality at this point. The maternal imago, all-powerful, needed neither a paternal nor a personal penis. The son could only engage in a deathlike struggle in which the object at stake was not primarily his penis and his sexual desire, but his entire self, his life.[1] It was evident that my hasty interpretation was due to *my own anxiety* in this two-dimensional relationship, and that I was seeking to bring in, at any cost, some paternal dimension. Thus I

[1] We had to wait two more years to analyze effectively Paul's oedipal castration anxiety, along with its quota of homosexual fantasies and anxieties. These were largely responsible for his inability to accept feelings of rivalry, and resolve his many work problems. By then I was no longer a strangling female, but a male rival who he imagined was more successful professionally than he, and who would certainly throw him out of analysis if he began to succeed in his own profession!

substituted the *mother with a penis* for the *omnipotent phallic mother* who would mangle and devour young Frankensteins. Although there are many links between the two fantasies, their difference is highly important — as this session clearly demonstrated. Perhaps I had been protecting myself unconsciously from the devouring cannibalistic son! Paul had offered me a phobia, and I had given him a fetish in return. His associations went round in circles in an attempt to use my interpretation, until I decided to tell him that I considered it erroneous; I reformulated the important split in the two female representations instead. That I had "gone astray in my interpretations" delighted Paul and also allowed him to take up his own discourse once more, free from countertransference interference.]

PZ: Once I put a spider and an earwig together into a spider web. They fought to the death...both dead. It was atrocious to watch. I used to like watching the spiders strangling the flies with their silken threads. You know they're frightfully aggressive and poisonous.

[Paul evoked many other long-past entomological dramas of which he had been the theatrical director. Wasps, bees, ants, and worms were his principal players in an ever-repeated primal scene of insect dimensions, in which crushing, strangling, and the poisonous sting played their inexorable role while providing a framework to contain the little boy's intense sexual anxiety. As time went by, it seems the perverse solution of strangling his penis was lost (perhaps exposing him to the risk of a psychosomatic regression instead!). But something was also gained. It is worth noting that today Paul is a learned though nonprofessional entomologist, and that this sublimatory activity continues to give him pleasure. Paul then went on to talking about his own sex life as though he too interpreted the insect battles in terms of primal-scene fantasy.]

PZ: When I feel like making love and Nadine rejects me, I get urticaria around my genitals.

JM: As though you produce urticaria in place of love-making?

PZ: Exactly! Just like masturbation.

JM: What does urticaria make you think of?

PZ: Ugh! Ants, worms, things wriggling everywhere. Horror. Just talking about it makes me itch all over. When Nadine refuses sex for days on end, that's just the way I feel — as though I were covered with insects. I itch everywhere, even in the places where there's no urticaria. My hair gets greasy and sticks to my scalp. I feel dirty and have to keep taking showers.

[Traces of hysterical conversion and of obsessive-compulsive behavior are briefly visible here, but poorly organized. The insect games and childhood sexual fantasies are replaced by skin sensations and anal fantasy, as though Paul's skin becomes enraged when Nadine pushes him away, and his whole body image becomes permeated with fecal imagery.]

JM: What do you think this skin language signifies?

PZ: It reminds me of my mother. She had horrid
        skin eruptions. Good heavens! Exactly like my
        penis the other day, covered with sores. It used
        to make me itchy to look at her [Paul twists his
        hands in the air and scratches at his skin and
        rubs it as though brushing off insects].
        [I reflected about all Paul had told me of his
        mother, seductive and frustrating at the same
        time. He had been breast-fed until he was four;
        there were many latency memories of games of
        an erotic kind with her, yet she disliked being
        touched. He now seems to be living out a
        regressive fantasy of being inside her skin (a
        desire to fuse? to undo separations?), and of be-
        ing punished for it (the skin sores? a fantasy
        castration on his own skin?). Whatever the an-
        swers may be, it seems certain that Nadine's
        present coldness, coupled with my imminent
        departure, have contributed to reactivating sex-
        ual interdictions of an archaic kind with regard
        to his mother.]

JM: So you are getting into your mother's skin?

PZ: God damn! Becoming my mother is no solu-
        tion! Besides the idea is horrendous. Having a
        sexual desire for her doesn't bother me — I've
        always known that I found my mother sexually
        attractive. What eats me up is the idea of being
        inside her skin. I feel crawly all over.
        [We get some inkling of a primitive desire to be-
        come one with his mother — whether in response
        to genital impulses or to the threat of separation
        (Nadine, the analyst), so that the original li-
        bidinal object, the mother's body and genital, is

endowed with oral-castrative and anal-exuding toxic fantasy, as an archaic line of primal defense. But the self-object confusions, due in part to the particular nature of Paul's relationship with his mother and the oedipal organization to which it gave rise, could only lead to displacements, condensations, projections, and counterprojections in a never-ending series — the mother's body — pits contents — her skin — the penis-neck to be strangled — the crowd-woman — the spider.

Paul's whole archaic drama would seem to have found — and lost — a multitude of psychic expressions and temporary "solutions" throughout his childhood. Some are only just returning to his mind; others were clearly given up without compensation in the form of new psychic constructions: for example, the insect theater, half eroticized and half sublimated, had given way to a sexual perversion, a hysterical conversion, a phobia, an authentic sublimation, and a psychosomatic malady.]

JM: Our time is up for today.

PZ: O.K. I just wanted to say that I'm beginning to see there's something wrong in my relations with women. Nadine, you, my mother — I've plenty to occupy me for the summer vacation!

One might postulate that Paul's true illness was not his gastric ulceration, but the profound split between psyche and soma, between his thinking self and his emotional life, on which his psychic structure was built. This formed the core of his illness. The soma was, so to speak, left to cope alone with psychological dangers that could not be represented psychically. There is reason to hope that the chasm between the real body and the imaginary somatic self had become narrower, and that the "delusional" body with its deranged somatic functioning was gradually becoming a symbolic one.

Chapter XI

Psychic Pain and the Psychosoma

Pain is a bridge that spans psyche and soma and as such presents particular interest to those whose work brings them into contact with human suffering. Whether it be physical or mental, it is pain that brings the patient to seek help, presenting the therapist with a complex challenge. The ineffability of pain makes it only approximately transmissible to another person. Once communicated, accurately or not, it places the therapist before the necessity of proving the value of his theoretical knowledge and his therapeutic skill.

From the point of view of analytic research and practice it is the field of *psychic pain* that forms a basic dimension to our daily work. Physical pain is not our concern except insofar as it becomes part of the analytic discourse and thus takes on symbolic significance. At least this is our pretension, and perhaps at heart we wish to avoid problems that may be considered specifically somatic. But the distinction between physical and mental pain is not as clear as we would like to believe, no clearer in point of fact than the intrication of the biological and the erogenic body. The language of pain always contains an inherent contradiction and inevitably presents us with a paradox.

Let us take the case of a hysterical patient who suffers from violent headaches each time he is to engage in a sexual adventure. Is he suffering from physical or psychic pain? Are we justified in proposing that mental suffering frequently provokes physical suffering? Might the opposite not be equally true? The link between these two fields of suffering is such that pain in one area inevitably affects the other — at least to the extent that the psychosoma functions as a whole and that body and mind are in contact with one another. However, it may happen that the paths that allow of such intercommunication are blocked, or that the messages are received but wrongly interpreted, so that physical pain and affective pain are confused or substituted for one another as part of psychic defense. It is frequently difficult to decide at what point an analysand is laying emphasis on his physical suffering in order to avoid recognizing mental pain. Patients who talk of their tiredness in place of recognizing depressive affect and the painful ideas associated with it are a commonplace occurrence in clinical practice. And the contrary situation, that of the analysand who ignores the signs of physical illness and instead attempts to find vairous "psychological" causes for his pains is equally as well-known. There are narcissistic factors involved in both situations, but the problem is more complex than that.

It is evident that a person who enjoys good physical and mental health is not invaded by pain. But the absence of suffering may itself be deceptive. It is possible for certain people to deny any awareness of mental pain and even to become insensible to physical pain. The psychic representation of the pain in these instances is either repressed, repudiated from consciousness, or otherwise stifled — at which point the suffering in question no longer exists for the individual concerned. Such an outcome is consequent on important psychic and somatic dysfunction of which the patient remains unaware, since he lacks any psychic recognition of the existence of his pain. From this point of view, it might be held that *pain is basically a psychological phenomenon.* The exclusion from consciousness of ideas and fantasies is, of course, familiar territory, and has formed the basis of psychoanalytic research for nearly a century. But the repudiation from consciousness of affective states, and the scrambling of messages from the soma have received significantly less attention. Yet these questions were given considerable importance by Freud from the beginnings of psychoanalytic discovery. And indeed such phenomena continue to play an important role in analytic work and may even render it inoperative if we do not manage, with the help of our analysands, to highlight these areas of impediment. We might, of course, believe that the attempt to throw light on such obscure phenomena as states of pain is like trying to solve the fundamental enigmas of life, and that the psychosoma is beyond our analytic scope as far as its somatic dysfunction may be concerned. As the observer of purely psychic phenomena, what may the analyst hope to detect with regard to the body, its somatic functioning, and its affective repercussions? Clearly there is nothing to observe unless these states give rise to psychic representations capable of being communicated.

If we wish to explore further the significance of somatic events as they appear in the psychoanalytic discourse we must first question *the status of the body as an object for the psyche*. It seems evident that without a body there can be no psyche; and no one would contest, at least from the psychoanalytic viewpoint, that psychic processes originate in and develop out of biological ones. The paradox reappears: *the body, if it is not able to achieve psychic representation, has no existence for the ego*. The analyst only has access to the "somatic self" to the extent that his analysand is able to apprehend it psychically himself, and provided also that the representations are communicable and that the patient is willing to transmit them.

The gap between the somatic self as the psyche is able to perceive it, and its embodiment in reality, may be astonishingly large. Every analyst has observed situations in which the patient claims to be in excellent physical health, denying evident signs to the contrary, until he falls seriously ill. Before then the illness, though real, had *no psychic existence* for him. Another commonplace example is the analysand who believes and therefore "knows" he is physically ill while in reality he enjoys perfect health. The only "truth" is that acknowledged psychically by the subject; we can scarcely expect him to communicate another one. Any ideas about his soma that differ from his own mental representations run the risk of being rejected as absurd. We might indeed say that the body about which we talk, of which we are conscious, with which we live, is nothing but *a system of psychic facts*.

This statement can be corroborated even with regard to the reflected visual image of the body. A patient overwhelmed by psychotic anxiety may, in his attempt to deal with it, create the delusion that one side of his body is missing. It would be useless to explain to him that this is erroneous, since others can clearly perceive both sides of his body. He "knows" the truth, that is, the facts accepted by his ego as true, and he is then likely to suspect those who say anything to the contrary of lying to him. Should these rational folk place him before a mirror, he will rapidly conclude that the image in the glass is not his own.

In fact the inability to recognize one's mirror image is not confined to those who are deluded. One of my patients, who lived in self-sought solitude in order to protect his creative narcissistic universe, claimed he never looked in the mirror and felt no need to. Whenever he accidentally caught a glimpse of his reflection, it required a short lapse of time for him to recognize the image as his own, and he felt impelled to verify that he was looking into a mirror and not at another person. He was perpetually astonished that others recognized him so readily. "My image of myself? But I have no such image. What would I want it for?" Another analysand, considerably more disturbed, discovered during a psychotic episode that her body "was another being," and that by placing herself before the glass she was able "to communicate with herself for the first time on certain matters."

Both these patients were communicating certain psychic "truths" concerning their somatic selves, and in ways which we have all known in childhood. For the infant ("infans": unable to speak) whose psyche is not yet formed by words, *his body is an object belonging to the external world* insofar as his psyche is able to be aware of it. He will need several years in order to attain psychosomatic unity, to believe that he lives *inside* his body, and to be capable of saying "*I* feel well, strong, sick, sad . . ." and so on. The feeling of identity is structured around the conviction of being contained in one's own skin, and the certitude that the soma and the self are indissociable. It is therefore surprising to discover that many adults do not possess this representation of the psychosoma. Once again the split between body and mind is not restricted to those who are governed by psychotic thinking. The analyst discovers with surprise that certain of his patients do not inhabit their bodies, while others have no mental awareness of perceptible somatic states; certain body parts, erogenic zones, and sense organs may also be eclipsed through their failure to achieve psychic representation. The gestalt of the somatic self is totally dependent on the ego's system of psychic representation. Representations that have been *repressed* are of course relatively accessible to both analyst and analysand in the course of analytic work, but those that have been ejected from the psyche in more radical fashion, as in the cases cited above, will only find their place in the analytic discourse inadvertently, or become perceptible through *the analyst's impression that something is missing.*

The psychosomatic image plays a fundamental role in ego identity, and the manner in which a person experiences his body tells us much about the structure of his relations with others. Neurotic relationships are dictated to a large extent by the nature of repressed fantasies attached to the erogenic zones and their significance. We might call this the "neurotic" body. But when the body no longer signifies that which separates one subject from another, and inside from outside, and when a person does not firmly believe that he inhabits his body, then relations with others run the risk of being confused or even terrifying. A similar predicament may create confusions between one part of the body and another, or condensation in the representation of the different zones and organs in the body image. This constitutes the "psychotic" body. It should be noted that this particular "body" resembles closely the "body" in repressed neurotic fantasy, and of course is familiar to every dreamer.

For others again the body as a psychic object is neither a neurotic nor a psychotic one, but an apparently disinvested one; its somatic and affective messages are not considered as the bearers of forbidden impulses, or feared as signs of extraterritorial power. Because of other psychic forces which remain obscure, the mental representations of the soma are disavowed, or decathected, or if registered, are denuded of meaning, and rejected from consciousness. Relations with others tend frequently in such cases to follow the same pattern, that is, the psychic reality of others or the significance of one's relation to them appears to be decathected. This deaf-and-dumb relation between psyche and soma is the hallmark of the "psychosomatic" body.

It should be pointed out that we all possess all three of these "bodies" with their potential symptomatology. The different organizations of the ego-body relation that I call the psychosoma are best studied in people in whom there is a notable predominance of one of the three somatopsychic modes. I shall discuss this more fully in the next chapter.

In order to better understand the psychic functioning behind the "psychosomatic" body, which is our chief concern in this chapter, the question of *the representation of pain*, whether physical or mental, is a central issue. But this presents a particular difficulty. From the standpoint of analytic observation of psychosomatic phenomena, we are faced with the lack of the very representations we wish to study. What trace can we expect to find of a missing representation?

As far as physical pain goes, there are many circumstances in which it is relatively easy to observe the psyche's capacity to refuse recognition of suffering: self-mutilators are able to remain completely insensible to the pain they inflict on themselves during moments of great psychic tension; catatonic patients, along with certain mystics such as fire-walkers, feel no pain in circumstances in which others would suffer considerably. It is a well-known fact that physical suffering may be *eroticized* to such an extent that, far from feeling pain, the person has an orgastic experience. Patients who "somatize" when under stress provide a final example. A certain number are capable of ignoring the body's distress signals until they fall gravely ill. The case of Paul Z (see Chapter X) is an example. I have also noted the same phenomenon in a number of patients with pulmonary tuberculosis.

Through the intricate interplay of splitting mechanisms, projection, and psychic repudiation, the human mind is able to avoid, deny, or even totally destroy any trace of its perception of physical pain, thus revealing a dislocation in psychosomatic unity.

The question of psychic factors that might be common to psychotic states, mystic experiences, sexual perversions, and psychosomatic manifestations arises here, as well as the recognition that these different psychic phenomena are within the reach of everyone at certain times, and form part of the archaic substratum of the human mind. Whatever may be the answer to these different enigmas, for the present it may at least be asserted that all of them are evidence of attempts at self-cure in the face of overwhelming conflict concerning, among other factors, that collection of psychic "facts" which constitutes for every individual his psychosomatic self. We might note, in passing, that the word "psychosomatic" in psychoanalytic language invariably refers to the pathology of the psychosoma, as though we lacked a concept of nonpathological psychosomatic unity. If the mysteries of psychosomatic pain and illness are difficult to conceptualize, the grasp of what might constitute psychosomatic health and psychosomatic pleasure would appear to be even more elusive — whether this be the pleasure of the body in good health, sexual pleasure, or the overall pleasure in feeling fully alive. It seems important to note that these are all essentially psychosomatic events.

The psyche's capacity to ignore physical pain is similarly able to deny mental pain. This similarity, however, arouses more perplexity than enlightenment, in view of the radical difference between the psychic and the physical. Yet it is certain that for the infant there is no distinction between painful physical sensations and painful affective states. Lacking the capacity for symbolic representation, the infant can neither think about his body and its sensations, nor recognize his own painful affective states. He can only *react* to these different forms of suffering at the moment they occur. The often advanced idea of a common psychosomatic matrix from which body and mind eventually develop entails a measure of theoretical incoherence. Would it not be more feasible to postulate that, from the beginning of psychic life, there is a "psyche" whose task is to register somatic presentations in pictographic fashion? Following the work of Castoriadis-Aulagnier (1975), we might posit the existence of an original or *primordial process* (to be distinguished from primary and secondary processes) that persists throughout life in everybody's mental functioning.[1] Without such an assumption the nursling would respond neither to bodily needs nor to the id impulses, and indeed would be exposed to the risk of biological extinction. But the complicated task of symbolization is no spontaneous matter. The eventual capacity of the growing infant to encode linguistically his bodily and emotional experiences is uniquely dependent on the nature of his tie to his mother, for it is she who, in the first instance, must *interpret* her baby's cries and gestures (Chapter IV on "primitive communication" centered on the capturing, in the clinical situation, of signs that might indicate some breakdown in this early communication between mother and baby). The mother also gives her child the words for his different body zones and conveys to him their meaning. She transmits the extent of fantasy space that the erogenous zones may occupy, and in particular the nature of the relation between each zone and its complementary object. The latter is the cornerstone on which the psychosoma schema will be constructed.

[1] I am indebted to Castoriadis-Aulagnier for her enlightening model of the mind-body relation and the activity of mental representation, as well as the concept of a *primordial process* to which I shall make further reference.

One further fundamental structuring element in the infant's psychosomatic organization is the mother's role in giving him *the words for his affects*. Lacking a language for his emotional states, he is incapable of dealing with them adequately. Thus it is within the unique mother-infant sphere that the child may hope to acquire a body which shall have symbolic meaning, and thus become conscious of its many messages and capable of elaborating symbolically, through verbal thought and imagination, the physical and emotional events that are truly his. This early psychic foundation will determine to a considerable extent the adult potentiality to capture and recognize one's personal psychic reality and to be able to communicate it to others. The gradual acquisition of an intact psychosomatic unity demands therefore that the body image, the erogenous zones and the affects and sensations belonging to these, be accessible to the symbolic process.

It is evident that a serious break in the transmission of affect is potentially dangerous. Affective inertia has been studied principally as a manifestation of certain psychotic states (such as the marked hypothymia associated with schizophrenia syndromes). However, this same affective apathy may be subtly present in other, nonpsychotic mental organizations. We have already seen in the portrait of the "anti-analysand" (Chapter VI) one expression of this symptom and the severe resistance to which it may give rise in the analytic situation. My intention in this chapter is to indicate its importance from the point of view of the psychosoma and of the implied threat to psychosomatic unity. *Affect,* in contradistinction to *ideational rep-*

resentation, is a borderline concept involving both body and mind and can in no way be envisaged as a purely psychic phenomenon. This vital bridge provides, well before the acquisition of language, the earliest elements of what will become a symbolic structure to represent the somatic self. These same elements are also providing the future imaginary habitation for the ego, and more specifically for the "I" of the verbal child. The comprehension of psychosomatic pathology will inevitably lead us to a particular interest in the registering of affective states, and the ways in which they are captured by the mother.

The recognition of the infant's affective experience, first by the mother, later by the child himself, is destined to play a primordial role in the construction and the maintenance of psychosomatic integrity as well as contributing a vital factor to the understanding of its pathology. Language itself reveals to us the extent to which sentiment and emotion are deeply rooted in the soma. Every metaphor carries the indelible imprint of its bodily origin. Human beings, to the extent that they are aware of their feelings, will readily communicate to those around them that they feel "crushed" by events, "torn" with sorrow, "stifled" with rage, "heartsick" with disappointment, "stabbed" or "burned" by the pain of treachery, and so on. Other metaphors, equally evocative, are currently called upon to communicate delight and happiness. This intimate interpenetration of psyche and soma through the bridge of affect becomes a serious matter if the circulation is blocked, and particularly if the path is closed to the affect of *pain.* Although the metapsychological problem of affect is fraught with complexity, its biological function is readily accessible. The transmission of affective reaction is destined to provide the psyche with important information concerning the body and its most urgent needs; in addition, it has a role to play in warning the psychic apparatus of approaching situations of psychological stress, or of privation. Should this precious link be friable or even completely severed, the consequences could be serious. The seminal papers of Engel (1962, 1967) give valuable insight into this aspect of psychosomatic dysfunction. Feelings of distress, despair, fervor, guilt, and rage may remain inaccessible to psychic representation and thus unavailable as information which would permit the person to think clearly, finally to take adequate action. Psychological as well as biological integrity might be said therefore to be endangered when physical and mental pain fail to achieve psychic representation.

"Pain: present at the periphery, is at the junction of body and mind, of life and death," writes Pontalis in his sensitive book on psychic pain (1977). Pontalis goes on to trace Freud's line of research throughout his continuing attempts to define the mechanisms at work in the phenomenon of pain and to distinguish between the experience of psychological as opposed to physical pain, as well as the factors that distinguish (or fail to distinguish) the unpleasure of anxiety from the pain of mourning.

It is not my intention to dwell on these subtle differences; important though they may be, their total rejection from the psyche has similar effects on the psychic economy. The nonrecognition of anxiety-arousing factors and the stifling of depressive affect are equally threatening to the unity of the psychosoma. When the psyche remains consistently deaf to painful affect, it is not surprising that this broken link between mind and body offers a favorable territory to pathological psychosomatic manifestations. Where there should have been some form of psychological adjustment, the soma, left to itself, must now take independent action, and will do so in accordance with its own biological savoir which cannot fail to be an inadequate and indeed faulty response to the stressful circumstances in question.

Psychoanalytic research into psychosomatic illness has given rise to two important concepts dealing with this question of flattened affect, namely: the concept of *operational thinking* (allied to the notion of an "operational" personality pattern) devised by research analysts of the Paris School (Marty et al., 1963) and the concept of *alexithymia* elaborated by Nemiah and Sifneos (1970a, 1973). Operational thinking refers to a pragmatic way of thinking about people and events, and implies a form of object relationship with impoverished libidinal cathexis and a lack of emotional response to crucial moments or traumatic losses in the lives of the people concerned. The observational research on which these concepts are based was confined largely to initial interviews in psychosomatic units with patients who had been sent because of their somatic symptoms. The first recorded interview of this type that I was privileged to hear has left an indelible memory. It provides a classical example of what is intended by the term *pensée opératoire*. A young woman suffering from an acute and violent attack of ulcerative colitis describes the onset of her illness but denies any unusual circumstances which may have occasioned stressful feelings at that time. Only in response to the insistence of the examiner does she consent to an attempt to reconstruct the preceding weeks. In a small unemotional voice she then relates the facts of a brutally abrupt abandonment by her fiancé during their vacation together; later in the interview she adds that she was also pregnant, and that this fact had to be dealt with as well as hidden from her parents. The young patient gave the impression of someone who is forbidden to reveal the slightest trace of emotional pain and instead must make the effort to minimize what could hardly have failed to be a traumatic situation over which she had no control. At the time it seemed to me that this young person had been rendered incapable, for unknown reasons, of carrying out the work of mourning, not only for her lover but also for her baby. She had fallen physically ill, much as a small infant might in a situation of catastrophic abandonment by the maternal object, when still at an age too tender to allow of psychic elaboration and verbal thought. However, the adult who reacts to painful circumstances of rejection by uncontrollable and continuing diarrhea raises many a complex question, the more so in view of the apparent absence of concern or emotional pain. It would be misleading to say that the patient quoted here was simply *denying* her feelings; she was quite unaware of them. It is conceivable that a baby, on the other hand, cannot reflect on his affective experience and *needs a maternal object to think for him*. This important function has been described in Bion's writings as the mother's capacity for "reverie," or for being a "container" for her baby's states of pain, which allows her to respond adequately to his needs.

This forms part of what I have called *primitive communication* between mother and child. In Chapter IV I cited the case of a patient who did not suffer from any manifest psychosomatic disturbance, to illustrate how perturbation in this early phase of development may profoundly affect the adult capacity to think about and effectively deal with emotional pain.

It may be noted in passing that the adults who are capable of stifling psychic pain to a marked degree, at times when one would expect an intense emotional reaction, often give the impression of being impavid, imperturbable, and able to deal adequately with no matter what catastrophes may befall them. This might be regarded as an *overadaptation* to external reality. It is more likely that such "strength" in the face of stressful events is a sign of fragility rather than force in the structure of the personality.

When the lack of reaction is particularly marked, however, this gives an impression of schizoid detachment or of psychopathic cynicism rather than adequate adaptation. Such was the case of a patient with a so-called "psychosomatic" personality pattern who, while driving, had run over a woman pushing a baby in a pram, seriously wounding both of them. When asked by the analyst in an initial interview what he had felt about this accident, he replied, "Oh, I didn't worry; I am fully insured"! It is difficult to foresee whether such a patient may one day become less fully "insured" against the psychological path of recognizing that he could find within himself the desire to kill a mother and her baby.

Another patient suffered a near-fatal attack of ulcerative colitis following a car accident in which her

parents and fiancé were killed; her only affective comment was, "I knew I'd have to pull myself together."
We might wonder whether she could come to face the
psychological truth behind her brutal statement that
she must "pull herself together," namely, that the multiple accident had shattered her inner world and that
she herself was in danger of falling apart.

The concept of *alexithymia,* as its name suggests,
concerns the specific inability of a person to name his
emotional states or to recognize the existence of his
affectivity. As with the research into operational thinking, the observations that have given rise to this concept have been based on preliminary interviews and
brief psychotherapy experience. Sifneos attributes this
apparent lack to a difficulty in linguistic symbolization. Other publications (Sifneos, 1974; Nemiah and
Sifneos, 1970b) suggest an irreversible physiological
defect. This seems like a hasty and uncreative hypothesis. Although it is evident that a gap in symbolization would give rise, in situations of psychic conflict, to
a weakened capacity for reflecting about oneself and
one's relation to the world of others, the reasons for
such a psychic "lack" raise questions that lead, from a
psychoanalytic standpoint, to *a consideration of the
vicissitudes of psychic representation and the transformations to which affective experience is subjected
when split off from any mental representation.* Since
we are concerned here with the representation of the
body and the capturing of affective accompaniments of
instinctual presentations, it is highly probable that the
phenomena associated with psychosomatic pathology
have to do with psychobiological processes of a primitive and preverbal order, and that these have failed to

be transformed into authentically symbolic processes capable of psychic representation. One important question: what factors in the psychic structure might be responsible for the continuing exclusion from psychic awareness of information so indispensable to psychosomatic well-being? Let us reiterate that somatic phenomena as a response to overwhelming affective experience and traumatic events is within the capacity of anyone, even though he may, in contra-distinction to many grave psychosomatic sufferers, possess many other modes of psychic management to deal with mental conflict and pain. *Can we then be content with the explanation of a lack — symbolic, libidinal or physiological — to explain such universal phenomena?* This notion only serves to define in the negative an organization that gives rise to many a mysterious reaction, and for which we have yet to devise satisfactory hypotheses. If "lack" there be, it is more likely to reside in our inadequate knowledge. The same may be said of the "psychosomatic personality" which, although clinically observable, is not restricted to those who "somatize," and indeed provides little theoretical enlightenment.

Somewhere in the psychological history of the individual, the apparent "void" must contain a positive significance. The two concepts mentioned above have contributed richly to enlarging our observational field; further psychoanalytic research into the mysterious psychosomatic "leap" is now needed. Other analysts have also brought thoughtful and thought-provoking hypotheses. We saw in Chapter IX that a third line of approach sought to give symbolic meaning to psycho-somatic symptoms, along the lines of neurotic symbolization. Even if the unconscious "meanings" attributed to ulcers, ulcerative colitis, and the like contribute little to our understanding of the causes, it seems to me that the hypothesis of an *archaic form of hysteria* of a psychobiological order is not to be excluded, particularly in view of the fact that psychosomatic symptoms frequently take on a neurotic-hysterical significance. It is a common observation that patients may obtain a much more stable psychosomatic equilibrium in the course of their analyses following the exploration of their oedipal structure and the conflicts to which it gives rise; but the narcissistic economy that maintains the image of the self, and is subtly expressed in the nature of relations with others, continues to threaten the psychosomatic equilibrium should conflict arise in object relations or in the narcissistic investment of the self.

A further contribution to the understanding of psychosomatic phenomena comes from observational research with psychotic patients. Pankow (1969), who has studied at length the nature of the body image and its diagnostic and dynamic value in distinguishing hysterical from psychotic states and psychic structures, notes that many a psychotic patient will tend to fall physically ill at times when his psychotic dissociation is beginning to heal. The psychotic, she claims, is not "in his skin," and feels himself to be without limits; he lacks an internalized image of himself and his body, which otherwise would enable him to maintain a unified image of himself among others. "At what moment," writes Dr. Pankow, "might we presume that a psychotic patient is living inside his own skin?" Certain phenomena are suggested as points of reference, including the capacity of the patient to suffer somatically (fever, digestive upsets, asthmatic phenomena, dermatosis) following a phase of dissociation or delusion. She concludes that "the patient may come to inhabit his body by means of psychosomatic suffering." The phenomena described by Pankow are also observable in the analytic situation with patients who are much less ill than those she is studying—that is to say, patients for whom the meaning of words and the use of language is not disturbed, but who may nevertheless maintain relations with their entourage based on psychotic mechanisms—for example, a relationship in which another person unconsciously represents a part of the subject himself and assures him of his subjective identity. Disturbance in the relationship with such a privileged object may also provoke psychosomatic reactions; these may be of a serious nature, but frequently of a benign order, bringing in their wake a sudden realization of self and of physical and psychical boundaries such as Pankow describes. It should be noted also that such breaks in a narcissistic tie of this kind can give rise to acute *psychotic* episodes in predisposed patients.

One of my patients who had never, in four years of psychoanalysis, been aware of the slightest physical disturbance, directed most of her psychic energy to maintaining mirrorlike relations with friends and lovers. As she began to give up her druglike dependence on others and to reflect more deeply about herself, she became aware, as she put it, "of a new dimension of myself which I have never missed before. I am now able to be sick sometimes; I catch a cold, I have a slight fever, I get weary, I have a backache, and these signs are quite precious to me. They make me aware that I have a body, which needs loving, that I have limits. It makes me feel much more alive, and gives me the possibility of caring for myself and my body."

Looked at uniquely from this point of view, we might be tempted to say that the recognition of being possessed of a body capable of suffering (as well as of pleasure) is indeed progress. It is evident that awareness of somatic pathology implies intrinsically that the "I" recognizes its body as a personal possession, and that the psychosoma is functioning as a unity. Psychosomatic illness may be capable of mobilizing valuable self-awareness and to this extent may be assimilated to many another traumatic experience, such as physical accident, that allows an individual to invest differently his body, its boundaries, and its biological functioning. Such reawakened cathexes, however, enter into the category of "secondary benefits," and the phenomena cannot be satisfactorily interpreted from a teleological standpoint that may propose a given patient allowed himself to fall ill *in order to* "find" himself or to draw upon himself the attention of others. His somatic illness might acquire such significance, but only as an aftereffect, not as a causal factor.

Coming back to the notion of a "psychosomatic personality," I would like to add that my personal clinical experiences lead me to suspect that the apparent detachment and delibidinized object relations maintained by "operational" ways of thinking and feeling, and the poverty of affective expression in communication with others conceal a positive aim — the precocious creation of a protective psychic barrier. It seems to me highly probable that such an organization represents a massive and archaic form of defense against mental pain in all its forms — in relation to oneself, to instinctual demands, and in contact with others. The roots of such defense must be linked to the way in which any interaction with another person is invested in the unconscious fantasy of the individual. Obviously this kind of defense is extremely dangerous to the mental and physical well-being of the person so afflicted, in that it runs the risk of confounding the distinction between inner and outer and between mental pain and physical pain. The supposed danger of the Other gives rise to his being accorded an extremely reduced psychic space — an urgent measure to avoid an introjective identification, with implosive and disintegrative propensity.

It has become evident to me in the course of my analytic work with such patients that this way of coping with the self-world relation is equivalent to the maintaining of a "sterile" space, apparently denuded of affect and libidinal cathexes, a space created in an attempt to preserve ego identity. The patient may protect himself not only against the fear of the potential frustration inherent in all object relations, but also against the unconscious fantasy of being unable to contain and elaborate the overwhelming emotion that threatens constantly to emerge in the contact with others. Such fears reveal themselves eventually to concern a fantasy of being unable to resist the absorption of other people's problems, their psychic pain, and even their physical afflictions. A fantasy of permeability, of interpenetration, without any assurance of one's capacity to master such confusion of identity, carries the concomitant risk of mutual, and potentially mortal, destruction. The story of Sabine (see Chapter VIII) is a case in point. It is perhaps pertinent to mention that this patient's analysis allowed of the complete disappearance of incapacitating psychosomatic symptoms (rheumatoid pathology) of which she had made no mention in the first two years of her analytic work with me.

The notion of an "empty" or "sterilized" space which I am proposing—whether this be the "alexithymic" defect or the "operational" relationship—is more easily perceived with analysands who are not "typical psychosomatics." Patients who have a series of psychic defenses at their disposal, such as neurotic and character symptoms, along with sporadic, or recurrent, psychosomatic manifestations, such as isolated allergic reactions, digestive upsets, cardiovascular incidents, or immunological failure during periods of stress, are exceedingly common in psychoanalytic practice. With patients whose defensive network is reduced to an armor-plated shell, many years may be required before the rejected representations and the stifled affects which surround this "sterilized" space become visible and available to verbal thought and psychic elaboration.

A writer who had come to analysis because of severe work inhibitions and considerable anxiety generated by unacceptable homosexual impulses, suffered also from several atypical skin allergies. In the course of the analysis it became evident that his psychic "skin" was fragile and liable to get "burnt" on the slightest provocation; his constantly recurring incidents of difficulty with others gave a somewhat persecutory nuance to the analytic discourse. His double sensitivity—somatic and psychic—to contact with the external world was expressed in two different modes which seemed to indicate two ways of coping with a basic unconscious danger. Whenever it befell this patient to witness a minor accident in which a passerby might, for example, crush a finger, or have his skin scratched or scorched, the patient himself would immediately suffer from pain in his own finger or from skin-burn, and so on. These would seem to be psychobiological reactions of a primitive kind, a sort of "archaic hysteria" in which anxiety is less attached to the phallic-sexual level than in hysteria, and more closely linked to confusion concerning body limits between one person and another. This raises the question of "archaic sexuality" in which the instinctual impulses tend toward a global corporal union with the Other. As with conversion hysteria, this instinctual desire might be considered to be blocked, leaving the symptom as the only visible trace of its existence. However, the difference between this "psychosomatic hysteria" and neurotic hysteria is considerable. In the Freudian concept, the neurotic symptom is a substitute for the patient's sexual activity (Freud, 1905a); Dora's nervous cough expressed the unconscious fantasy of oral coitus that Dora believed to be the erotic relationship of her father with Frau K. We might also deduce from Freud's theorization that in the second phase of the analysis, in which Dora's homosexual attachment to Frau K is revealed, the same "nervous cough" had acquired further significance — it might now be considered as an identification with Dora's father, in order to live out an unconscious fantasy of access to the longed-for object.

Dora's repressed wishes, attached to both the heterosexual as well as the homosexual Oedipus complex, therefore achieve expression through the symptom. In the case of the "skin-burned" analysand, the sexual conflict is a more primitive one, but the symptom reveals the same underlying dynamic significance: the defense against the double oedipal wish and the accompanying castration fears are replaced by the defense against the *wish* for fusion and the accompanying *fear* of dedifferentiation.

This same patient revealed a more complex defensive structure in relational situations where he risked being "scratched" or "scorched" in his contact with others. He was, for example, incapable of listening to stories of misfortune or recitals of masochistic behavior without being plunged into violent anger with the speaker. He would give vent to this anger in a way that effectively prevented any dangerous identification with the other person. The patient's fragility in situations of potential fusion-confusion led him to avoid on all possible occasions any risk of being exposed to either the physical or the psychological pain of others. It was as though *the pain of the Other immediately became experienced as his own.* The analysand showed no trace of that disaffected or sterilized void between himself and the others which I have found to be typical of "somatizing" patients. This no doubt protected the patient against more serious psychosomatic disorganization, although keeping him in a situation of continual neurotic suffering and continuing neurotic character problems of a paranoid kind. His fear of *becoming the Other* revealed its unconscious counterpart, his fear of a *wish to absorb and be absorbed* in relation to the Other, in a symbiotic or fusional fashion. Any such fantasies mobilized intense horror in the patient, and he came to recognize that he maintained a permanent struggle against their arousal.

This kind of psychic conflict is by no means rare in analytic practice. It gives rise to many different "solutions," with perturbing consequences, such as sexual problems of various kinds arising from physical disintegration fears or the danger of losing one's psychic limits. This anxiety can well give rise to an "addictive" form of sexuality which seeks to confirm bodily and psychological boundaries, a form of "operational" sexuality that might be assimilated to "operational thinking"—a common though not invariable sexual pattern with severely somatizing patients in which the sexual partner runs the risk of being ignored as a separate person with his own psychic space and his own desires. This element is often discernible in perverse sexual relations, although it may prevail in heterosexual relationships also (see Chapters I and II).

The search for the feared-and-desired fusion with Another is also clearly apparent in other addictive patterns. Drug and medicament addiction, extreme dependence on tobacco or alcohol, and bulimia are all common examples in which a nonhuman object plays an unconscious *maternal* role in a desired fusional union. All such addictive "objects" seem to me to belong to the category of *pathological* transitional phenomena.

Further exploration of the psychic economy of the addictive personality goes beyond the aim of this chapter. I would simply like to emphasize that in the case of the "scorched" patient mentioned above, we have a privileged glimpse *in statu nascendi* of the kind of psychic pain that would contribute, in others, to the creation of a protective characterological shell, a defensive organization that today we might call "psychosomatic," or "schizoid," or "narcissistic." The victims of this emptied-out space are liable to be deaf to their own suffering as well as to that of others. The only visible sign of the lost suffering is the "void."

We might also notice the similarity between the facilitating terrain that such sterilized space provides between the subject and his internal and external objects and the phenomena manifested in certain psychotic states. Rosenfeld (1965) describes this kind of psychic management in term of projective identification and suggests that it is often possible to retrace the roots of the mechanisms of projection in the analysis of schizophrenic patients where it may be observed that such patients, at the moment when they draw close to another person, whether in hatred or in love, are in danger *of being confused with the object of their passion.* Nevertheless, in spite of the similarity, there is an important difference. The psychotic organization in itself represents a global defense against an apprehended, though inexplicable or incoherent threat. The psychic work involved serves to provide a "meaning" through delusional formations to explain the suffering; as Freud (1911) put it in the Schreber case, it is an attempt at recovery, an attempt to recreate a new vision of the world "in which it may once again be possible to live." But this attempt at self-cure interferes subsequently with the functioning of the ego; language itself becomes threatened with losing its symbolic and semantic function by being subjected to primary-process thinking. Such a denouement is avoided in the organization described here; in the place of the neo-reality created by psychotic thought, to fill up the incomprehensible void, there is this "nothing" which offers itself to the primordial psychic process that underlies both primary and secondary processes, thus short-circuiting the capturing of instinctual pulsation and leaving an exposed field in which psychosomatic processes may manifest themselves.

What may we envisage as taking place in those sectors of psychic life in which there is no protective buffering in the form of either neurotic or psychotic defenses? What may arise in situations of narcissistic loss or instinctual dissatisfaction? In the absence of neurotic and psychotic symptoms or symptomatic behavior to fill the empty space of non-represented impulses, the soma itself tends to respond — but in accordance with what logic? And in the name of what defensive goals?

To find tentative answers to these questions I have only my observations of patients in analysis — those who suffer predominantly from psychosomatic disorganization, as well as those who, while having sudden psychosomatic manifestations, also possess well-constructed neurotic, narcissistic, or borderline psychic structures. It is instructive in such cases to note the specific moments at which psychosomatic problems arise. The response of the soma to imminent situations of psychic pain and stress appears incoherent in most circumstances, and in any case, totally inefficient for dealing with the stressful situation. But the slow establishing of temporal links and the close observation of the nature of objectal ties provide a number of useful clues. At least a certain "significance" to psychosomatic explosion has become apparent for me, even though the "meaning" has nothing in common with the underlying, language-structured unconscious that contains the key to neurotic and psychotic symptoms and their specific modes of thought. In order to pursue this question of "significance" I shall now leave to one side all the economic factors that appear to obstruct the creation of psychological defenses and to predispose an individual to psychosomatic afflictions in his psychic attempts at self-cure.

Let us go back to the "skin-burned" patient. Quite clearly his skin reacted as though it had been physically attacked (which, incidentally, recalls the somatic responses induced by hypnotic suggestion; if the soma "believes" that it has been burned, it is quite logical that the somatic organization will produce physiological reactions intended to deal with the anticipated damage). When the perception of another person becomes fused with one's own image (as is frequently the case with young children) any affective mobilization due to the sight of the Other being scratched or skin-burned may then be captured and registered psychically in such a way as to precipitate a rapid somatic response, such as a nursling might have in a state of distress. The patient described also suffered at other moments from skin allergies which appeared to arise in a variety of circumstances that were less obvious to him than the witnessing of a skinned or scorched person. The facilitating situations included overwork, mourning situations, and anxiety (imperceptible to the patient at the beginning of his analysis) in situations that aroused forbidden erotic fantasies. My hypothesis in such instances is the following: *in face of the pre-*

monitory threat to the infantile ego, the psyche refuses all recognition of suffering; thereupon the soma prepares itself to combat a biological danger. In patients who are the target of massive psychosomatic explosion, the mistaken "reply" of the soma is more difficult to decipher. I have frequently noticed in analysands who were inclined to severe attacks of respiratory illness, their tendency to fall ill in the midst of the "cold" climate of abandonment and the "hot, stifling" atmosphere of unwelcome aspects of a love relationship. Instead of exploring the strong emotions that might be expected to arise (which these patients would begin to do after a year or more of analytic work) they would develop rhinitis, hay-fever, asthma and eczema. Without some psychic guidelines, the soma is inevitably going to respond mistakenly.

Let us refer once more to the young ulcerative colitis patient described above. Following the brutal abandonment by her fiancé at the time she was pregnant, instead of containing and elaborating emotional reactions to this tragedy, her body, on its own, reacted as though it had been invaded by poisonous substances capable of producing death, and which had therefore to be expulsed physically.

Although analytic work on the basis of the patient's associations to the precipitating factors of psychosomatic illness do in fact give rise to many a hypothesis of the hidden dramas at stake, and even though in certain cases these reconstructions are followed by considerable modification in the psychosomatic pathology, they nevertheless cannot be taken as *sufficient* explanation, although I am of the opinion that we are dealing with a central and necessary element for the comprehension of such phenomena.

The body and somatic function respond following their own autonomous paths; in line with somatic logic, they will attempt to "expulse" or to "retain," or even to do the two at the same time (as we might conjecture to be the case in asthmatic states and colonic dysfunction). It is beyond my field of research to explore the innumerable unanswered questions that touch upon the different forms of psychosomatic expression, for example the difference between symptoms attached to the bodily systems in communication with the external world — the skin, the respiratory apparatus, the elimination and alimentary systems — and those whose functions are directed internally, such as cardiovascular and immunological dysfunctions. Whatever the answers may be, it seems probable that in these affections we are witnessing the effects of *archaic biological processes whose aim is fundamentally to adapt and to conserve life forces* — a strange psychosomatic irony!

In sum, I believe that the "operational" sectors of thought, behavior, and personality and the "sterilized" spaces that have been created to produce such pragmatic ways of being, are barriers constructed to ward off dangers that can neither be captured as psychic representations nor verbalized; these might be considered as primitive attempts of the organism to protect itself in the field of the Other. When the subject feels threatened by each pictographic representation of his instinctual life because it is felt to be unacceptable to the Other, the psyche might be thought to make a colossal effort to *conserve* its vital forces by becoming deaf to instinctual appeal — rather like the autistic child who refuses to live because he is so afraid of death. Such a cleavage between psyche and soma would of course facilitate psychosomatic disorganization. Situations capable of invoking psychic pain and conflict that are refused access to psychic representations will then tend to be taken over by that implacable information-processing machine, the body, which will reply in place of the subject's psyche. If this story without words could be told, it would surely appear that the soma is responding intelligently, given its own logical codes, when it replies to psychological threats as though they were biological ones. Although psychosomatic illness runs the risk of precipitating the individual into premature death, the fundamental aim of this anachronistic defense may nevertheless be survival.

Chapter XII

Three Heads and Three Bodies

In every discourse that expresses ideas about the body and sex, none is as strange or anxiety-inspiring as that wrought by psychotic thinking.

Christine, a young girl of eighteen, was sent to me by her parents mainly because of difficulties with her school work. Christine herself explained after her second interview that she suffered from "solidification inside her head" and a fear of losing the sight of one eye. In reply to my questioning, she confided her secret: the troubles inside her head were due to her being influenced by cats. The cats "magnetized" her after several hours of study, and especially when she left the house. Even in bed she was tormented by these "magnetic" cats, but she had found a remedy against their influence. She now slept with a little wooden cross squeezed between her legs. Here was a new version of a familiar story, that of the "influencing machine" with its power over the body and the instincts — a machine constructed with the rich material of the primary process, an escaped dream that Christine offered me as reality. In the hope of bringing her problem a little closer to her instinctual reality, I asked whether, in describing the uncanny power of the cats, she was not in reality talking about her own "pussy." "Well, of course," she acquiesced without difficulty, and added, "anybody could see that!" She then went on to describe her fight against masturbation and the magic influence of the cross to protect her in the night against bodily disintegration. The tenor of her disordered associations revealed the extent to which she felt her sexual drives as threatening, not only to her entire body, but to her psychic identity as well. In her delusion she possessed nothing but a symbolic body; in the place of her genital, nothing but words. The body did not fulfill its primary symbolic function as a "container" which would have allowed her to distinguish between inner and outer worlds, between dream and fantasy, between herself and others. I might add that Christine rapidly lost her delusional fantasy about cats, and was able once more to go out in the streets, but her thinking remained profoundly psychotic. Nothing but an intricate system of splitting permitted her to gain apparent insight into the connections between her delusional beliefs and her sexual impulses. This did not markedly modify her relation to her body or to the bodies of others. The splits were maintained, and her ego continued to be dominated by primary-process thinking.

In neurotic structures the "I-body" relationship is notably different. The psychotic part of the personality, which flies in the face of the impossible, is confined to the world of dreams or seeks sublimatory transformation. The neurotic conflict leaves the field of the impossible to struggle instead with that which is possible but *forbidden*. By the very fact that this is rooted in

the *bidden* and the interdictions that have been pronounced, these injunctions have retained their symbolic significance and may therefore find myriad ways
of expressing themselves through repressed thoughts
and fantasies which provide the raw material to build
the drama we call the symptom. For the neurotic has
acquired the right to perceive his body, his psychosoma, as a unified whole. In order to achieve this, he
has been obliged to give up the illusion of the omnipotence of thoughts and wishes, but he has also had
to pay the price of renouncing his sex organ as an instrument of pleasure. Sexual fulfillment becomes
costly, and in many cases may only seek realization in
neurotic symptomatology, or punishment through
neurotic suffering. Although his symptoms are a
mystery to him, the neurotic sufferer readily accepts
that he himself is the author of his symptomatic creation and that the solution is to be found within himself
(he cannot permit himself to blame cats, cosmic rays,
or the concierge). Unlike the psychotic or those who
have created sexual perversions[1] to escape mental
conflict, he is unable to experience his body as the
plaything of destiny and his symptom as a natural
given.

Whereas the normal-neurotic person has at his disposal the psychic representation of his body as a container within which his ego "lives," the psychotic does
not possess this reassuring illusion. The psychotic use of
the body representation reveals to what extent the

---

[1]The perverse invention functions psychically like a psychotic delusion
with regard to the body, but its psychotic dimension is confined to the
relatively narrow area of the sexual act due to erotization of the conflicts
at stake.

body is perceived as vulnerable and permeable, capable of being controlled from outside and of being confused with someone else's body. The body zones and functions are astonishingly scattered in the subject's mind, so that his corporal space is constantly experienced as being torn to pieces in the contact with others or threatened with disintegration by the upsurge of any strong affect. Thus delusional reconstruction is required in order to give meaning to relations with others. Such was the case with Christine.

Again, this way of perceiving the relationship between two bodily entities is the raw material from which not only delusions are constructed, following the mechanisms of primary-process thinking, but also repressed fantasies, neurotic symptoms, and dreams. All delusional thinking would make "sense" if it were introduced by the phrase: "I dreamed that. . . ." The "I" of the psychotic, like that of the dreamer, or the unconscious fantasy of the neurotic whose symptom expresses itself corporally, is not basically "embodied" and can with impunity do away with the inconvenience of otherness, the difference between the sexes, or the inevitability of death; in all these circumstances, the body in its reality is transcended.

As regards emotional experience, we observe that in acute psychotic states affects are intense and uncontrollable, whereas in psychosomatic organizations affect is manifestly flattened, raising the question whether such emotional stifling may in certain cases favor the production of psychosomatic phenomena. The following vignettes illustrate a neurotic and a psychosomatic "head," different from Christine's psychotic "head."

John, twenty-six, sought help because of the intolerable anxiety he experienced whenever he had a date with a girl who attracted him sexually. Fierce headaches frequently prevented him from keeping these appointments. The violence of his symptoms had increased since his parents had moved to Paris, although he did not live with them. "I must be nuts to put on such a circus about going to bed with girls," he exclaimed during his first interview. Although he had not the slightest acquaintance with psychoanalysis (how rare and pleasing today!), the young man had already proposed an "analytic" interpretation of his headaches — an inner theater whose play and characters he did not understand, but it was nevertheless his; moreover he knew it had to do with his love life and sexual anxiety.

During the first weeks of his treatment he developed his parental portraits. "My mother is rather young and seductive. She acts like one of my girl friends with me. Christ! How I would have liked a little grey-haired mother with a black shawl around her shoulders!" The father: "A big, violent man who controlled everything but was generous nevertheless." A box on the ears was his customary reply to any foolishness. One day the patient brought the following dream: "I was in my mother's bedroom; it was as though I were going to sleep in her bed or something stupid like that, and then I heard my father's footsteps on the staircase. Suddenly I was the one at the bottom of the stairs and starting to go up. My father came down with that terrible look on his face that he always had when I was a kid. He raised his hand to slap me and, as he did so, his hand became bigger and bigger . . . enormous. I've never seen an arm so big. He was going to strike me on the head. I was sure he was going to kill me. I woke up with a start, and I had the most terrible headache." Then he added: "Psychoanalysis is a stupid thing. Imagine telling such nonsense. And with it all my headaches are even worse!"

This dream, which is transparent for the psycho-analyst, even in its manifest form, was certainly not so for my patient. It took him more than a year to place all the characters in their roles in this drama and to discover the subtle complications of the relationship between himself and them: the seductive and rejecting mother, the kind but castrating father who was at the same time an idealized phallic figure, the "enormous arm-hand-penis" which had so impressed the little boy of the past. This dream conveys rather clearly how the psyche may make hysterical use of the body representation and its symbolization possibilities. The head — in the patient's unconscious language, his penis — is threatened because of the incestuous and childlike attachment of the boy for his mother. An attachment that had been well repressed but with which his ego had nevertheless to deal. The infantile ego had ruled for him that all women were his mother and therefore forbidden. His symptom, as we see in his dream, has been constructed through the symbolic language of the body as a castration at the hands of the father.

After two years the headaches had completely disappeared and the young man was engaged in a sexual relationship that was totally satisfactory to him. At this point he escaped from the analysis. Perhaps I should add that he escaped while keeping intact all aspects of the homosexual oedipal conflict which had just begun to reveal itself through his dreams and associations, as well as in his external reality where his fixation on an idealized father-boss rendered him incapable of leaving his present job to the detriment of his professional life.

Of course, not all headaches reveal themselves capable of hysterical transcription. I recall in this respect the care of a migraine patient, formerly tubercular, who also suffered from asthma and an anguishing tachycardia at moments of wakening. Near forty years of age, Victoria had come to France to take up a post with an important international organization. Her work, which she carried out with verve and efficiency, had to do with helping people of backward countries. Her devotion to these people as well as to her friends was recognized by everyone. Her love life was in a state of chaos, and she was completely dissatisfied with it. Her lovers, also disfavored by circumstances, brought out in Victoria the desire to save them. Gay, energetic, stimulating to everyone, she nevertheless sought analysis because of an ill-defined depressive state. She had grown afraid of not being able to maintain her sparkling image.

Victoria rarely dreamed or day-dreamed. In view of the absence of dreams and her tachycardia upon awakening, I asked her to imagine a scene, any scene, which might be invented to accompany her somatic experience. "Say just any old thing? I'm not crazy enough for a thing like that!" But at her next session: "Well, I have a dream for you. Good. I dreamed that my alarm clock went off. I saw I was going to be late to work, and I jumped out of bed. I ran a bath. I put on the dress I had laid out the night before. And—would you believe it—my alarm clock went off. I woke up with a terrible headache."

Where then was the dream? There certainly must have been one, but it had been buried a thousand leagues from the place where my patient was, hidden away behind archaic anxiety which existed before there were words to communicate it. A few weeks later, however, Victoria brought me her first real dream: "Someone called me to come and look at the corpse of a woman. In reality it was the body of Mrs. X, the wife of my boss, but in the dream she had the same name as I do. Suddenly the body started to walk very slowly toward me. I screamed. 'But don't you see she is still filled with anxiety!' The others replied that it was of no importance; she was going to be buried just the same. She trembled as though begging me to come to her aid, then leaped toward me, and her icy hands closed around my neck. I could not move I was so cold. I tried to scream, but no sound came from my throat. I awoke with a headache and a sore throat, but I had no tachycardia."

In fact this waking tachycardia did not reappear during the next five years of Victoria's analysis. The asthma also disappeared after eighteen months, but the migraine headaches were more tenacious.

The mother of this patient had been of fragile physical and mental health, which had rendered Victoria's childhood traumatic. She did everything she could to help her mother, and while still very young was capable of handling many tasks most children would be unable to assume. However, we can see from this fragment of her analysis, at what price she had developed her strength of character. Her need to push fantasy and emotion aside, her clinging to the real and tangible, and the compulsion to be constantly active had been attained at the price of her inner life, and at the cost of being unable to depend on the help of others without anxiety.

The contrast between the two migraine sufferers is striking from several points of view. I shall take the example of the dreams alone. On the one hand, we have the dramatic stage play of the hysterically structured analysand, a play involving the oedipal objects and the child and adult selves, but built around a theme created by the childhood self to protect his sexuality. The psychosomatic patient, on the other hand, is trying to protect her psychic life from dissolution. She seeks through constant activity to escape from anxiety of psychotic dimensions concerning archaic objects and the danger of a mortal fusion. These had been dealt with by disavowal and refusal to allow psychic space for painful affect until the experience of the analysis provided a sufficiently safe space in which these primitive anxieties could come to the surface as dreams and fantasies.

Christine who dreams while wide awake, John who dreams while sleeping, Victoria who cannot dream — show us three patterns of psychic functioning.

I hope these truncated clinical excerpts may serve to provide my readers with a glimpse into the complex links between mental functioning and the psychic representation of the somatic self, and into the different symptomatic expressions to which these patterns may give rise.

Chapter XIII

Plea for a Measure of Abnormality

I was once invited to take part in a psychoanalytic colloquium on the following theme: "Pathological and pathogenic aspects of normality"—a provocative title and raising an important question, if only for the fact that the participants were stimulated to assess the concept of normality. What is "normality" from a psychoanalytic viewpoint? And, supposing we manage to define such a commodity, could it be endowed with varying qualities: a "good" normality and a "bad" one? No sooner had I begun to reflect upon the problem, than I became aware that over and beyond the attempt to define "abnormal" normality I was far from being able to conceptualize the structure of "normal" normality. In the midst of these questionings one further doubt clouded my mind, a matter rather delicate to formulate. For several years I have spent much of my time with *analysts* (and of course, with analysands); could I be sure I even knew what constitutes a "normal" person? My colleagues have never appeared to me to be eminently "normal" people; as for myself, I feel quite at home with them. Who are we, who am I,

463

to judge what is normal or abnormal?

The more I thought about it, the more I became convinced that "normality" is not, and never could be, *a psychoanalytic concept*; the very notion is unequivocally anti-analytic.

For an analyst to speak of normality is like trying to describe the dark side of the moon. We can imagine it of course, even send up a rocket and take some photos and, on this basis, build up theories about how it *ought* to look. But where does that lead us? It is not our country, scarcely even our planet. The neuroses with their secret psychotic center, the psychoses with their thick neurotic fringe—this is our family, our terrain, where we all speak, with certain variations of dialect, the same language. But this apart, we must ask the question whether something called a "normal personality structure" could really exist. And even if it exists, why must we leave our familiar analytic field, so comfortably abnormal, to search for traces of the normal? So that we may explain to these "normal" people how sick they really are? There is the further complication that those who proclaim themselves normal—though we may consider their normality pathological or even pathogenic—do not want any truck with us. Not only do they escape our contact, they are indeed suspicious of us. I am reminded of a time when I offered a bunch of asparagus to the elderly farm-hand who had helped to till the soil in my country garden. He vigorously refused my offer. "You don't care for asparagus?" I asked. "Couldn't rightly say," he replied, "never tasted 'em. Folks around here don't eat stuff like that"! It is possible that analysts are a luxury item, like asparagus; you need to have developed a taste for it. That we may consider ourselves highly edible changes nothing — and in any case is not specific to analysts. One of life's over-all aims, is to possess something that others may need or desire, so, why should we concern ourselves with these "normals" who want nothing to do with analysts? Our narcissism (normal? pathological?) sees to it that those who ask *nothing* of us, hold little interest for us. But let us put aside our prejudices and let us aim for the moon.

Although it is conceivable that an analyst might op-pose "normal" and "neurotic" it is equally feasible to suggest that it is "normal to be neurotic." This brings us face to face with two distinct dimensions of the concept of normality. To say that neurosis is a normal phe-nomenon is to refer to an idea of *quantity:* the *statis-tical norm.* If on the contrary we seek to contrast "nor-mal" and "neurotic," this is based on the notion of *quality:* a "normally acceptable" idea of the norm for a given society — and for which I propose the term *nor-mative norm* (in contrast to the statistical norm) with a view to maintaining the distinction between attributes of quantity and quality. The normative norm desig-nates a state of being toward which one tends and wherein is included the notion of an *ideal.* So now we have statistical normality and normative normality over and above our elusive pathological normality.

The quantifiable, the statistical norm, indubitably has sociological research value, but its psychoanalytic interest is relatively unimportant. What is of interest to psychoanalysis is normality from the normative aspect (which, we are well aware, includes a vagueness of limits and shifting superego elements). From this van-tage point the analyst might be tempted to formulate a number of questions. I have chosen a few which are of interest to me:

— Are there any "normal" analysts?
— Is there such a thing as "normal" sexuality?
— Are there any "psychoanalytical norms"?

Let us leave the terra firma of the quantifiable, with its statistical curves (and their built-in trompe-l'oeil) for the shifting sands of the normative and see whether we may begin to map out its contours. But now we are back at the beginning: What is a normal human being? My dictionary (Webster) informs me that "normal" means: conforming to rules, regular, average, or ordinary. Might this help us to track down the pathogenic "regulars" and the "ordinary" pathologicals? The "regular guy" is everywhere; those who desire above all to "conform to the rules," the "good children," are constantly with us also; many people wish to appear to conform, at least in the eyes of others. But who, in his heart of hearts, aspires to be "average" or "ordinary"?

Without leading us too far astray this short excursion into lexical erudition highlights the fundamental *ambivalence* attached to the concept of normality — that is to say, approbation and condemnation at the same time. If one finds it unenticing to be "ordinary," this does not mean that one wishes to be thought *abnormal*. The ambiguity implicit in the term might already indicate to us that it pertains to two different sectors of our psychic being, one that seeks to obey the laws, and another that seeks to circumvent them. But quite apart from this inherent ambivalence, the normative is always a subjective value. The idea that each person has formed of his own "normality" can only be understood in relation to reference points: normal as compared with what? In the eyes of whom? Whether one judges oneself, or others, to be normal or abnormal, this judgment is obligatorily relative to a *preexistent norm.* The earliest conception of all future norms is furnished, obviously, by the family. For the child (and there is very little difference for the adult) the "normal" is that which is *heimlich,* the recognizable, that which is accepted *at home. Das Unheimliche,* the disquieting unfamiliar, the *uncanny,* so vividly described by Freud, is the essence of the "abnormal," that which arises from within and in so doing casts its dark shadow upon the familiar background—that which will or will not be *accepted by the family. Das Unheimliche,* that which does not belong "at home," represents, as Freud demonstrated, a special category of that which is familiar, recognizable, normal. The apparent opposition fades away. The wish to escape conformity is the desire to transgress the family-transmitted laws, whereas the contrary wish, to "be normal," is fundamentally aimed at deserving the parents' love by respecting their rules and adopting their ideals—a narcissistic goal destined to be embodied in an ego ideal which in turn will leave its imprint on the instinctual aims. Children make valorous efforts to behave "normally." I am reminded of a certain little boy and his father on a visit to the zoo. The child did everything he should not do—he leaned too far over the bear-pit, he threw pebbles at the seals, and pushed his way rudely among the other visitors. Finally, the exasperated father shouted: "How many times must I tell you—behave like a human being!" The little boy looked at his father sadly: "Daddy, what do you have to do to become a human being?"

How does one fit into the norm? The answer is evident — for every child, the norm is the identification with the parents' desires. This family norm will therefore be "pathogenic" or "normative" according to its coincidence with or derivation from the norms of the society to which the parents belong.

In psychoanalytic theory this norm is defined in terms of the concept of an "oedipal organization" within each individual, a *normalizing structure* in the sense that it pre-exists the birth of the child and is destined to structure psychically the child's future intra- and interpersonal relations. Is the solving of the oedipal conflict the factor that will bring forth "good" normality? But everybody finds some kind of "solution" to the unacceptable oedipal situation. Whether it be a neurotic, psychotic, perverse, or psychosomatic solution, or a mixture, the task of distributing these according to a normative scale is an exceedingly delicate one. Certain psychoanalytic writings would seem to incarn some such ideal in a mythical being who displays a "genital character" — that is, someone who loves his neighbor as much as he loves himself; and he is compared with a less highly esteemed small brother known as a "pregenital character" (but the latter has the privilege of also being able to hate his neighbor). And now we have, in inverse position, yet another — the subject of our discussion — he who is *afflicted with normality*, who suffers from a normality symptom. What are the manifestations of this affliction? We might suppose that these "normal" people are the ones who would give the impression of "conforming to the rules," of "fitting into the norm," the "regular guys" — that is, they would appear to be free of psychological symptoms except that they might suffer from psychosomatic symptoms or subtle character pathology. At first glance there is nothing *unheimlich*, nothing uncanny about these people. The normality symptom, invisible to the naked eye, hides behind an asymptomatic screen. I tried to draw a psychological portrait of analysands of this kind (Chapter VI) and named them "robot analysands" in that they functioned with an unshakable system of preconceived ideas which prevented any further thought and gave to the ego structure the force of a programmed robot. This infallible thought structure enables these patients to maintain a certain psychic equilibrium in face of unrecognized archaic anxieties. They are often tempted to undertake an analysis for reasons other than psychological suffering, but nevertheless present themselves as authentic neurotic sufferers (in which they are not mistaken), although their symptoms do not truly interest them. Once engaged in an analytic relationship, it is the anlayst who suffers; he is disavowed as a separate being, as though any recognition of difference would bring the threat of castration and death. The analyst is treated as though he might attack the patient's most vital defenses. But these are not the patients I wish to discuss here. Others, who resemble them in certain respects, but who proclaim themselves to be *normal* also seek psychoanalysis these days, frequently to please some other person.

Mrs. N (for Normal) seats herself comfortably in the armchair facing mine (not perched on the edge of it, as many patients are in their first interviews). Slim and elegant, she holds her head high and looks calmly into my eyes. The thought crosses my mind that she is more at ease than I am, and I have an urge to say, "Now tell me what's wrong!" as though to create a balance of power, but she takes the initiative.

Mrs. N: No doubt you're wondering why I've come to see you. Well, my Doctor told me I should do an analysis. My marriage has been going badly for some time, and I'm really tired out. We're both forty-five, and we have three children. I love my husband and my daughters, but lately he has been making life impossible. He's always in a bad mood...complains about the slightest thing...drinks a bit much...and recently I discovered he has a mistress. It's quite intolerable...particularly since there is absolutely no reason [Mrs. N stops as though she has now given me all the basic elements of the situation].

JM: You do not feel you have contributed anything yourself to the problems between you and your husband?

Mrs. N: Frankly, I don't. I've looked into it, but I haven't changed at all. I don't see what more I could have done. I love him. There's no problem.

JM: You feel that he is the one with the problem?

Mrs. N: Well — yes I do, rather.

JM: And yet it is you who has come to see me. Do you feel you might have some problems that could be talked over?

Mrs. N: Me? No, not really. No. In fact I've always felt quite good about myself — always felt confident you might say.

Attempts to explore the possibility that the changes

in her husband might have made her feel less confident led us nowhere. During my own two interviews with Mrs. N, this phrase constantly recurred: "I've always felt rather good about myself." Effectively, Mrs. N did seem to feel rather good and confident about herself; if problems there were, they were somewhere outside, external to herself. What was Mrs. N seeking? What did she really want — that what went on outside herself should be as ordered, as well arranged, as she was inside herself?

What more can I say about Mrs. N? Member of a wealthy upper-class family, religiously oriented without bigotry, affectionate without excess, patriotic but not chauvinistic, slightly aligned with the intellectual left — Mrs. N felt worthy of her family lineage. Like the other women of the family, she was a good housekeeper, concerned herself with her servants, her children, and her husband. To the latter, she was faithful, and she was not frigid. In winter she went skiing, in the summer to the seaside. She kept up numerous civic and social activities. During her second interview she went as far as to say that she could not see what psychoanalysis could do for her. I was rather of her opinion, but I must admit asking myself if it were possible that some people might feel *too good* about themselves.

But what does this mean? Too good for analysis? Or for the analyst? Mrs. N was a "normal" woman, in her own eyes as well as those of her family, her neighbors, and her friends. What more could one ask? It seems that the psychoanalyst asks for something more. As analysts we cannot avoid the troubling impression that something is lacking in these so-called "normal personalities." Our only hope (and however could we justify it?) would be that this normal person should *come to suffer from his normality.* As long as Mrs. N remains incapable of putting herself in question, in no matter what dimension of her daily existence or personal history—incapable of asking herself what she genuinely thinks of her married life and her partner, of facing up to what her husband may feel about her, of putting in question the foundation for her feelings, impressions and convictions, finally of asking herself whether there might be a measure of illusion in her way of seeing her world, perhaps even a lack of imagination on her part —then she remains in my opinion unanalyzable.

We must ask ourselves, however, *whether it is normal to put oneself in question in this manner.* Is it normal to put in doubt one's object choices, one's rules of behavior, one's religious and political beliefs, even one's esthetic tastes? Surely not, no more than it would be to doubt one's own identity. "Who am I?": A question for philosophers and fools. To be a witness to one's own division, to seek for sense in the nonsense of symptoms, to doubt all that one is or has ever been—these are the signs by which a person reveals himself as an eventual candidate for a psychoanalysis—precisely in virtue of these "abnormal" questions. Those who consider themselves normal, who create no such problems for themselves, who do not doubt their good sense or their essential goodness, nevertheless come too, nowadays, seeking analysis. To what end? What is even more troubling is the fact that we analysts regard them as armor-plated and *ill* people! An illness for which psychoanalysis can do nothing. Whence comes this illness? Does it arise from feeling "too good" about oneself? Are such people "ill" simply because they suffer less than we do?

It should be pointed out that if the psychoanalyst considers the too-well-adapted with suspicion, they from their side do not consider the psychoanalyst as one of them either. What sort of figure does the analyst cut in the eyes of "normal" mortals? No doubt we can be fitted into a statistical curve, but we do not readily fit into the normative norm of these normal others. In this respect I would like to recount a story that dates back some fifteen years ago. A fourteen-year-old girl whose parents were analysts, like many adolescents, considered herself well fitted to judge the adult world. In her school there was considerable talk about psychoanalysis, and the students even wrote papers on different aspects of the subject. For the first time, her parents' professional work took on a certain value in her eyes. She asked if she could, like a grown-up, meet some of the analyst friends about whom she had heard so much. Her mother suggested she come to the country the following Sunday and take part in a luncheon to which she planned to invite an assortment of analysts of varying persuasions. The friends came, ate well, drank well, talked at length — about sex and perversion, about their colleagues and the Psychoanalytic Society — until late in the day. That evening the parents asked the girl for her impressions. "Well," she said, "your friends are a fair bunch of creeps." Her parents invited her to be a little more precise. "Do you ever listen to yourselves?" she asked. "Have you ever noticed that you only have two subjects of conversation? Analysts don't talk about anything but the penis and the Psychoanalytic Society! You find that *normal*, huh?"

When thinking about it, I realized that, normal or not, there was a certain truth to this young lady's opinion. Analysts in social gatherings do not talk like other people. One might even wonder if, when they talk of "the penis and the Psychoanalytic Society," it might not be one and the same thing. A more disquieting fact I have observed is that, as the years go by, the established analysts talk more and more about the Society and less and less about the penis. Is this a "normal" development? Whatever the answer may be, there is little evidence that analysts belong to a "normal" category of persons. It is indeed interesting to note that the writings of American colleagues, in spite of a culture pattern that sets high value on the capacity for adaptation, conformity, and decision-making, have been the most insistent in warning against the danger of accepting "normal" people as candidates for psychoanalytic training. It would appear that the "too-well-adapted-to-life" citizens do not make gifted analysts. Those who recognize within themselves neither symptom nor psychic suffering, who have never been touched by the torture of self-doubt or the fear of the Other, are perhaps little apt to understand these psychic ills in other people.

So much for the "normality" of analysts. What about sexuality? Is there such a thing as a "normal sexual pattern"? This would appear to be a thoroughly "psychoanalytic" question. From 1905 on Freud underlined the fact that the frontier between so-called normal sexuality and deviant sexuality was difficult to distinguish. Having characterized neurosis as the "negative" and perversion as the "positive" of one and the same complex of sexual conflicts, he then added: "...in the most favorable cases, which lie between these two extremes, they may by means of effective restriction and other kinds of modification bring about what is known as normal sexual life" (Freud, 1905b, p. 172). It is clear that Freud considered man's sexual life to be the target of many hazards, and a successful sexual life as something of a luxury. In contrast, he found that the credulity of love and the overestimation of the charms and perfections of the love object were of a remarkable banality. In this respect, Freud made a distinction between the erotic life of antiquity and that of the our epoch — or rather of his, since the sexual mores have changed considerably. The Greeks, he claimed, glorified the drive to the detriment of the object, whereas modern man idealizes the object and looks upon the drive with contempt. We might, of course, question the ancient "glorification" because of the nostalgia and fantasy it contains, but we might likewise question the overestimation of the sexual object today. Certain musical comedies, the ubiquitous sex shops, pornographic films and the like, would all appear to idealize the *drive* as such, in all its different erotic forms, while the *object* has become indistinct or interchangeable.

In psychoanalytic practice, we observe changes that tend in the same direction. A few years ago, we found on the analyst's couch numerous patients suffering from diverse neurotic sexual problems, frequently in a context in which the sexual object was loved and highly esteemed. "I love her, yet I cannot make love to her." Today there are more analysands who say: "I make love with her, but I do not love her." Here are two clinical vignettes that highlight, in condensed fashion, these two positions in relation to the objects of desire.

Gabriel, thirty-eight, has suffered for many years from persistent sexual impotence. "Last night, I tried to make love to her. Nothing worked! And to think that makes three years I've been in love with her. I'm so afraid of losing her. I said, 'Look, I want to make love to you, but it [indicating his penis] doesn't want to.'"

Pierre-Alain has been coming for two years, twice a week, for psychotherapy. I am still not sure whether he would be capable of accepting an analysis with its more rigid conditions. He is a typical young man of the times. His long hair is held in place by a hairband; he talks of "grass" and "acid," and of the paintings of Vasarely, which, with the "babes" seems to fill up the empty spaces of his existence. Twenty-seven years old, he sought therapy because of severe work inhibitions in an intellectual field, but also because of his unsatisfactory relationships and his feeling of loneliness. He has four or five girl friends with whom he maintains sexual relations, but complains that he is incapable of loving any of them — except on rare occasions when wandering through one of his sought-after chemical paradises. There he meets signs, so he feels, of his unconscious life and the impression of being in love. One day he recounted: "I had sex yesterday afternoon with Pascale, and then last night I took Francine to bed. I made love to her too, but only because I had an erection. She doesn't excite me very much — but neither does Pascale. Still, I'm not a homosexual. I tried it once with a guy. Stupid! I'll stick to women!"

Gabriel lays emphasis on the *importance of the drive*

and finds his symptom arises in his sexual activity, whereas Pierre-Alain places it on the side of the object and finds his symptom in his object relations. Their two problems might be subsumed by the remark each one made about his penis. Gabriel: "*I* want to, but *it* doesn't." Pierre-Alain: "*It* wants to, but *I* don't." One complains of an executive lack and the other of an affective lack. Everyone would say that Gabriel has a sexual problem, whereas Pierre-Alain, who has not the slightest functional difficulty, might be considered by some as symptom-free. Gabriel dreams of a sexual activity like Pierre-Alain's.

Statistically, with respect to his age and sociocultural group, the sexual preoccupations of Pierre-Alain are within the norm, yet most analysts would probably agree that beneath his "normal" sexual appearance this patient conceals problems that are more complex than those of Gabriel. They would say that an object relationship in which erotism is linked to feelings of love is the more normal. Is this a countertransference prejudice? The norm, sexual or otherwise, always has a sociotemporal dimension. The recent rebellion of homosexuals against the discrimination from which they suffer may seem abnormal to certain people, whereas others, particularly young adults, consider the "gay liberation front" perfectly normal. Why, they exclaim, should anyone accept persecution simply because he does not practice the same sexuality as the "old man." In point of fact, are these questions truly *psychoanalytic* problems? I do not think so. It is not the analyst's function to decide what his analysands are to do with their lives, their children, or their sex.

If Gabriel, impotent, and Pierre-Alain, incapable of love, are both psychoanalytic "cases," it is not because of their sexual behavior, but because *they put themselves in question.* If judgment there be, it can only be concerned with the analyzability of the patients who seek help, and the form of analytic help best suited to their needs. The patients discussed here have quite different psychic structures. Gabriel's repressed fantasies, impregnated with anxiety and phallic castration fears, find expression within the body, thereby mastering the fantasied danger in symbolic fashion. For Pierre-Alain, the fantasied danger is a more global one, a sort of "primary" castration anxiety of a global kind. Pierre-Alain resembles a baby who has lost the breast and is frantically trying to find it through drugs, other people, and his genital apparatus. He has a "thirst" for others, and his penis functions to this effect. It enables him to make some form of contact with the Other. Moved by his own particular castration fantasy, he hurtles himself across the space that separates him from others — like a trapeze artist circling toward unknown hands — with only one demand to make of them: *they must be there.* My observations and reflections on changing sexual mores lead me to conclude that (quite apart from the question of basic differences of psychic structure between one individual and another) *sexual norms change continually, but castration anxiety remains. It has simply found new disguises.*

Of what consists the normality of so-called normal people? Is a normal person someone who needs analysis or someone who does not? Some authors have suggested, and not without reason, that a person needs to be in excellent psychic health if he hopes to be able to make use of a classical psychoanalysis. People who "need" analysis, as popular parlance would put it, are not necessarily analyzable (as every analyst has discovered to his dismay). Although the experience of psychoanalysis theoretically should benefit most "normal neurotics," this must be predicated on the desire of the patient to undergo this experience, because he believes that he harbors problems to which psychological answers might be found. However, if it is statistically normal to be neurotic, it is even more normal to be unaware that this is so, or to acknowledge neurotic failings even when these appear evident. I come back therefore to the question formulated earlier: is it *normal* (not only statistically but also normatively) to put oneself in question, to question one's cherished beliefs and their origins, to examine attentively the established orders and all one has been taught to accept without question — that is, to question the order that reigns within ourselves, within our family backgrounds, or within the social group to which we belong? Most people, it must be admitted, do not ask themselves such questions. The viewpoint of the analyst as well as the analysand does not fit within the norm. We evolve, with our patients, in a rarefied atmosphere. Why should we become preoccupied with those who call themselves normal, particularly if their sole motivation for seeking analysis arises from the idea that "it is normal to be psychoanalyzed"? The major aim of such an analysis could only be to bring to light psychic pain, which till then had not been recognized as such, and to make the patient capable of suffering. Do we wish to bring the plague to the whole world?

Normality when glorified as an ideal is certainly to be regarded as a symptom; but what of the prognosis? Is it curable? Man is not easily cured of his character traits. No doubt we all harbor chimeric beliefs to which we cling more dearly than to life itself. Might "normality" be nothing more than a chimera? Is the "normal man" a creature of the imagination who believes he is self-evident, to be found everywhere, a well-established reality, convinced of his conformity? This state of self-esteem might conceivably enable a person to maintain his psychic equilibrium; it might also make him inaccessible to analysis. It may be added that of all the narcissistic character traits that man may construct for himself, the reputation for being "normal" is probably the one that brings the largest number of secondary benefits! However, even if the belief that some people have in their normality is for analysts a sign of pathology, this does not give us the right to try at all costs to open their eyes, to force them to face the deceits and disguises of the human spirit. Analysis leads us after all to come to know all that we have passed our lives in wishing *not* to know; to recognize all that is most painful and most scandalous in the depths of our being — not only the forbidden erotic desires, but also our infantile avidity for what we do not possess, our unsuspected selfishness, our childlike narcissism, and our murderous aggression. Why should anyone seek to possess this knowledge? Who wants to question all that he knows, all that he is? Let the analyst keep for himself this questionable treasure, proclaim those who live at a comfortable distance from their unconscious.

Might one of the side benefits of analysis be that it enables us to live with "normal" people? We are a marginal minority, and as such are interested in other marginal people who resemble us. Indeed, should psychoanalysis one day cease to be a marginal discipline that seeks to question the established order of beliefs and prejudices (should it cease to be "beyond the norm"), then it shall have ceased to fulfill its function.

If the conviction of "being normal" is a character defense that blocks the liberty of individual thinking, why are people so afflicted in such large numbers? What are the signs and what is the cause of this affliction? Permit me to narrow the question by pointing out certain signs to the contrary, since it is frequently easier to appreciate what an entity is not rather than what it is. I would willingly contrast the so-called normal personality, from a statistical as well as a normative standpoint, with what might be called the creative personality (irrespective of neurotic, psychotic, or characterological symptoms). Most people are sadly uncreative in the commonly accepted sense of the word (artistic or intellectual creation, political or scientific genius, etc.). But in a larger perspective, it must be recognized that man *always creates something* in the space that separates him from the Other or from the fulfillment of his desires. These diverse "creations" require as much energy, passion, and innovation as the socially recognized ones. They may take the form of a neurotic symptom, a perversion, a psychosis, a criminal career, a work of art, or an intellectual production. The important clinical differences that distinguish these various inventions is not in question here, for that has to do with the specific "abnormality" which is the domain of psychoanalysis. My interest is centered for the time being on those individuals who appear to create nothing either sublime or pathological. But they do in fact create the protective shield we call normality. Such a person respects the ideas that have been handed down to him as he respects the rules of society; there is no apparent conflict, for the wish to transgress these rules of thought and behavior does not appear, even in imagination. The nostalgic fragrance of Marcel Proust's madeleine awakens no remembrance of things past, and he will waste no time in searching for *les temps perdus*. Yet he too has lost something precious. In the construction of his solid wall of normality, the richness of fantasy seems to be lacking; or perhaps it would be nearer the truth to say that this restraining wall keeps the subject *out of contact with himself and his imaginative life*.

Children who vociferously question every perception that is new to them, who imagine the unimaginable with facility before becoming "normalized," are, in contrast to most adults, authentically innovative and formulate creative questions. I have in mind a faraway memory of my son, aged three, watching me pouring tea. "Hey Maman, what makes the tea stand up in the cup when you pour it out of the pot?" I looked, as though for the first time, at that column of tea which effectively "stood up" between the teapot and the cup. Moreover I was incapable of providing a plausible explanation. Why does this childlike questioning eye with its passionate vigilance become lost to the majority of adults? At what moment do the shutters fall into place, and what determines their subsequent transparence or opacity? Fall they must, because the curious gaze of children is quickly apprehended as transgression. The astonished concentration of the little boy on the column of tea *has become detached from his mother's body* and its mysteries. He has begun to understand that one no longer asks questions about the columns of water that pour from human bodies; and even less about the phallic column of his father, its lack in his mother, and the unimaginable conjunction between the parents. Should he fail to find new symbolic links to the objects of his passionate curiosity by turning his eyes elsewhere, he risks losing forever the open-eyed questioning attitude of the child and henceforth will keep his eyes on the ground. We all have within us locked doors and dark areas where no light may fall and no doubt may penetrate, so that new and unusual connections of ideas and perceptions will not arise. How many adults are capable of questioning the obvious? How many are able to draw with the serious and sophisticated naivety of children? Or see in everyday objects something fantastic that the others no longer see? An Einstein? a Picasso? a Freud?

A handful only — artists, musicians, writers, scientists — escape the icy shower of *normalization* that the world pours upon them. Indeed each child must pass this way, must take his place in the order of things; but does it have to be at the price of the loss of that magical time when all thoughts, fantasies, and feelings were at least thinkable, representable? To hold fast to the hope that all might be questioned, that each desire may be fulfilled, that everything can be transformed into its opposite or even cease to exist, is to defy the laws and challenge the logic upon which human relations are built and regulated. Thus all art, every invention, each new thought is at the same time an act of transgression. Small wonder that new and curious connections become forbidden. How many of us can even equal in our waking lives the creativity of our own dreams? Men of genius and certain madmen perhaps.

Others no longer even know how to dream. If the

psychotic wipes out the distinction between inner and outer, between desire and its fulfillment, the most affected of our so-called normal folk block all inter-penetration between the world within and perceptions of the outside world; the fluid of psychic life no longer flows. The unusual, the unknown, and the unexpected will not light a fire in conscious thought; they may even pass unperceived. Rather like *Das Unheimliche* — that Freud derived from its opposite, the familiar — normality, following the same trajectory, comes ever closer to its opposite, the "abnormal," in this respect. This ego quality, this good common sense that never confuses inner and outer, nor desire and realization, leaves the imaginary world behind to concentrate ex-clusively on external reality with its concreteness and its mastery over emotion. Such clinging to the factual world may go so far as to *cripple symbolic functioning*, thus opening a dangerous door to the explosion of the imaginary in the soma itself.

Obviously the child, who does not yet know the "norms" life imposes, must submit, little by little, to the normalizing effect of his environment and family structure, with their ideals and interdictions, if he hopes to take his place one day as an adult among adults. But to be caught in the grip of an overly power-ful social ego, over-reasonable and overadapted, is no more desirable than the dominance of unleashed in-stinctual forces. The point at which the "norm" becomes the straitjacket of the soul and the cemetery of imagina-tion is a delicate one to define. No doubt it originates in that primordial relationship with the breast-mother, the baby's universe, wherein evolve his first creative psychic acts — his capacity to hallucinate this mother-

universe and eventually to recreate her inside himself
to help support the intolerable reality of her absence
and otherness. It is possible that some, even many, renounce too early the magical omnipotence of their infantile megalomania, give up too early their transitional objects, resolve too readily, perhaps too well,
their incestuous oedipal longings?

Faced with the difficulty of "becoming a human being" it is always possible to respond by an overadaptation to the world of external reality, by becoming "supernormal." Thereafter the feverish forces
of life may become entrapped in a closed-circuit
system; these forces, to become creative, must be
filtered through the representational symbolic world or
their effects may become purely destructive, and when
conflict goes unnoticed, even put life itself in danger.
What lies beneath this solid protective wall of the "too-
well-adapted-to-life" people? A budding psychosis? Is
it possible that when "normality" is worshipped as an
ideal state it serves the function of maintaining a well-
compensated psychotic state? There is a growing body
of evidence to support the hypothesis that both
psychotic and psychosomatic accidents are cloaked for
many years in unimpeachable "normality," and that
the maintenance of this character defense is something
of a hazard to health in the event of sudden environmental stress.

Even though such people rarely turn to psychoanalysis, I would not say that our science can do
nothing for the "supernormal." The analytic process is
itself a *creative process*, and these individuals carry
within themselves all the elements for creating *their*
analyst and *their* psychoanalytic adventure, like every-

body else. If once engaged in this adventure nothing happens to transform their way of experiencing themselves and the world, it may be that *we* have failed to understand their communication and to detect their cry of distress.

We must also admit in respect to "normal" people that they are the pillars of society and that without them the social structure would be in imminent peril. The normal man will never overthrow the Monarchy and he will willingly die for the Republic. But analysts, beware! For whom tolls the bell? For them, for me, for you? We may likewise run the risk of dying locked in our identity as "analyst." This is a fate that pursues us all. The analyst who believes himself to be "normal," and capable of deciding on "norms" of behavior for his patients, runs the risk of being extremely detrimental to the creative unfolding and self-discovery they seek. No analyst, according to Freud (1910), may hope to take his patients beyond the point at which he can no longer put *himself* in question.

References

Bak, R. (1956), Aggression and perversion. In: *Perversions: Psychodynamics and Therapy*, ed. S. Lorand. New York: Random House, pp. 231–240.

Barnes, M. & Berke, J. (1971), *Two Accounts of a Journey Through Madness*. London: MacGibbon and Kee.

Berne, E. (1949), *The Mind in Action*. London: Lehman.

Bion, W. R. (1959), Attacks on linking. In: *Second Thoughts*. London: Heinemann, 1967, pp. 93–109.

_____ (1962), *Learning from Experience*. London: Heinemann.

_____ (1963), *Elements of Psycho-Analysis*. London: Heinemann.

_____ (1967), *Second Thoughts*. London: Heinemann.

_____ (1970), *Attention and Interpretation*. London: Heinemann.

Bouvet, M. (1967), *La relation d'objet*. Paris: Payot.

Brunswick, R. M. (1940), The preoedipal phase of the libido development. *Psychoanal. Quart.*, 9:293–319.

Castoriadis-Aulagnier, P. (1975), *La violence de l'interprétation*. Paris: Presses Universitaires de France.

Chasseguet-Smirgel, J. (1971), La hiérarchie des actes créateurs. In: *Pour une psychanalyse de l'art et de la créativité*. Paris: Payot, pp. 102–103.

David, C. (1971), *L'état amoureux*. Paris: Payot.

Deutsch, H. (1932), On female homosexuality. *Psychoanal. Quart.*, 1:484–510.

_____ (1944–1945), *The Psychology of Women*, Vols. 1 & 2. New York: Grune & Stratton.

Engel, G. (1962), Anxiety and depression withdrawal. *Internat. J. Psycho-Anal.*, 45:84–96.

_____ (1967), Psychoanalytic theory of psychosomatic disorder. *J. Amer. Psychoanal. Assn.*, 15:344–356.

487

Fain, M. (1971), Prélude à la vie fantasmatique. *Rev. Franç. Psychanal.*, 35:291–364.

―――― & David, C. (1963), Aspects fonctionels de la vie onirique. *Rev. Franç. Psychanal.*, 27:241–343.

―――― & Kreisler, L. (1970), Discussion sur la genèse des fonctions représentatives. *Rev. Franç. Psychanal.*, 34:285–306.

Federn, P. C. (1952), *Ego Psychology and the Psychoses*. New York: Basic Books.

Freud, A. (1936), *The Ego and the Mechanisms of Defense*. New York: International Universities Press, 1946.

Freud, S. (1887–1902), *The Origins of Psycho-Analysis*. London: Imago, 1954.

―――― (1893), Drafts A and B, the aetiology of the neuroses. *Standard Edition*, 1:177–184. London: Hogarth Press, 1966.

―――― (1897), Letter 79. In: *The Origins of Psychoanalysis: Letters to Wilhelm Fliess, Drafts and Notes: 1887–1902*. New York: Basic Books, 1954, pp. 238–241.

―――― (1905a), Fragment of an analysis of a case of hysteria. *Standard Edition*, 7:7–122. London: Hogarth Press, 1953.

―――― (1905b), Three essays on the theory of sexuality. *Standard Edition*, 7:125–231. London: Hogarth Press, 1953.

―――― (1908), On the sexual theories of children. *Standard Edition*, 9:205–226. London: Hogarth Press, 1959.

―――― (1910), Future prospects of psycho-analysis. *Standard Edition*, 11:141–151. London: Hogarth Press, 1957.

―――― (1911), Psycho-analytic notes on an autobiographical account of a case of paranoia. *Standard Edition*, 12:3–84. London: Hogarth Press, 1958.

―――― (1914), On narcissism: An introduction. *Standard Edition*, 14:67–104. London: Hogarth Press, 1957.

―――― (1915a), The unconscious. *Standard Edition*, 14:159–216. London: Hogarth Press, 1957.

―――― (1915b), A case of paranoia running counter to the psycho-analytic theory of the disease. *Standard Edition*, 14:261–272. London: Hogarth Press, 1957.

―――― (1917), Mourning and melancholia. *Standard Edition*, 14:234–258. London: Hogarth Press, 1957.

―――― (1920), The psychogenesis of a case of homosexuality in a woman. *Standard Edition*, 18:145–172. London: Hogarth Press, 1955.

―――― (1922), Some neurotic mechanisms in jealousy, paranoia, and homosexuality. *Standard Edition*, 18:221–234. London: Hogarth Press, 1955.

―――― (1923), The infantile genital organization. *Standard Edition*, 19:141–148. London: Hogarth Press, 1961.

―――― (1924a), The economic problem of masochism. *Standard Edition*, 19:157–172. London: Hogarth Press, 1961.

_____ (1924b), The loss of reality in neurosis and psychosis. *Standard Edition*, 19:183–190. London: Hogarth Press, 1961.

_____ (1925), Some psychical consequences of the anatomical distinction between the sexes. *Standard Edition*, 19:243–260. London: Hogarth Press, 1961.

_____ (1927), Fetishism. *Standard Edition*, 21:149–158. London: Hogarth Press, 1961.

_____ (1931), Female sexuality. *Standard Edition*, 21:223–246. London: Hogarth Press, 1961.

_____ (1933), Femininity. *Standard Edition*, 22:112–135. London: Hogarth Press, 1964.

_____ (1940), Splitting of the ego in the process of defense. *Standard Edition*, 23:271–278. London: Hogarth Press, 1964.

Garma, A. (1950), On the pathogenesis of peptic ulcer. *Internat. J. Psycho-Anal.*, 31:55–125.

_____ (1957), Oral digestive superego aggressions and actual conflicts in peptic ulcer patients. *Internat. J. Psycho-Anal.*, 37:75–86.

Gide, A. (1920), *Corydon*. Paris: Gallimard.

Gillespie, W. H. (1956a), The general theory of sexual perversion. *Internat. J. Psycho-Anal.*, 37:396–403.

_____ (1956b), The structure and aetiology of sexual perversion. In: *Perversions: Psychodynamics and Therapy*, ed. S. Lorand. New York: Random House, pp. 28–41.

Giovacchini, P. (1977), Countertransference with primitive mental states. In: *Countertransference*, ed. L. Epstein & A. Feiner. New York: Jason Aronson, 1979, pp. 235–266.

Glover, E. (1933), The relation of perversion-formation to the development of reality-sense. In: *On the Early Development of Mind*. New York: International Universities Press, 1956, pp. 216–234.

_____ (1960), *The Roots of Crime*. New York: International Universities Press.

Green, A. (1973), *Le discours vivant*. Paris: Presses Universitaires de France.

Grunberger, B. (1971), *Narcissism: Psychoanalytic Essays*. New York: International Universities Press, 1979.

Hellman, I. (1954), Some observations on mothers of children with intellectual inhibitions. *The Psychoanalytic Study of the Child*, 9:258–273. New York: International Universities Press.

Itten, J. (1961), *The Art of Color*. New York: Van Nostrand, Reinhold.

Jacobson, R. (1962), *Selected Writings*. The Hague: Mouton.

Jones, E. (1927), The early development of female sexuality. *Internat. J. Psycho-Anal.*, 8:459–472.

_____ (1932), The phallic phase. *Internat. J. Psycho-Anal.*, 14:1–33, 1933.

Kernberg, O. (1975), *Borderline Conditions and Pathological Narcissism*. New York: Jason Aronson.

Khan, M. M. R. (1969), Role of the "collated internal object" in perversion-formations. *Internat. J. Psycho-Anal.*, 50:555–565.
Klein, M. (1921–1945), *Love, Guilt and Reparation and Other Works.* London: Hogarth Press, 1975.
—— (1932), *The Psycho-Analysis of Children.* London: Hogarth Press, 1959.
—— (1950), *Contributions to Psycho-Analysis, 1921–1945.* London: Hogarth Press.
—— Heimann, P., Isaacs, S. & Rivière, J. (1952), *Developments in Psychoanalysis.* London: Hogarth Press.
Kreisler, L., Fain, M. & Soulé, M. (1974), *L'enfant et son corps.* Paris: Presses Universitaires de France.
Kohut, H. (1971), *Analysis of the Self.* New York: International Universities Press.
Kurth, F. & Patterson, A. (1968), Structuring aspects of the penis. *Internat. J. Psycho-Anal.*, 49:620–628.
Lacan, J. (1956), Réponse au commentaire de J. Hyppolite sur la "Verneinung." In: *Écrits.* Paris: Seuil, 1966, pp. 381–400.
—— (1959), D'une question préliminaire à tout traitement possible de la psychose. In: *Écrits.* Paris: Seuil, 1966, pp. 531–584.
—— (1966) *Écrits.* Paris: Seuil.
Laplanche, J. & Pontalis, J. -B. (1973), *The Language of Psycho-Analysis.* New York: Norton.
Leduc, V. (1966), *Thérèse et Isabelle.* Paris: Gallimard.
Levi-Strauss, C. (1949), *Les structures élémentaires de la parenté.* Paris: Presses Universitaires de France.
Lewin, B. (1948), The nature of reality, the meaning of nothing, with an addendum on concentration. *Psychoanal. Quart.*, 17:524–526.
Lichtenstein, H. (1961), Identity and sexuality. *J. Amer. Psychoanal. Assn.*, 9:179–260.
Loriod, J. (1969), Observation clinique d'un malade psychosomatique. *Rev. Franç. Psychanal.*, 33:255–272.
Mahler, M. (1952), On child psychosis and schizophrenia: Autistic and symbiotic infantile psychoses. *The Psychoanalytic Study of the Child,* 7:286–305. New York: International Universities Press.
—— (1970), *On Human Symbiosis and the Vicissitudes of Individuation.* New York: International Universities Press.
—— & Gosliner, B. (1955), On symbiotic child psychosis. *The Psychoanalytic Study of the Child,* 10:195–212. New York: International Universities Press.
Marty, P. & Fain, M. (1965), A propos du narcissisme et de sa genèse. *Rev. Franç. Psychanal.*, 29:561–572.
—— & M'Uzan, M. de (1963), La pensée opératoire. *Rev. Franç. Psychanal.*, 27:345–356.
—— —— & David, C. (1963), *L'investigation psychosomatique.* Paris: Presses Universitaires de France.

McDougall, J. (1964), Considérations sur la relation d'objet dans l'homo-
sexualité féminine. In: *Recherches psychanalytiques nouvelles sur
la sexualité féminine*, ed. J. Chasseguet et al. Paris: Payot.
———— (1970), Homosexuality in women. In: *Female Sexuality*, ed. J.
Chasseguet et al. Ann Arbor: Michigan University Press.
———— (1980), La sexualité perverse et l'économie psychique. In: *Les
grandes découvertes de la psychanalyse*, ed. J. Chasseguet & B.
Grunberger. Paris: Tchou.
Meltzer, D. (1967), *The Psycho-Analytical Process*. London: Heinemann.
Miller, I. (1969), Unconscious fantasy and masturbatory technique. *J.
Amer. Psychoanal. Assn.*, 17:826–847.
Modell, A. (1973), Affects and psychoanalytic knowledge. In: *Annual of
Psychoanalysis*, 1:117–124. New York: Quadrangle.
Montgrain, N. H., et al. (1975), Préliminaries à une étude psychana-
lytique du transsexualisme. *L'Evolution Psychiatrique*, 3:637–654.
M'Uzan, M. de (1972), Un cas de masochisme pervers. In: *La sexualité
perverse*. Paris: Payot.
Nemiah, J. & Sifneos, P. (1970a), Affect and fantasy in patients with psy-
chosomatic disorders. In: *Modern Trends in Psychosomatic
Medicine*, ed. O. Hill. London: Butterworths, pp. 26–34.
———— ———— (1970b), Psychosomatic illness: A problem in communica-
tion. *Psychother. Psychosom.*, 18:154–160.
———— ———— (1973), The prevalence of "alexithymic" characteristics in
psychosomatic patients. *Psychother. Psychosom.*, 22:255–262.
Nunberg, H. & Federn, P., eds. (1974), Discussion on masturbation.
Minutes of the Vienna Psychoanalytic Society, 3 & 4. New York:
International Universities Press.
Painter, G. (1965), *Marcel Proust: A Biography*. London: Chatto &
Windus, p. 267.
Pankow, G. (1959), Dynamic structurization and Goldstein's concept
of the organism. *Amer. J. Psychoanal.*, 19:157–160.
———— (1969), *L'homme et sa psychose*. Paris: Aubier-Montaigne.
Pontalis, J. -B. (1977), *Entre le rêve et la douleur*. Paris: Gallimard.
Reich, A. (1951), The discussion of 1912 on masturbation. In: *The Psy-
choanalytic Study of the Child*, 6:80–94. New York: International
Universities Press.
Rosen, I., ed. (1964), *The Pathology and Treatment of Sexual Deviation*.
London: Oxford University Press.
Rosen, V. (1967), Disorders of communication in psychoanalysis. *J.
Amer. Psychoanal. Assn.*, 15:467–490.
Rosenfeld, H. (1949), Remarks on the relation of male homosexuality to
paranoia, paranoid anxiety and narcissism. In: *Psychotic States*.
New York: International Universities Press, 1965, pp. 34–51.
———— (1965), *Psychotic States*. New York: International Universities
Press.
———— (1971), A clinical approach to the psycho-analytic theory of the

life and death instincts. *Internat. J. Psycho-Anal.*, 52:169–178.

Sachs, H. (1923), Zur Genese der Perversionen. *Internat. Z. Psychoanal.*, 9:172–182.

Sami-Ali, (1969), Etude de l'image du corps dans l'urticaire. *Rev. Franç. Psychanal.*, 33:121–226.

Schmiderberg, M. (1956), Delinquent acts as perversions and fetishes. *Internat. J. Psycho-Anal.*, 37:422–424.

Segal, H. (1956), Depression in the schizophrenic. *Internat. J. Psycho-Anal.*, 37:339–343.

Sifneos, P. (1974), Reconsideration of psychodynamic mechanisms in psychosomatic symptom formation. *Psychother. Psychosom.*, 24:151–155.

Socarides, C. (1968), *The Overt Homosexual.* New York: Jason Aronson.

Sperling, M. (1955), Psychosis and psychosomatic illness. *Internat. J. Psycho-Anal.*, 36:320–327.

———— (1968), Acting-out behaviour and psychosomatic symptoms. *Internat. J. Psycho-Anal.*, 49:250–253.

Spitz, R. (1949), Autoerotism: Some empirical findings and hypotheses on three of its manifestations in the first year of life. *The Psychoanalytic Study of the Child*, 3/4:85–120. New York: International Universities Press.

———— (1962), Autoerotism. *The Psychoanalytic Study of the Child*, 17:283–315. New York: International Universities Press.

Stoller, R. S. (1968), *Sex and Gender.* New York: Science House.

Stone, L. (1961), *The Psychoanalytic Situation.* New York: International Universities Press.

Strachey, J. (1934), The nature of the therapeutic action of psychoanalysis. *Internat. J. Psycho-Anal.*, 15:127–159.

Tausk, V. (1912), On masturbation. *The Psychoanalytic Study of the Child*, 6:61–79. New York: International Universities Press, 1956.

———— (1919), On the origin of "influencing machine" in schizophrenia. *Psychoanal. Quart.*, 2:519–556, 1933.

Torok, M. (1964), The significance of penis envy in women. In: *Female Sexuality.* Ann Arbor: University of Michigan Press, 1970, pp. 167–168.

Viderman, S. (1970), *La construction de l'espace analytique.* Paris: Denoël.

Winnicott, D. (1935), The manic defence. In: *Collected Papers.* New York: Basic Books, 1958, pp. 129–144.

———— (1948), Reparation in respect of mother's organized defence against depression. In: *Collected Papers.* New York: Basic Books, 1958, pp. 91–96.

———— (1951), Transitional objects and transitional phenomena. In: *Collected Papers.* New York: Basic Books, 1958, pp. 229–242.

———— (1960), The theory of the parent-infant relationship. In: *The*

Maturational Processes and the Facilitating Environment. New York: International Universities Press, 1965, pp. 37–55.

_____ (1971a), *Playing and Reality.* London: Tavistock Publications.

_____ (1971b), The use of an object and relating through identifications. In: *Playing and Reality.* London: Tavistock Publications, pp. 86–94.

Yahalom, I. (1967), Sense, affect and image in the development of the symbolic process. *Internat. J. Psycho-Anal.*, 48:373–383.